ANCIENT ASTROLOGY

IN THEORY AND PRACTICE

Ancient Astrology in Theory and Practice:
A Manual of Traditional Techniques
Volume One: Assessing Planetary Condition

By Demetra George

First published in 2019 by

RUBEDO PRESS
Auckland · New Zealand
ISBN: 978-0-473-44539-3

Second edition, with minor corrections, March 2019

Design and Typography
by Aaron Cheak

The cover image represents the astronomical ceiling
from the Temple of Hathor at Dendera, as illustrated in
Description de l'Égypte, ou Recueil des observations et des recherches
qui ont été faites en Égypte pendant l'expédition de l'armée française
(Commission des sciences et arts d'Egypte; Paris: Imprimerie impériale, 1809–1822)
The illustration facing page 23 is a representation of the geocentric
or Ptolemaic universe, from Bartolomeu Velho's *Cosmographia*
(Bibilotèque nationale de France, Paris, 1568)

SCRIBE SANGUINE QUIA SANGUIS SPIRITUS

ANCIENT
ASTROLOGY

IN THEORY & PRACTICE

A Manual of Traditional Techniques

DEMETRA GEORGE

VOLUME ONE
ASSESSING PLANETARY CONDITION

RUBEDO
2019

CONTENTS

VOLUME ONE

Assessing Planetary Condition

LIST OF FIGURES

LIST OF TABLES

SYMBOLS AND ABBREVIATIONS
USED IN THIS BOOK

PLANETS

☉	Sun
☽	Moon
☿	Mercury
♀	Venus
♂	Mars
♃	Jupiter
♄	Saturn
⊗	Part of Fortune
Φ	Part of Spirit
☊	North Node
☋	South Node
℞	Retrograde

SIGNS

♋	Cancer
♌	Leo
♍	Virgo
♎	Libra
♏	Scorpio
♐	Sagittarius
♑	Capricorn
♒	Aquarius
♓	Pisces
♈	Aries
♉	Taurus
♊	Gemini

ASPECTS

☌	Conjunction
✳	Sextile
☐	Square
△	Trine
☍	Opposition

ABBREVIATIONS

ASC	Ascendant
DSC	Descendant
MC	*Medium Cœli* (Midheaven)
IC	*Imum Cœli* (Lower heaven)
CCAG	*Catalogus Codicum Astrologorum Græcorum* (Catalogue of Greek Astrological Codices)

ACKNOWLEDGEMENTS

———

Demetra George would like to thank Robert Schmidt, Ellen Black, Alan White, Chris Brennan, Benjamin Dykes, James Holden, Robert Zoller, Robert Hand, Malcolm Wilson, David Calderwood, Tony Howard, Jeanette Girosky, Scott Silverman, Alecs Garrett, Priscilla Costello, Curtis Manwaring, Bill Johnston, Slaven Slobodnjak, Marcus Kuenzel, Dennis Harness, Claudia Lapp, Gary Rabidou, Paul Saffel, Douglas Bloch, Bruce Schennum, Leisa Schaim, and Aaron Cheak. Diagrams courtesy of Katy Mumford, Lara Wollock, and Aaron Cheak. All translations are her own unless otherwise noted.

The publisher would like to thank Austin Coppock, Chris Brennan, and Tony Howard for the series of fortunate events that brought this book to Rubedo Press. Particular thanks is owed to Leisa Schaim, who made a truly heroic effort in her detailed proof of this volume (any lingering errors are, of course, the responsibility of the publisher alone). The deepest gratitude, however, must be given to Demetra George, who has been both an absolute pleasure to work with, and an honour to learn from.

Foreword

CHRIS BRENNAN

———

IT IS AN HONOR FOR ME TO WELCOME AND INTRODUCE THE PUBLICATION of *Ancient Astrology in Theory and Practice: A Manual of Traditional Techniques*, by Demetra George. This book provides a comprehensive overview of the techniques of what has come to be known as Hellenistic astrology, which was practiced in the Mediterranean region around the time of the Roman Empire. This is not meant to be a purely historical survey, but is instead designed with the intent of teaching contemporary astrologers how to use ancient astrology in practice. The goal of the book, then, is to help revive an astrological tradition that has been lost for centuries until now.

I first met Demetra as a student at Kepler College. She was teaching a course on Hellenistic astrology, which I took in the second year of the program in 2004. The primary text was a 150-page sourcebook of translations from a number of Greco-Roman astrologers, prepared by Robert Schmidt based on translations that he had been working on over the course of the past decade through Project Hindsight. These primary texts were meant to be read alongside an extensive set of lessons and commentary that Demetra had prepared for the course. However, due a communication error, I didn't receive Demetra's notes until a few weeks into the semester.

I struggled through the lessons initially, because even though the excerpts in the sourcebook had been translated into English, it was difficult to understand the meaning the original authors were trying to convey without context. The ancient astrologers' approach to the field, and the technical terms they used to describe it, were so radically different from modern western astrology that my prior knowledge was of little use. Despite these issues, I stuck with the course. Though I wasn't able to comprehend everything I was reading, I could tell the texts contained something extremely valuable. Eventually Demetra realized that I was missing an integral part of the course, and she sent me her written notes. Suddenly everything I was reading made sense and became much easier to understand. Working through the ancient texts went from being an agonizing and bewildering struggle to a more approachable and enjoyable exercise, because I now had a guide to help initiate me and lead the way.

This book is rooted in the course lessons that Demetra wrote all those years ago, and has grown to include more than a decade of additional historical, conceptual, and technical research that she has done in this field. Demetra is not only uniquely qualified to write this book due to her background in ancient Greek and the history of astrology, she is also a gifted teacher known among her many students for her ability to make complex concepts understandable. It is also fitting that Demetra should be one of the first astrologers to publish a work on ancient astrology of this kind, because due to either luck or fate, she was the very first subscriber to the Project Hindsight translation series in the early 1990s, and also the person to whom Robert Schmidt dedicated his first published volume of his final translation series in 2009.

In the mid-1990s, there was much excitement in the astrological community surrounding the translations that were being produced by Project Hindsight and the quest to revive ancient astrology through this community-funded translation project. However, the revival didn't impact mainstream practice as quickly as one might have expected given the initial enthusiasm surrounding the material. This is because astrologers who purchased the translations generally found them just as difficult to understand as I did during my early attempts to read them. It took the efforts of astrologers like Demetra to not only translate the Greek texts, but also to unpack the concepts they contained, before the techniques would start to be adopted more widely. In some instances this work involved quite a bit of reconstruction, since the texts that have come down to us are often fragmentary. This process was then followed by a period of starting to put the techniques into practice, testing them out, and refining them. Over time, ancient astrology has been slowly brought back to life, and some Hellenistic techniques such as whole sign houses, sect, and annual profections have started to enter the mainstream of contemporary astrological practice.

When she was in college, Demetra initially trained to be a math teacher. Though she pursued a career as an astrologer instead, she is known among her students for her innate ability to break down advanced concepts and teach them in a way that is approachable for beginners. This talent was first demonstrated with her second published book, *Astrology For Yourself* (1987), a workbook for modern astrology. The book you are about to read represents a similar approach, now applied to ancient astrology. While Demetra does not shy away from delving into more complex technical concepts, she recognizes the importance of written exercises and the educational value of the workbook format to help commit complicated principles to memory.

In many ways this book represents the culmination of numerous threads in Demetra's life, and the intersection of several paths that have made her uniquely qualified to help revive and teach ancient astrology. I consider myself incredibly fortunate to have learned from Demetra at the point in my career when I did, and I am excited for those of you who are beginning a journey into ancient astrology through her work. Good luck in your studies.

CHRIS BRENNAN
Author of *Hellenistic Astrology:*
The Study of Fate and Fortune
September 24, 2018

Preface

MY LONG AND WINDING ROAD TO
HELLENISTIC ASTROLOGY

———

❡ IN THE FINAL DECADES OF MY LIFE, AS I REFLECT BACK UPON THE PATH
that brought me to writing this practical manual of ancient astrology, it seems
as if this destination was already embedded in the fate-lines of my birth. My an-
cestry arises from the land of Greece. All of my Greek grandparents immigrated
to the United States at the beginning of the twentieth century. In my early years,
I was raised by both of my grandmothers and learned Greek as my first language. By day, I accompanied them to the Greek Orthodox Church where I was
immersed for hours at a time in the chanting of the liturgies, enchanted by the
wafts of incense and the luminescent glow of candles. By night, my *yia-yias* held
me spellbound with the myths of the Greek gods and goddesses in lieu of other
bedtime stories.

It was only when I went to kindergarten that my family realized I needed to
learn English. Between the ages of six and eight, the outer circumstances of my
life began to change as Pluto crossed my Ascendant. No longer in daily contact
with my grandparents, I lost my memory of the Greek language. But the stories
lay sleeping deep inside of me, waiting to be awakened at some future time.

In the spring of 1970, after studying mathematics, physics, and philosophy at
college, I was living on a commune in the remote mountains of Southern Oregon. I found myself isolated with other young spiritual seekers surrounded by a
metaphysical library of dozens of books on astrology, tarot, numerology, eastern
religions, and yogic practices. In the summer of 1971, while I was pregnant with
my first child, I taught myself how to cast a chart using Llewellyn George's *ABC
Horoscope Maker and Delineator*. I deepened my studies with correspondence
lessons from the Rosicrucian Society in Oceanside, California. I attended my
first astrology conference in April 1973, drawn to San Francisco to hear Dane
Rudhyar teach on person-centered humanistic astrology.

But the very first person who spoke to me as I stood in the lobby waiting for
the doors to the auditorium to open was Eleanor Bach. She had just published
the *Asteroid Ephemeris*—in fact she carried copies hot off the press in her satchel.

Upon hearing that my name was Demetra, and that I lived on a commune growing organic food, she made rapid associations with Ceres, the asteroid goddess of agriculture (the Roman version of the Greek Demeter). She opened the ephemeris and discovered this asteroid was opposite my Sun! She then gave me a copy of her book. This was the kiss that awoke the sleeping beauties, and the stories of the Greco-Roman goddesses once again came to life inside me.

When I returned to my alternative country life, well outside the box of the mainstream astrological community, I simply retold the myths of Ceres, Pallas, Juno and Vesta in my chart readings as a way to access their astrological meanings. Transiting Uranus in Libra was conjunct my natal Jupiter/Juno, and the doors to a brilliant new world of wisdom were suddenly flung open; but the soil from which they arose were rooted in my ancient lineage.

By 1980 I was moved to set down my insights about the asteroids thanks in large part to the encouragement and assistance of Douglas Bloch. But it took another six years for the book to be published, with the support of the Dobyns/Pottenger/Michelsen family at Astro Communications, to whom I'm eternally grateful. In June 1986, Tony Joseph, my mentor/teacher in using myth as the basis for astrology, passed away well before his years, and one week later, my book *Asteroid Goddesses* was in print. The following week was the first United Astrology Conference (UAC), and due to a last-minute cancellation, I was given an opportunity to present this material. In the midst of my Uranus opposition, my national and international astrological career was launched, and my reputation grew as a modern mythic archetypal astrologer with an inclination towards women's spirituality.

The Pluto transit to my Ascendant during my childhood that had severed my connection to my Greek roots moved onto my Imum Cœli (IC) in 1989, bringing me back to the old homeland. I took my first trip to Greece on a tour led by a friend of a friend and experienced the power of sacred sites that are still vibrant with ancient energies. Somewhere along the way I realized that I could be a tour guide too.

1992–1993 was a threshold year in my life. In July 1992 I attended the American Federation of Astrologers Convention in Chicago, the place of my birth. There I met Robert Zoller and Robert Schmidt, both of whom would become my teachers in ancient astrology. But at the time I had no idea who they were professionally. In September of that year, I led my first archetypal astrology/mythology/archaeology tour to Greece and was impressed by the qualities of one of our participants who facilitated past-life regressions. I arranged to have a session with her the following spring. My focus was to gain insight into why I had lost knowledge of the Greek language and what I had to do to reclaim it.

Given my romantic expectations of what would surface, the images that emerged during the regression were puzzling. I found myself in the seventeenth century as a young woman somewhere on the west coast of the English Isles, perhaps in Wales. My grandfather observed the stars as part of his work preparing mapping charts for celestial navigation. He sent me to a nearby abbey where I learned Greek and Latin, and I ended up in a large city associated with occult circles and spent the remaining years of my life transcribing and translating ancient astrological texts.

A few days after the regression, I spoke for the Boston NCGR. While there, I became curious about a brochure I found on my hostess Joyce Levine's coffee table: *Archive for the Retrieval of Historical Astrological Texts* (ARHAT), which explained Rob Hand's latest endeavor. The following weekend I was at the Northwest Astrological Conference (NORWAC) in Seattle, where Robert Hand and Robert Schmidt announced Project Hindsight, an organization started along with Robert Zoller with the mission to translate the corpus of ancient Greek and Latin astrological texts. It turns out that I was the first subscriber to the project, instantly handing over my credit card based upon the sequence of events of the previous week. I had returned to Greece to connect with the person who would help reveal my past life, which was to be a foreshadowing of the destination ahead. And within two weeks, the vision began to come into physical manifestation.

During the next three years, I gradually crossed the bridge between my identity as a modern feminist goddess astrologer to that of a student of ancient astrology. Both passions ultimately had their origins in the classical antiquity of my ancestors. My books, *Mysteries of the Dark Moon*, and *Finding Our Way Through the Dark*, were published in the early 1990s, completing my mythological and astrological studies of the Moon Goddess. The middle of that decade was marked by my attendance at the historic Project Hindsight Conclaves. Here, in a spirit of intoxicating excitement, students, scholars, and astrologers converged to reveal the origins of our tradition. I had only the vaguest idea of exactly what the three Roberts (Schmidt, Hand, and Zoller) were saying, but emotionally speaking, I was overcome with the conviction that it was extremely important, and that it would revolutionize the shape of astrology's future.

By 1997, my children were grown and on their own. I had been patiently waiting for this time when I would have the opportunity to return to university and obtain my graduate degree. That summer, I moved away from the Oregon Coast, my home for almost twenty-five years, and enrolled in the Classics Department at the University of Oregon. At the time, I was thinking that I would develop the language skills in ancient Greek and Latin to further my mytho-

logical research, but the universe had other plans for me. Midway through the
program, I was contacted by Kepler College, which had just received authori-
zation to grant bachelor's degrees in astrology. They asked me to be part of its
first-year faculty to teach the history of ancient astrology. I would have the right
degree—an M.A. in Classics to satisfy the requirements of the Washington State
Board of Education—at just the right time: the opening of the college. Using the
Hellenistic time-lord procedure of Zodiacal Releasing from the Lot of Spirit, a
"loosing of the bond" had just occurred (May 1998), spinning my life into an
entirely new direction.

Malcolm Wilson, my advisor par excellence, prepared me for the job. The
next two years were an intensive period of assembling the history of astrology
from its Babylonian origins through to the Hellenistic, Arabic, and Medieval
periods, as viewed through the lens of politics, philosophy, and religion. I grad-
uated in June 2000 and Kepler College opened its doors the very next month.
Over the next six years, I taught the history of ancient and Medieval astrology as
part of Kepler's first-year program, and as an adjunct professor at the University
of Oregon for several terms.

Kepler's final symposium of the first-year college program in spring 2001
was held to coincide with the NORWAC conference so that our students could
attend both gatherings. Representatives from Project Hindsight had a booth at
the trade show where they were promoting their translations, recordings, and
an upcoming intensive course in Hellenistic astrology. Alan White gave an im-
promptu talk, and the Kepler students were intrigued about the astrological
techniques practiced during the period that they had just been studying from a
historical perspective. In fielding their questions to me, I realized how important it was that I attend Robert Schmidt's upcoming Hellenistic intensive being
held that summer.

During one week in July 2001, the tower of astrology that I had carefully
constructed over twenty-five years fell like a house of cards. The very foundations of how I thought about and practiced astrology were overturned. But in
the midst of this catastrophe was the wildly thrilling excitement of the beginner's mind. I had an opportunity to rebuild the edifice of my practice utilizing
the wisdom of the ancients. "What a tragedy it would have been", I thought, "had
I dedicated my life to astrology and never opened this ancient treasure chest".

I returned to Kepler College the next semester with the conviction that the
techniques of Hellenistic astrology should be added to the curriculum in order
to keep integrity between the historical and practical educational objectives. Because the founders of Kepler College, like the general community, were not yet
aware of the newly-released Hellenistic material when they designed the pro-

gram, there was no space for it. However, Dennis Harness, who was slated to give a module on Vedic astrology during the second year, generously offered to open up his course so that we could do a cross-cultural comparative study of eastern and western astrological traditions. That winter, I spent four months in Virginia, staying at the home of Alan White with weekly visits to Robert Schmidt in nearby Maryland. Under their instruction and with their assistance, I designed the beginning and intermediate courses in Hellenistic Astrology, which I taught and refined at Kepler College over the next five years.

In 2004, a young student named Chris Brennan enrolled in the course, which ultimately inspired him to pursue Hellenistic Astrology as a dedicated field of study. Thirteen years later, he brought this to fruition with the publication of *Hellenistic Astrology: The Study of Fate and Fortune.* In many ways, my years teaching at Kepler College were the high point of my professional career. I had the opportunity for creative collaboration with Nick Campion, Robert Hand, Lee Lehman, Dennis Harness, Maria Mateus, Georgia Stathis, Bruce Scofield, Maggie McPhearson, and others. We were gifted with students who were eager and dedicated to learning the very best we collectively had to offer. However, the wheel turns, and in the fall of 2006, I left Kepler College as transiting Saturn crossed my Ascendant, and my path took another bend in the road.

In the intervening decade I wrote *Astrology and the Authentic Self* (2008) as a bridge book introducing modern astrologers to the simpler doctrines of ancient astrology which could be easily integrated into their modern practices. I have since focused upon teaching ancient astrology to individual students over a lengthy series of one-on-one conversations. I took this approach because I wanted to make sure that each student actually understood the material and knew how to practically apply it. In addition, I wanted to discover where the students had difficulty in comprehension so that I could develop better ways of presenting the teachings.

I have reexamined the primary source texts, compared various translations, and have done my own translations in order to clarify and deepen my understanding of the doctrines. In the process, my studies took me into the Arabic and Medieval material to see how certain doctrines were transmitted, where they were preserved, and how they changed or fell out of the tradition. For this, much gratitude goes to Robert Schmidt, Benjamin Dykes, James Holden, Robert Hand, and Robert Zoller for the many translations they have published and their responses to my many questions.

Ancient Astrology in Theory and Practice is the result of my efforts to decipher the core principles of traditional astrology and make them accessible to the modern practitioner. It is not an exhaustive study, but one which will allow a person to understand the rationale behind many techniques of the Hellenistic, Medieval, or Renaissance traditions, along with examples and self-guided exercises for their application. There will undoubtedly—and hopefully—be works by others that will follow this, adding to our body of knowledge. I am grateful, honored, and humbled to have been a small part of this living link in the transmission of traditional astrology.

The final and seventh major work that is still ahead of me is the completion of a set of my own translations in the Hermetic medical astrology, *iatromathematika*, with accompanying historical and contextual commentary. This includes a text on the construction of healing amulets based upon the thirty-six star decans, a katarchic treatise on diagnosing and prognosticating the course of an illness based upon the motion of the Moon, and the earliest herbal giving the zodiacal correspondences for botanical medicinal plants with instructions and timing for the preparation and administration of remedies. With the grace of the heavenly deities, I pray that I will have the years of life and soundness of mind to make this last offering at the temple of Lady Astrologia.

DEMETRA GEORGE
December 16, 2016

INTRODUCTION
AND OVERVIEW

Introduction

———

EARLY PEOPLES HAVE LOOKED TO THE HEAVENS AS A SOURCE OF SPIRITUAL guidance for earthly affairs since at least the third millennium BCE. Western astrology originated in Mesopotamia, was consolidated during the Hellenistic-Egyptian era, diffused throughout the Roman Empire, returned to the Persian and Islamic empires in late antiquity, reintroduced into Medieval Europe in the twelfth century, spread northwards into France, Germany, and England during the Renaissance, and eventually made its way to America and the Antipodes in the twentieth century. It also spread eastwards. During the first century CE, it spread to India and from there to Tibet, China, Southeast Asia and Japan. Now, in the twenty-first century, Asian countries are experiencing a burgeoning interest in both modern and traditional astrology as transmitted from the western cultures.

Astrological doctrines are received, translated, adapted, practiced, and then, in turn, passed on to others, influencing the philosophical systems, religious beliefs, and political history of each host culture. They have sparked passionate debates about the nature of the cosmos, fate, free will, the soul, and the life of the stars. *Ancient Astrology in Theory and Practice* is primarily a practical treatise on how to apply ancient astrological techniques to the analysis and interpretation of charts. However, before we begin, it is important to start with a brief historical tour in order to follow the trail of this ancient wisdom. Contemporary astrologers are the heirs to a rich and profound tradition that inspires a sense of awe in this deep discipline.[1]

---

1   For further reading on the history of astrology, see: Chris BRENNAN, *Hellenistic Astrology: The Study of Fate and Fortune* (Denver, CO: Amor Fati Publications, 2017); Nicholas CAMPION, *A History of Western Astrology, Volume 1: The Ancient and Classical Worlds* (London: Bloomsbury Academic, 2009); CAMPION, *A History of Western Astrology, Volume 2: The Medieval and Modern Worlds* (London: Bloomsbury Academic, 2009); James Herschel HOLDEN, *A History of Horoscopic Astrology* (Tempe, AZ: American Federation of Astrologers, 1996); James Herschel HOLDEN and Kris Brandt RISKE, *Biographical Dictionary*

The term "traditional astrology" is now being used as an umbrella term that includes Babylonian astral divination, Hellenistic, Arabic, Medieval, and Renaissance styles of astrology. Its principles are similar to, but not identical with, the Vedic tradition that is practiced in India. Other broad terms, such as "ancient astrology", "Greek astrology", and "classical astrology", are often used interchangeably with "traditional astrology". Collectively, however, "traditional astrology" describes the techniques of a very wide-ranging lineage, spanning a time period from 2000 BCE–1700 CE.

BABYLONIAN ASTROLOGY (2000 BCE–100 BCE)

Divination from celestial bodies in regards to the general conditions of the land, nation, and king was practiced as early as the third millennium BCE in the cultures of Mesopotamia, China, and the Indus Valley. However, the earliest evidence for natal astrology appears for the first time at the end of the fifth century BCE in Babylonian cuneiform texts. Natal astrology, i.e., looking to the positions of planets in zodiacal signs at the moment of birth in order to make determinations regarding *individual* character and destiny, was thus contrasted against astrology employed for the purposes of determining *national and royal* destiny. This more "individualized" astrology emerged several thousand years after the previous, more general kind of celestial divination had been in practice. The surviving evidence of Babylonian natal astrology is currently limited to a handful of nativities, a few rudimentary interpretive manuals, and ephemerides and diaries listing the positions of planets in signs, their conjunctions with fixed stars, the risings and settings of planets, and the visibility of the lunar phases.

Transmission. The Greeks first fully encountered Babylonian proto-astrology in the fourth century BCE when they colonized the lands of the Ancient Near East following the conquests of Alexander the Great. In 290 BCE, a Babylonian priest of Bel named Berossus traveled to the Greek island of Kos—home to a center of Hippocratic medicine and an Asclepian healing sanctuary—where he opened a school of astrology for the Greeks.

of Western Astrologers (Tempe, AZ: American Federation of Astrologers, 2013). Robert SCHMIDT, while producing the seminal translations (with commentaries) of many of the Greek texts, also contributed short biographical entries on the Hellenistic astrologers in his *Sourcebook of Hellenistic Astrological Texts: Translations and Commentary*, trans. Robert SCHMIDT (Cumberland, MD: Phaser Foundation, 2005).

HELLENISTIC ASTROLOGY (150 BCE–625 CE)

The idea of divination by the stars spread from Babylonia eastwards into the Indus Valley, northwards, and westwards. It entered Egypt, where there was a mingling of cultures, religions, and philosophies in the new cosmopolitan capital of Alexandria under the rule of the Greek Ptolemaic kings. Drawing upon the longstanding Babylonian tradition of astral omen divination and the indigenous Egyptian use of the thirty-six star decans for calendrical and ritual purposes, the founders of Hellenistic astrology added the components of Greek philosophical thinking and mathematical astronomy.

It was in this milieu that the kind of astrology we recognize today—featuring an Ascendant, planets in signs and houses, aspects, lots (Arabic parts), and a variety of timing methods—emerged in Egypt around 150 BCE. With the Roman conquest of Egypt in the first century BCE, Hellenistic astrology spread to all areas of the Roman Empire. The first Roman emperors had court astrologers as political advisors. Over the next seven hundred years (150 BCE–625 CE), hundreds of astrological texts were written in Greek, and a few in Latin, by authors from various ethnicities and cultures throughout the Mediterranean Basin and regions of the Ancient Near East—Egypt, Asia Minor (Turkey), mainland Greece, Syria, Rome, and North Africa.

The names of prominent Hellenistic astrologers whose texts are extant, translated into modern languages, or widely quoted by other ancient astrologers include: Nechepso and Petosiris of Egypt, Thrasyllus of Alexandria, Marcus Manilius of Rome, Balbillus of Rome, Dorotheus of Sidon, Teucer of Babylon, Vettius Valens of Antioch, Claudius Ptolemy—an Egyptian-born Roman citizen of Alexandria, Antiochus of Athens, Porphyry of Tyre, Firmicus Maternus of Rome, Paulus of Alexandria, Hephaistio of Thebes, and Rhetorius of Egypt.

Transmission. With the advent of the Christian era, Hellenistic astrology was virtually forgotten in western Europe due to the loss of the Greek language and the condemnations against pagan practices by both the church and state. Some Greek astrological texts were preserved in the monastic libraries of the eastern Christian Byzantine Empire, but generally it was forbidden to read them. Before their disappearance in the west, some texts had made their way to the cultures of Persia and India, where they were translated into Pahlavi and Sanskrit. The doctrines were subsequently adapted to the philosophies and social customs of their new host cultures.

PERSIAN ASTROLOGY (226 CE–632 CE)

Around the second century CE, Sassanian Persian rulers wanted to use astrology to predict the future victories or defeats of rulers and dynasties, and to justify the legitimacy of the current rulers as ordained by the stars—as had their Babylonian predecessors. They arranged to have Hellenistic astrological texts translated from Greek into the Persian Pahlavi language. Persian astrologers applied natal techniques to general (mundane) astrology, and attempted to determine past and future history—the fates of nations and dynasties—by innovating new astrological methods such as the Jupiter/Saturn cycle, and the Aries ingress chart. They also adapted Hellenistic time-lord procedures to long-range planetary periods based upon the Zoroastrian theory of the millennia and the Indian theory of the *yugas*.

Transmission. The Sassanian Persian kings had invited not only Hellenistic astrologers to their courts to translate their texts from Greek, but also Syrian, Chinese, and Indian astrologers. Ideas and techniques were exchanged between all these cultures, brought back to their respective homes, and incorporated into each individual tradition. The Arabs conquered the Persians in 632, and within a century, their caliphs established the House of Wisdom, a center where Islamic scholars translated Persian and Indian astrological texts into Arabic. Following tradition, the rulers used astrology to politically legitimize the authority of their new dynasty, as well as to time their military and political actions. The foundation of their capital city at Baghdad was elected by three Persian astrologers (July 21, 762, 2:40 p.m., LMT).

ARABIC ASTROLOGY (600 CE–1300 CE)

The Arabs translated many Persian Pahlavi versions of the Hellenistic texts; when they had exhausted those sources, they sent emissaries as well as raiding parties to Byzantium to procure more texts written in Greek, including Ptolemy's *Tetrabiblos*. Many Indian astrological and astro-medical texts were also translated into Arabic. The following centuries saw the golden age of Arabic astrology, with authors from all over the Islamic empire writing in Arabic. By the eleventh century there were hundreds of Arabic works on astrology by dozens of authors. Many changes were made to the doctrine, including different approaches to house systems, aspects, rulerships, and the addition of many Arabic parts to the Greek system of lots, and the twenty-eight lunar mansions derived from the twenty-seven Indian *nakshatras*. The Arabic period saw the rise and popularity of interrogational (horary) astrology, and the introduction of new doctrines such as the translation and collection of light.

Prominent Arabic-era astrologers include: Nawbakht the Persian, Theophilus of Edessa, Masha'allah from Basra, Omar Tiberiades of Persian descent, Abu Ali al-Khayyat, Sahl ibn Bishr, Abu Ma'shar, Al-Kindi, Abu-Bakr, Al-Rigal, and Al-Biruni.[2]

Transmission. While astrology flourished brilliantly between the seventh and tenth centuries in the Arabic period, in the western world knowledge of astrology had been either forgotten, or relegated to the realm of the "evil and forbidden". However, in the tenth century, Arabic astrological works began to trickle into the Eastern Roman Empire at Byzantium, where numerous works were translated into Greek. These included not only the original Hellenistic works that had gone through Persian and Arabic translations, but also the new works of the Arabic astrologers themselves. Astrology consequently flourished in the court of the Byzantine emperor Manuel I (1143–1180 CE), who used it extensively in his political affairs, even composing a Christian defense of the subject.[3]

Meanwhile, in the west, the wealth of the Arabic astrological literature had found its way to the Moorish libraries and bookshops in southern Spain. When Latin Christendom conquered Spain in 1085, European scholars flocked to Spain to partake of the Classical heritage that had been preserved by the Arabs as well as the Arabs' own rich intellectual tradition. Again, the very first works to be translated were the astrological treatises that cited the works of the Hellenistic authors. Soon after, Medieval astrologers began to compose their own compendia.

Among the scholars who produced the first translations of Arabic astrological texts into Latin were John of Seville, Hugo of Santella, Plato of Tivoli, Hermann of Carinthia, and Robert of Chester. Abraham ibn Ezra, a Spanish Jew, translated the Arabic and created his own texts in Hebrew.

MEDIEVAL/BYZANTINE ASTROLOGY (1200–1500 CE)

At the beginning of the twelfth century, there was virtually no technical knowledge of astrology in western Europe. However, by the end of the century, there were hundreds of translations as well as new works by Latin astrologers. The Me-

---

2 English translations of many of these works are now available through the efforts of Benjamin Dykes through Cazimi Press.

3 Demetra GEORGE, "Manuel I Komnenos and Michael Glykas: A Twelfth-Century Defense and Refutation of Astrology" in *Culture and Cosmos* (Autumn/Winter 2001, Spring/Summer 2001, Spring/Summer 2002). Demophilus is the name of a Byzantine astrologer working in Constantinople from the tenth century and John Camaratus wrote an astrological treatise in the court of Manuel I.

dieval astrology of the thirteenth and fourteenth centuries was thus dependent upon the Latin translations of the Arabic treatises, which in turn were formulated from the Persian and Indian adaptations of some (but not all) of the Hellenistic texts authored over a thousand years earlier. In Byzantium, from the twelfth century on, thousands of astrological manuscripts were compiled. And in the fourteenth century, astrologers revised many of these Classical and Byzantine texts. Because the texts were copied and recopied, they have been preserved; but because they were often revised, portions of the original tradition have also been obscured.

Because astrology could be validated as a legitimate science within the prevailing Aristotelian cosmology, it was taught—especially in the form of medical astrology—at numerous Medieval universities. It was also sought as a form of guidance by nobles and the wealthy. Notable Byzantine era astrologers include John Abramius and Eleutherius Zebelanos, while the most important Medieval European astrologers include Guido Bonatti in Italy, Leopold of Austria, Johann Müller (Regiomantanus) in Germany, and Symon de Phares in France.

Transmission. The fall of Constantinople to the Turks in 1453 resulted in the influx of Greek scholars and texts to Italy, contributing to the rebirth of the Classical paganism and humanism that characterized the Renaissance. The Arabic *Picatrix*, a text of astral magic, and Ficino's translation of the *Corpus Hermeticum*, opened the way for the proliferation of a Hermetic magical astrology. This movement existed side by side with the practice of a more scientific astrology that was derived directly from the Classical Greek tradition. From the tensions between the magical and cosmological approaches, a desire emerged to purify astrology from its magical affiliations, and to reframe it as more scientific.

In the sixteenth century, Greek manuscripts that had not passed through Arabic translations became directly available. The work of Claudius Ptolemy, based upon Aristotelian natural philosophy, rose to prominence and was championed as particularly representative of this non-magical, more scientific tradition. Ironically, Ptolemy himself—a Roman citizen born in Egypt—may not have been a practicing astrologer, but rather an academic who was more concerned with making astrology conceptually consistent within the context of his cosmological model. Because of this, the contents of the *Tetrabiblos* were not wholly representative of mainstream Hellenistic astrological doctrines. Nevertheless, Ptolemy's work became an important reference for the Renaissance tradition that would become so influential to the work of William Lilly and other seventeenth-century astrologers, both in England and on the Continent.

RENAISSANCE ASTROLOGY (1500–1700 CE)

The first part of the Renaissance period saw an increase in the popularity of astrology. There were movements to test and refine the system, advances in techniques, better calculations for planetary positions, and the incorporation of astrological motifs into art and literature. The invention of the printing press allowed for the widespread publication and distribution of almanacs, putting astrology into the hands of the common people. This also gave rise to a plethora of predictions and prophecies, many about cataclysmic events that caused widespread panic but which did not eventuate. The spiritual and magical dimensions of astrology, which led to doubts about the possibility of free will, were attacked by both the Catholic and Protestant churches, which condemned all forms of divination. Notable astrologers from the Renaissance period include: Luca Gaurico, Johann Schoner, Jerome Cardan, Tycho Brahe, John Kepler, Jean Baptiste Morin, and Placidus.

Transmission. With the acceptance of Copernicus' heliocentric model of the universe, combined with an upsurge in experimental science and mechanistic materialism, astrology lost its scientific rationale and fell into disrepute over the next few centuries. However, in the sixteenth and early seventeenth centuries, a number of astrological works were published in England.

SEVENTEENTH-CENTURY ENGLAND

Despite the Copernican revolution, astrology survived and flourished in England for another century. The leading figure of golden-age English astrology was William Lilly, who read most of the Latin works on astrology. His major work was a 900-page tome entitled *Christian Astrology*, a detailed treatise on horary, and some natal, astrology with numerous case examples. He includes an extensive bibliography of over two-hundred astrological works from his library. Other important astrologers from this period include Nicholas Culpepper, John Gadbury, Henry Coley, John Partridge, and John Whalley.

By the eighteenth century, under the influence of the Enlightenment, astrology was no longer deemed worthy as a topic of study and discussion within intellectual circles. Diluted, the tradition disappeared and went underground again. However, by the end of the nineteenth century, several movements would contribute to the resurrection of astrology, albeit in a new form. The Spiritualist movement, which sought unseen causes behind manifest phenomena; the Theosophical movement, which brought the eastern doctrines of karma and reincarnation to the west; and the discovery of the unconscious in depth psychology:

all served to stimulate a renewed interest in astrology as a tool for self-real-
ization and self-understanding. The concepts embedded in these systems of
thought would inform the humanistic, psychological, and spiritual astrologies
of the twentieth century. Here, the birth chart would be viewed as the map of
the psyche and soul, rather than the events fated to befall the native. This reconstruction, begun on the European Continent and especially in England, would
make its way to America to be taken up by the New World.

Alongside the occult and psychological currents at the close of the nineteenth century, developments in European academic circles would have an
equally significant impact on the future of the astrological discipline. A small
group of scholars, led by the Belgian Franz Cumont, a historian of astrology,
embarked upon a program to collect and edit all of the Greek astrological manuscripts that lay scattered throughout the libraries, monasteries, and private col-
lections in Europe and Russia. The result of this painstaking and laborious work
was the twelve-volume *Catalog of Greek Astrological Codices* (CCAG), which
took fifty years to complete.[4] However, until recently, no one in the academic
community (who was also fluent in ancient Greek) was interested in bringing
these texts into English translation.

MODERN ASTROLOGY (20TH–21ST CENTURIES)

Until recently, the only ancient astrological works that were available in English
translation were Manilius' Latin *Astronomica* (as early as 1697), Ptolemy's *Tetrabiblos* (in 1940 by F. E. Robbins), and the *Mathesis*, the Latin work of Firmicus
Maternus (partially translated into English by Jean Rhys Bram in 1975). David
Pingree produced an English version of Dorotheus' *Pentateuch* in 1976, but this
was from the Arabic translation of the Persian translation of the original Greek.
Until the last decade of the twentieth century, these four texts constituted the
extent of our direct knowledge of ancient Hellenistic astrological texts.

Ultimately, it was left to the astrological community to reclaim its own history. In 1993, Robert Schmidt, Robert Hand, and Robert Zoller initiated Project
Hindsight to translate the corpus of ancient astrological material from Latin and
Greek into English. In its first years, this effort was widely supported by sub-
scribers from the astrological community. James Holden began his own translations of these ancient texts in the 1950s, which for the most part he retained as
a private hobby. All of his translations were published before his death in 2013.

---

4   Franz CUMONT and Franz BOLL, eds, *Catalogus Codicum Astrologorum Græcorum*, 12
     Volumes (Brussels: Lamertin, 1898–1953). Henceforth CCAG.

As we approach 2020, many of the primary works of the Hellenistic, Arabic, and Medieval astrologers are now available in English translation due to the dedicated efforts of James Holden, Robert Schmidt, Benjamin Dykes, Robert Hand, Robert Zoller, Meira Epstein, and Eduardo Gramaglia. A list of these works is included in the bibliography of primary source texts. Thus, for the first time since their composition in antiquity, the astrological heritage is available to be read, studied, and mined for its insights into how astrology was conceptualized and practiced for the first seventeen centuries of the common era. Contemporary astrologers are therefore on the brink of one of the most exciting periods of astrological history: a renaissance in astrological thought that has historically taken place whenever the writings of the ancients have been rediscovered and translated.

Prominent among early twenty-first-century astrologers actively involved in conveying the astrology of the ancients to the contemporary astrological community are figures such as James Holden, Olivia Barclay, Robert Schmidt, Robert Zoller, Robert Hand, Alan White, Geoffrey Cornelius, Demetra George, Chris Brennan, Benjamin Dykes, Deborah Houlding, Lee Lehman, Meira Epstein, John Frawley, Christopher Warnock, Dorian Greenbaum, Bernadette Brady, Zdenek Bohuslav, Karine Dilanyan, Eduardo Gramaglia, Helena Avelar, Luis Ribeiro, Guiseppe Bezza, and Hakan Kirkoglu.

A MODERN MANUAL OF TRADITIONAL TECHNIQUES

The present book is written as a practitioner's guide for contemporary astrologers—both seasoned professionals as well as new students—who are eager to avail themselves of an astrological tradition that had been practiced for over two-thousand years. More specifically, this guide is designed to lead modern astrologers through a step-by-step process that will enable them to utilize the principles of ancient astrology in order to build a more solid structure for the interpretation of the natal chart. In order to anchor the theory and concepts into immediate practical application, I include detailed analysis of two example charts, plus hands-on exercises and instructions for understanding the individual's chart. Definitions, vocabulary, ample illustrations, and tables organize and systematize the traditional astrological techniques and provide a foundation for understanding primary source texts.

My own training, both in the focus of study and in the ancient Greek language, is primarily grounded in material from the Hellenistic era. However, over the last two decades I have increasingly cross-referenced the transmission of the doctrines in the Arabic and Medieval traditions. As a result, *Ancient*

Astrology in Theory and Practice gives you the foundational training for the study and practice not only of Hellenistic, but also Arabic, Medieval, and Renaissance astrological traditions. But beyond that, it supports the integration of the fruits of these ancient astrological wisdom teachings in a manner that can strengthen and deepen the way we read charts today.

The book begins simply, but gets increasingly more complex with each successive technique. Some may find the material overwhelming. However, my conviction, based upon my experience with many students whom I have guided through this process, is that if you diligently do each exercise as it appears in the text, you will be able to understand the principles and acquire the foundation for what comes next. The key to mastery lies in doing the exercises.

In the second century, Vettius Valens wrote an instructional book for one of his students which included an oath for astrologers to use the information wisely and responsibly. He compared the path to learning certain teachings to an initiate's path up a mountain peak to a temple where one could communicate with the celestial gods. The rewards far outweighed the effort it took to arrive at the destination.

> And just as a person might climb up with great effort through steps and twisting curves to some mountain peak and come upon a temple furnished with extravagant statues of deities made of gold and silver and ivory or purple vestments, this person would believe that the climb was not to be regretted nor was tiring and would worship with pleasure imagining that he is conversing with the heavenly gods, so in the same way for those who trust in our precepts.[5]

I am humbled to have the opportunity and honor to be a living link in the transmission of the ancient astrological doctrines that were formulated and practiced by our predecessors.

---

5   VALENS, *Anthology 7*, Preface.

PRIMORDIAL GOD (PROTOGENOS) OF LIGHT &
BIUE, BLUE EITHER OF THE HEAVENS

KHAOS, EAR
EREBOS -
MIST OF
DARKNESS

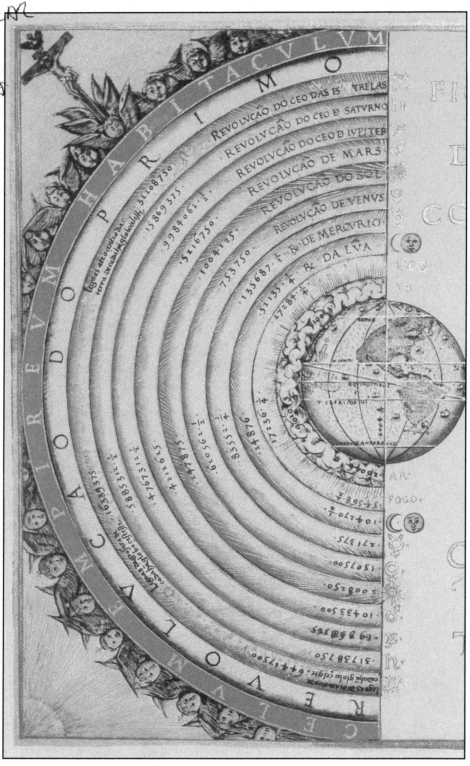

CHAPTER 1

The Hierarchy of the Cosmos

———

ANCIENT PHILOSOPHERS ENVISIONED A GEOCENTRIC COSMOS WHERE the earth formed the center of an ordered system surrounded by seven wandering planets and a multitude of stars. The heavens above were a realm composed of a fifth divine element called *aithēr*. According to Plato, the cosmos was alive and infused with soul and intelligence. At the top of the hierarchy, located at the extremities of the cosmos, stood a principle of unity, of eternal and unchanging being, which different philosophers called "The Good" (Plato), "The Prime Mover" (Aristotle), "The One" (Plotinus), and which later became identified with the Christian God.

Below the principle of unity in the cosmic hierarchy were a plethora of celestial bodies, "the visible appearances of the gods", which were divided between the fixed stars (which had regular motions) and the wandering planets (which had irregular motions, and traveled along their courses in nested concentric spheres). The fixed stars were considered to be more divine than the planets. Because they were seen to move across the night sky with perfectly regular and circular motion—a prime feature of divinity—they were believed to be closer to the source of unity.

The planets occupied the space between the fixed stars and the Earth. Thus they were thought to be slightly less divine because of both their greater distance from the source and their erratic movements. At the center and bottom of the hierarchy was the Earth, terrestrial in nature, composed of the four elements of fire, earth, air, and water, in a constant state of flux and change, coming to be and passing away. The Earth was populated with mortals who were primarily composed of the same physical elements as the Earth, but who also contained a spark of the divine, known as the soul.

This hierarchy and arrangement of the celestial bodies informed astrologers as to the nature and ranking of the various criteria for assessing a planet's condition. When this model was perceived through the lens of the astrologers, a certain band of the fixed stars formed the images of the zodiacal constellations

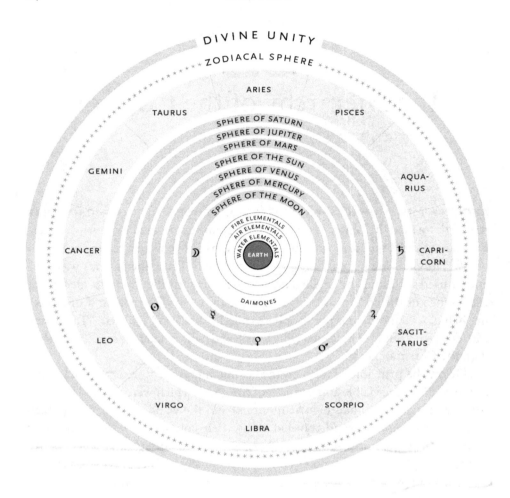

FIGURE 1. DIVINE UNITY & COSMIC HIERARCHY

The totality of divine unity encompasses the fixed stars (the sphere of the zodiac), the planetary spheres (Saturn, Jupiter, Mars, Sun, Venus, Mercury, Moon), the daimones, the sublunary elements (the spirits of fire, air, water), and finally, at the very center, earth itself.

against whose background the sun and planets seemed to move. These images later became the basis for the meanings of the twelve zodiacal signs. Because of the fixed stars' closer proximity to the source and the regularity of their motion, the symbolism of the zodiacal signs has the greatest quality of divinity in the astrological trinity of sign, planet, and house. From the earliest time period of Babylonian astrology, the zodiacal constellations were understood as "stations for great gods", celestial palaces where the planetary gods resided. Hellenistic astrology rephrased this concept of the zodiacal sign in terms of an *oïkos*: a domicile or residence for a planetary lord. When a planet is located in its own zodiacal domicile—its sign of rulership—it was considered to be just as powerful as when a lord is in residence on his own estate.

Following the fixed stars in the descending cosmological order were the spheres of the planets: Saturn, Jupiter, Mars, the Sun (in the center of the planetary order), Venus, Mercury, and the Moon, which was closest to Earth. The originators of western astrology in Babylonia identified the planets with the gods of their pantheon. When knowledge of Babylonian astronomy came to the Greek world in the sixth century BCE, the Greeks gave the planets the names of their own gods that most closely resembled the attributes of their Babylonian counterparts. But rather than identifying the planet *as a god*, the Greeks placed the planets under the auspices of a particular god. For example, the Babylonian Nebu, the scribe god, metamorphosed into the "star of Hermēs", which we know as Mercury.

The planets did not demonstrate perfectly regular motion—they went forwards and backwards; they seemed to slow down, stand still, and then moved quickly forward again; they also wandered north and south of the ecliptic, and sometimes disappeared altogether from sight. They moved at different speeds, both within their own cycles as well as relative to one another. Periodically, a planetary god would come into alignment with another, only to then separate, hurrying forward to stand at right angles and then at a diameter. For these reasons they were considered to be erratic, and even though they represented gods and goddesses, they were seen as slightly less divine than the fixed star zodiacal constellations. Certainly in Greek mythology, the Olympic gods were far from perfect, having many human frailties; but they were still immortals.

Hellenistic astronomers and astrologers charted these multitudinous movements, and labeled them as planets in direct, stationary, and retrograde motions; making heliacal risings and settings; *cazimi*, combust, and under the beams; conjunct one another, sextile, square, trine, and opposed. The planetary gods were rollicking about the heavens, traveling to different celestial palaces, engaging in friendly and adversarial relations, and ever negotiating about the fates of the mortals below, whose lives were under their jurisdiction. When a planet was traveling faster than its average speed, direct in motion, and visible relative to the Sun, its condition was regarded as good because it was moving quickly and directly toward bringing about its matters in ways that could be seen. And when a planet was in harmonious aspect configuration with a benefic planet, it was thought to have the support to bring forth its best expression.

And then there was the terrestrial earth, where mortals were born into the conditions of living human experience, and then died. Like the four elements of which the earth and mortals were composed, mortals were subject to the ever-changing forces of generation and corruption, coming into being and then passing away. Ancient astrologers structured and divided the realms on earth in accordance with the great circles—the horizon, meridian, and ecliptic. They noted the places relative to the earth where the Sun rose, culminated overhead, set beneath the horizon, and descended to the deepest place under the earth. They divided these great circles by twelve, resonant with the twelve zodiacal signs, and each sector became a location where the various good and bad activities of the human experience took place: vital life force, money, siblings, parents, children, illness, spouses, death, religion, honors, friends, and afflictions.

The planets held a special role in the astrological cosmos as mediators between the divine and terrestrial, between the zodiacal signs and the houses. They transmitted the energies of the divine star signs, stepping down the frequencies for human assimilation, and anchoring them into the earthly sphere and human experience through the topics of the twelve houses. The Moon in particular, because she was closest to the earth and moved so quickly, made contact every month with each of the other planets via her conjoinings and aspects, gathering up their effluences and bringing down their significations into the physical body of earth and her inhabitants.

HIERARCHY OF PLANETARY CONDITION

Traditional astrologers made a distinction between a planet's celestial condition and its terrestrial disposition. This was called a planet's essential and accidental dignity by Medieval astrologers. A planet's celestial condition describes how the planet is situated in the sky on a particular day. For the most part, with the exception of the Moon's position, this will be the same for everyone born on that day. Celestial condition is based upon three general categories.

The terminology in the following table will be covered in the subsequent chapters of this book.

Table 1. Hierarchy of Planetary Condition

COSMOS	COSMOLOGICAL FACTORS	CONDITION
Fixed stars	*Decans* *Zodiacal signs*	*Rulership systems.* *Sect rejoicing by zodiacal sign.*
Planetary spheres	*Solar phase synodic cycle*	*Planetary speed, direction, visibility, & phase. Sect rejoicing by solar phase. Lunar applications, phases, nodes, & eclipses. Aspect testimony & relations, bonification & maltreatment.*
Earth	*Houses*	*Active/strong and inactive/weak houses. Fortunate and unfortunate houses. Sect rejoicing by hemisphere. Joys of the houses.*

[handwritten: CONJUNCTION of ♃ planet]

The first and most important consideration is the planet's ZODIACAL SIGN RULERSHIPS. This reflects the greater divinity ascribed to the fixed stars which in turn lend their images to the zodiacal signs. The zodiacal signs as domiciles provide the resources and powers that a planet utilizes in its expression.

Next in importance is a planet's ORBITAL RELATIONSHIP TO THE SUN, for the Sun represents the heart and center of the solar system. The planet's speed, direction, and visibility are all derived from its solar phase relationship and play important roles in how effectively it functions.

The third factor in the hierarchy of a planet's celestial condition is the AS-PECT CONFIGURATIONS it makes with other planets. These provide one of the social systems of alliances and cooperation or enmities and obstacles that planetary gods encounter in attempting to shape the life of the native in accordance with his or her fate.

Once a planet's celestial condition has been determined, the next step is to examine where that individual was born into time and space on a particular day and moment. Like the game of musical chairs in which children dance around a circle of chairs, when the music stops, they sit upon the chairs directly underneath. In a similar fashion at the moment of birth, the planets pause and drop into the houses which stand on earth below their revolving motion. Some of these houses signify the good things of life, and others, more difficult experiences. A planet's own nature, along with its celestial condition, determines how these good and bad human experiences will unfold for the native.

The basic rule for assessing planetary condition is: *The better the planet's condition, the better the outcome.* As Jean Baptiste Morin, a sixteenth-century French astrologer, wrote:

> Every planet in good celestial state, such as in its own sign or exaltation or triplicity, oriental to the Sun and occidental to the Moon, free from adverse aspects to malefics, in direct and rapid motion, etc., is said to be a benefic universally and for the whole world, and so will be a benefic for any individual born at that time—in whatever house it may appear—and this is even more certain if it receives the favorable rays of the benefics. For the good or evil of a planet's nature or condition is neither abolished nor altered by the houses but is merely given a specific determination, and the planets are more effective in their action the more their celestial state is in conformity with their natures [...]
>
> Furthermore any planet in adverse celestial state, such as in exile, retrograde, in bad aspect to the malefics, and receiving no good aspects from the benefics, can be considered to be malefic universally and for the whole world and so also for any individual born at that time—no matter in what house it falls by either location or rulership—because such a condition vitiates the planet's nature [...]
>
> Finally a planet in an intermediate state such as peregrine and adversely configured by benefics—or favorably so by malefics—will act in a moderate way in producing good and evil. But one should observe that the more ways a planet is assisted in its celestial state the more good it is likely to produce, but the more ways it is impaired the more it will incline to cause evil.[1]

We will now proceed to unpack this paragraph in the balance of this book. We will present the traditional approach to the planets, signs, solar and lunar phase, and aspects. We will examine the celestial condition of each planet in the example charts, and then you will have the guided opportunity to repeat this process with your own chart. Once we know exactly what we can expect from each planet, in terms of both its strengths and weaknesses, we can then begin the process of interpreting its meaning in a particular chart as we place the planets into the wheel of houses and experiences of the human condition on earth.

In the context of discussing planetary condition, one final but important comment must be made about the terms "good" and "bad" (benefic and malefic, favorable or unfavorable, fortunate or unfortunate, as well as several other sets of synonyms). Modern psychological approaches emphasize that the counseling

---

1   Jean Baptiste MORIN, *Astrologica Gallica*, 21, 2.2, trans. Baldwin.

astrologer never uses the words good or bad in speaking to a client. For the most part, this distinction has dropped out of many modern interpretation books. Editorial guidelines in some astrological publishing houses disqualified these words from the texts. However, the notion of benefic and malefic is a fundamental consideration in traditional astrology.

When I use the phrase "good condition", I mean the conditions that lead to long life, good health, prosperity, happiness, and success in one's endeavors. When I use the phrase "bad condition", I mean the conditions that lead to short life, poor health, poverty, suffering, and failure in one's endeavors. It is based upon the recognition that the human condition is filled with both good and bad experiences, and the astrological chart reflects that reality. Whether or not a person can do something to change the indications of the chart is another discussion altogether that entails beliefs about fate and the efficacy of spiritual practice and free will. But in this work, our lens is what the chart itself indicates about the good and bad of the life of the native based upon the principles of traditional astrology. When using these insights in astrological counseling, you must filter them through your own belief system regarding the roles of human choice, intentionality, and free will.

CHAPTER 2

The First Five Steps

IN LEARNING TRADITIONAL ASTROLOGY

———

IF YOU HAVE A BACKGROUND IN MODERN ASTROLOGY, there are several conceptual and methodological shifts that are necessary before you can approach the traditional methods of viewing and interpreting charts. This might seem disconcerting at first, as it calls into question some of the most basic understandings that inform your astrological practice. You shouldn't have to reject what you already know and have found valuable. But it will be useful to temporarily shelve these perspectives as you explore traditional techniques. Otherwise, you will likely face ongoing confusion and difficulty mastering the system. At the conclusion of your studies of this material, you can then make an informed decision as to how you want to continue, which techniques and ideas to integrate into your current practice, and which parts of your current practice you might want to revise.

From this point on we may speak of the "native" and the "nativity". These words come from the Latin verb *natus* which means "to be born". Thus, the "native" is the person whose chart we're reading (the person who is born) and their nativity is the astrological chart depicting the arrangement of the planets at the time of birth.

STEP ONE: SUSPEND USE OF THE
TWELVE-LETTER ALPHABET

The basic components of astrological symbolism are planets, zodiacal signs, and houses. From the beginning of the astrological tradition, planets had special correspondences with certain signs and houses that were considered more conducive and beneficial to the expression of each planet's essential nature. We will discuss the specifics of these associations in later chapters that cover various zodiacal-sign rulership systems and the planetary joys of the houses.

However, the planet/sign and planet/house correspondences of traditional astrology differ from the modern *twelve-letter alphabet* system popularized during the second half of the twentieth century. The twelve-letter alphabet teaches that the meanings of a particular planet, sign, and house are derived from the same principle, such as Mars, Aries, and the first house, and are thus interchangeable in interpretation. The same would hold true for Venus, Taurus, and the second house; Mercury, Gemini, and the third house; etc.

But from the traditional standpoint, while Mars is associated with Aries as its lord, there is no basis for its association with the first house, nor is there any particular correspondence between Aries and the first house. This operating principle is especially evident and problematic in many modern "cookbook style" interpretation guides that present the same interpretation of a planet—for example, Mars—in either Gemini or in the third house. A traditional astrologer would have completely different criteria for delineating the meaning of Mars in a sign versus in a house, and would not equate Gemini with the third house.

STEP TWO: USE ONLY THE SEVEN VISIBLE PLANETS

Evidence of divination by astrology goes back to the second millennium BCE when cuneiform texts identified the seven visible planetary bodies: Sun, Moon, Mercury, Venus, Mars, Jupiter, and Saturn. These were the only planets known to ancient peoples, since Uranus, Neptune, Pluto, and the asteroids weren't discovered until after the invention of the telescope in the seventeenth century. Thus, the systems of traditional astrology, as practiced by Babylonian, Hellenistic, Arabic, Indian, Medieval, and Renaissance astrologers, were developed and refined over a 4000-year period based solely upon the seven visible planets. The North and South Nodes of the Moon as well as Lots (Arabic parts) were also a part of the symbol systems of traditional astrology, but the outer planets and asteroids were not.

Sun   Moon   Mercury   Venus   Mars   Jupiter   Saturn

FIGURE 2. THE SEVEN VISIBLE PLANETS

You should certainly continue to include the outer planets and the asteroids (as I do) in your chart analysis. But you will learn to regard them in different ways than the seven original planets. And you will learn how to extract much more information about the chart from the seven visible planets.

STEP THREE: USE TRADITIONAL RULERSHIPS

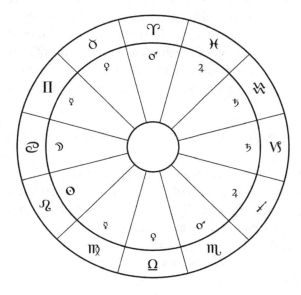

FIGURE 3. TRADITIONAL SIGN RULERSHIPS

Most astrologers are aware of planetary rulerships, whereby each of the planets is said to rule a sign: for example, the Sun rules Leo. The ancient terminology states that each planet is the "lord" of a particular sign; when it happens to be located in that sign in a particular chart, it is thought to possess certain powers. There is general agreement between traditional and modern thought that the Sun rules Leo, the Moon rules Cancer, Mercury is the ruler of Gemini and Virgo, and Venus is the ruler of Taurus and Libra. But then the traditional and modern systems begin to diverge. When the modern planets Uranus, Neptune, and Pluto were discovered, they were assigned as rulers of the signs Aquarius, Pisces, and Scorpio respectively, displacing the ancient rulers: Saturn, Jupiter, and Mars. This stems from modern astrologers noticing an affinity between each of the new planets and these three signs that traditionally had dual rulership. The rationale for the traditional system of rulerships was based upon a geometrical substructure depicted by the *thema mundi*, the symbolic chart of the creation of the world, rather than upon the modern principle of affinities between planet and sign. The *thema mundi* will be discussed further in the section on zodiacal signs.

When practicing traditional astrology, it is necessary to use the traditional rulers of all twelve signs as indicated in the diagram above. In particular, use Saturn as a ruler for Aquarius as well as for Capricorn, Jupiter as the ruler of Pisces as well as for Sagittarius, and Mars as the ruler of Scorpio as well as for Aries. This is especially important when determining which planet is the ruler of a particular house in order to interpret the meaning of that house in an individual chart. For example, if someone were to ask about the topic of relationships—signified by the seventh house—and that house is occupied by the sign Pisces, you would look to the planet Jupiter rather than to Neptune to make your judgment.

STEP FOUR: USE WHOLE SIGN HOUSES

For the first seven hundred years of horoscopic astrology during the Hellenistic and Arabic eras, the house system of choice was whole sign houses, where signs and houses are coincident. Each house contains all thirty degrees of one—and only one—sign. This differs from the quadrant house systems used in modern astrology, such as Placidus, Porphyry, Regiomontanus, and Koch, where houses are of unequal size and can contain a varying number of degrees of one, two, or even three different signs. Ancient astrologers were aware of and discussed other house systems such as Porphyry and equal houses, but used these sparingly and only for specialized inquires (FIGURE 4).

In whole sign houses, all of the degrees of the rising sign occupy the first house and all planets in that sign are read as first house planets, regardless of their degree. For instance, even if a planet is at three degrees of a sign and the rising sign is twenty-eight degrees of the same sign, the planet is still read as a first house planet. The Ascendant degree is a point floating somewhere in the first house. While it still marks the horizon, designating which degrees of your rising sign are above the horizon and which are below the horizon, it does not divide the first house from the twelfth house. The sign following the rising sign occupies the entirety of the second house, and all planets in that sign are considered second house planets, etc.

Planets may occupy different houses in a whole sign house system as compared to a quadrant house system. When considering one's own chart for the first time using whole sign houses, if planets shift houses, this different perspective can initially cause an identity crisis for many astrologers. But you are asked to reflect upon and consider the changes as you work through the process. As you look at the example chart, note which planets change house position.

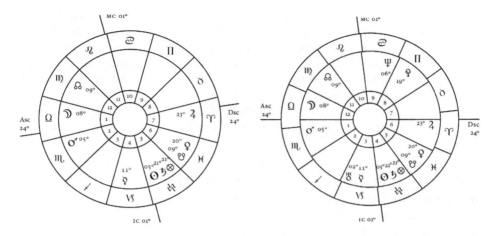

FIGURE 4. CHART OF MARIA VON TRAPP:
WHOLE SIGN VERSUS PORPHYRY HOUSES

25 January 1905, 23:50, Tyrol, Austria. LEFT: *Whole Sign houses (signs and houses are equal).* RIGHT: *Porphyry houses (first house begins from the Ascendant degree). Note that, in this example, the Whole Sign chart uses the traditional seven planets, while the Porphyry chart includes the trans-Saturnian planets, Uranus, Neptune, and Pluto:* ♅ ♆ ♇.

STEP FIVE: PLANETARY CONDITION

While the first four steps mentioned above are primarily shifts of technique, this fifth step entails a major conceptual shift. In the modern approach, all of the planets in a particular chart are considered equal in their capacity to bring about their matters; they are thought to do so in different ways depending upon their sign, house, and aspects. Interpretation involves blending together various combinations of keywords.

However, in the traditional approach, some planets are more capable of manifesting their significations in stable, consistent, long-lasting, and beneficial ways for the individual. Prior to interpreting the meaning of a planet in a particular chart, therefore, the astrologer must first determine its *condition*. This is based upon a number of different criteria such as a planet's sect, zodiacal sign rulerships, its phase relationship to the Sun, and its aspects. Each of these factors was thought to have an influence on the planet's capacity to bring about positive outcomes for the individual.

Ancient astrologers taught that the better a planet's condition, the more support a planet has and the better job it can do. Vettius Valens wrote in the second century:

> The benefic stars that are suitably and well-situated bring forth their
> own matters according to their nature and the nature of their zodi-
> acal sign, with the additional mixture of the aspect testimonies and
> co-presences of each star. When they are unfavorably situated, they
> are indicative of reversals and obstacles. Likewise, even the malefic
> stars, when they operate suitably and are of the sect, are givers of good
> and indicative of greater rank and success. But when they are in un-
> profitable places, they bring about banishment and accusations.[1]

A paraphrase of this paragraph might read that if the benefic planets (e.g.
Jupiter, Venus) are in good condition, they bring about their own significations
in accordance with the sign that they occupy, but if in poor condition, they bring
about reversals. In a similar way, the malefic planets (e.g. Saturn, Mars) when in
favorable condition bring forth good outcomes, great position, and success; but
in poor condition, malefic planets bring about disasters and accusations.

So, if a traditional astrologer wanted to interpret how the planet Mars located in the second house might be expected to operate in terms of the person's
ability to generate financial resources to support their livelihood, Mars would
first be subject to an exhaustive analysis based upon its sect, four kinds of sign
rulership (domicile, exaltation, triplicity, bound), its phase relationship to the
Sun (speed, visibility, direction, heliacal rise/set), and its aspects from benefic
and malefic planets. If the condition of Mars was determined to be good, the
astrologer could then indicate stable and fortunate money matters. However, if
the condition was judged to be bad, the reading would signify challenges and
conflict in generating resources, or financial instability.

Look at the example chart of Maria von Trapp, the real-life heroine behind
The Sound of Music (FIGURE 4). If one were to inquire about the topic of wealth, a
traditional astrologer would begin to assess the chart in the following manner. The
second house signifies money. It is occupied by the sign of Scorpio, whose ruler is
Mars, which belongs to the sect of this nocturnal chart. Because Mars is located
in its own sign of rulership, the primary indication is good for wealth. Since Mars
also rules Aries, which is located in the seventh house, part of the wealth comes
from marriage. Maria was an orphan who married a wealthy baron, and her husband was a high-ranking military officer (Mars). Here is an example of Valens'
teaching where a malefic planet (Mars) in good condition brings about a great
position for Maria—who became a baroness. Note that using Pluto as the ruler of
Scorpio would not yield the same clear delineation. A full analysis would factor

---

1   Vettius VALENS, *Anthology* 1.1.

in a number of other variables, but this simplified version suffices to illustrate the point.

This book will thoroughly explore planetary condition as a preliminary to interpretation. You will not only learn how to determine if a planet is strong or weak in its overall ability to do good for the individual, but also in which particular ways it is strong or weak. In the process, you will learn how ancient astrologers thought about sect, zodiacal signs, houses, aspects, and phases.

Some of this material will give you the rationale for many astrological doctrines you have been taught as givens and provide a better foundation for any kind of astrology you do. Other parts of this material may challenge your previous ways of thinking and interpretation, and require you to either re-evaluate or defend your former beliefs. In any case, how you think about and practice astrology will be deepened, stimulated, and expanded.

A REMARK ON FATE AND FREE WILL

Some astrologers who have been trained in the modern approach may be taken aback at the seemingly deterministic language in which this book is written. Indeed, I am sometimes asked if I believe that the planets themselves are the causes of good and bad experiences in a person's life. In this book I want to communicate the tradition of ancient astrology as it was conceptualized and practiced by its founders and by the many generations of astrologers that have preceded us. At the same time, my intention is to make whatever insights and benefits this system offers available to the contemporary practitioner—short of totally reframing it to accommodate the sensibilities of the modern mindset and belief system.

This is a challenge because the ancient astrological teachings were recorded from the perspective that the planets shape the good and bad events of a person's life. This is antithetical to the contemporary worldview and predominant religious convictions that it is the will of a person, not the planets, that is the source of all of a person's actions. The dichotomy between the fate compelled by the stars and the free will of the human soul was a major topic of debate in the philosophical and religious circles of the ancient world. Furthermore, questions concerning the efficacy of prayers, sacrifices, and salvation to avert negative stellar indications, whether planetary appearances are signs or causes, as well as whether the stars could be inherently bad were contemplated and discussed by ancient thinkers as they still are today.

Did the ancients believe that the planets are the actual physical causes of human actions and terrestrial events? Yes, some astrologers did. Claudius Ptolemy adapted Aristotelian natural philosophy as a basis for the explanation of astro-logical influences. The motions of the Sun and Moon were the causes of heating and cooling on the earth which precipitated the change and transformation of the four elements into each other by means of hot, wet, cold, and dry forces. Since humans were composed of the same elements as the earth (albeit with a spark of the divine thrown in for good measure, according to some spiritual philosophers), the planets were likewise, at least in part, the physical causes of human activity. However, Ptolemy himself also conceded that there were addi-tional factors to consider.

Do I believe that planets operate as actual physical causes of human ac-tions? Not in so far as some kind of electromagnetic or other vibrational forces are emitted by planets, travel through the solar system and impact humans at birth to make them do good or bad things over the course of their lives. Nor do I believe that the planets are embodiments of astral gods who force their wills on mortals. However, the traditional view of astrology is that the conditions of planets at birth and subsequently over time describe the complex web of inter-dependent causes that surround an individual. These circumstances predispose a person to make certain choices, followed up by words and actions whose even-tual outcomes are better or worse in relation to their own best interests.

The planet is not physically forcing a person to take a certain action—this is the gap where some kind of free will exists. However it often does describe how the results of that action will turn out in the end. In my attempt to report the tradition as it was recorded and as best as I have been able to understand it, the language of causation that I use often reflects the syntax of the ancient astrologers themselves.

PART ONE

PLANETS AND SECT

CHAPTER 3

The Planets

———

WESTERN ASTROLOGY ORIGINATED IN MESOPOTAMIA, WHERE EARLY astronomers identified the seven visible planets. In their cosmological system, the celestial bodies were understood as one of the manifestations of the divine. The planets were named after the gods and goddesses and imbued with their mythic and religious attributes. When the planets appeared in the sky, the planetary deities were thought to be communicating their wishes and intentions to humanity. The role of the astrologer was to carefully observe the motions and positions of the planetary gods, note the corresponding terrestrial effects, and convey this information to the kings who could then rule the country in accordance with divine intention. The practice of astrology was motivated by the desire to know whether or not the planetary gods were favorably disposed to the outcome of various events on earth. If not, there was recourse to a set of rituals, the *namburbi*, to try to persuade the god to change his or her mind. This speaks to an early view of astrological prognostication as not absolutely deterministic.

THE NAMES OF THE PLANETS

When the astronomical knowledge of the Babylonians was introduced into Greece around the sixth century BCE, Greek astronomer-philosophers, most likely the Pythagoreans, gave the planets the names of the Greek gods who most closely resembled their Babylonian counterparts. For example, the Greeks identified the planet that the Babylonians had named Inanna/Ishtar, the goddess of love, with the "star of Aphroditē" which we know today as Venus. One way of understanding the meaning of a planet is to become familiar with the mythic attributes and deeds of the god or goddess who shares the same name. This archetypal approach reaches back into the heart of astrological origins that was predicated upon the divine nature of planetary energy.

Below is a table of the corresponding planetary names from the Babylonian, Greek, Roman, and Indian astrological traditions.[1] A table comparing the significations of the planets and the attributes of the corresponding deities is included at the end of this section.

Table 2. English, Roman, Greek, Babylonian, & Indian Planetary Deities

ENGLISH	ROMAN	GREEK	BABYLONIAN	INDIAN
Sun	*Sol*	*Hēlios*	*Shamesh*	*Surya*
Moon	*Luna*	*Selēnē*	*Sin*	*Chandra*
Mercury	*Mercurius*	*Hermēs*	*Nebu*	*Budha*
Venus	*Venus*	*Aphroditē*	*Ishtar*	*Shukra*
Mars	*Martus*	*Ares*	*Nergal*	*Kuja*
Jupiter	*Jove*	*Zeus*	*Marduk*	*Brihaspati*
Saturn	*Saturnus*	*Kronos*	*Ninurta*	*Shani*

Hellenistic, Arabic, Medieval, and Renaissance astrology differed from the Babylonian. While the planets still carried the names of the gods, the planets were increasingly disassociated from divine forces. After the second century, astrology took a scientific turn where terrestrial events were seen as the results of physical causes due to planetary motion rather than divine intention. Ancient astrologers were certainly cautious of the increasing influence of the monotheistic Christian and Islamic religions and did not want to present an alternate polytheistic pantheon of deities. Or they may have thought that it was more advantageous, both from a scholarly as well as a political standpoint, to position astrology as a science rather than as religion. The exception to this is found in the hermetic spiritual and magical traditions, an underground stream of astrological transmission, where planetary gods were invoked for intercession in human affairs. Nevertheless, the significations of the planets continued to reflect many qualities of the deities who shared their names. Modern archetypal psychology sees a correspondence between the ancient deities and the archetypes of the psyche: the planets represent the various parts of the personality whose nature can be approached through mythological investigation.

[1] Greek technical terms have generally been transliterated according to the conventions established by Robert SCHMIDT in his introduction to book 7 of Vettius Valens' *Anthology*. These conventions have been followed by most scholars and translators of traditional astrology, such as Dorian GREENBAUM, Benjamin DYKES, and Chris BRENNAN.

THE TRADITIONAL
SIGNIFICATIONS OF THE PLANETS

The Sun signifies the matters concerning soul, the Moon that concern
the body, Saturn possessions, Jupiter money, Mars military matters,
Venus matters of desire and partnership, Mercury custom and character and speech.—TEUCER OF BABYLON.[2]

Each planet has a basic nature that is expressed on several different levels of
reality. From a cosmological perspective that envisions the world as ensouled,
the planets represent the gods, who mediate and transmit the energies of the
divine realms to mortals, regulating and governing human life. Each planetary
god represents some faculty of the soul which links human consciousness to divine consciousness. In accordance with the principle of "as above, so below", as
the planetary energy descends and becomes more coalesced into physical form,
a planet likewise represents certain human character traits, parts of the body,
types of people, occupations, and concrete objects. The Hermetic principle of
correspondences links each planet to entities in the plant and mineral kingdoms, such as specific herbs and flowers, stones, colors, metals, and tastes, geographical areas, a day of the week and hours of the day. And in a more scientific
conception of the astrological cosmos based upon the Aristotelian principles of
natural philosophy, each planet is understood as some combination of the four
qualities of hot, wet, cold, and dry.

Each planet had authority over one of the seven days of the week, as well as
over the hours of each day. The Sun had authority over Sunday, the Moon over
Monday, Mars over Tuesday, Mercury over Wednesday, Jupiter over Thursday,
Venus over Friday, and Saturn over Saturday. The first hour of each day, beginning at sunrise, was governed by the planet that ruled that day. The subsequent
hours were then subdivided with each planet, in turn, having authority over
a certain portion of the day, based upon the Chaldean order of the planets—
Moon, Mercury, Venus, Sun, Mars, Jupiter, and Saturn.

The planetary ruler of the day and executor of the hour were considered in
all kinds of astrological inceptions (electional charts) in the determination of
auspicious times to initiate events. The planet ruling the day and hour at which a
person was born was also a consideration in natal charts. In addition, planetary
days and hours were an important component of astral magic rituals in which
invocations and supplications were made to the planetary gods on the day and

hour that was sacred to the deity who had authority over the particular thing being requested. For example, love magic rituals were considered to be more potent when enacted on a day and hour that Aphroditē ruled. Finally, planetary days and hours were considered in charts that looked to the time a person took ill in order to judge the outcome of the disease, or for the times to pick, prepare, or administer botanical medications.

Modern astrology has reframed the ancient understanding of the planets. The ancient planetary gods and goddesses have now withdrawn into the recesses of the psychological unconscious. When the astrological chart is viewed as a map of the psyche, the planets represent the active forces of the psyche or the various parts of the personality. In lay language we can recognize them as the many people/voices inside our own being who play different roles in our lives and have different agendas, needs, desires, and directives. When astrology moves into psychological terrain, integration of the "Jungian Self" can be likened to recognizing, expressing, balancing, and harmonizing the functions represented by the various planets. Remember that the basic natures of each planet reach back into the archetypal realm of the great celestial gods of old.

The main source in the ancient literature for an exposition concerning the planets is *The Nature and Force of the Seven Planets* by Teucer of Babylon.[3] Teucer's work was used as the basis for much, but not all, of Vettius Valens' chapter on the planets, as well as Porphyry's *Introduction* to the *Tetrabiblos*, and Antiochus of Athens' *Summary*.[4] Claudius Ptolemy wrote about the planets in terms of their qualities of hot, wet, cold, and dry, which was incorporated into Hephaistio of Thebes' comments on the planets.[5]

THE TWO LIGHTS: THE SUN AND THE MOON

There are two lights in the sky. The Sun shines by day and orders the seasons of the year, while the Moon illuminates the night and regulates the weeks of the month. Ancient astrologers called them the Celestial God and Goddess, which manifested as the terrestrial King and Queen, and then, the father and mother. These luminaries had more extensive roles than the other planets in the interpretation of the chart. Paulus said that they rule everything, and being sovereigns of all things, they obtained dominion over all.[6]

---

3   This text has been translated by James HOLDEN and is included in an appendix of his
     translation of the RHETORIUS *Compendium*.
4   VALENS, *Anthology* 1.1; PORPHYRY, *Introduction* 1.4, 1.45; ANTIOCHUS, *Summary* 1.1.
5   PTOLEMY, *Tetrabiblos* 1.4; HEPHAISTIO, *Apotelesmatics* 1.2.
6   PAULUS, *Introduction* 3.

THE SUN is nature's fire and it represents the light of the intellect, the organ of mental perception, the life breath and its movement. It represents the soul, as the divine part of the human mind. It is recognized for its heating and somewhat drying qualities. It indicates the paternal and ruling person, public reputation, people of nobility and high repute, and honors. The Sun rules the head, the right eye, the heart; gold, wheat and barley; the color yellow, the bitter taste, and Sunday. The poetic name of the Sun was *Phōs* or light itself.

The planetary gods associated with the Sun are Shamesh, Heliōs, and Apollō—all were portrayed with beams of light emanating from their heads and they were connected to divination and oaths.

The nature of the Sun is to build. Its essence, according to Valens, is the ruler of light. From a modern perspective, it is the archetype of the Leader and Illuminator.

THE MOON reflects the light of the Sun to earth and represents a person's life, the entire physical body, and conception. It is recognized for its humidifying qualities and is slightly warming. It indicates the mother and women who rule; legitimate marriage; the mistress of the house, the nurse, and the matters of the household; the city and assemblies of people; and voyages and travel. It rules over the left eye, the stomach, breasts, spleen, and marrow; silver and glass; the color green, the salty taste, and Monday.

The poetic name of the Moon, *Selēnē*, means the bright or flashing flame. The Moon was linked to the Babylonian god Sin, who measured time. In Greece and Rome, the Moon was envisioned as the goddess Selēnē who watches over the sleep of mortals, then Artemis and Diana as the virgin huntress of the new moon and overseer of childbirth.

The nature of the Moon is to nourish. Its essence, according to Valens, is foresight. From a modern perspective, it is the archetype of the Caretaker.

The Sun and Moon as luminaries are referred to as the king and queen. This suggests that the roles of the other five planets fall under their auspices and, much like the ministers of a king and queen, assist in bringing about the various matters of a person's life in accordance with their own natures.

THE FIVE PLANETS

SATURN was associated with the destructive life force in nature due to its excessive cold, moderately dry, and constricting qualities. It was seen as a source of sorrow, misery, long-lasting punishment, grief, captivities, and mishaps. It brought slander, disrepute, and trouble. It signified very old persons, matters that are long-lasting, old doings; help from ancient or obsolete things or older persons; and elder brothers. Saturn also designated those who do not marry, widowhood, orphanhood, and childlessness. The Saturnine character was described as dark, downcast, disposed to silence, incapable of emotional display, austere, solitary, and black-clad. It indicated laborers and farmers because of its rule over the land; work at waterside trades; tax and custom collectors; and those who are renters of property. It indicates long-lasting chronic complaints from cold and moisture, and rules over the thighs, knees, lymph, bladder, and kidneys, as well as hidden injuries and gout. Saturn is castor-like in color, astringent in taste, linked to the metal lead, and associated with Saturday.

When Saturn is in good condition, it gives authority over fields, building, watery property, abundance, property of others, inheritance and windfalls, power to subordinate and suppress others, or to benefit from the losses of others. When Saturn is in bad condition, it brings debt, imprisonment, false accusations, banishment, and chronic misfortune.

The poetic name of Saturn was *Phainōn*, which means the shining one. The Babylonians named this planet Ninurta, their god of agriculture and irrigation, war, sickness, and death. The Greek Kronos was associated with old age and death and the Roman Saturnus was a god of agriculture.

The nature of Saturn is to endure. Its essence, according to Valens, is ignorance and necessity. From a modern perspective, it is the archetype of the Elder.

JUPITER was associated with the warm and moist power that is productive of life force and signifies magnificence, reputation, dignity, prosperity, abundance, inheritance, knowledge, and justice. It represented relief from troubles, freedom from bondage, friendships with great men, and the favor of leaders and the masses. It is the main significator of childbearing and children. It rules over the thighs, feet, liver, sperm, uterus, and the body's right side. Its color is light grey, it is sweet in taste, its metal is tin, and its weekday is Thursday.

When Jupiter is in good condition, it indicates those who receive honors and renown, who are well spoken of because of their goodness and piety, who are happy in marriage and children, and rich in friendships. However, when Jupiter is in poor condition, it decreases the powers of the high-minded and begrudges progress in life.

The poetic name of Jupiter was *Phaethōn*, which means the radiant one. The Babylonians knew this planet as Marduk, and to the Greeks he was Zeus. Both of these deities battle a dragon, establish order in the cosmos, and become the supreme leader of the gods. Protectors of the state, both are guardians of law and justice, and rule wisdom and human fate.

The nature of Jupiter is to expand and affirm. According to Valens, it is the ruler of rank, crowns, and zeal. From a modern perspective, it is the archetype of the Sage, Priest, and Great Man.

MARS was understood by ancient astrologers as the dry, fiery, and hot power that is destructive of the life force as it appears both in nature and in human character. This planet was associated with violence, wars, anger, murder, danger, recklessness, the hunt and chase, combat, torture, and bloodshed. It led to estrangements, breaches in friendship, enemies, lawsuits, theft, and taking away of belongings. It signifies lies, reproaches, and perjury. It governs those who gain their ends through the use of fire or iron. Sexually, it was connected with the procreative impulse and sexual intercourse, as well as adulteries, ruination of women, and abortion. In the body, it was said to rule the head, seat, genitals, blood, sperm duct, bile, adrenals, and the elimination of excrement; it brings fevers, inflammations, ulcerations, and pustules. Its color is red, it is acidic in taste, its metal is iron, and its day is Tuesday.

When Mars is in good condition, it can make the person daring, valiant, courageous, indomitable, and conversant in danger; it signifies military leaders, warriors, and success in warfare. However, when it is in poor condition, it makes the native a wrong-doer; blasphemous, uncontrollable, and reckless; and it may bring severe bodily suffering.

The poetic name of Mars is *Puroeides*, which means the fiery one. The Babylonians knew him as Nergal, the god of the underworld, fevers, plagues, and war, whom the Greeks associated with Arēs, their own god of war, violence, and anger. The Roman Martus was a protector of the empire through his military prowess and valor.

The nature of Mars is to energize. Its essence, according to Valens, is action and effort. From a modern perspective, it is the archetype of the Warrior and Competitor.

VENUS was associated with the moist and warming power that is productive of the life force and signifies desire, love, beauty, cleanliness, purity, and religious worship. She also signifies female persons—the mother, sister, and daughter; she rules over marriage, and benefits from royal women. She makes for a cheerful and friendly character. She is associated with cosmetic adornment, wearing of gold, skill in the arts of the Muses (singing and painting), and theatre. Venus is also associated with embroidery, dyeing, and unguents; crafts masters or trade; and work with precious stones. Venus rules the neck, face, the sense of smell, the front parts of the body, the parts of intercourse, the lungs, and bile. Venus corresponds to the color white, the greasy taste, precious stones, the olive, and Friday.

When Venus is in good condition, she brings beauty of appearance, distinction, and purity; popular esteem and praise from superiors; an affectionate nature; erotic love; wealth and success. However, when in poor condition, she lessens the limits of beneficence and brings jealousy and hate at the end of one's successes.

The poetic name of Venus is *Phōsphoros*, the torchbearer (later, in Latin, *Lucifer*). The Babylonians knew the planet Venus as Inanna and Ishtar, the goddess of love and the fertility of the land, while to the Greeks this planet was the star of Aphroditē, goddess of beauty and desire.

The nature of Venus is to magnetize. Its essence, according to Valens, is love, desire, and beauty. From a modern perspective, it is the archetype of the Lover and Harmonizer.

MERCURY is the bestower of forethought and intelligence, and rules over practical wisdom, education, reason, and knowledge. His qualities are quickly changing, sometimes wet and sometimes dry. He is connected with language, communications, friendship, fellowship, numbers and accounts, weights and measures, coins, sports, commerce, business, marketing, and banking. He can make orators, philosophers, scribes, doctors, architects, musicians, astrologers, prophets, diviners, augurs, and dream interpreters. He indicates younger persons, children, and nurslings. He gives the capacity for display of skills, as well as deception, lies, thievery, and sleight of hand. He rules the hands, shoulders, fingers, joints, intestines, arteries, tongue, and the sense of hearing. His correspondences are the color blue, sharpness in taste, copper or brass and coins used in commerce, and Wednesday.

When Mercury is in good condition, it makes a person industrious, sound of judgment, successful in intellectual matters, sociable, ingenious, and respected. When in bad condition it can lead to disturbances of the mind, madness, ecstasy, and melancholy—all things capricious in their final outcomes.

The poetic name for Mercury is *Stilbōn*, which means the gleaming, glittering, or glistening one. The Babylonians associated this planet with Nebu, the god of scribes, bestower of human wisdom, and inventor of writing. The Greeks placed this planet under the auspices of Hermēs, the winged messenger of Zeus, patron of writing, the sciences, commerce, travel, athletics and luck. Hermēs was also the protector of thieves, and a psychopomp or guide through the underworld.

The nature of Mercury is to communicate. Its essence, according to Valens, is law, friendship, and trust. From a modern perspective, it is the archetype of the Messenger.

On the following page is a comparative table of the similarities and differences between Babylonian and Greek deities associated with the same planet, as well as the astrological significations of the planets as given by Vettius Valens, based on his descriptions in Anthology 1.1.

Table 3. Attributes of the Babylonian and Greek Planetary Deities

PLANET	BABYLONIAN	GREEK	MEANING (V. VALENS)
SUN	SHAMASH *God of justice, divination, oaths, solar disc of radiating sunbeams*	HĒLIOS *God who sees all, phœbus, brilliant, witness to oaths, drives chariot of sun across the sky; cults on Kos and Rhodes* APOLLŌ *God of divination, healing, and music*	*Light of the mind, organ of perception of the soul, kingly office, persons of high repute, judgment, crowns of office, popular leadership, father, height of fortune*
MOON	SIN *God of wisdom, measurer of time*	SELĒNĒ *Goddess of full moon who watches over sleep of mortals* ARTEMIS *Goddess of new moon, childbirth, animals, & the hunt* HEKATĒ *Goddess of waning moon, crossroads & the underworld*	*Reflection of solar light, life, body, mother, conception, queen, wanderings, legal marriage, housekeeping, property, gathering of crowds, home, ships, receipts and expenditures*
MERCURY	NEBU *Scribe god, commerce, writer of destinies, source of human wisdom*	HERMĒS *Winged messenger of Zeus, patron of writing and sciences, esp. math and astronomy; commerce, travel, athletics, luck. Psychopomp/ guide to underworld, protector of thieves*	*Letters, education of children, commerce, disputation, speech, brothers, youth, theft, bestower of intellectual and practical wisdom, augurs, interpreter of dreams, lawyers, orators, philosophers, temple-builders, searchers of the sky*
VENUS	INNANA/ISHTAR *Goddess of love as evening star, fertility of the land, goddess of war as morning star*	APHRODITĒ *Goddess of love, beauty, sexual desire, pleasures*	*Desire, erotic love, arts, gold jewelry, festivities, precious stones, music, friendships, acquisitions of belongings, weddings, painting, reconciliations for the good*
MARS	NERGAL *God of underworld, fevers, plagues, identified with Erra as god of war*	ARĒS *God of war, brutality, rage, patron of soldiers*	*Violence, war, adultery, plundering, anger, combat, enemies, bloodshed, iron, military generals, warriors, ruination of women, loss, banishment, sexual intercourse, breaches of friends, murder, imprisonment*

PLANET	BABYLONIAN	GREEK	MEANING (V. VALENS)
JUPITER	MARDUK *Battles dragon Tiamat, established order and organization in the cosmos, guardian of justice and law, presides over council of other 6 planetary gods, determines men's fate*	ZEUS *Battles the dragon Typhœus, and establishes order and organization in the cosmos, leader of the gods, guardian of justice and the law, protector of the state, god of wisdom, manifests as lightening and thunder, controls fate of humans*	*Begetting of children, erotic love, alliances, knowledge, abundance, justice, sovereignty, mediation of disputes, confirmation of good things, friendship with great men, great gifts, freedom, deliverance from evils, trusts, inheritances*
SATURN	NINURTA *God of war and god of agriculture, lord of the Earth, regulates irrigation, god of sickness and death*	KRONOS *Father Time, rules over old age and death, god of agriculture*	*Solitary, deceitful, miserable, violent actions, depressions, long-lasting punishments, tears, accusations, concealments, captivity, childlessness, orphanhood, laborers and farmers, authority over earth, tax and custom collectors, forced activities*

The traditional meanings differ, but also overlap, with the more modern meanings attributed to the planets from an archetypal perspective.

Table 4. Modern Archetypal Meanings of the Seven Planets

PLANET	MODERN ARCHETYPE
SUN	*Leader, illuminator*
MOON	*Mother, caretaker*
MERCURY	*Messenger, trickster*
VENUS	*Lover*
MARS	*Warrior*
JUPITER	*Sage, priest, wise man*
SATURN	*Elder*

CHAPTER 4

Classification

BENEFIC AND MALEFIC

———

THE PLANETS ATTEMPT TO BRING FORTH THEIR OWN SIGNIFICATIONS into the life of the individual. In order to do so, they must mediate between the zodiacal signs and the houses. They draw upon the resources and powers of the zodiacal signs that they occupy, and as active agents, they bring about their significations into the earthly life of an individual through the houses in which they are placed and in accordance with the houses they rule. Based upon their condition and position, they will accomplish this more or less effectively and more or less in the individual's best interests. We are now ready to begin our discussion about the factors that contribute to a planet's condition, which influences its ability to bring about its most beneficial outcomes for the native.

The planets are classified according to four categories: elemental qualities, benefic and malefic nature, masculine and feminine gender, and day and night sect.

QUALITIES	Planets can be classified as *hot, cold, moist, and dry*.
NATURE	Planets can be classified as *benefic*, "doers of good", or *malefic*, "doers of bad".
GENDER	Planets can be classified as belonging to either the *masculine* gender or the *feminine* gender.
SECT	Planets can be classified as belonging either to the *diurnal* (day) sect or to the *nocturnal* (night) sect.

Table 5. Classifications of the Planets

HOT	Sun, Mars, Jupiter, Venus, Moon	CHANGEABLE	Mercury
COLD	Saturn		
MOIST	Moon, Venus, Jupiter	CHANGEABLE	Mercury
DRY	Mars, Sun, Saturn		
BENEFIC	Jupiter, Venus	CHANGEABLE	Mercury
MALEFIC	Saturn, Mars		
MASCULINE	Sun, Jupiter, Saturn, Mars	ANDROGYNOUS	Mercury
FEMININE	Moon, Venus		
DIURNAL	Sun, Jupiter, Saturn	COMMON	Mercury
NOCTURNAL	Moon, Venus, Mars		

ELEMENTAL QUALITIES OF THE PLANETS

In the centuries preceding the development of Hellenistic astrology, successive generations of Greek philosophers were speculating upon the primal elements that comprised the world, and in turn, the human body which was made of the same constituent parts. They proposed that all matter in the sublunar realm was composed of the four elements of fire, earth, air, and water, which were constantly in a state of change due to the qualities of heat, coldness, wetness, and dryness.

In the second century CE, Claudius Ptolemy attempted to give a firm philosophical foundation to Hellenistic astrology based upon the tenets of Aristotle's natural philosophy. He associated each of the planets with some combination of the hot, wet, cold, and dry qualities that were involved in the transformation of matter (*Tetrabiblos* 1.4). He derived these correspondences from the relative proximity of the planets to the obvious heating power of the Sun and the humidifying power of the Moon.

The Sun was found to be heating and somewhat drying. The Moon had moist exhalations that both ripened and putrefied organic matter, but was also slightly warming. Saturn cools and moderately dries. Mars primarily dries and burns. Jupiter has a temperate active force that warms and moistens at the same time. Venus is similar to Jupiter in her temperate nature, but she primarily moistens and then warms. Mercury sometimes dries and sometimes moistens.

When these principles entered into Hellenistic medical astrology (*iatro-mathematika*), diseases were classified as hot and cold. Hot diseases were indicated by configurations of the Moon with the hot planets Mars and the Sun, and cold diseases were signified by the Moon's configurations to the cold planet Saturn, and occasionally Mercury. Hellenistic texts contain extensive passages detailing the type, course, and prognosis of illness based upon the qualities of the planets. The doctrine of the elements and qualities, when applied to mainstream medicine, would take shape as the theories concerning the Hippocratic humors and the Galenic temperaments. However, it was only during the Medieval period that humors and temperaments were grafted onto medical astrological theories.

BENEFIC AND MALEFIC NATURE OF THE PLANETS

Recognizing the existence of both positive and negative outcomes in the world, ancient astrology classified the seven visible planets as having a benefic, malefic, or common nature (able to go either way). On an impersonal level, this distinction speaks to the productive and destructive aspects of the life force—both of which have roles in the cycle of living things.

Venus and Jupiter are classified as benefic planets whose nature better enables them to bring about positive outcomes in the life of the individual, events that are productive of prosperity, success, and happiness. The Greek term, *agathopoios*, means "a doer of good".

Mars and Saturn are classified as malefic planets that are indicative of problematic or destructive outcomes in the life of the individual, events that characterized by poverty, failure, and suffering. Their Greek term, *kakopoios*, means a "doer of bad".

Mercury is classified as "common". It has the capacity to change depending upon which planet it is most closely connected—benefic when with Venus or Jupiter, or malefic when with Mars or Saturn.

There is some disagreement as well as omission in the texts about the Sun and Moon. Some authors saw the Sun as changeable like Mercury, while others placed it with the benefics.[1] The authors are silent about the benefic or malefic nature of the Moon. Both lights may have had a variable nature depending upon

---

1   PTOLEMY, *Tetrabiblos* 1.5; RHETORIUS, *Compendium* 1.2.

the sect of the chart. For the most part, when there is a reference to the benefics or malefics, the author is speaking primarily about Venus and Jupiter or Mars and Saturn.

Ptolemy gave a scientific explanation for this, explaining that Venus and Jupiter are benefic because they abound in the hot and moist qualities, which are conducive to the growth of living things.[2] The cold and dry qualities that are destructive to life are associated with Mars and Saturn, and thus predispose these planets to being malefic in nature. If you plant a seed and give it warmth and moisture, the plant will grow; but if it lies in frozen ground without any water, it will not sprout.

One could also look to how the Greeks themselves viewed their gods—Arēs (Mars) had a lust for bloodshed and battle and was hated by everyone, while Aphroditē (Venus), the embodiment of beauty, was loved and desired by all. Zeus (Jupiter) was the god of abundance, wealth, and justice, while Kronos (Saturn) represented suffering, confinement, and avarice.

A subtle but important point to note is that the planets themselves are not intrinsically good or bad, but the actions that are undertaken by the individual under their auspices can lead to positive or negative, constructive or destructive outcomes in a person's life. In the philosophical circles of antiquity, the position that no planet was inherently bad was a lively topic of debate. The Neoplatonic philosopher Plotinus argued that there are no bad planets because they are divine and they do not contain a cause of evil in their nature.[3] The astrologers themselves recognized this point in the premise that under certain circumstances a malefic planet could bring about beneficial outcomes, while a benefic planet could be limited in the amount of good it could do. According to Rhetorius:

> Malefic planets well-situated by phase, sect, and house magnify the fortunes, while benefic planets badly situated can hinder the fortunes.[4]

Each planet starts off at a baseline of benefic or malefic, but in any given chart a variety of factors can modify its expression from the median baseline towards one pole or the other. The baseline for benefic planets is that they are predisposed to bringing about fortunate outcomes. When Venus and Jupiter are in good condition, they accentuate their own most positive significations as well as the topics of the house they occupy; but in poor condition they are limited in

---

2   PTOLEMY, *Tetrabiblos* 1.6.
3   PLOTINUS, *Enneads* 2.3.1–2.
4   RHETORIUS, *Compendium* 1.2.

the amount of good they can do, or the good is unstable and erratic. The baseline for Mars and Saturn is that they present obstacles and conflicts in the houses they occupy; but if they are in good condition they can bring wealth and leadership and success, albeit with some struggle and persistence. However, when the malefic planets are in poor condition, this is the indication of severe difficulties as regards the houses they occupy and rule.

Table 6. Range of Benefic and Malefic Outcomes

RANGE	BENEFIC (GOOD) VENUS/JUPITER	MALEFIC (BAD) MARS/SATURN
Best	*Very good*	*Not very bad*
+	*Quite good*	*Somewhat bad*
o	*Good*	*Bad*
-	*Somewhat good*	*Quite bad*
Worst	*Not very good*	*Very bad*

A variety of factors can predispose these planets to act better or worse than their natural tendency, which you will learn as you progress in this study. Before we move on to the next category, we will pause first and complete this exercise to anchor what we have learned so far.

→   EXERCISE 1
In order to consolidate your understanding of the basic features that comprise a planet's nature, complete exercise 1:
Characteristics of the Planets

EXERCISE 1

CHARACTERISTICS OF THE PLANETS

For each planet:

1.   *Enter its deity namesake and its associated archetype.*
2.   *List several significations, drawing on traditional meanings (after Valens), and modern ones that you are already familiar with.*
3.   *Describe the elemental quality of the planet (hot, cold, moist, and dry).*
4.   *Note its essential nature: benefic, malefic, or common (changeable).*
5.   *Note its gender (masculine, feminine, or androgynous).*

REFLECTION AND ANALYSIS

1.   Think about the connection between a planet named after a mythic deity and its significations, its natural power/quality, and why it is considered a benefic or malefic influence. Can you recognize a continuum that informs the composite depictions of each planet in the astrological literature?
2.   Do you think that Hellenistic astrology was a fusion of an earlier, mythopoetic view of the cosmos with a newer, more rational and scientific explanation based upon natural philosophy? Or do you think that it stood on its own as a new scientific discipline severed from its earlier mythic roots?

SUN

Deity SHAMESH, HELIOS, APOLLO
Archetype LEADER. ILLUMINATOR
Significations ~~TO BUILD~~; LIGHT of the INTELLECT; SOUL
Quality - HEATING & SOMEWHAT DRYING
Essential Nature TO BUILD
Gender YANG, M
DIURNAL

MOON

Deity SELENE; SIN, ARTEMIS & DIANA
Archetype MOTHER; CARETAKER
Significations - REFLECTS LIGHT of the SUN, PERSON'S LIFE
Quality HUMIDIFYING & SOMEWHAT WARMING (HOT) MOIST
Essential Nature TO NOURISH; FORESIGHT
Gender F
NOCTURNAL

MERCURY

Deity HERMES
Archetype MESSENGER; TRICKSTER   BESTOWER of
Significations COMMUNICATION; SKILLS; INTELLECT; EDUCATION
Quality CHANGEABLE
Essential Nature COMMUNICATION; LAW, FRIENDSHIP TRUST
Gender ANDROGYNOUS
COMMON

VENUS

Deity APHRODITE; INANNA & ISHTAR
Archetype ~~COMB~~ LOVER & HARMONIZER
Significations PRODUCTIVE; DESIRE, LOVE, BEAUTY,
CLEANLINESS
Quality HOT MOIST
Essential Nature BENEFIC - MAGNETIZE
Gender F

MARS

Deity ARES
Archetype WARRIOR; competitive
Significations BURN, destructive, war, RUINATION
Quality HOT, DRY
Essential Nature malefic : ~~~~ FIERY
Gender M

JUPITER

Deity ZEUS
Archetype SAGE.PRIEST, WISE MAN
Significations — MAGNIFICENT
HOT *Quality* warm; moist; pleasure like fire; ~~stabilize~~
Essential Nature Benefic
Gender M

SATURN

Deity NENTYA; KRONOS
Archetype ELDER
Significations LONG LASTING; sorrow - ENDURE; TIRELESS
 NECESSITY
Quality COLD; DRY; CONSTRICTING
Essential Nature rule with abundance / DEBT; malefic
Gender M
  (GOD CONDITION -
      (FIEND)

CHAPTER 5

Gender

OF THE PLANETS

———

ANCIENT ASTROLOGY CLASSIFIES THE PLANETS BY MEANS OF MASCULINE and feminine gender. The Sun, Mercury, Mars, Jupiter, and Saturn belong to the masculine gender; the Moon and Venus belong to the feminine gender; Mercury is common.[1] This is one of the few clear instances where the gender of planets seems to correspond directly to the gender of their divine namesake (i.e., god or goddess). However, there exist a number of astrological conditions that make a planet, whatever its essential gender, shift towards a more masculine or feminine expression.

In this context, masculine and feminine do not refer solely to male and female, but rather to the two basic kinds of energy. Ancient philosophers such as Plato defined masculine energy as initiating action and feminine energy as receiving the action. Ptolemy explains the assignment of gender to the planets in terms of the qualities, where moisture is primarily associated with the feminine and dryness with the masculine.[2] In modern astrology you may have heard gender distinctions referred to as positive or negative polarities, or as yang and yin.

The rationale is that if a planet occupies masculine conditions, it will tend to initiate the action. If a planet occupies feminine conditions, it will tend to be the recipient of action. The masculine energy is characterized by faster movement, and welcomes change. Thus the events of planets in masculine conditions occur sooner. Feminine energy moves slower, is resistant to change, and thus the outcomes of planets in feminine conditions come about later. For the most part, masculine planets act more in accordance with their basic natures when they occupy masculine conditions, as do feminine planets in feminine conditions.

---

1 See PTOLEMY, *Tetrabiblos* 1.6; HEPHAISTIO, *Apotelesmatics* 1.2.
2 PTOLEMY, *Tetrabiblos* 1.6.

Planets are modified towards becoming more masculine or more feminine by the following conditions:[3]

1. ZODIACAL SIGN
2. SOLAR PHASE
3. CELESTIAL LATITUDE
4. QUADRANT LOCATION

Table 7. Gender of Planets

	MASCULINE PLANETS	FEMININE PLANETS
PLANET	*Sun, Mercury, Mars, Jupiter, Saturn*	*Moon, Venus*
	MASCULINIZING CONDITIONS	FEMINIZING CONDITIONS
SIGN	*Aries, Gemini, Leo, Libra, Sagittarius, Aquarius*	*Taurus, Cancer, Virgo, Scorpio, Capricorn, Pisces*
PHASE	*Morning, ahead of Sun*	*Evening, behind the Sun*
QUADRANT	ASC to MC DSC to IC	MC to DSC IC to ASC
LATITUDE	*North*	*South*

PLANETS AND GENDER

The GENDER OF THE ZODIACAL SIGN in which a planet is located is the first and most important factor in this evaluation. The masculine signs are Aries, Gemini, Leo, Libra, Sagittarius, and Aquarius, which correspond to the fire and air elements. The feminine signs are Taurus, Cancer, Virgo, Scorpio, Capricorn, and Pisces, which belong to the earth and water elements. Masculine planets act more in accordance with their essential nature when they occupy the masculine signs, while feminine planets act more in accordance with their basic nature when they occupy feminine signs.

Just as it is easier to be ourselves and do our best when we are in an environment that supports and enhances our basic nature, planets also operate better in

3   ANTIOCHUS, *Thesaurus* 1.1; RHETORIUS, *Compendium* 1.1.

zodiacal signs that have a similar pace to their own. When a masculine planet is located in a feminine sign, its ability to act is slowed down, which might be a source of frustration or boredom. If a feminine planet is located in a masculine sign, it may feel pressured and rushed to act before it is ready, thus becoming a source of tension or fear. With a boom of laughter, the late, great Alan White would illustrate this principle with the example of two teenagers making out at the drive-in movie—the boy wants to speed things up while the girl urges to slow it down.

While in general, a planet's condition is improved when it is located in a zodiacal sign that is of the same gender, this is not an absolute rule. There is no value judgment here between the fast and the prolonged; between the early blooming and the late; the context of each situation determines which kind of energy is more advantageous. And sometimes what is best is for the fast to slow down, as with the inflammation rate of an illness.

A planet's SOLAR PHASE is the second condition for assessing gender modification. A planet becomes more masculinized when it is seen in the morning sky rising before (ahead of) the Sun, and more feminized when it appears in the evening sky after (following) the setting Sun. We might imagine that most people are energized and ready for activity in the morning and inclined towards rest and relaxation in the evening.

To determine if a planet is of the morning or of the evening phase, turn the chart around so that the Sun is at the position of the Ascendant—the sunrise point. Remember that the planets move according to diurnal motion, so at sunrise they ascend over the Ascendant and move in a clockwise direction where the Midheaven is noon, the Descendant is sunset, and the Nadir is midnight. If the planet in question is of the morning, it has risen before the Sun and is ahead of the Sun (up to the Sun's opposition degree), but will have zodiacal longitude that is less than the Sun. (Sun at 15° Leo, Mercury at 25° Cancer). If the planet in question is of the evening, it has risen after the Sun and is behind the Sun (up to the Sun's opposition degree), but will have zodiacal longitude that is greater than the Sun. (Sun at 15° Leo, Mercury at 5° Virgo). The Sun can be anywhere in the chart; the determining factor is simply whether the planet in question is ahead of the Sun or behind the Sun in its diurnal motion. We will explain morning and evening star/planets more fully in Part Three.

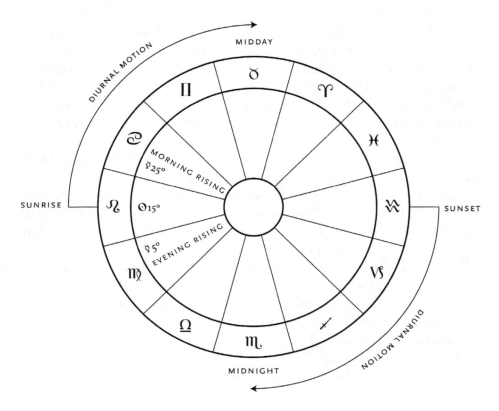

FIGURE 5. MORNING AND EVENING PLANETS

Sun rising at 15° Leo (descending at 15° Aquarius). Mercury at 25° Cancer rises in the morning, before sunrise; Mercury at 5° Virgo can be seen appearing in the evening sky after sunset.

The advanced student can fine-tune this assessment by noting that the masculinizing sector of the solar phase cycle extends forward from the fifteenth degree ahead of the Sun until the one-hundred-and-twentieth degree from the Sun, or just before the retrograde station. The feminizing sector of the solar phase cycle extends backwards from the fifteenth degree behind Sun until the one-hundred-and-twentieth degree from the Sun, or just after the direct station.

A planet's quadrant location also influences its gender modifications. The houses in the quadrant from the Ascendant to the Midheaven are masculine; those from the Midheaven to the Descendant are feminine; the houses from the Descendant to the IC degree are masculine, and those from the IC to the Ascendant are feminine. A planet becomes more masculine when in the masculine quadrants, perhaps because the motion of the Sun is rising towards its

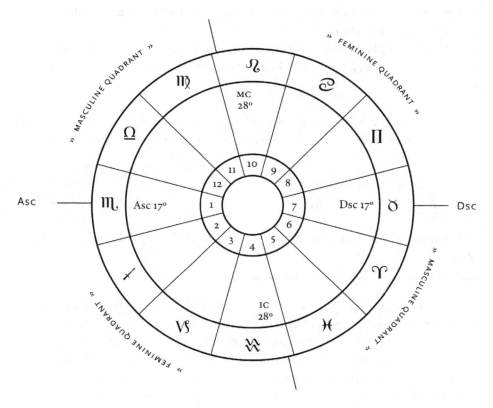

FIGURE 6. MASCULINE AND FEMININE QUADRANTS

Moving in diurnal motion, the masculine quadrants stretch from ASC to MC, and from DSC to IC. The Feminine quadrants stretch from MC to DSC, and from IC to ASC.

culminating or anti-culminating points. A planet becomes more feminine when in the feminine quadrants, perhaps due to the declining direction of the Sun. It is not altogether clear from the texts whether these quadrants are demarcated by whole sign or by exact degrees of the angles, although Paulus does specify exact degree in his discussion on this matter.[4]

The final gender modification is a planet's celestial latitude. Celestial latitude is the distance of a planet north or south of the ecliptic. A planet north of the ecliptic becomes more masculine, while a planet south of the ecliptic becomes more feminine. Many astrological software programs contain reports for a planet's latitude. Be sure to distinguish this from a planet's declination, which is its

4   PAULUS, *Introduction 7.*

distance north or south of the celestial equator, and which is used in many "out of bounds" interpretations.

Similar to a planet's basic benefic or malefic nature, a planet's masculine or feminine gender can be modified in a number of ways that influence its expression.

Table 8. Range of Feminized and Masculinized Planetary Expressions

	← FEMININE CONDITIONS	NEUTRAL CONDITIONS	MASCULINE → CONDITIONS
FEMININE PLANET	*Extremely feminine*	*Feminine*	*Masculinized feminine*
MASCULINE PLANET	*Feminized masculine*	*Masculine*	*Extremely masculine*

Rhetorius, shaped by the cultural norms of his day, concludes that masculine planets in masculine conditions make men willful and daring, while making women insubordinate and shameless. Likewise, feminine planets in feminine conditions make men soft and cowardly, and women modest, dignified, and obedient.[5] However, remember that many interpretations of the symbols cannot help but reflect the customs and values of the day. In the contemporary world, a planet's gender modifications may provide valuable insights into the expression of shifting gender fluidity (e.g., in the LGBTQIA community).

5   RHETORIUS, *Compendium* 1.

EXAMPLE CHARTS

We will now introduce the two example charts that will be used throughout the remainder of this book—the horoscopes of JACQUELINE KENNEDY ONASSIS, *and* PABLO PICASSO *(reproduced on the following two pages). We will begin by examining these charts in relation to gender modification.*

JACQUELINE KENNEDY ONASSIS: The masculine Sun is located in the masculine sign Leo; the feminine Moon is in the masculine sign Aries; morning phase Mercury is in masculine Leo; feminine Venus is in masculine Gemini; masculine Mars is in feminine Virgo; masculine Jupiter is in masculine Gemini; and masculine Saturn is in masculine Sagittarius. Note that both feminine planets—Moon and Venus—find themselves in masculine signs, propelling them to more activity and possibly pointing to the stress of overdoing or difficulty with expressing vulnerability and receiving help. Mars is located in the feminine sign of Virgo, slowing down its impulsiveness based upon discrimination and analysis of the impulse.

PABLO PICASSO: All of the planets are in signs contrary to their natural gender. The masculine planets are in feminine signs, and both feminine planets are in masculine signs. This might suggest a certain energetic discomfort inside one's own skin, being prompted to act more slowly when the impulse is to go fast and vice-versa. It can also point to an expression of gender that does not polarize to male and female stereotypes.

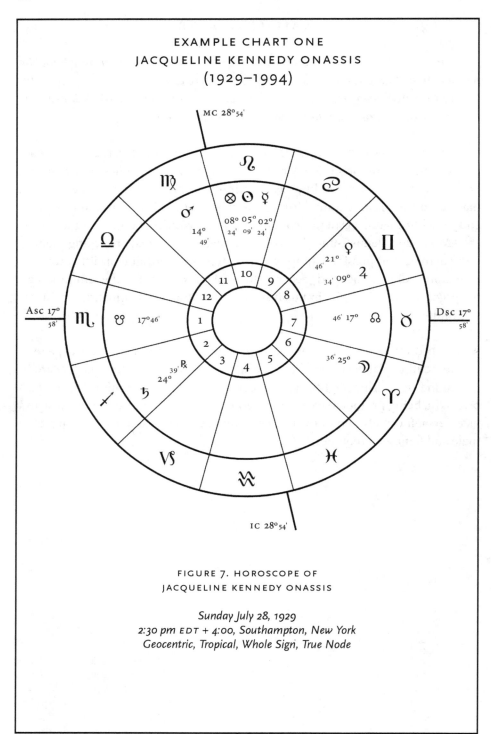

EXAMPLE CHART ONE
JACQUELINE KENNEDY ONASSIS
(1929–1994)

FIGURE 7. HOROSCOPE OF
JACQUELINE KENNEDY ONASSIS

Sunday July 28, 1929
2:30 pm EDT + 4:00, Southampton, New York
Geocentric, Tropical, Whole Sign, True Node

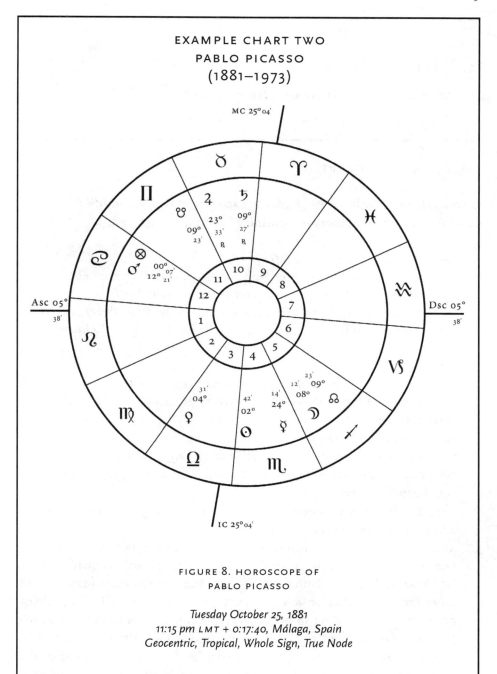

EXAMPLE CHART TWO
PABLO PICASSO
(1881–1973)

FIGURE 8. HOROSCOPE OF
PABLO PICASSO

Tuesday October 25, 1881
11:15 pm LMT + 0:17:40, Málaga, Spain
Geocentric, Tropical, Whole Sign, True Node

EXERCISE 2

GENDER MODIFICATIONS OF THE PLANETS

USING YOUR OWN CHART

Investigate how the baseline gender of each planet can be modified by its conditions, becoming more masculinized or more feminized.

1. *Note the gender of the planet (M/F).*
    If the planet is masculine, enter M. If the planet is feminine, enter F.
2. *Note the gender of the sign in which the planet is located (M/F).*
    Note the zodiacal sign that each planet occupies and enter the gender of the sign. The MASCULINE SIGNS are: *Aries, Gemini, Leo, Libra, Sagittarius, and Aquarius.* The FEMININE SIGNS are: *Taurus, Cancer, Virgo, Scorpio, Capricorn, and Pisces*).
3. *Determine if the planet is in a sign of its own gender (Y/N).*
    If the gender of the planet is the same as the gender of the sign it occupies, enter Y. If not, enter N.
4. *How might this affect its activity? (e.g. more active/passive).*
    Consider how the gender of a planet's zodiacal sign relative to its own natural gender modifies its expression. Masculine conditions predispose a planet to be more active, move faster, and to bring its events about sooner. Feminine conditions predispose a planet to be more receptive, to move slower, and to bring its events about later.
5. ADVANCED: *What other factors modify the gender of a planet?*
    For an advanced exercise, consider how conditions such as quadrant, solar phase, and celestial latitude incline a planet towards more masculine or more feminine behavior. MASCULINIZING CONDITIONS include: rising before the Sun; location in quadrants from the degrees of the ASC to the MC and from the DSC to the IC; and north celestial latitude. FEMINIZING CONDITIONS include: rising after the sun; location in quadrants from the degrees of the MC to the DSC and from the IC to the ASC; and south celestial latitude.

Planet	Gender of planet	Gender of zodiac sign	Planet in sign of own gender?	Effect (active vs. passive, etc.)	Other factors
SUN	M	M	NO	FQ	
JUPITER	M	M F	YES	ACTIVE – F.Q	
SATURN	M	M F	NO	MQ	
MERCURY	M/F ANDROGYNOUS	M F	✓	FQ	
MOON	F	F	✓	FQ	
MARS	M	M F		MQ	
VENUS F	F Q		FQ		

REFLECTION AND ANALYSIS

MOON: Mercury: Jupiter, Venus

1. Which planets' gender is in accordance with the gender of their sign?
2. Which planets are made more masculine? Jupiter
3. Which planets are made more feminine?
4. Is there a predominance of masculinized or feminized energy in the chart, or is there a balance?
5. What does this suggest about the overall speed or pace of life?
6. If the feminine gender planets are in masculine conditions, do you experience them as more assertive, or pressured to be more active than your natural inclination?

7. If masculine gender planets are in feminine conditions, do you experience them as more receptive, or do you feel confined and frustrated by their slower pace?

_____

CHAPTER 6

Sect

OF THE PLANETS

Since the whole is administered by the Sun and the Moon and none of the things that exist in the cosmos come into being apart from the rulership of these stars, it is necessary to explain the solar and lunar sect, what each has been allotted and how everything comes together through these. The Sun was allotted the day and the morning rising and the masculine zodiacal signs; it has as its spear-bearing guards the star of Saturn and the star of Jupiter. The Moon was allotted the night and the evening rising and the feminine zodiacal signs; it has as its spear-bearing guards the star of Mars and the star of Venus. The star of Mercury is regarded as common in nature; when rising in the morning it rejoices with the Sun, but rejoices with the Moon when evening rising. — PAULUS.[1]

THE THIRD CLASSIFICATION OF PLANETS IS ACCORDING TO SECT. Sect comes from the Greek word *hairēsis*, which can mean a faction, an alliance, identification with a school of thought, or even a political party or team. Many traditional astrological doctrines are based upon the social customs of the ancient world. Sect doctrines reflect the system of alliances and enmities, the determinations of friends and foes based upon these alliances, and the shifting balance of power as to which side holds the position of privilege and dominance. The sect of the chart and the sect status of a planet were among the very first considerations in the analysis of a planet's condition.[2]

---

1   PAULUS, *Introduction* 6.
2   PTOLEMY, *Tetrabiblos* 1.7; PAULUS, *Introduction* 6; RHETORIUS, *Compendium* 2; PORPHYRY, *Introduction* 4; HEPHAISTIO, *Apotelesmatics* 1.2; VALENS, *Anthology* 3.5.

DIURNAL AND NOCTURNAL SECT

Ancient astrology defines two sects, a diurnal (day) sect and a nocturnal (night) sect. If a person is born during the day, the sect of their chart is diurnal; a birth during the night denotes a nocturnal sect chart.

There are many techniques in traditional astrology in which sect plays a significant role. A planet's sect status determines how much authority and freedom a planet has to bring forth its positive significations on behalf of the individual. Sect also tells us which other planets a planet can best rely upon to support its own agenda. The interpretation of planets indicative of favorable or unfavorable outcomes due to their sect status was a primary feature of ancient astrology, and this distinction has for the most part been lost to modern practice.

The sect of a chart was the starting point for many considerations such as the length of life calculations; evaluations of the overall eminence of a person's life; the formulas for many of the lots (better known today as Arabic Parts); and the planetary significators for particular topics such as parents.

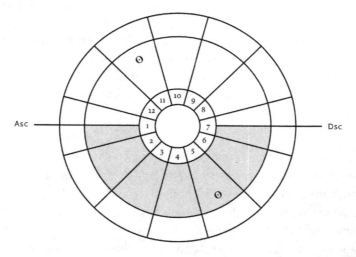

FIGURE 9. DIURNAL AND NOCTURNAL CHARTS

Diurnal (day) chart: Sun above horizon (ASC–DSC axis)
Nocturnal (night) chart: Sun below horizon (ASC–DSC axis)

In order to determine the sect of a chart, first look at the degrees of the Ascendant and Descendant and visually connect them with a line. If you are using the whole sign house system, most computer displays and printouts will have the symbol for the Ascendant (ASC) and Descendant (DSC) points floating somewhere in the first and seventh houses. This is the axis you want, not the horizontal line that marks the cusp of the 1st house that is displayed when using quadrant house systems such as Placidus. (You may want to review the section on Whole Sign houses in the Introduction.) This axis, demarcated by the exact degrees of the Ascendant and Descendant, marks the horizon—where sky meets earth. However, it is not depicted as visually accurate in most computer print-outs generated with the whole sign house system.

If the Sun lies above the line of the horizon, that person was born during the day and has a diurnal sect chart; if the Sun is located beneath the horizon line, that person was born at night and thus has a nocturnal sect chart. You can confirm this by looking at the time of birth and noting if it occurred by day or night.

→ EXAMPLE CHARTS

CHART I is *diurnal*. The Ascendant/Descendant axis from 17° Scorpio 58' to 17° Taurus 58' demarcates the horizon. The Sun at 5° Leo is above the horizon. The birth time is 2:30 PM, during the day.

CHART II is *nocturnal*. The horizon is marked by the axis from 5° Leo 38' to 5° Aquarius 38', and the Sun is at 2° Scorpio below the horizon. The birth time is 11:15 PM, during the night.

THE SUN AND MOON AS SECT LEADERS

The two sects reflect the primacy of the Sun and Moon as the two great lights which illuminate the sky. The ancient authors related how everything in the created world arises from these two stars. The Sun predominates by day, while the Moon reigns supreme by night. The Sun is the sect leader for diurnal charts (individuals born during the day), while the Moon is the sect leader for nocturnal charts (individuals born at night). The divine manifestation of the Sun and Moon are the solar God and the lunar Goddess. Their earthly representatives are the King and Queen, the archetypal Father and Mother.

On the broadest level of interpretation, the illuminating power of the Sun represents the mind and the realm of thought, while the reflective power of the Moon represents the body and realm of sensation. The sect of the chart helps the astrologer determine which of these two faculties predominates in the life of an individual, where a soul animating a body incarnates into time and space with a physical destiny to unfold. We might speculate as to whether this implies that the native is more of a solar type or lunar type, and which luminary directs the course of the life. The ancient texts do not give an explicit definition of what the sect of the chart means in the interpretation of the native's character, only that the planets which belong to the sect of the chart have more beneficence.

From a modern perspective one could propose that diurnal individuals belong to the solar sect school of thought, where the Sun represents the mind and soul,[3] the light of consciousness, an objective state of awareness, the use of reason, and an inclination to bring things to light and illuminate them. Nocturnal individuals belong to the lunar school of thought where the Moon represents the body,[4] the depth of intuitive perception arising from the physical senses, a subjective state of awareness, the use of instinct, and understanding by delving deep into underlying causes.

→   EXAMPLE CHARTS

Who is the sect leader of the chart?
CHART I is diurnal and the sect leader is the Sun.
CHART II is nocturnal and the sect leader is the Moon.

SECT MATES

The Sun and Moon are the respective leaders of the diurnal and nocturnal sects, but to the extent that sect is defined as a school of thought, each sect is comprised of additional followers. The two sect leaders have their own team members, called sect mates, which are drawn from the remaining five planets.

Table 9. Diurnal and Nocturnal Sect Mates

SECT	DIURNAL		NOCTURNAL
Sect Leader	*Sun*		*Moon*
Benefic Planet	*Jupiter*		*Venus*
Malefic Planet	*Saturn*		*Mars*
Common	*Morning star*	*← Mercury →*	*Evening star*
	Mercury	*goes either way*	*Mercury*

---

3   VALENS, *Anthology* 1.1.
4   VALENS, *Anthology* 1.1.

Jupiter and Saturn belong to the day sect while the planets Venus and Mars belong to the night sect. This is the case in each and every chart, regardless of whether the chart is diurnal or nocturnal. But Mercury (as always) can go either way. In some charts it belongs to the diurnal sect and in other charts it aligns with the nocturnal sect. Mercury rising before the Sun in the morning belongs to the diurnal sect; but when Mercury rises after the Sun and is thus seen in the evening, it belongs to the nocturnal sect.

→ EXAMPLE CHARTS

Does Mercury belong to the diurnal sect or to the nocturnal sect?

CHART I: If you turn the chart ¼ of the way to the left so the Sun appears on the ASC/eastern horizon, you can see that Mercury has just risen above the ASC preceding the Sun. Thus it is a morning star. You can double check by noting that Mercury at 2° Leo is at a lesser zodiacal degree than the Sun at 5° Leo, going in the natural order of the zodiac. Thus Mercury belongs to the diurnal sect in this chart.

CHART II: This time turn the chart ¼ way to the right so again the Sun seems to be on the ASC/eastern horizon. The Sun comes up and over the ASC first and Mercury follows afterwards. You would not see Mercury in the morning sky because the Sun will be too bright by the time Mercury rises. However, just after the Sun sets in the evening, it will be dark enough to see Mercury's appearance, which is traveling behind the Sun. Thus Mercury is an evening star in this chart. That Mercury at 24° Scorpio is at a greater zodiacal degree (in the natural order of the zodiac) than the Sun at 2° Scorpio confirms our answer. Thus Mercury belongs to the nocturnal sect in this chart.

→ SEE FIGURE 5: MORNING & EVENING RISING (*chapter 5, page 64*)

Note that while Mercury, in the first chart, is a diurnal sect member, it is because Mercury rises ahead of the Sun, not because it is a diurnal chart. If Mercury rose after the Sun, it would belong to the nocturnal sect, even in a diurnal chart. The same for Mercury belonging to the nocturnal sect in the second example chart. It is because Mercury rose after the Sun, not because it is a nocturnal chart.

The sect leader and its sect mates operate as a team in order to bring about the destiny of an individual. One might think that the respective planets of each sect have alliances of friendship and cooperation based upon common interests or agendas, while planets of opposing sects can have intrinsic enmities between them because they follow a different system of thought (values, beliefs, agendas, or affiliations).

Notice that each sect is led by one of the lights, the Sun or Moon, and contains one benefic planet, Jupiter or Venus, and one malefic planet, Saturn or Mars. Mercury tips the balance and can belong to either sect depending upon its relationship to the Sun.

Hellenistic astrologers gave various explanations as to why certain planets belonged to each sect. One line of thinking proposed that the natural activities of certain planets were more suitable by day or by night. Jupiter's significations of pursuit of wisdom or achievement of good reputation operate better during the "heat and vigor" of the daytime hours, while Venus' inclinations towards pleasure, relaxation, and lovemaking operate better by the "moisture and gift of rest" at night.

Ptolemy proposed that the warmth of the day lessens the destructive, cold qualities of Saturn, so it can act in a more beneficent manner; the coolness of night likewise tempers the destructive, fiery nature of Mars, where its injurious power is moderated.[5] Porphyry links the assignment of planets to sect on the basis of the number of solar phases a planet makes—Jupiter and Saturn make fewer solar phases and therefore are more similar to the Sun, while Venus and Mars make more solar phases and are thus more similar to the Moon.[6]

When evaluating a chart in terms of sect, it is helpful to investigate how well the members of each sect operate together as a team with their leader. One way to do this is to see if they are connected by whole sign aspects with each other and with the sect light, and whether those aspects are sympathetic (sextile and trine) or unsympathetic (square and opposition).

→ EXAMPLE CHARTS

Assess the internal integration and harmony between the members of each sect.

CHART I: The diurnal sect is composed of the Sun, Jupiter, Saturn, and Mercury. The Sun as the sect leader is co-present in the same zodiacal sign as his sect mate, Mercury, sextile Jupiter, and trine to Saturn. They are all configured to one another in a harmonious manner. The nocturnal sect is composed of the Moon, Venus, and Mars. The Moon as

5   PTOLEMY, *Tetrabiblos* 1.7.
6   PORPHYRY, *Introduction* 2.

sect leader is sextile to Venus, but in aversion to Mars; Venus and Mars square one another. The Moon is disconnected from Mars, and Mars and Venus have an antagonistic relationship. Clearly the diurnal team has better internal organization and communication than does the nocturnal team.

CHART II: The nocturnal sect is composed of the Moon, Venus, Mars, and Mercury. The Moon as sect leader has a sextile to Venus, but does not aspect either Mercury or Mars. Mercury and Mars are trine and thus have good communication. The diurnal sect is composed of the Sun, Jupiter, and Saturn. The Sun as sect leader opposes his sect mates Jupiter and Saturn and has an adversarial relationship with them. Both sects have some internal cohesion amidst considerable problems in connections and communications.

→ EXERCISE 3

Using your own chart, complete exercise 3:
Sect Determinations

EXERCISE 3

SECT DETERMINATIONS

Using your own chart, answer the following questions in a notebook.

1. *Where is the Sun in your chart?* Is it above or below the horizon as marked by the degrees of your ASC/DSC axis? *BELOW*
2. *Is the sect of your chart diurnal or nocturnal?*
3. *Does your time of birth correspond to day or night?* Keep in mind the variations of day and night due to the season of the year.
4. *Based upon the sect of your chart, which of the two luminaries is your sect leader, the Sun or Moon?*
5. *Do you feel more aligned to the solar/diurnal sect of thought, or to the lunar/nocturnal sect of thought?* When you seek to know and understand, is it more fruitful for you to try to shed light upon the situation or to go deep within to feel your way?
6. *Is Mercury morning rising (before the Sun) or evening rising (after the Sun)?*
7. *Does Mercury belong to the diurnal or nocturnal sect in your chart?*
8. *List which planets belong to the diurnal sect and which belong to nocturnal sect.*
9. ADVANCED: *Evaluate the internal cohesion and connection of the planets in each sect based upon the whole sign aspects between them.*
10. *Is one sect better integrated and more harmonious as a team than the other?*

INTERPRETATION USING SECT CONSIDERATIONS

Sect was a very important factor in the interpretation of planets, as the sect of the chart pointed to which set of planets, the diurnal or nocturnal, were predisposed to having the potential to bring forth better outcomes in the life of the person. The basic principle of interpretation using sect considerations is that planets which belong to the same sect as the sect of the chart can bring about more fortunate circumstances and final outcomes than those planets which belong to the contrary sect. The planets of the contrary sect are limited or compromised in their capacity to act in ways that consistently bring about lasting and favorable results. And as with the other planetary conditions, these baseline judgments can be modified and mitigated by other factors, which we will address in the appropriate sections.

The first step in using sect considerations in interpretation is to identify the sect of the chart as either a day or a night chart. The next step is to distinguish which planets belong to the same sect as that of the chart and which planets belong to the contrary sect. Finally, pay attention to the benefic planet of the same sect as the chart, and even more so to the malefic planet of the contrary sect.

In a day chart, the Sun is the sect leader and along with its diurnal sect mates, Jupiter, Saturn and a morning star Mercury, these planets belong to the same sect as the chart. You may see this written variously as the "planets of the sect in favor", "planets of the sect", or "planets in sect". They operate with privilege, have the authority to pursue their agenda, and have the home advantage to bring forth their most beneficial significations. The malefic qualities of Saturn tend to be suppressed, turned away from the individual, or used to benefit the native albeit at the cost of others.

In a diurnal chart, the nocturnal sect planets—Moon, Venus, Mars and an evening star Mercury—are contrary to the sect (sometimes called "out of sect"). They have less authority to pursue their agenda and in some instances their actions do not result in favorable outcomes for the individual. They may struggle to accomplish their matters. It may be the case that Venus' benefic qualities are somewhat lessened, while the aggressive qualities of Mars can become accentuated. Given additional factors, Mars can turn reckless or destructive in some diurnal charts. Keep in mind that this is destructive in regards to one's own best interests, not necessarily towards others.

Conversely, in a nocturnal chart, the Moon is the sect leader and along with its sect mates Venus, Mars, and evening star Mercury. These planets belong to the same sect as the sect of the chart. They are more well-disposed to pursue their own agenda and actualize beneficial outcomes in accordance with their natures for the individual.

In a nocturnal chart, the planets that belong to the diurnal sect—the Sun, Jupiter, Saturn, and morning star Mercury—are contrary to the sect of the chart (some say "out of sect"). They have less freedom and efficacy to do good for the individual. Saturn can be particularly difficult in nocturnal births where its qualities of negation, frustration, and denial are more emphasized. However, be aware that there are a number of other factors which we will describe later that can modify these statements from their baselines.

Imagine the government of a country that has two political parties. If one party is in charge, those officials have greater authority and license to advocate for their platforms, which in theory are the policies that most benefit the citizens. You might think that the planets that belong to the sect of the chart function in a similar manner to the legislators who hold the majority in the legislature and thus have a mandate to rule and implement their policies. In actuality, the extent of the good that they can bring about corresponds to their overall condition, which consists of a number of other factors.

Lest anyone get confused by the above example, the sect that is in charge is not due to having more members, but whether they are members who belong to the same sect as the sect of the chart.

Here are several examples illustrating how Hellenistic astrologers employed sect considerations. In this first example, note how the same planet in the same sign/house is interpreted in a very different way:

> Saturn [...] posited in the fourth house will, if it holds this house by day, make those greedy for money, and custodians of gold and silver. But if it was in this sign/house by night, it dissipates the paternal inheritance and will cause the quick death of the father.[7]

> Mars there [in the 5th house] by night brings about the existence of many good things, high repute and being honored by the populace and [these natives] command kinsmen… But, if Mars is there by day, it makes living abroad as a mercenary harmful and dangerous.[8]

The malefic planets Saturn and Mars, while still being true to their essential natures, can operate in benefic ways if they belong to the same sect as the chart but can be especially destructive if they are contrary to the sect of the chart. One of Saturn's natural significations is wealth, especially from land and buildings. Since it is a diurnal planet, in a day chart it brings about accumulation or over-

---

7   FIRMICUS MATERNUS, *Mathesis* 3.3A.8, trans. HOLDEN.
8   RHETORIUS, *Compendium* 57.

sight of money, while in a night chart it can destroy either the inheritance from the father, or the father himself (fourth house signification). Mars has to do with leadership; as a nocturnal planet in a night chart, it works on behalf of the best interests of the individual and can point to renown and honor, but in a day chart accentuates its significations of danger and violence.

The interpretation of sect is even more influential when a planet holds a prominent ruling position due to its location in the angular houses, in particular the first or tenth houses. In these cases, the effects of its sect status, for better or worse, are especially pronounced. The fourth-century Roman astrologer, Firmicus Maternus, instructs:

> Take note also, if it is a diurnal nativity, where those stars are placed that rejoice in diurnal genitures and where those are that rejoice in nocturnal ones. For if the stars that rejoice by day hold the principal places in a diurnal nativity and are found in the first angles, they denote the greatest increases in good fortune. But if the stars that we have said rejoice by night hold the principal places in a diurnal nativity or possess the first angles of the nativity, they indicate unlimited misfortunes with continual disasters.
>
> We ought to observe this also in nocturnal genitures, but with a changed order of power, for if in a nocturnal geniture the stars which we have said rejoice by night possess the principal houses or the first angles of the nativity, in a similar fashion they denote the greatest increases of good fortune. But if in nocturnal nativities those that we have said rejoice in diurnal association possess the principal houses or the first angles of the nativity, they make the whole adornment of good fortune to be entangled with woeful occurrences of misfortunes.[9]

In a day chart, when the diurnal planets are placed in the first or tenth houses, they bring about the greatest good fortune, but the nocturnal planets are much more problematic. The reverse is true in night charts, where the nocturnal planets in the first or tenth houses indicate great increase of fortune, but the diurnal planets entangle one in misfortune.

Beyond different interpretations concerning how the planets operate in the various houses, sect status helps the astrologer to identify which of the two malefic planets in a given chart is the better advocate for the native's best interests and which is potentially the greater indicator of difficulties. Sect status helps the astrologer to judge whether Mars or Saturn will act as "friend" or "foe".

9   Firmicus Maternus, *Mathesis* 2.22.11–12, trans. Holden.

In the course of Valens' discussion regarding the use of the triplicity lords of the sect light in order to judge happiness and eminence in a person's life, he tells us to take note of the aspects made by Saturn and Mars to a planet in question, and then to adjust our interpretation in accordance with the sect of the chart. Pay attention to how problematic the malefic contrary to sect operates when it is also square or opposed to a planet, and more so if that planet is a ruler of the chart. But when a malefic belongs to the sect in favor and is in otherwise good condition, it can be a "bestower of good".

> If, for example, Saturn is found in opposition or in square for night births, it will bring about reversals, ruin, dangers, injuries, and diseases, as well as sluggishness in enterprises. For day births, Mars causes hot, reckless men, precarious in their activities and in their livelihoods. They experience imprisonment, trials, abuse, cuts, burns, bleeding, and accidents/falls. But if these stars happen to be configured properly, in their own sects, they are actively positive. As a result, these stars are not to be considered malefics in all cases; they can be bestowers of good.[10]

Sect status helps the astrologer to distinguish which of the two malefic planets, Saturn or Mars, is working for the individual and which can be the cause of problems and setbacks. In a diurnal chart, Saturn can be a powerful ally, like a bodyguard defending a person's interests, and given certain other supportive testimony, it has the capacity to bring forth its positive significations such as wealth and land. But for diurnal births, Mars symbolizes the enemy provoking attacks, and can lead to enmities, anger, violence, illness, and recklessness. By contrast, in a nocturnal chart, Mars can act as a warrior fighting for you, and can even point to leadership qualities; but Saturn by night can block success and bring hardship, especially due to deprivation, denial, and rejection.

This rule holds true for the benefic planets as well, but to a somewhat lesser extent. The nature of both Jupiter and Venus is to do good, bringing about fortunate outcomes. However, in diurnal charts Jupiter is positioned to do the greater good, while Venus can be somewhat limited in her freedom to bring about her best significations. Conversely, in night charts, it is Venus who has the potential to bring about more good fortune, while Jupiter is more constrained. This is not to say, for example, that a well-placed Venus in a day chart does not signify good things happening to the individual, but the question arises as to whether these pleasurable activities are in the person's long-term best interests. For example:

10   VALENS, *Anthology* 2.2.

being popular at school, with numerous dates, friends, parties, and admiration may be good, but the excessive pursuit of these pleasurable activities can undermine one's academic achievement.

At this point, the first-time student of Hellenistic astrology may begin to worry if an important planet in their own chart, such as the Ascendant ruler, belongs to the contrary sect. What does this mean? It may simply be that the person has to work harder to bring about the things that the planet represents; those things may not come as easily, they may encounter setbacks due to circumstances, and consequently may have to develop more realistic expectations of what is feasible. Keep in mind that sect status is only one of a number of other considerations, and can be mitigated or counteracted by other factors that affect the overall performance and judgment of a planet's function.

In summary, when a planet belongs to the same sect as the chart, the benefic planet of that sect increases in its overall benefic capacity to do good for the native and the malefic planet of the sect decreases in its tendency to do bad. When a planet belongs to the sect contrary to the sect of the chart, the benefic significations of the benefic planet are more constrained and the malefic significations of the malefic planet are increased.

A few words need to be said here about whether the good we're discussing is for the native or for others. Antiochus explains that under certain circumstances, Saturn "can benefit a native though by assigning an increase to them to the detriment of another".[11] The action of a malefic, while beneficial for the individual may be seen and experienced as something bad by others. Victory in a competition or war is good for the winners, who may not be good people, but bad for the losers who may not be bad people. This dichotomy raises thorny ethical issues for the astrologer as advisor or for the lawyer as criminal defender. Valens points out that malefic planets operate differently in the charts of eminent people than for those having mediocre nativities. They can contribute to success and reputation in great nativities, but may have dire consequences for others.[12]

→ EXAMPLE CHARTS

> CHART 1 is a diurnal chart. Thus the Sun is the sect leader, and along with its sect mates Jupiter, Saturn, and morning star Mercury, these planets belong to the same sect as the sect of the chart and have greater freedom to pursue their beneficial agendas for the individual. The

11   ANTIOCHUS, *Summary* 1.1.
12   VALENS, *Anthology* 7.2.

Moon, Venus, and Mars are contrary to the sect of the chart. Saturn is potentially the more sympathetic malefic, while Mars is the more problematic malefic. Jupiter is the more helpful benefic, while Venus is limited in its beneficial outcomes.

CHART II is a nocturnal chart. Thus the Moon is the sect leader, and along with its sect mates, Venus, Mars, and evening star Mercury, these planets belong to the sect of the chart and have greater freedom to pursue their beneficial agendas for the individual. The Sun, Jupiter, and Saturn are contrary to the sect of the chart and are more constrained in their efforts to do good for the individual. Mars is potentially the more sympathetic malefic, while Saturn is the more problematic malefic. Venus is the more helpful benefic, while Jupiter is limited in its beneficial outcomes.

Although we are not yet learning how to interpret houses according to traditional guidelines, based upon your current analysis of birth charts, imagine how in a day chart you might emphasize the more positive significations of Saturn's ranges of meanings relative to its house location, while considering the more problematic meanings of Mars in its house location. And then do the reverse for a night chart. For example:

By day, Saturn in the tenth—hard work leads to professional success; by night, Saturn in the tenth—frustrations and delays in professional advancement.

By day, Mars in the sixth—conflict and aggression with co-employees lead to being fired from a job; by night Mars in the sixth—a competitive and aggressive nature leads to having the best employee performance in one's job.

→   EXERCISE 4

Using your own chart, complete exercise 4:
Identifying Benefics and Malefics by Sect

EXERCISE 4

IDENTIFYING BENEFICS AND MALEFICS BY SECT

Using a notebook, answer the following questions to identify which planets belong to the same sect as the chart, and which planets belong to the contrary sect.

1. *What is the sect of the chart?*
2. *Which planets are in the same sect as the sect of the chart?*
3. *Which planets are in the contrary sect to the sect of the chart?*
   What is the advantage of planets belonging to the same sect as the chart? Take a moment and reflect upon the placements of Saturn and Mars in your chart based only upon sect considerations. The malefic that belongs to the same sect as the sect of your chart works on your behalf. The malefic that belongs to the contrary sect of your chart presents the greater difficulties.
4. *Which of the two malefics is your friend?*
5. *Which of the two malefics is your foe?*
6. *The benefic that belongs to the same sect as your chart is potentially the more benefic of the two.*
7. *Which of the two benefics is potentially more helpful to you, Jupiter or Venus?*
8. *Think about which houses each benefic and malefic occupy in your chart.*
9. *Which house topic is potentially the source of the greater good due to the presence of the benefic of the sect?*
10. *Which house topic is potentially limited in the amount of expected good due to the presence of the benefic contrary to sect?*
11. *Which house topic is potentially the source of greater problems due to the presence of the malefic of the contrary sect?*
12. *Which house topic is potentially the source of limited bad or even some good due to the presence of the malefic of the sect?*

So far, based upon sect considerations, we have determined whether a chart is diurnal or nocturnal, which planets belong to each sect, which sect or team of planets has the potential capacity for actions that are more fortunate for the native, and in any given chart which of the two benefic planets is more benefic as well as which of the two malefic planets is more malefic.

CHAPTER 7

Planetary Joys

AND SECT REJOICING

———

In diurnal births, the Sun, Saturn and Jupiter rejoice in masculine zodiacal signs when they operate in good houses, and especially when
Saturn and Jupiter are rising in the morning. In nocturnal births, the
Moon, Mars, and Venus rejoice when rising in the evening and occupying feminine zodiacal signs, the latter two stars having been sta-
tioned as spear-bearing guards of the Moon. — PAULUS.[1]

THE CONCEPT OF JOYS AND REJOICING ABOUNDS THROUGHOUT THE
traditional literature. Rejoicing comes from the Greek word *chairō* which can be
translated as "to take delight in". When a person is happy, he or she tends to do
a better job in all their endeavors. In a similar way, when planets are located in
certain houses, hemispheres, zodiacal signs, and phases, they occupy environ-
ments that are supportive of the expression of their basic natures. Consequently,
they take delight, are exceedingly happy, and are more likely to bring forth better
and more beneficial outcomes for the individual.

In assessing a planet's capacity to bring about positive outcomes, the primary sect consideration is whether or not it belongs to the sect of the chart. For a
more nuanced analysis of sect, there are several sect-rejoicing conditions that
fine-tune the understanding of how the planet functions, giving subtle detail to
the interpretation. While sect-rejoicing conditions are not as important as other
factors in the overall analysis of a planet, in some cases they can be a tie breaker
when trying to determine the planet that is in the best condition, a judgment
call used in the preliminary step of many procedures.

The main sect-rejoicing conditions are as follows:

1. Rejoicing by Hemisphere
2. Rejoicing by Zodiacal Sign
3. Rejoicing by Solar Phase

1   PAULUS, *Introduction* 6.

REJOICING BY HEMISPHERE

> By day, the diurnal planets rejoice when they are above the earth,
> while the nocturnal planets rejoice when they are below the earth.
> And again, by night, the nocturnal planets rejoice when they are
> above the earth, while the diurnal planets rejoice when they are below
> the earth. — RHETORIUS.[2]

Depending upon their sect, planets prefer being located in light or dark envi-
ronments because these locations are more comfortable and aligned with their
essential natures. It is the Sun's location in the chart that determines the hemispheres of day and night.

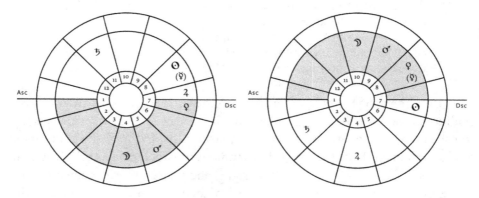

FIGURES 10 & 11. SECT REJOICING BY HEMISPHERE:
DIURNAL CHARTS (LEFT) & NOCTURNAL CHARTS (RIGHT)

Diurnal sect planets rejoice above the horizon (day) in diurnal charts.
Nocturnal sect planets rejoice above the horizon (night) in nocturnal charts.

The line of the horizon which separates the sky from the earth is the same as
the line that separates the two hemispheres of the chart into the day and night
sectors. This horizon line is represented by the exact degrees of the Ascendant/
Descendant axis in the birth chart. It divides the chart into an upper and lower
hemisphere. The hemisphere that contains the Sun is where it is day. The hemisphere that does not contain the Sun is where it is night. Depending upon the
time of birth, the Sun can be located either above or below the horizon and thus
the day hemisphere can be either above or below the horizon.

2   RHETORIUS, *Compendium* 44.

When the Sun is located above the horizon, the daytime is in the upper hemisphere. This would correspond to a birth time of approximately 6am to 6pm, depending upon sunrise and sunset times in accordance with the seasons and latitude. The day portion of the chart includes some of the degrees of the first house that are above the ASC axis, the eleventh, tenth, ninth, and eighth houses, and some degrees of the seventh house above the DSC axis. Night and dark are below the horizon of this axis.

However, when the Sun is placed beneath the horizon in the lower hemisphere, the daytime part of the chart is likewise in the lower hemisphere and covers some of the degrees of the first house below the ASC axis, the second, third, fourth, fifth, and sixth houses, and some of the degrees of the seventh house below the DSC axis. Night-time births correspond to birth times from approximately 6pm to 6am. If this is confusing to you, imagine that someone born at midnight would have the Sun located around the fourth house. If you looked outside, it would be night in the sky above and daytime would be below the earth on the other side of the world.

→   MAKE SURE YOU UNDERSTAND THIS CONCEPT PROPERLY
    BEFORE PROCEEDING

When using the whole sign house system, parts of the first and seventh houses are above the horizon and parts are below. In CHART 1, the ASC degree is 17° Scorpio 58'. The portion of the sign Scorpio that extends from 0° to 17° Scorpio 58' is above the horizon in the upper hemisphere, and the part from 17° Scorpio 58' to 30° Scorpio is below the horizon. The same applies for the seventh house, where part of the sign Taurus is above in the upper hemisphere, and part is below in the lower hemisphere.

The diurnal sect planets rejoice when occupying the day hemisphere of the chart, while the nocturnal sect planets rejoice when they occupy the night hemisphere of the chart. Keep in mind that night is not necessarily the same hemisphere as where the Moon is located, but rather the hemisphere where the Sun is not.

The diurnal planets—Jupiter, Saturn, and a morning star Mercury—rejoice when they are in the same hemisphere as the Sun. The day-time environment is more conducive to the expression of their significations. In a diurnal chart, this is when they are above the horizon along with the Sun. In a nocturnal chart, they want to be beneath the horizon, in the company of the Sun. Remember, whichever hemisphere the Sun is in, that is where it is day and that can be either above or below the horizon.

The nocturnal planets are happier and feel more comfortable in their environment when they are placed in the dark, night-time hours of the chart. The nocturnal planets—Moon, Venus, Mars, and an evening star Mercury—rejoice when they are in the opposite hemisphere than the Sun. If the Sun is above the horizon, the nocturnal planets want to be below in the lower hemisphere; but if the Sun is below the horizon, the nocturnal planets want to be above, in the upper hemisphere.

A common error here that many beginning students make is to think that the nocturnal planets want to be with the Moon, but this is incorrect if the Moon should happen to be in the same hemisphere as the Sun. Another error is that the lower hemisphere is always the darker subjective realm of awareness—this is not the case if the Sun is located there.

→   EXAMPLE CHARTS

Determine in which hemisphere each planet is located and thus whether it rejoices by hemisphere. If so, its condition is improved to bring forth better outcomes. If not, it does not rejoice. But this does not mean that its condition is worsened. It simply remains neutral.

CHART I IS A DIURNAL CHART. The upper hemisphere is where it is day and the lower hemisphere is where it is night. THE SUN always rejoices by hemisphere as it defines the category. MARS, a nocturnal planet, does not rejoice in the upper day hemisphere. MERCURY, a morning star diurnal planet, rejoices in the upper day hemisphere. VENUS, a nocturnal planet, does not rejoice in the upper day hemisphere. JUPITER, a diurnal planet, rejoices in the upper day hemisphere. THE MOON, a nocturnal planet, rejoices in the lower hemisphere where it is night. SATURN, a diurnal planet, does not rejoice in the lower night hemisphere.

ANALYSIS: *Two of the three diurnal planets (excluding the Sun), Mercury and Jupiter, rejoice by hemisphere; one, Saturn, does not. Only one of the nocturnal planets, the Moon, rejoices by hemisphere; the other two, Mars and Venus, do not.*

CHART II IS A NOCTURNAL CHART; the lower hemisphere is where it is day and the upper hemisphere is where it is night. MARS, a nocturnal planet, rejoices in the upper night hemisphere. JUPITER, a diurnal planet, does not rejoice in the upper night hemisphere. SATURN, a diurnal planet, does not rejoice in the upper night hemisphere. THE MOON, a nocturnal planet, does not rejoice in the lower day hemisphere.

MERCURY, an evening star nocturnal planet, does not rejoice in the lower day hemisphere. THE SUN defines the category. VENUS, a nocturnal planet, does not rejoice in the lower day hemisphere.

ANALYSIS: *Only one planet in this chart, Mars, rejoices by hemisphere.*

→ EXERCISE 5

Using your own chart, complete exercise 5:
Sect-Rejoicing by Hemisphere

EXERCISE 5

SECT-REJOICING BY HEMISPHERE

Using your own chart, answer the following questions to identify which planets rejoice by hemisphere.

1. *What is the sect of your chart (diurnal or nocturnal)?*
2. *What hemisphere is the Sun located in, upper or lower?*
   This hemisphere is the DAY sector.
3. *In your chart, is the upper hemisphere the day sector or the night sector?*
4. *In your chart, is the lower hemisphere the day sector or the night sector?*
5. *Jupiter is a diurnal planet. Is it located in the day hemisphere of the chart along with the Sun?* If so, it rejoices. If it is located in the opposite hemisphere than the Sun, it does not rejoice.
6. *Does Jupiter rejoice by hemisphere?*
7. *Saturn is a diurnal planet. Is it located in the day hemisphere of the chart along with the Sun?* If so, it rejoices. If it is located in the opposite hemisphere than the Sun, it does not rejoice.
8. *Does Saturn rejoice by hemisphere?*
9. *Does Mercury belong to the diurnal or nocturnal sect?* If it belongs to the diurnal sect and is located in the same hemisphere as the Sun, it rejoices. If it belongs to the nocturnal sect and is located in the opposite hemisphere than the Sun, it rejoices.
10. *Does Mercury rejoice by hemisphere?*
11. *The Moon is a nocturnal planet. Is it located in the opposite hemisphere than the Sun?* If so, it rejoices. If it is located in the same hemisphere as the Sun, it does not rejoice.
12. *Does the Moon rejoice by hemisphere?*
13. *Venus is a nocturnal planet. Is it located in the opposite hemisphere than the Sun?* If so, it rejoices. If it is located in the same hemisphere as the Sun, it does not rejoice.
14. *Does Venus rejoice by hemisphere?*
15. *Mars is a nocturnal planet. Is it located in the opposite hemisphere than the Sun?* If so, it rejoices. If it is located in the same hemisphere as the Sun, it does not rejoice.
16. *Does Mars rejoice by hemisphere?*

REFLECTION AND ANALYSIS

1. Which diurnal planets rejoice by hemisphere?
2. Which nocturnal planets rejoice by hemisphere?
3. How do you think that location in the appropriate hemisphere by sect enhances the beneficial expression of your planets' behaviors?
4. How do you think that location in the contrary hemisphere by sect detracts from the beneficial expression of your planets' behaviors?

REJOICING BY ZODIACAL SIGN

Again, in the same way they assigned six of the signs to the masculine and diurnal nature and an equal number to the feminine and nocturnal. — PTOLEMY.[3]

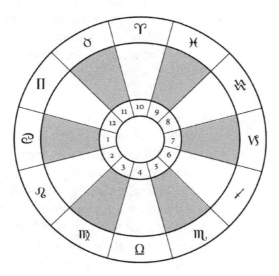

FIGURE 12. SECT REJOICING BY ZODIACAL SIGN

One way that zodiacal signs function is similar to filters that shape and color the manner in which the planets express their significations. Like the planets, the zodiacal signs are classified according to masculine and feminine gender. The masculine energy of speed, action, and outer activity passes through Aries, Gemini, Leo, Libra, Sagittarius, and Aquarius (the fire and air signs). The fem-

3   PTOLEMY, *Tetrabiblos* 1.12.

inine energy of a ~~more leisurely~~ pace, receptivity, and inner reflection passes through ~~Taurus, Cancer, Virgo, Scorpio, Capricorn, and Pisces~~ (the earth and water signs).

The diurnal planets rejoice in the active, diurnal, masculine signs and the nocturnal planets rejoice in the more relaxed, nocturnal, feminine signs. Morning star Mercury prefers the diurnal signs, while evening star Mercury prefers the nocturnal signs.

The one inconsistency in this classification is Mars. In his discussion on gender considerations, Rhetorius relates how Mars in masculine signs in the charts of men makes men more manly,[4] but sect considerations suggest that Mars acts better when in the nocturnal signs. The Hellenistic astrologers themselves seem conflicted on the Mars issue. Paulus affirms that nocturnal planets rejoice in nocturnal feminine signs. However, Antiochus and Porphyry, while affirming that diurnal planets rejoice in diurnal signs, were silent on the corollary of nocturnal planets rejoicing in nocturnal signs.

For now, let us deem that the diurnal planets rejoice in the masculine diurnal signs and the nocturnal planets rejoice in the feminine nocturnal signs, and suspend our judgment about Mars. Mars will continue to present problems. It may be that Mars must be examined on a case-by-case basis.

→   EXAMPLE CHARTS

CHART I: The diurnal SUN rejoices in the diurnal masculine sign Leo. Diurnal JUPITER rejoices in the diurnal masculine sign Gemini. Diurnal SATURN rejoices in the diurnal masculine sign Sagittarius. Diurnal MERCURY rejoices in the diurnal masculine sign Leo. The nocturnal MOON does not rejoice in the diurnal masculine sign Aries. Nocturnal VENUS does not rejoice in the diurnal masculine sign Gemini. Nocturnal MARS rejoices in the nocturnal feminine sign Virgo by sect, but not by gender. One might speculate that the warrior is not happy being slowed down by thought and analysis, but his actions do have better outcomes.

ANALYSIS: *The diurnal planets all rejoice by zodiacal sign, but all the nocturnal planets are uncomfortable in their signs, with the possible exception of Mars.*

CHART II: The diurnal SUN does not rejoice in the nocturnal feminine sign Scorpio. Diurnal JUPITER does not rejoice in the nocturnal fem-

4   RHETORIUS, *Compendium* 1.1

inine sign Taurus. Diurnal SATURN does not rejoice in the nocturnal feminine sign Taurus. Nocturnal MERCURY rejoices in the nocturnal feminine sign Scorpio. The nocturnal MOON does not rejoice in the diurnal masculine sign Sagittarius. Nocturnal VENUS does not rejoice in the diurnal masculine sign Libra. Nocturnal MARS rejoices in the nocturnal feminine sign Cancer by sect, but not by gender. One might speculate that the warrior is not happy being overly concerned for his prey, but his actions as protector of the vulnerable have better outcomes.

ANALYSIS: *The only planet that rejoices by zodiacal sign is Mercury. All the others do not, with the possible exception of Mars.*

→ EXERCISE 6

Using your own chart, complete exercise 6:
Rejoicing by Zodiacal Sign

EXERCISE 6

REJOICING BY ZODIACAL SIGN

Using your own chart, answer the following questions to identify which planets rejoice by zodiacal sign.

1. *Is the diurnal sect Sun in a diurnal masculine sign?*
    Does it rejoice?
2. *Is diurnal sect Jupiter in a diurnal masculine sign?*
    Does it rejoice?
3. *Is diurnal sect Saturn in a diurnal masculine sign?*
    Does it rejoice?
4. *If Mercury is in the diurnal sect, is it located in a diurnal masculine sign?*
    Does it rejoice?
5. *If Mercury is in the nocturnal sect, is it located in a nocturnal feminine sign?*
    Does it rejoice?
6. *Is the nocturnal sect Moon in a nocturnal feminine sign?*
    Does it rejoice?
7. *Is nocturnal sect Venus in a nocturnal feminine sign?*
    Does it rejoice?
8. *Is nocturnal sect Mars in a nocturnal feminine sign?*
    Does it rejoice?

REFLECTION AND ANALYSIS

1. Which diurnal sect planets rejoice by zodiacal sign?
2. Which nocturnal sect planets rejoice by zodiacal sign?
3. How many planets in your chart rejoice by zodiacal sign?
4. How do you think that the planet's location in a zodiacal sign that is harmonious with its sect affiliation enhances its beneficial expression in your life?
5. If planets are located in zodiacal signs that are not harmonious with their sect affiliation, do you have a sense of discomfort with the beneficial expression of that planet's functions in your life?

SECT-REJOICING BY SOLAR PHASE

The third means of sect-rejoicing is determined by a planet's solar phase. As mentioned before, when a planet rises in the morning before the Sun, it partakes of the heat and vigor of day and becomes more masculine. It thus follows that the diurnal planets—Saturn and Jupiter—rejoice when they are morning stars preceding the Sun.

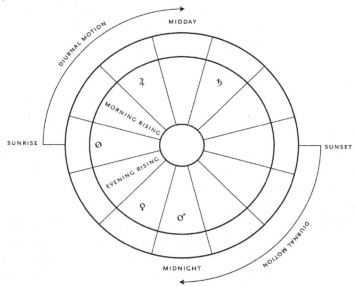

FIGURE 13. REJOICING BY SOLAR PHASE

Jupiter and Saturn rejoice when they rise before the Sun.
Venus and Mars rejoice when they rise after the Sun.

Conversely, when a planet is immersed in the coolness, moisture, and rest of evening, it is made more feminine. Therefore, following this reasoning, the nocturnal planets—Moon, Venus and Mars—rejoice when they are evening stars rising in the night sky after the Sun sets.

Mercury can rejoice either in the morning or in the evening, happily partaking of whichever environment its sect mates prefer.

However, Mars continues to give trouble. As a masculine gender planet, we must ask to what extent Mars rejoices when it finds itself in feminine conditions. Most of the astrologers, except Paulus, were silent on Mars rejoicing in the nocturnal signs. And later in the tradition, contrary to the earlier guidelines, Rhetorius states that Mars rejoices when it is a morning riser.[5] There seems to have been an understanding of how destructive Mars can become when overheated and an attempt to manage and temper its bad behavior through aligning it with the night energies. But Mars, if anything, is irascible and struggles against being pigeon-holed and controlled.

The only planets that can be evaluated according to rejoicing by solar phase are Venus, Mars, Jupiter, and Saturn. This is because the Sun is the reference point for this consideration; Mercury's sect is defined by its solar phase; and the Moon does not revolve around the Sun, but rather the earth.

An early Hellenistic astrologer wrote that the Moon in a day chart rejoices when it is waxing, but in a night chart rejoices when it is waning.[6] We will look at this more carefully in the chapter on solar and lunar phases.

To determine a planet's solar phase, follow the general guidelines given for Mercury rising ahead of the Sun in the morning, or appearing after the Sun in the evening. It might be helpful to draw a line from the Sun to its opposition point which is the dividing line between morning and evening rising, relative to the Sun. Looking to the diurnal (clockwise) motion as a planet rises over the ASC, culminates at the MC, sets at the DSC, and anti-culminates at the IC, you can see if that planet has risen before the Sun or after the Sun.

The diurnal planets do better when they are of the morning, and the nocturnal planets do better when they are of the evening. However, we are using the word rejoice in this context in a general sense. As we will see later, "rejoicing by solar phase as a morning or evening star" will have more strict parameters as a certain segment of the morning or evening arc (from 15 to ~120 degrees ahead of or behind the Sun). But for now, let us keep it simple so you can practice recognizing whether a planet is ahead of or behind the Sun in its diurnal clockwise motion.

→ EXAMPLE CHARTS

CHART 1: Diurnal JUPITER rejoices as a planet of the morning because it is ahead of the Sun. Diurnal SATURN does not rejoice as a planet of the morning because it is behind the Sun. Nocturnal VENUS does not rejoice as a planet of the morning because it is ahead of the Sun. Nocturnal MARS is an evening star. Does it rejoice rising behind the Sun?

ANALYSIS: *Jupiter and Mars rejoice by solar phase, but Saturn and Venus do not.*

5   RHETORIUS, *Compendium* 1.44.
6   SERAPIO, *Definitions.*

CHART II: A line drawn from the Sun at 2° Scorpio goes to 2° Taurus. Keeping the diurnal (clockwise) motion of the planets in mind, you can see that both Jupiter and Saturn have risen before the Sun and thus are of the morning. If the position of one of those planets had been at 1° Taurus or 25° Aries, it would have been of the evening. It is the axis of the Sun and its opposite polarity point that demarcates the difference between being ahead of the Sun (of the morning) and being behind the Sun (of the evening).

Diurnal JUPITER is a planet of the morning and rejoices because it rises ahead of the Sun. Diurnal SATURN is a planet of the morning and rejoices because it rises ahead of the Sun. Nocturnal VENUS is a planet of the morning and does not rejoice because it rises ahead of the Sun. Nocturnal MARS is a planet of the morning. Does it rejoice?

ANALYSIS: *All the planets are of the morning, rising ahead of the Sun. However, the diurnal planets both rejoice in this condition by solar phase while the nocturnal planets do not.*

→   EXERCISE 7

Using your own chart, complete exercise 7:
Rejoicing by Solar Phase

EXERCISE 7

REJOICING BY SOLAR PHASE

Using your own chart, answer the following questions to identify which planets rejoice by solar phase.

1. *Is diurnal Jupiter a morning star, rising ahead of the Sun?* If so, it rejoices. Does Jupiter rejoice according to solar phase?
2. *Is diurnal Saturn a morning star, rising ahead of the Sun?* If so, it rejoices. Does Saturn rejoice according to solar phase?
3. *Is nocturnal Venus an evening star, rising after the Sun?* If so, it rejoices. Does Venus rejoice by solar phase?
4. *Is nocturnal Mars an evening star, rising after the Sun?* If so, it rejoices. Does Mars rejoice by solar phase?
5. *If you have a diurnal chart, the Moon will rejoice if she is waxing, increasing in light.* Does the Moon rejoice by sect and phase?
6. *If you have a nocturnal chart, the Moon will rejoice if she is waning, decreasing in light.* Does the Moon rejoice by sect and phase?

We are not analyzing the Sun because the Sun determines the category. We are not analyzing Mercury, because Mercury's solar phase determines its sect status.

REFLECTION AND ANALYSIS

1. Which diurnal sect planets rejoice by solar phase?
2. Which nocturnal sect planets rejoice by solar phase?
3. How many planets in your chart rejoice by solar phase?
4. Do you have a sense that the diurnal planets that rejoice as morning stars take the lead in your life?
5. Do you have a sense that the nocturnal planets that rejoice as evening stars bring up the rear in your life?
6. Do you experience more happiness or contentment in regards to the significations of your planets that rejoice by solar phase?

ADVANCED CONSIDERATIONS

Before we conclude this section, there is another important point to note. The interpretive texts often delineate Saturn, Jupiter, and Mars using the qualifiers by day or night, but when writing about Venus and Mercury, the terms used are morning appearance or evening appearance, which James Holden, referring to Latin Medieval astrological terminology, has translated as matutine (morning) and vespertine (evening).

Because Venus can never be more than 48° away from the Sun, it is almost always in the same hemisphere as the Sun and thus she rarely rejoices by hemisphere. This may contribute to the situation in which many people have problems with their love lives. It is only when the Sun is close to the horizon (sunrise or sunset birth times) that Venus has the possibility of rejoicing in the hemisphere opposite the Sun. The same is true for Mercury, who cannot be more than 28° from the Sun—it will rarely be in the opposite hemisphere than the Sun and so its solar phase is more relevant in sect-based interpretations.

For this reason, the ancient astrologers, when giving delineations of the planets Venus and Mercury, often looked more to their solar phase to determine how they might function. Therefore, since Venus and Mercury rarely rejoice by hemisphere, their solar phase becomes a stronger factor in nuanced interpretations. However, in cases where they do rejoice by hemisphere, it is especially noteworthy as this is not a common improvement of their condition.

As we shall see, there are many other factors that also have an influence on our final judgment about the condition of a planet, but sect is the starting point and baseline for many of the other modifications.

SUMMARY OF MAIN POINTS
CONCERNING SECT AND SECT-REJOICING

IF THE SUN IS ABOVE THE HORIZON:

> The SECT of the chart is *diurnal*.
> The SUN is the *sect leader*.
> The DIURNAL PLANETS—Sun, Jupiter, Saturn, and a morning star Mercury—*belong to the same sect as the sect of the chart* (and the nocturnal planets are contrary to the sect of the chart).
> The DIURNAL PLANETS have *more freedom* to bring about beneficial outcomes, and the NOCTURNAL PLANETS are *more constrained*.
> JUPITER is the *greater benefic*.
> MARS is the potentially *more problematic malefic*.

IF THE SUN IS BELOW THE HORIZON:

> The SECT of the chart is *nocturnal*.
> The MOON is the *sect leader*.
> The NOCTURNAL PLANETS—Moon, Venus, Mars, and evening star Mercury—*belong to the same sect as the sect of the chart* (and the diurnal planets are contrary to sect).
> The NOCTURNAL PLANETS have *more freedom* to bring about beneficial outcomes, and the DIURNAL PLANETS are *more constrained*.
> VENUS is the *greater benefic*.
> SATURN is the potentially *more problematic malefic*.

SECT-REJOICING CONDITIONS:

> The DIURNAL PLANETS rejoice when located in the *same hemisphere as the Sun*, and the NOCTURNAL PLANETS rejoice when in the *hemisphere opposite the Sun*.
> The DIURNAL PLANETS rejoice in *diurnal zodiacal signs*; the NOCTURNAL PLANETS rejoice in the *nocturnal zodiacal signs*.
> The DIURNAL PLANETS rejoice as *morning stars* ahead of the Sun, and the NOCTURNAL PLANETS rejoice as *evening stars* following the Sun.

JUDGING THE NATIVITY

Let us now put all this information together in our master template. Focusing only upon sect conditions at this point, we can begin our process of finding the best planet in the chart as well as the planet that is most challenged. This will become a critical factor later on when we begin to interpret the planets in the houses in which they are located and the houses which they rule.

The most important part of this process is making the final judgment about each planet. For me, initially this was very difficult because my training as a modern astrologer stressed that nothing in the chart is bad. Planets in various signs and houses described the wide range of ways that planets could potentially manifest equally well. But the traditional-minded astrologer must undo this thinking pattern. It is necessary to stand back and be dispassionate about the factors that make a planet function optimally, as opposed to those that put it at a disadvantage in terms of its predisposition to bring about favorable outcomes for the person.

And, in some fundamental way, if you cannot bring yourself to make these judgments, it is pointless to continue with this way of evaluating a chart. But keep in mind that the value here is in knowing when something is a problem, and then presenting the information in a way that is helpful and guides the client toward solutions.

I will describe my own thinking about how to judge each planet to give you an idea of how to proceed and what to look at. But in the end, each astrologer must make his or her own judgments. While there are right and wrong determinations of the conditions, there are no absolute right or wrong evaluations by astrologers concerning what these conditions mean. This is what separates the art of astrology from the science of astrology.

→ EXAMPLE CHARTS

We will now tabulate all the determinations we have made about each planet's sect status and sect-rejoicing. Here we will see how much more we can learn about each planet's condition and ability to bring forth its significations in positive ways for the individual. For each planet, we are noting whether it belongs to the diurnal or nocturnal sect; to the same sect of the chart or the contrary sect; if it is a benefic or malefic, and especially if it is the benefic of the sect or the malefic contrary to the sect of the chart; and whether it rejoices in each of the sect-rejoicing conditions. Then we will give it an evaluation based only upon sect criteria.

CHART I: DIURNAL SECT

Planet: sign and degree	Sect of planet: day or night	Same or contrary sect	Benefic/ malefic	Rejoice by hemi- sphere	Rejoice by sign	Rejoice by solar phase	Judg- ment
SUN 5° Leo	Day	Same	N/A	N/A	Yes	N/A	A
JUPITER 9° Gem	Day	Same	Benefic of sect	Yes	Yes	Yes	A+
SATURN 24° Sag Rx	Day	Same	Malefic of sect	No	Yes	No	B-
MERCURY 2° Leo	Day	Same	N/A	Yes	Yes	N/A	A-
MOON 25° Aries	Night	Contrary	N/A	Yes	No	No	B-
VENUS 21° Gem	Night	Contrary	Benefic contrary to sect	No	No	No	C-
MARS 14° Virgo	Night	Contrary	Malefic contrary to sect	No	Yes	Yes	C

In general, give a higher evaluation to the luminary, benefic, and other planets of the sect in this order, with sect-rejoicing as a modifier.

In this diurnal chart, the SUN as sect leader belongs to the same sect as the sect of the chart, the favored position. The only rejoicing condition that applies to it is its zodiacal sign, as it rejoices in a masculine sign. I am giving the Sun an A.

JUPITER is the benefic of the sect in favor. It is the planet that has the freedom and authority to do the best benefic work, and it rejoices in all three of its sect-rejoicing conditions—hemisphere, zodiacal sign, and solar phase. I am giving it an A+ based only on sect conditions, but I am aware that it is in Gemini, the sign of its detriment, so this may detract from its overall grade later on.

SATURN is a malefic, but in the same sect as the sect of the chart, so it is positioned to do better than its baseline. But it only rejoices in its zodiacal sign, not by hemisphere or phase, so it is not a very happy Saturn. I think it gets a B-.

MERCURY belongs to the sect of the chart and is thus positioned to do well. As a diurnal planet, Mercury rejoices in the diurnal sign Leo. Its solar phase is not applicable and its presence in the same hemisphere as the Sun is not unusual. I am going to give it an A-.

THE MOON, as the sect leader for the nocturnal planets, belongs to the contrary sect and thus is more limited in her position to do her best for the individual. She rejoices by hemisphere, but not in the fiery masculine diurnal sign of Aries. As a waning moon she does not rejoice in this day chart. I am giving her a B-.

VENUS is very challenged. Although a benefic by nature, she is a nocturnal sect planet in a day chart and therefore does not belong to the sect of the chart. She is not in a position to bring forth her full positive significations. And Venus is quite unhappy, not rejoicing by hemisphere, sign, or phase. I am giving her a C-.

MARS, a member of the contrary sect of this day chart and thus the problematic malefic, does not rejoice by hemisphere. He is an evening star in a feminine nocturnal sign, which makes us think he is not intrinsically happy, but the outcomes of his actions will be better for the individual. The tempering of his nature can lead to careful deliberation and restraint, rather than critical aggression. So I am giving him a C and know to watch him carefully.

My final analysis is that the *diurnal team* that belongs to the privileged same sect as this day chart is overall quite powerful, with the Sun as strong leader, Jupiter as most favorable benefic, Mercury quite good, and Saturn the weakest link, but still functional. All planets are well-aspected to the Sun by whole sign aspects—Mercury conjoins, Jupiter sextiles, and Saturn trines the Sun. They are well-connected and have internal cooperation as a team.

The *nocturnal team*, of the contrary sect, is definitely challenged. The Moon as leader is middling; Venus occupies conditions that are totally unsuitable to her nature, and it is hard to predict whether Mars' malefic tendencies will be let loose or tensely constrained. While the Moon has a sextile to Venus, she is not connected to Mars, and Mars is square Venus. Thus there is some internal disconnect and struggle among the nocturnal team members.

CHART II: NOCTURNAL SECT

Planet: sign and degree	Sect of planet: day or night	Same or contrary sect	Benefic/ malefic	Rejoice by hemi- sphere	Rejoice by sign	Rejoice by solar phase	Judg- ment
SUN 3° Scorpio	Day	Contrary	N/A	N/A	No	N/A	C
JUPITER 23° Taurus Rx	Day	Contrary	Benefic	No	No	Yes	C+
SATURN 9° Taurus Rx	Day	Contrary	Malefic contrary to sect	No	No	Yes	C
MERCURY 25° Scorpio	Night	Same	Neutral	No	Yes	N/A	B
MOON 9° Sagit- tarius	Night	Same	N/A	No	No	No	C+
VENUS 5° Libra	Night	Same	Benefic of sect	No	No	No	B-
MARS 13° Cancer	Night	Same	Malefic	Yes	Yes	No	B-

THE SUN as leader of the diurnal sect in a nocturnal chart is not in the position to do his best and he does not rejoice in the sign of Scorpio. I give the Sun a C.

JUPITER, while a benefic planet, does not have the position to bring about the full measure of its beneficence in this nocturnal chart. It only rejoices by solar phase, but not by hemisphere or zodiacal sign. Therefore I give it a C+.

SATURN, the malefic contrary to sect, with only one sect rejoicing condition, presents a big problem to the individual. I give it a C.

MERCURY is a nocturnal planet in a nocturnal chart and thus belongs to the sect of the chart. It rejoices in a nocturnal sign but not by hemisphere. I am going to give it a B. I will wait until we complete the remaining sections on the criteria for evaluation in order to determine if it is operating as a benefic or malefic.

THE MOON is the sect leader in this nocturnal chart. However, she does not rejoice in the same hemisphere as the Sun nor by zodiacal sign. As a waxing moon she does not rejoice in this night chart. So I am giving her a C+.

VENUS, the more powerful benefic in this nocturnal chart, does not rejoice by hemisphere, not by solar phase as a morning star, nor in the diurnal sign of Libra. But I am giving her a B-, because she is the benefic of the sect in favor.

MARS, the potentially helpful malefic of the sect of the chart, rejoices in the hemisphere opposite that of the Sun, and also reluctantly rejoices in the nocturnal sign of Cancer. Mars is a morning star, becoming more masculinized, but also more aggressive. I am giving it a B-.

In the final analysis, the *diurnal planets* in this chart are contrary to the sect of this night chart, so immediately some of their score, relative to their ability to do good for the individual, drops down.

→ EXERCISE 8

Using your own chart, complete exercise 8:
Final Judgments for Sect and Sect Rejoicing

EXERCISE 8

FINAL JUDGMENT FOR SECT AND SECT-REJOICING

Using your own chart, complete the following exercise to form a final judgment for each planet based on sect factors.

This exercise integrates all the factors we have looked at so far. This enables us to arrive at a judgment for each planet concerning its ability to bring forth beneficial outcomes for you based upon each planet's sect status and sect-rejoicing.

SECT OF CHART: (DIURNAL/NOCTURNAL)

Planet: sign and degree	Sect of planet: day or night	Same or contrary sect	Benefic/malefic	Rejoice by hemisphere	Rejoice by sign	Rejoice by solar phase	Judgment:
SUN			N/A	N/A		N/A	
JUPITER							
SATURN							
MERCURY						N/A	
MOON		N/A					
VENUS							
MARS							

1. *Sect of the chart: enter* DAY *(diurnal) or* NIGHT *(nocturnal).*
    Diurnal is Sun above horizon as defined by degrees of ASC/DSC axis; nocturnal is Sun below horizon).

2. *Planet: enter the zodiacal sign and degree of each planet.*

3. *Sect of the planet: enter the sect of each planet—*DAY *(diurnal) or* NIGHT *(nocturnal).* This will always be the same for each planet, except Mercury who will vary from chart to chart depending upon its solar phase (diurnal = of the morning; nocturnal = of the evening).

4. *Same sect or contrary sect: if the sect of the planet is the same as the sect of the chart, enter* SAME. *If the sect of the planet is different than the sect of the chart, enter* CONTRARY.

5. *Benefic or malefic: for Venus, Jupiter, Mars, and Saturn, enter whether the planet is a* BENEFIC *or* MALEFIC. *This will be the same for every chart. Note the planet that is the benefic of the sect and the planet that is the malefic contrary to the sect.*
    You can make this evaluation for the Sun, Moon, and Mercury after you have examined all of the other criteria.

6. *Rejoice by hemisphere: if the planet rejoices by hemisphere (diurnal planets in same hemisphere as Sun, nocturnal planets in opposite hemisphere than Sun), enter* YES. *Otherwise enter* NO.

7. *Rejoice by zodiacal sign: if the planet rejoices by zodiacal sign (diurnal planets in diurnal fire/air signs, nocturnal planets in nocturnal earth/water signs), enter* YES. *Otherwise enter* NO.

8. *Rejoice by solar phase: if the planet rejoices by solar phase (diurnal planets of the morning, nocturnal planets of the evening) enter* YES. *Otherwise enter* NO.

9. *Judgment: the most important criterion is whether or not the planet belongs to the same sect as the sect of the chart. This places it in a position to more effectively bring about its benefic significations, whether it is a benefic planet or a malefic planet.*
    If the planet is the benefic of the sect of the chart (Jupiter in a day chart, Venus in a night chart), this enhances its benefic powers. If the planet is the benefic of the contrary sect (Jupiter in a night chart, Venus in a day chart), its benefic powers are limited (in accordance with its overall condition). If the planet is the malefic of the sect of the chart, it can potentially use its malefic nature on behalf of the best interests of the individual. If the planet is the malefic of the contrary sect, it is more likely to use its malefic nature to bring about outcomes that are not in the best interests of the individual.
    The above factors establish the baseline. The three sect-rejoicing conditions

serve to bring the baseline of the planet's condition slightly towards more benefic or towards less benefic.

10. *Grade: now come to a judgment for each planet. Beginners, look to the sect status of the planet, identify the benefic of the sect and the malefic contrary to the sect, and sect-rejoicing (if you feel comfortable with synthesizing these additional factors). Intermediates, integrate the sect-rejoicing conditions. Above all, be sure to give each planet a grade—*A, B, C, D, E, OR F *with pluses or minuses.*

This is the art of judgment. Learning how to make this evaluation and feeling confident about your process is the key to later easily and accurately interpreting the planet in its house location. With practice, this process will get easier. Your thinking and hence understanding of the chart will shift from fuzzy to clear. You can change your mind about the grade later on after you have evaluated a number of charts and you become more proficient in the process.

REFLECTION AND ANALYSIS

1. What is the sect of your chart?
2. Based upon the sect of your chart, which of the two luminaries is your sect leader, the Sun or Moon?
3. Do you feel more aligned with the solar/diurnal sect of thought or with the lunar/nocturnal sect of thought? When you seek to know and understand, is it more fruitful for you to try to shed light upon the situation or go deep within to feel your way?
4. Based upon the sect of your chart, which of the two benefic planets is more of an ally? Think about how this planet, in accordance with its sign, house, and overall condition, is predisposed to bring about the most positive outcomes in your life.
5. Based upon the sect of your chart, which of the two malefic planets is more of a problem? Think about how this planet, in accordance with its sign, house, and overall condition, is predisposed to bring about the greater difficult outcomes in your life.
6. Based upon sect-rejoicing conditions, which planets are the happiest? Which planets are not happy? Think about whether your happy planets belong to the sect of the chart or not. Are the activities of these planets ultimately serving your best interests or not?
7. Based upon sect and sect-rejoicing conditions only, which planet is in the best condition?
8. Based upon sect and sect-rejoicing conditions only, which planet is in

the worst condition?

9. Which sect's planets, the day or night, are in overall better condition?

10. Do these planets belong to the same sect as your chart or not?

11. Do the planets that are predisposed to bring about more beneficial outcomes rejoice or not? What does this suggest to you in reflecting upon your life?

12. Look back at your grading of each planet in case you now want to change anything.

13. Write a sentence for each planet where you summarize its condition based upon its sect and give your reasoning for the grade you assign to it.

CHAPTER 8

Summary

———

THE ORIGINS OF ASTROLOGY WERE BASED UPON THE BELIEF THAT THE planets were one of the *visible manifestations of the gods* and that each planet's significations corresponded to the attributes of the deity after whom it was named. A planet's basic nature is derived from its special essence in the cosmic soul, and is the underlying principle that gives rise to all of its various significations in human and terrestrial life.

Planets can be classified according to masculine and feminine GENDER, benefic and malefic NATURE, and diurnal and nocturnal SECT. Gender shapes the relative speed and outward or inward orientation of the planet. Essential benefic or malefic nature determines the baseline of actions that promote well-being or actions whose results are self-destructive.

Planets that belong to the same SECT as the chart are more effective in bringing forth favorable outcomes in the life of the individual. The BENEFIC planet, Jupiter or Venus, that belongs to the sect of the chart is best positioned to do the greater good. The malefic planet, Saturn or Mars, of the contrary sect can present more difficult problems to the individual.

The three SECT-REJOICING CONDITIONS of *hemisphere, zodiacal sign,* and *phase* give the subtle nuances to enhancing or constraining a planet's activity. When planets occupy hemispheres, zodiacal signs, phase relationships to the Sun, quadrants, and latitude directions that are compatible with their inherent gender and sect status, they rejoice and their events are more beneficial for the individual.

Think about how much you have gleaned so far about the relative strengths and weaknesses of each planet. You are now making your first judgments about each planet and beginning to see which of the planets is leading out front in the individual's journey to fulfill his or her destiny, which planets are managing to keep up the pace, and which are falling behind. Suspect that some of these initial judgments will undoubtedly be modified with each additional category of criteria.

Looking ahead, after factoring in the zodiacal sign, solar and lunar phase conditions, and aspect considerations, you will make a final judgment about each planet. Then you will be ready to interpret it in the houses. By this time you will have a good sense of how positive or how problematic the planet will be relative to the topic of the house in which it is located, and the houses which it rules.

PRIMARY SOURCE READINGS
FOR PART ONE: PLANETS AND SECT

SIGNIFICATIONS OF THE PLANETS

VALENS   *Anthology* 1.1: The Nature of the Stars.
TEUCER   The Nature and Force of the Seven Planets (CCAG 7, pp. 213–224:
              translation by J. HOLDEN in RHETORIUS, *Astrological Compendia*).
ANTIOCHUS   *Summary* 1.1: The Seven Wandering Stars.
PTOLEMY   *Tetrabiblos* 1.4: The Power of the Wandering Stars.
              Tetrabiblos 2.8: The Quality of the Predicted Event.
PORPHYRY   *Introduction* 2: Changes Produced by the Transfers of the Sun,
              Moon, and Stars.
              Introduction 45: What Sort of Body Part Each Star Rules.
HEPHAISTIO   *Apotelesmatics* 1.2: The Power of the Seven Wandering Stars.

CLASSIFICATIONS OF THE PLANETS

PTOLEMY   *Tetrabiblos* 1.5: Beneficent and Maleficent Planets.
              Tetrabiblos 1.6: Masculine and Feminine Planets.
              Tetrabiblos 1.7: Diurnal and Nocturnal Planets.
PORPHYRY   *Introduction* 4: Diurnal and Nocturnal Stars.
FIRMICUS   *Mathesis* 2.8: Stars that Rejoice by Day or Night.
PAULUS   *Introduction* 6: The Sects of the Two Luminaries.
HEPHAISTIO   *Apotelesmatics* 1.2: The Power of the Seven Wandering Stars.
RHETORIUS   *Compendium* 1: Stars that Become Masculine and Feminine.
              Compendium 2: The Sects of Stars.
              Compendium 44: When the Stars Rejoice.

PART TWO

SIGNS AND RULERSHIPS

CHAPTER 9

The Zodiacal Signs

―――

IN THE HEAVENS

ON A SPIRITUAL LEVEL THE PLANETS ARE THE VISUAL APPEARANCES of the gods. These divine emanations of the planetary gods take form in the terrestrial realm as multiple physical manifestations in the mineral, vegetative, animal, and human kingdoms. In the human personality, the planets symbolize the active forces in the psyche that motivate a person towards his or her destination and destiny. In the previous section, we explored how each planet's gender, benefic or malefic nature, and sect status indicates the extent to which the planet is positioned to bring about this destiny in the best possible manner.

We now turn to a discussion of the twelve zodiacal signs, the next important category in the assessment of a planet's condition. The zodiacal signs represent the celestial abodes of the planets. They shape the characteristics of the planets' behaviors and appearances, the manner in which they bring their significations about, the resources that they have available in order to accomplish their agenda, and the special powers that are available to them when occupying certain zodiacal signs.

Let us begin by saying a few words about the zodiac, which consists of a circle of images of living beings in the sky. These images form the backdrop for the movement of the planets as we gaze at them in the night sky. We will distinguish between two different zodiacal systems—the sidereal and the tropical zodiacs.

THE ZODIACAL CONSTELLATIONS
AND ZODIACAL SIGNS

The zodiac is the fundamental frame of reference used by both astronomers and astrologers to locate the positions of planets in the starry heavens. Zodiac comes from the Greek word *zōidion* (pl. *zōidia*) which means a small image of a living creature. The Greek names of the zodiacal constellations are Aries the Ram, Taurus the Bull, Gemini the Twins, Cancer the Crab, Leo the Lion, Virgo the Virgin, Libra the Scales, Scorpio the Scorpion, Sagittarius the Archer, Capricorn the Ibex or Goat-Fish, Aquarius the Water-pourer, and Pisces the Fishes.

This twelve-fold zodiac, that is now the basis of both Western and Eastern astrology, has its origins in the observations of Babylonian astronomers during the second millennium BCE. Standing on Earth and looking outwards toward the cosmos, the Sun appears to move along a path called the ecliptic. All the planets and the Moon travel within a band that is approximately eight degrees on either side of the Sun. As these early peoples observed the passage of the Sun, Moon, and five visible planets across the night sky, these wandering celestial bodies seemed to follow this path against the background of certain fixed stars. The ancients imagined groupings of fixed stars to be similar to the shapes of animals or humans and designated them as the zodiacal constellations. An ancient astronomer could then point to a planet such as Mars and say that it was in some constellation such as the Bull or the Scorpion.

The Babylonians first gave the zodiacal and other extra-zodiacal constellations their names around 1300 BCE. Originally their zodiac consisted of eighteen constellations that marked the monthly passage of the Moon as recorded in the eighth-century *Mul Apin Star Catalog*. During this same period in the Indus Valley in India, Hindu astronomers had designated twenty-seven star groups called *nakshatras* to mark the passage of the Moon. By the fifth century BCE the Babylonians had scaled down their zodiac to twelve constellations that marked the yearly passage of the Sun. While each of the twelve designated constellations were not an equal length of thirty degrees each, the divisions were made as equal thirty-degree segments in order to correspond to the twelve months of the year of an already existing solar calendar.

In 336 BCE the Greek astronomer Eudoxus of Cnidus, a student of Plato's, wrote a handbook for a globe on which the constellations were mapped. He followed many Babylonian designations for the constellations, but changed their names to Greek, following most of the conventions with a corresponding term. The names of ten of the twelve Babylonian zodiacal constellations were simply converted to the Greek equivalent of the same word, such as the *Mastabbagalgal*, the Great Twins (Gemini), and the *Urgula*, the Lion (Leo).

SIDEREAL AND TROPICAL ZODIACS AND PRECESSION

There are two different zodiacs in use—the sidereal zodiac and the tropical zodiac. The frame of reference for the sidereal zodiac (sidereal means star) is the

Sun's apparent movement against the background of the constellations of fixed stars, as discussed above. The frame of reference for the tropical zodiac is the seasonal path of the Sun relative to the Earth.

As the Sun travels north and south of the equator during its annual journey, its yearly course is marked by four critical turning points, known as the solstices and equinoxes. Each of these turning points initiates one of the four seasons.

At the Winter Solstice, the Sun reaches its southernmost declination, where daytime hours are shortest. It then moves in a northerly direction and the light hours begin to increase. At the Spring Equinox, the Sun crosses the celestial equator where day and night hours are equal. It reaches its northernmost declination at the Summer Solstice, the longest day of the year. It then turns south and crosses the celestial equator again at the Fall Equinox, equalizing day and night. Now the night continues to increase until the Sun reaches the Winter Solstice again.

This path of the Sun is divided into twelve equal thirty-degree segments of zodiacal signs. The beginning of the seasons—Spring, Summer, Fall, and Winter, as marked by the equinoxes and solstices—correspond to the first degree of Aries, Cancer, Libra, and Capricorn, respectively. The equal divisions of the remaining signs complete the zodiacal circle.

Astronomers, Hindu Vedic astrologers, and some "western sidereal" astrologers use the sidereal zodiac, while most western astrologers use the tropical zodiac in order to denote the location of the planets. This has generated tremendous confusion among both astrologers and the non-astrological public, resulting in a host of controversies due to the use of the same term to designate different frames of reference.

These two different zodiacal locational systems were not much of a problem when Hellenistic astrology was first being formulated in the early centuries of our era. At that time, the zodiacal constellations were roughly aligned with the seasonal zodiacal signs (see FIGURE 14). Looking out from Earth, the Spring Equinox point at 0° Aries was approximately in the same line of vision as the beginning of the constellation Aries. Valens and others noted that in their era the Spring Equinox point was at 8° Aries.[1] However, this is now much more of a problem because the two zodiacs have separated over the intervening time by about 24° (see FIGURE 15). This is due to the astronomical phenomenon of precession.

[1]   VALENS, *Anthology* 9.12P, trans. RILEY.

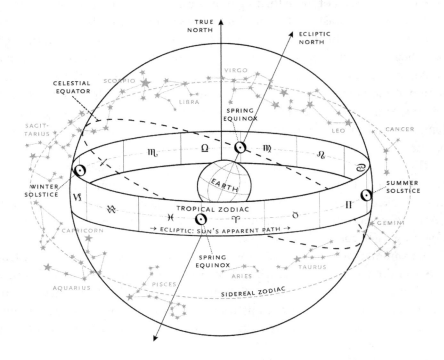

FIGURE 14. TROPICAL AND SIDEREAL ZODIACS
CIRCA THIRD CENTURY CE

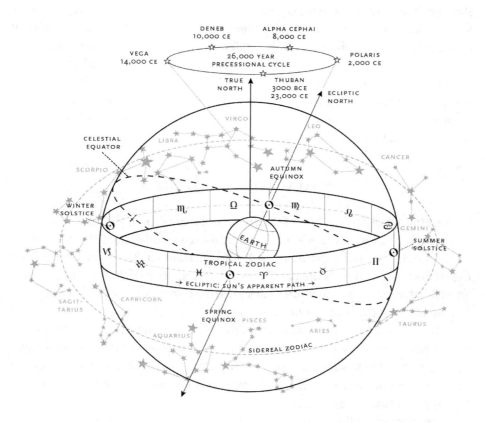

FIGURE 15. EQUINOCTIAL PRECESSION
CIRCA 2,000 CE

Precession is the slow wobbling movement that the earth makes on its axis due to its tilt, like the spinning of a top (a child's toy). As the earth makes this slow turning movement, its axis traces a circle in the sky that takes 26,000 years to complete. As it does so, its alignment against the relatively fixed sidereal frame shifts backwards through the zodiac at the rate of one degree for every seventy-two years. The two zodiacs that were aligned in the second century will not realign now for another 24,000 years. The Spring Equinox point of the tropical zodiac (0° Aries) is now located at 6° Pisces in the sidereal zodiac. In 2016, tropical astrologers locate Saturn in Sagittarius, but in the night sky it is in the sidereal constellation of Scorpio.

WHICH ZODIAC TO USE?

In examining the descriptions of the characteristics of the zodiacal signs, we will discover that historically both zodiacs contributed significations that we continue to associate with the nature of each sign. Certain attributes are drawn from the sidereal constellation images that are representative of their corresponding animal behaviors, and other attributes are drawn from the tropical characteristics based upon the qualities of air and light in the various seasons.

The sidereal zodiac speaks to our relationship to the many distant stars in our galaxy, some of which no longer exist, even though we still see their light. Thus it may address more transpersonal perspectives about the nature of the soul's consciousness, its development over long expanses of time, and our relationship to a galactic awareness.

The tropical zodiac addresses our relationship to our own nearby star, the Sun. As the center of our solar system, it regulates both the day and night cycle as well as the seasonal cycle. Its significance is directed more to the personal and immediate issues of this particular life.

Both systems offer valid and worthwhile perspectives. Each system has an internal integrity that when used in a consistent manner, brings forth accurate insights into character and destiny. In the remainder of this book, we will be using the tropical zodiac for our frame of reference in order to locate a planet's position. This is the system that most western astrologers, both traditional and modern, have followed since about the fourth century CE.

CHAPTER 10

Functions and Classifications

OF THE ZODIACAL SIGNS

———

THE ZODIACAL SIGNS SERVE THREE PRIMARY FUNCTIONS IN THE OVERALL structure and internal integrity of the birth chart:

1. as *images* that shape behaviors and physical characteristics
2. as *configurations* which act as a network of familial relationships
3. as *residences* which provide resources and powers

The broad brushstrokes of this organization reflect in part the social customs of the Hellenistic world, where there were clear rules and distinctions establishing one's position in the network of alliances and enmities and the various ways in which wealth, resources, and power were distributed.

Hellenistic astrologers often used two Greek words, *zōidion* and *oikos*, when writing about the zodiacal signs. *Zōidion* means a small image of a living thing, and *oikos* means a home or dwelling place. These two notions about the zodiacal signs can be traced back to the second millennium BCE Babylonian creation myth, the *Enuma Elish*:

> He [Marduk] constructed stations for the great gods,
> Fixing their astral likenesses (*images*) as the stars of the Zodiac.
> He determined the year and into sections he divided it;
> He set up three constellations for each of the twelve months.[1]

This verse suggests that the images of the constellations were set up as the dwelling places for the planetary gods, and these stellar images marked each segment of the twelve-month year.

---

1   *Enuma Elish* v. 1–4. Translation by E. A. SPEISER in *Ancient Near Eastern Texts Relating to the Old Testament*, 3rd edition, edited by James PRITCHARD (Princeton, 1969).

ZODIACAL SIGNS AS IMAGES

> The ancients divided the zodiac into twelve sections, attributing a
> name to each from the smaller living beings upon the earth that are
> for the most part sympathetic and placing their images in the stars as
> constellations in these regions as it was approved. — HEPHAISTIO.[2]

The earliest comprehensive source of the zodiacal signs is found in the writings
of Teucer of Babylon, which date to around the first century CE.[3] The form and
content of the descriptions of the zodiacal signs remained relatively consistent
from the Hellenistic through to the Arabic, Medieval, and Renaissance texts. To
get a sense of how ancient astrologers understood the zodiacal signs, here is a
detailed explication of the entry on Aries.

TEUCER OF BABYLON ON ARIES "THE RAM"

Teucer begins by listing various characteristics and categories of the signs such
as gender, modality, appearance, animal attributes, and general behavior traits:

> It is masculine, tropical, spring, equinoctial, ascending, four-footed,
> lives on dry land, royal, barren, changeable, high-spirited, fiery, mid-
> heaven of the cosmos, rising and falling, terminal, licentious, ardent,
> mutilated, fleshy, weak-eyed, servile, semi-vocal, unruly, authorita-
> tive, looking towards the southeast.

He then describes Aries in terms of the rulership, as well as detriment and
fall, of various planets in accordance with systems of domicile, exaltation, and
triplicity rulers:

---

2   *Apotelesmatics* 1.1.

3   This excerpt (edited in the CCAG 7, pp. 194–96) is a translation from a compilation made
    by RHETORIUS OF EGYPT around the late sixth century. He drew primarily upon the
    work of the first-century astrologer, TEUCER OF BABYLON (i.e., the city Babylon in Egypt,
    not Mesopotamia), who was a principal source on the zodiacal signs and planets for
    other astrologers as well, including VALENS (*Anthology* 1.2). Teucer's account includes the
    mention of a number of "non-standard" constellations called the *dōdekaōros*, which may
    be Egyptian constellations as some of the images and names correlate to Egyptian deities.
    Rhetorius' text also draws from the writings of Claudius PTOLEMY, and thus is represen-
    tative of the accumulated understanding of his day regarding the nature of the zodiacal
    signs. An English translation of Rhetorius' text of Teucer for all of the twelve zodiacal
    signs is contained in RHETORIUS' *Compendia*, translated by James Holden. MANILIUS
    (*Astronomica* 2.150–692), PAULUS OF ALEXANDRIA (*Introduction* 2), and HEPHAISTIO
    OF THEBES (*Apotelesmatics* 1.1) also contain entries detailing the twelve zodiacal signs.

It has thirty degrees, a degree contains sixty minutes, and the first minute contains sixty seconds, and so on. It is the domicile of Mars, the exaltation of the Sun around the nineteenth degree, the fall of Saturn around the twenty-first degree, the triplicity by day of the Sun, by night of Jupiter, and common to both [sects] of Saturn, and the detriment of Venus.

Teucer designates the three decans of the zodiacal sign and the other constellations that rise along with that of Aries:

It has three decans. These stars rise alongside the first decan: Athene, the tail of Cetus, a third of Triangulum, the Cynocephalus bearing the lamp and the head of Ailouros of the *dōdekaōros*. The stars that rise with the second decan are Andromeda, the middle of Cetus, the Gorgon and the sword of Perseus, half of Triangulum, and the middle of Ailouros of the *dōdekaōros*. The stars that rise with the third decan are Cassiopeia sitting upon her throne, Perseus with his head downward, the head of Cetus, the remainder of Triangulum, and the tail of Ailouros of the *dōdekaōros*.

In this next paragraph, each of the three decans is correlated to a planet that was thought to have influence over that ten-degree sector. Each decan was said to have the "face" or countenance of a certain planet that reflects the earlier Egyptian depictions of the decans as the images of various deities:

The first decan has the countenance of Mars, the second of the Sun, and the third of Venus.

Teucer then gives us the degree intervals or boundaries within the zodiacal sign that are each governed by a different planetary bound lord:

And it has the bounds/terms of the five planets: from the first to the sixth [degree], Jupiter, from the seventh to the twelfth, Venus, from the thirteenth to the twentieth, Mercury, from the twenty-first to the twenty-fifth, Mars, and from the twenty-sixth to the thirtieth, Saturn.

He gives us the climes, the geographical areas that are under the dominion of Aries, as well as ailments, body parts, and letters of the alphabet:

The climes that are subject to this zodiacal sign are Persia, according to Ptolemy, Britain, Galatia, Germany, Palestine, Idoumea, and Judea. The parts of the body it rules are the head, face, all of the conditions and mishaps that occur around the head, weak sight, paralysis, hardness of hearing, blindness, scaly skin, canker sores, thinning of hair, baldness, mental stupor, wounds, and the usual things concerning the hearing and the teeth. It rules the letters *alpha* and *nu*.

Teucer describes the various parts of the Ram's body that rise successively and links each part to specific degrees of the sign:

> There arises from the first to the third the boundary of the sign, from the third to the seventh the head, from the eighth to the tenth the neck, from the eleventh to the thirteenth the chest, from the fourteenth to the eighteenth the waist, from the nineteenth to the twenty-first the hips, from the twenty-second to the twenty-fourth the back, from the twenty-fifth to the twenty-seventh the tail, and from the twenty-eighth to the thirtieth the feet.

Teucer concludes this section with a description of the physical appearance of a native who is born when Aries is rising or if the sign contains the Moon:

> It denotes in the appearance a long nose, black eyes, bald forehead, stately, slight build, good-natured disposition, thin legs, pleasant voice, and those who are generous.

Finally, he gives more specific details about a native's fate and destiny in regards to each of the three decans in the sign:

> And those born in the first decan are practical, ruling. They abandon or flee from their homeland, pass through much land and sea, are admired in foreign lands, going back and forth over time, and have injured many. There is not a good death for the father and his patrimony vanishes. They cast out their brothers. The secret places of the body will be diminished. Those born in the second decan will be wealthy, but continually experience sorrows and losses and the recovery of their possessions. Those born in the third decan suffer many things, partaking of dangers or imprisonment. Due to hatreds, they are dismissed in youth from their own family and return later, but are separated again. And for the most part, they do not bear children.

CHARACTERISTICS OF THE TWELVE
ZODIACAL SIGNS

In looking closely at the descriptions of the twelve zodiacal signs contained in the writings of the Hellenistic authors, we see that the characteristics of the signs are classified according to certain general categories. Some of the characteristics pertain to the descriptions of the living creatures—their appearances, behaviors, and environment:

1. Environment: terrestrial or celestial
2. Nature and appearance: human, beastly, winged, amphibious, scaly, four-footed
3. Physical appearance of humans based on Ascendant sign or Moon sign
4. Human personality traits, behaviors, body parts, illnesses, and fate

Other categories classify the zodiacal signs according to fundamental astrological doctrines:

5. Sect as diurnal or nocturnal
6. Gender as masculine or feminine
7. Modality (quadruplicity) as tropical, solid, or double-bodied (cardinal, fixed, or mutable)
8. Element (triplicity) as fire, earth, air, or water
9. Rulership as the domicile and detriment, exaltation and fall, triplicity, bounds, and decans of various planets

The zodiacal signs also gave indications to meteorological, mundane, and other correspondences:

10. Season of the year
11. Wind directions
12. Weather conditions
13. Names of fixed stars that are part of the constellation and the extra-zodiacal stars and constellations that rise, culminate, or set at the same time as the zodiacal constellation rise
14. Climes—geographical zones and countries
15. Letters of the alphabet

There are also a number of additional categories mentioned by the Hellenistic astrologers.

> He [Antiochus] makes distinctions about the zodiacal signs, which
> are tropical and which are double-bodied and which are solid, which
> have superfluous limbs and which are human in shape, which are mu-
> tilated and which are hairy, which incline towards sexual intercourse
> and are productive of sperm and offspring and which are unfruitful,
> which are vocal and which are mute, which are masculine and which
> are feminine, and that the masculine zodiacal signs are of the solar
> sect while the feminine are of the lunar sect.[4]

Drawing from the works of a number of Hellenistic astrologers, a sampling
of the characteristics of the twelve zodiacal signs has been assembled in the following table, classified by certain general categories. Keep in mind that in some
instances the assignment of certain characteristics to a zodiacal sign may vary
from one author to another. The categories of weather, paran constellations, decan interpretations, and geography are omitted in the following table. At some
point in your studies, you will want to read the full entries for all the signs in the
primary source texts.

4   ANTIOCHUS, *Summary* 2.

Table 10. Characteristics of the Zodiacal Signs

ARIES	THE RAM ♈
Astronomical features	*Northern · Commanding · Short Ascension · Crooked*
Characteristics	*Bestial · Quadrupedal · Terrestrial · Unprolific · Semi-vocal Single · Free · Licentious · Lewd · Mutilated · Violent*
Places/Winds	*Persia · (South) East Wind*
Classifications	*Masculine · Diurnal · Tropical · Spring · Equinoctial · Fiery*
Rulerships	DOMICILE *Mars* · DETRIMENT *Venus* EXALTATION *Sun (19°)* · FALL *Saturn (20°)*
	TRIPLICITY *Sun (D) · Jupiter (N)*
	BOUNDS *Jupiter 1-6° · Venus 7-12° · Mercury 13-20° Mars 21-25° · Saturn 26-30°*
	DECANS *Mars · Sun · Venus*
Parts of cosmos/ Human body/ Illnesses	*Head of the cosmos and cause of rank Head and Face Headaches, weak-sight, apoplexy, deafness, blindness, leprosy, scurvy, baldness, unconsciousness, wounds, maladies of hearing and teeth*
Personality traits [mostly Valens]	*Bright, notable, just, bold, authoritative, braggarts, great-souled, inconstant, haughty, threatening, quickly changing, well-off, unruly, irascible, kingly*
Physical appearance (ASC or Moon) [Teucer]	*Flushed-face, long-nosed, black-eyed, bald forehead, dignified, slim, shapely, skinny legged, pleasant voice, magnanimous*

TAURUS	THE BULL ♉
Astronomical features	*Northern · Commanding · Short Ascension · Crooked*
Characteristics	*Bestial · Quadrupedal · Terrestrial · Unprolific · Semi-vocal* *Single · Servile · Licentious · Lewd · Broken · Violent*
Places/Winds	*Babylon · South Wind*
Classifications	*Feminine · Nocturnal · Solid · Spring · Earthy*
Rulerships	DOMICILE *Venus* · DETRIMENT *Mars* EXALTATION *Moon (3°)* · FALL *none* TRIPLICITY *Venus* (D) · *Moon* (N) BOUNDS *Venus 1-8° · Mercury 9-14° · Jupiter 15-22°* *Saturn 23-27° · Mars 28-30°* DECANS *Mercury · Moon · Saturn*
Parts of cosmos/ Human body/ Illnesses	*Wealth-bringing [house] of the cosmos (Taurus on the 11th in the* *thema mundi)* *Neck, sinews of neck, tendons, gullet* *Swelling of glands of neck, suffocation and nostrils, injury and* *diseases of eyes, skin eruptions*
Personality traits [mostly Valens]	*Good, versed in a handicraft, hard-working, good at preserving* *things, pleasure-loving, music-loving, husbandmen, planters,* *builders, industrious, noble, indicative for estates and possessions,* *agricultural*
Physical appearance (ASC or Moon) [Teucer]	*Fuller in color, large mouth, sharp-haired, heavy-spirited, turned* *out of houses*

GEMINI	THE TWINS ♊
Astronomical features	*Northern · Commanding · Short Ascension · Crooked*
Characteristics	*Human · Rational · Winged · Barren · Vocal/Euphonious Whole · Dual · Free*
Places/Winds	*Cappadocia · (South)West Wind*
Classifications	*Masculine · Diurnal · Bi-corporeal · Spring · Airy*
Rulerships	DOMICILE *Mercury* · DETRIMENT *Jupiter* EXALTATION *none* · FALL *none*
	TRIPLICITY *Saturn* (D) · *Mercury* (N)
	BOUNDS *Mercury 1-6° · Jupiter 7-12° · Venus 13-17° Mars 18-24° · Saturn 25-30°*
	DECANS *Jupiter · Mars · Sun*
Parts of cosmos/ Human body/ Illnesses	*12th house of the cosmos Shoulders, arms, hands, fingers* [*No illnesses listed by Teucer or Valens*]
Personality traits [mostly Valens]	*Articulate, fond of discourse, those who work with letters and education, poetic, lovers of music, teachers of voice, interpreters, aptitude for commerce, critics of good and bad, initiates in occult matters, versed in business, wealthy*
Physical appearance (ASC or Moon) [Teucer]	*Swarthy, heavy beards, meeting eyebrows, bald foreheads, swift in walk*

CANCER	THE CRAB ♋
Astronomical features	*Northern · Commanding · Long Ascension · Straight*
Characteristics	*Bestial · Amphibious · Fertile · Mute · Single · Servile · Rough-skinned · Broken*
Places/Winds	*Armenia · North Wind*
Classifications	*Feminine · Nocturnal · Tropical · Solstitial · Summery · Watery*
Rulerships	DOMICILE *Moon* · DETRIMENT *Saturn* EXALTATION *Jupiter (15°)* · FALL *Mars (28°)* TRIPLICITY *Venus* (D) · *Mars* (N) BOUNDS *Mars 1-7° · Venus 8-13° · Mercury 14-19° Jupiter 20-25° · Saturn 26-30°* DECANS *Venus · Mercury · Moon*
Parts of cosmos/ Human body/ Illnesses	*Ascendant of the cosmos, breast and ribs of cosmos Chest, stomach, breasts, heart, spleen, hidden places Lichen-like skin patches, leprosy, apoplexy, dropsy, hunch-back, moles*
Personality traits [mostly Valens]	*Digging, fond of repute, popular, changeable, theatrical, cheerful, fond of pleasure and entertaining, inconstant in knowledge, wandering and sojourning abroad*
Physical appearance (ASC or Moon) [Teucer]	*Dark complexion, small-necked, chesty, bow-legged or moving sideways in walk, well-formed, the extravagances of others*

LEO	THE LION ♌
Astronomical features	*Northern · Commanding · Long Ascension · Straight*
Characteristics	*Bestial · Quadrupedal · Terrestrial · Semi-vocal · Barren · Single · Free · Lewd · Broken*
Places/Winds	*Asia · East Wind*
Classifications	*Masculine · Diurnal · Solid · Summery · Fiery*
Rulerships	DOMICILE *Sun* · DETRIMENT *Saturn* EXALTATION *none* · FALL *none* TRIPLICITY *Sun* (D) · *Jupiter* (N) BOUNDS *Jupiter 1-6° · Venus 7-11° · Saturn 12-18°* *Mercury 19-24° · Mars 25-30°* DECANS *Saturn · Jupiter · Mars*
Parts of cosmos/ Human body/ Illnesses	*Heart of the cosmos* *Heart and places around it, ribs, sinews, bones, hips, heart, eyesight, manliness*
Personality traits [mostly Valens]	*Well-tempered, intellectual, notable, good, unchangeable, just, hating work, insubordinate, despising flattery, puffed-up with intentions, beneficent, possibly tyrannical or kingly, imperious, irascible*
Physical appearance (ASC or Moon) [Teucer]	*Pale complexion, maimed, very sharp-eyed, big-mouthed, thin-set teeth, fine neck, short nose, broad-chested, flat-bellied, slim below, fine-boned, deep-voiced, hard-reared*

VIRGO	THE VIRGIN ♍
Astronomical features	*Northern · Commanding · Long Ascension · Straight*
Characteristics	*Human · Rational · Winged · Vocal · Barren · Dual · Free · Rough-skinned*
Places/Winds	*Greece and Ionia · South(west) Wind*
Classifications	*Feminine · Nocturnal · Bi-corporeal · Summery · Earthy*
Rulerships	DOMICILE *Mercury* · DETRIMENT *Jupiter* EXALTATION *Mercury (15°)* · FALL *Venus (27°)*
	TRIPLICITY *Venus* (D) · *Moon* (N)
	BOUNDS *Mercury 1-7° · Venus 8-17° · Jupiter 18-21° Mars 22-28° · Saturn 29-30°*
	DECANS *Sun · Venus · Mercury*
Parts of cosmos/ Human body/ Illnesses	*Cadent of the cosmos, southwest Belly, entrails, hidden parts, loins, upper intestines, insides*
Personality traits [mostly Valens]	*Fastidious, Set in the shape of justice, Industrious, Practices a handicraft, Concerned with Body, Mystical. Good, modest, involved with the mysteries, full of care, managers of properties of others, faithful, good at domestic affairs, writers, those who are supported by speeches and calculations, initiates into occult matters*
Physical appearance (ASC or Moon) [Teucer]	*Good complexion, shapely, easy to deal with, cheerful, kindly*

LIBRA	THE SCALES ♎
Astronomical features	*Southern · Obeying · Long Ascension · Straight*
Characteristics	*Human · Vocal · Unprolific · Single · Servile · Whole · Violent · Lecherous*
Places/Winds	*Libya & Cyrene, West Wind; Southwest Wind*
Classifications	*Masculine · Diurnal · Tropical · Equinoctial · Autumnal · Airy*
Rulerships	DOMICILE *Venus* · DETRIMENT *Mars* EXALTATION *Saturn (20°)* · FALL *Sun (19°)* TRIPLICITY *Saturn* (D) · *Mercury* (N) BOUNDS *Saturn 1-6° · Mercury 7-14° · Jupiter 15-21°* *Venus 22-28° · Mars 29-30°* DECANS *Moon · Saturn · Jupiter*
Parts of cosmos/ Human body/ Illnesses	*Subterranean zōidion of the cosmos* *Hips, buttocks, groin, colon, hind parts, bladder*
Personality traits [mostly Valens]	*Good and just, though malicious; desirous of the goods of others, lose what first acquire, ups and downs, live irregularly, oversee balances, measures and weights or supplies*
Physical appearance (ASC or Moon) [Teucer]	*Temperate persons, black-eyed, beautiful hair, patient and just*

SCORPIO   THE SCORPION ♏

Astronomical   *Southern · Obeying · Long Ascension · Straight*
features

Characteristics   *Bestial · Terrestrial · Scaly · Fertile · Mute · Single · Servile · Bro-*
                  ken · Violent · Humped · Cause of foul smells

Places/Winds   *Italy, North Wind*

Classifications   *Feminine · Nocturnal · Autumnal · Solid · Watery*

Rulerships   DOMICILE *Mars* · DETRIMENT *Venus*
                  EXALTATION *none* · FALL *Moon (3°)*

                  TRIPLICITY
                  Venus (D) · *Mars* (N)

                  BOUNDS
                  Mars 1-7° · Venus 8-11° · Mercury 12-19°
                  Jupiter 20-24° · Saturn 25-30°

                  DECANS
                  Mars · Sun · Venus

Parts of cosmos/ *Fifth house of cosmos*
Human body/   *Genitals, Bladder, Groin, Buttocks*
Illnesses   *Dimness of vision, weakness of sight, kidney stones, hemorrhage,*
                  strangury, tumors, tumors in throat, unspeakable vice, sexual
                  promiscuity, fistulas, cancer

Personality traits *Treacherous, knavish, rapacious, murderous, traitorous, liable to*
[mostly Valens]   *theft, secret plotters, thieves, perjured, covetous, privy to mur-*
                  der, sorcery, malicious doings, haters of own families, piercing,
                  cunning, irascible

Physical   *Dark complexion, dark eyes, austere, kinky-haired, weak-voiced,*
appearance   *courageous, swift, disdainful*
(ASC or Moon)
[Teucer]

SAGITTARIUS   THE ARCHER ♐

Astronomical features	*Southern · Obeying · Long Ascension · Straight*
Characteristics	*Terrestrial · Winged · Human & Bestial · Quadrupedal (2nd half) · Vocal (1st half) · Semi-vocal (2nd half) · Unprolific · Dual · Free (Broken) · Enigmatical · Sinewy*
Places/Winds	*Cilicia & Crete, East Wind*
Classifications	*Masculine · Diurnal · Bi-corporeal · Autumnal · Fiery*
Rulerships	DOMICILE *Jupiter* · DETRIMENT *Mercury* EXALTATION *none* · FALL *none* TRIPLICITY *Sun* (D) *· Jupiter* (N) BOUNDS *Jupiter 1-12° · Venus 13-17° · Mercury 18-21°* *Saturn 22-26° · Mars 27-30°* DECANS *Mercury · Moon · Saturn*
Parts of cosmos/ Human body/ Illnesses	*Cadent of the cosmos and house of slaves* *Thighs, groin* *Superfluous limbs, birthmarks, bald, weak sight, epileptics, pain in eyes, maimed by a barb, falling from heights, danger from quadrupeds, loss of limbs or injury by wild beasts*
Personality traits [mostly Valens]	*Good, just, great-souled, critical, generous, fond of brothers and friends, lose and reacquire possessions, prevail over enemies, lovers of reputation, versatile, notable, weave matters in a riddling fashion, authoritative, kingly*
Physical appearance (ASC or Moon) [Teucer]	*Moderate coloration, nicely shaped mouth, nice eyes, shapely form, swift, reckless, invincible, petty-minded, generally unstable*

CAPRICORN	THE SEA GOAT ♑
Astronomical features	*Southern · Obeying · Short Ascension · Crooked*
Characteristics	*Bestial · Amphibious · Unprolific · Semi-vocal · Dual · Servile · Enigmatic · Rough-skinned · Scaly · Broken · Violent · Licentious Lewd · Cause of evils, toils, troubles · Very wet*
Places/Winds	*Syria, South Wind*
Classifications	*Feminine · Nocturnal · Tropical · Solstitial · Wintry · Earthy*
Rulerships	DOMICILE *Saturn* · DETRIMENT *Moon* EXALTATION *Mars (28°)* · FALL *Jupiter (15°)* TRIPLICITY *Venus* (D) · *Moon* (N) BOUNDS *Mercury 1–7° · Jupiter 8–14° · Venus 15–22° Saturn 23–26° · Mars 27–30°* DECANS *Jupiter · Mars · Sun*
Parts of cosmos/ Human body/ Illnesses	*Setting/descendant of the cosmos Knees, sinews Dim sight, maiming because of spiny backbone, madness, distress from humors and fluxes, hunchbacks, disabled, lame*
Personality traits [mostly Valens]	*Stone-cutters, farmers, bad, good and simple at exposition, hardworking, full of care, sleepless, fond of laughter, planners of great works, makers of bad mistakes, fickle, mischievous, liars, culpable*
Physical appearance (ASC or Moon) [Teucer]	*Small face, slender ankles, fond of women, liars, conceited, servile, religious, loving his friends, dependable, those receiving aid so lack nothing, eloquent, foolhardy*

AQUARIUS	THE WATER-BEARER ♒
Astronomical features	*Southern · Obeying · Short Ascension · Crooked*
Characteristics	*Human · Rational · Winged · Vocal · Unprolific · Single · Free · Whole · Scaly · Violent · Wet · Very cold*
Places/Winds	*Egypt · West Wind*
Classifications	*Masculine · Diurnal · Solid · Wintry · Airy*
Rulerships	DOMICILE *Saturn* · DETRIMENT *Sun* EXALTATION *none* · FALL *none* TRIPLICITY *Saturn* (D) · *Mercury* (N) BOUNDS *Mercury 1–7° · Venus 8–13° · Jupiter 14–20° Mars 21–25° · Saturn 26–30°* DECANS *Venus · Mercury · Moon*
Parts of cosmos/ Human body/ Illnesses	*Eighth house of the cosmos, concerning death* *Lower legs, shins, legs, sinews* *Dropsy, arthritics, mental illness, castrated and wounded, elephantiasis, jaundice, black bile, disabled in a limb, hunchback, incontinent*
Personality traits [mostly Valens]	*Fearful, handicraft, malicious, haters of own families, single-minded, deceitful, treacherous, concealers, misanthropists, impious, accusers, betrayers of opinion and truth, begrudging, waterside trades, cause of troubles through struggles, working in hard materials*
Physical appearance (ASC or Moon) [Teucer]	*Good coloration, easy to heal, sensitive, vainglorious, fond of cleanliness, braggarts*

PISCES	THE FISHES ♓
Astronomical features	*Southern · Obeying · Short Ascension · Crooked*
Characteristics	*Bestial · Aquatic · Fertile · Mute · Dual · Servile · Licentious · Lewd · Sinewy · Scaly · Rough-finned · Broken · Wet*
Places/Winds	*Red Sea & India, North Wind*
Classifications	*Feminine · Nocturnal · Bi-corporeal · Wintry · Watery*
Rulerships	DOMICILE *Jupiter* · DETRIMENT *Mercury* EXALTATION *Venus (27°)* · FALL *Mercury (15°)*
	TRIPLICITY *Venus (D) · Mars (N)*
	BOUNDS *Venus 1–12° · Jupiter 13–16° · Mercury 17–19° Mars 20–28° · Saturn 29–30°*
	DECANS *Saturn · Jupiter · Mars*
Parts of cosmos/ Human body/ Illnesses	*Good cadent of the cosmos, the house of God Feet, soles, and sinews of feet, ankles Arthritics, gout, hunchbacks, rough-skinned or leprous, scurvy, scabs, promiscuous, diseases involving humors, eruptions*
Personality traits [mostly Valens]	*Inconstant, of two minds, change from bad to good, erotic, servile, popular, sociable, waterside trades, restless, cause of wandering, complicated*
Physical appearance (ASC or Moon) [Teucer]	*Pale complexion, nice hair, ingenious, hard-drinkers, spendthrifts*

In addition to the astronomical considerations above, the signs were also classified in accordance with the appearances of their images, which contributed other characteristics to each sign. Among the most referred to were the human/animal distinctions and how these related to categories of fertility, voice, and other behaviors. There is some variation in these classifications from one author to the next. In chart delineation, ancient astrologers looked to the zodiacal signs of the Ascendant, lord of the Ascendant, and the Moon (rather than the Sun) for these indications.[5]

> HUMAN (rational, pleasing appearance, beautiful voices, thrive in the east): Gemini, Virgo, Libra, Aquarius, and the first part of Sagittarius
> BESTIAL (named after animals): Aries, Taurus, Leo, Scorpio, Capricorn, and the last half of Sagittarius
> WINGED: Gemini, Virgo, Pisces, (Sagittarius)
> COMPLETE QUADRUPEDS (the four-footed animals): Aries, Taurus, Leo, Capricorn, and the last half of Sagittarius
> TERRESTRIAL (living on land): Aries, Taurus, Leo, Scorpio (Gemini, Virgo, Libra, Sagittarius)
> AMPHIBIOUS (living on land and water): Cancer, Capricorn, Aquarius
> AQUATIC (living in water): Pisces
>
> FERTILE (having many offspring, the three watery signs): Cancer, Scorpio, Pisces
> MODERATELY FRUITFUL: Taurus, Capricorn
> MODERATELY BARREN: Sagittarius, Aquarius
> UNPROLIFIC (having few children): Aries, Taurus, Libra, Sagittarius, Capricorn, Aquarius
> BARREN/STERILE: Gemini, Leo, Virgo
>
> VOCAL (capacity to be a good speaker): Gemini, Libra, latter part of Virgo, first part of Sagittarius, Aquarius
> SEMI-VOCAL/HALF A VOICE (shaped in images of animals bleating, lowing, roaring; those born of little discourse, speaking less, poor organization of words): Aries, Taurus, Leo,

---

5   These groupings are explicated by BONATTI, *Book of Astronomy* 2.20; DEVORE, *Encyclopedia of Astrology*; MANILIUS, *Astronomica* 2.150–270; and ANTIOCHUS, *Summary* 2.

Capricorn, and the last half of Sagittarius
MUTE/LACKING A VOICE (shaped in images of animals lacking a voice, stuttering, speak little): Cancer, Scorpio, Pisces

SINGLE FORM (keeping to an unshared estate): Aries, Taurus, Cancer, Leo, Libra, Scorpio, Aquarius
DUAL FORM (shared estate, companions both add and take away): Pisces and Gemini, Capricorn and Sagittarius, Virgo

FREE (running): Aries, Leo, Sagittarius; (standing erect with limbs perfectly poised): Virgo, Gemini, Aquarius
SERVILE (sitting fatigued, slouched, and weariness of mind): Taurus, Libra, Capricorn, Cancer, Scorpio, Pisces

LICENTIOUS/INDECENT: Aries, Taurus, Capricorn, Pisces, and Libra in part
LECHEROUS/LEWD: Aries, Taurus, Leo, Capricorn in part, Pisces, and Libra (because the constellation of the Goat rises with it)[6]
VIOLENT/DESTRUCTIVE (domicile or exaltation of malefic planets): Aries, Libra, Scorpio, Capricorn, Aquarius
BROKEN/IMPERFECT/MUTILATED (distortions of body and limbs): Taurus, Leo, Scorpio, Pisces, Capricorn, Cancer
ROUGH-SKINNED, LEPROUS, MANGY, SCURVY: Aries, Taurus, Cancer, Scorpio, Capricorn, Pisces
WHOLE/PERFECT (strong, robust, less liable to accidents): Gemini, Libra, Aquarius

In the ancient literature, many of these traits were associated with the Ascendant sign and the Moon sign, which both signify the physical body, rather than the Sun, which is more connected to the soul. When individuals act upon their core instincts, they may express some of the animal behaviors represented by images of the zodiacal signs prominent in their birth chart.

→ EXERCISE 9

Having reviewed table 10, complete exercise 9:
Characteristics of the Zodiacal Signs

6   See RHETORIUS, *Compendium* 76.

EXERCISE 9

CHARACTERISTICS OF THE ZODIACAL SIGNS

1. List whether each sign is terrestrial, aquatic, amphibious, human, or winged.
2. List some physical bodily characteristics for each sign.
3. List some human behavioral traits for each sign.

Sign	Terrestrial, aquatic, amphibious, human, winged?	Physical characteristics	Human behaviors
ARIES			
TAURUS			
GEMINI			
CANCER			
LEO			
VIRGO			
LIBRA			
SCORPIO			
SAGITTARIUS			
CAPRICORN			
AQUARIUS			
PISCES			

REFLECTION AND ANALYSIS

1. To what extent can you see a resonance in your own appearance and bodily image with the zodiacal characteristics of your Moon or Ascendant sign?

2. Can you recognize any of the animal behaviors associated with the images of your Moon or Ascendant sign in your core instinctual responses to situations?

CHAPTER 11

Zodiacal Signs

AS CONFIGURATIONS

———

SOME OF THE MEANINGS OF THE ZODIACAL SIGNS ARE DERIVED FROM the characteristics of the living beings associated with their images. Other meanings arise from the geometric patterns formed by the intervals between the zodiacal signs relative to their positions in the zodiacal circle. Yet still more meanings come from the special distances of the zodiacal signs relative to sensitive axes such as the solstices and equinoxes.

An underlying rationale that organized the astrological doctrines concerning zodiacal signs posited that zodiacal signs do not act only as individual separate entities but also as parts of larger networks of shared traits. We will first explore how the classifications well-known to modern astrologers—polarity, modality, and element—link zodiacal signs into certain family alliances with common behaviors and actions. We will then look to lesser-known zodiacal sign patterns, such as signs that command and obey, from which interpretive meaning is also derived.

In many introductory books on astrology, students learn the first set of principles that classify the zodiacal signs according to polarity, element, and modality. We will now revisit these doctrines from a traditional point of view and discuss the ways that ancient astrologers conceptualized how certain sets of zodiacal signs shaped the ways in which resident planets brought about their significations and events. This structure is also the foundation of aspect configuration theory.

The model that informs these classifications is a geometric substructure based upon the division of the circle by whole numbers, the conceptual meaning ascribed to each number, and the regular polygons that can be inscribed into the zodiacal circle. These polygons are the six-sided HEXAGON, the four-sided SQUARE, the three-sided TRIANGLE, and the DIAMETER that bisects the circle. When these geometric figures are inscribed within the twelvefold division of zodiacal signs, they link together certain sets of signs that are hence related to one another in specific ways. These sets describe traits that are shared by the zodiacal signs by virtue of being part of the same family.

THE HEXAGON: POLARITY AND GENDER

The six-sided hexagon figure links together two sets of every other sign, yielding the classification of signs into masculine and feminine gender. This category is better known to modern astrologers as the principle of polarity. Various authors refer to this classification as positive/negative polarity, yin/yang, or active/passive. Gender, as we learned in the previous section, is also the underlying quality of the classification of zodiacal signs as diurnal and nocturnal.

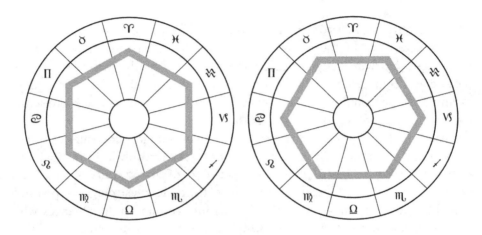

FIGURE 16. HEXAGONS LINK SAME GENDER

Left: The masculine gender/diurnal set consists of Aries, Gemini, Leo, Libra, Sagittarius, & Aquarius. Right: The feminine gender/nocturnal set consists of Taurus, Cancer, Virgo, Scorpio, Capricorn, & Pisces.

The nature of masculine energy is to speed up events. Therefore, the activities of planets occupying masculine gender signs proceed faster, and occur and conclude sooner. By contrast, the nature of the feminine gender signs is to move more slowly. Therefore, the activities of the planets occupying feminine gender signs proceed at a slower pace, occur later, and take longer to complete. For example, Mercury in a masculine sign is a quick thinker and fast talker, while Mercury in a feminine sign takes longer to formulate and communicate thoughts, with the possibility that they may be better-considered.

When zodiacal signs are linked by the sides of the hexagon, they share the same gender. They have an affinity based upon the speed and pace of the energy that they furnish to planets that reside in their signs, which shapes the way in which these planets bring about their significations. Planets occupying signs linked by the sides of the hexagon likewise have a simpatico relationship with one another by virtue of operating at the same pace. Later we will discuss how gender of the signs underlies the nature of the sextile aspect that connects every other zodiacal sign.

Table 11. Gender, Sect, Element

Gender	Signs	Geometrical figure (aspect)	Sect	Element	Mode of action
Masculine	♈ ♊ ♌ ♎ ♐ ♒	Hexagon (6 sides, sextile)	Diurnal	Fire Air	Speeds up Occurs sooner
Feminine	♉ ♋ ♍ ♏ ♑ ♓	Hexagon (6 sides, sextile)	Nocturnal	Earth Water	Slows down Occurs later

→ EXAMPLE CHARTS

In CHARTS I and II, you can look to see how each planet's events proceed faster or slower according to the gender of their signs. In CHART I, six planets occupy masculine gender signs and only one occupies a feminine gender sign. Sun and Mercury are in masculine Leo, Venus and Jupiter are in masculine Gemini, Saturn is in masculine Sagittarius, the Moon is in masculine Aries, and only one planet, Mars in Virgo, is in a feminine sign. We might expect the events of this person's life to move quickly.

In CHART II, the feminine planets Venus and the Moon are in the masculine gender signs while all the masculine planets occupy feminine signs. As a general overview, one might say that the feminine is speeded up while the masculine is slowed down. Perhaps this suggests a mixed or moderate pace, albeit with considerable frustrations, as each planet finds itself in a sign whose rhythm is counter to its own.

→ EXERCISE 10

Using your own chart, complete exercise 10:
Gender of a Planet's Sign

EXERCISE 10

GENDER OF THE PLANET'S ZODIACAL SIGN

Using your own chart, enter each planet's zodiacal sign, the gender of the planet, and the gender of the zodiacal sign.

Is the planet's action speeded up or slowed down by the gender of its zodiacal sign?

Planet's sign	Gender of Planet (M/F)	Gender of sign (M/F)	Action of planet (Faster or slower)
SUN			
JUPITER			
SATURN			
MERCURY			
MOON			
VENUS			
MARS			

REFLECTION AND ANALYSIS

1. How many planets occupy zodiacal signs where their actions move faster and their events occur sooner?
2. How many planets occupy zodiacal signs where their actions move more slowly and their events occur later?
3. Which planets occupy zodiacal signs of the same gender?
4. Which planets occupy zodiacal signs of the contrary gender?
5. In which instances, if any, do you experience an ease, pressure, or frustration at the pace at which these parts of your personality operate?

THE SQUARE: QUADRUPLICITY AND MODALITY

And again, when the Sun comes into the tropical zodiacal sign Cancer, it brings the summer turning (solstice). The air begins to be warmer and from this point on it subtracts from the magnitude of the day and adds to the magnitude of the night. Then the Sun comes into the solid and summer-like zodiacal sign Leo. It makes the air steadier and unchanging, still subtracting from the magnitude of the day and adding to the magnitude of the night. Then when the Sun comes into the double-bodied zodiacal sign Virgo, it alternates the air and makes it a mixture between summer and autumn. It further increases the night and lessens the day. In this tri-zodiac (quadrant), summer, which is fire, is completed. — RHETORIUS.[1]

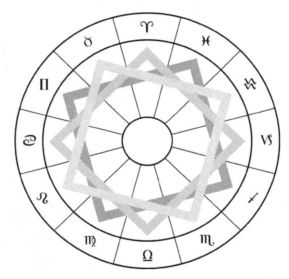

FIGURE 17. TETRAGON (FOUR-SIDED FIGURE)

The tetragon or square links four signs of the same modality:
cardinal, fixed, mutable.

When the four-sided square (tetragon) figure is inscribed into the zodiacal circle, it links together three sets of four signs each. Modern astrologers know this classification of the zodiacal signs as the cardinal, fixed, and mutable modalities. Traditional astrologers may use the word quadruplicity when speaking about the modalities because this term is derived from the root word for four. The four sides of the square connect three sets containing four zodiacal signs each.

1   RHETORIUS, *Compendium*, Preface.

These sets of quadruplicities were called the tropical, solid, and bi-corporeal (double-bodied) signs by Hellenistic astrologers. The nature of each set of quadruplicities was derived from the seasonal changes that occur in the air when the Sun passes through those signs in its yearly course. These descriptions help justify the use of the tropical zodiac in the later Hellenistic period that continued through subsequent Western traditions.

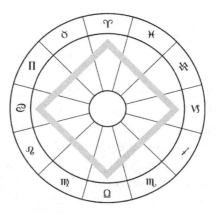

FIGURE 18. CARDINAL MODALITY
Cancer, Libra, Capricorn, Aries

The tropical (cardinal) zodiacal signs are comprised of Aries and Libra (the two signs that mark the spring and autumn equinoxes), and Cancer and Capricorn (the two signs that mark the summer and winter solstices). Each of these signs ushers in a new season with a turning in the air and a dynamic change of weather. Aries ushers in spring, Cancer summer, Libra autumn, and Capricorn winter.

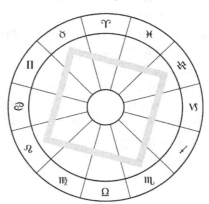

FIGURE 19. FIXED MODALITY
Leo, Scorpio, Aquarius, Taurus

The solstices mark a sharp turning of the Sun's northern or southern direction, and thus events signified by planets in the solstice signs of Cancer and Capricorn tend to have sudden reversals and changes in direction. The equinoxes mark the moment of equal length of day and night hours, followed by the increasing prevalence of day over night or vice versa. Thus events and topics signified by planets in the equinoctial signs of Aries and Libra are characterized by shifts in balance. Planets occupying tropical signs initiate new actions, proceed in sudden starts and stops, alternating

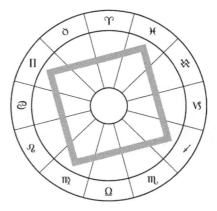

FIGURE 20. MUTABLE MODALITY
Virgo, Sagittarius, Pisces, Gemini

and shifting their emphasis. Their focus is more on generating dynamic energy to initiate endeavors rather than sustaining and completing what was started.

The solid signs are Taurus, Leo, Scorpio, and Aquarius—the fixed signs in modern astrology. These signs correspond to the second month in each season, when the air was seen to be calm and unchangeable. The events of planets occupying the solid signs are more stable, and the action proceeds towards completion in a focused and steady manner. The midpoint axis at 15° of the solid fixed signs indicates the points in the zodiacal circle that furnish the most concentrated and focused energy. It corresponds to the midpoint between a Solstice and an Equinox, and is celebrated by many cultures as a seasonal holiday (Candlemas in February, Beltane in May, Lammas in August, Samhain/Halloween in October).

The bicorporeal signs, also known as double-bodied signs, are Gemini, Virgo, Sagittarius, and Pisces. These are referred to as the mutable signs in modern astrology. Gemini is depicted as the twins, Virgo as a maiden with wheat, Sagittarius as a centaur (human/horse), and Pisces as two fishes. These zodiacal signs correspond to the third month in each season, marking the transition between the calm air in the solid sign that precedes it and the dynamic air in the tropical sign that follows it. During the bi-corporeal months, the air changes daily and is a mixture of both calm and energetic. The bicorporeal signs also signal the noticeable increase or decrease of the daylight hours. The quality of energy that flows through these signs is conducive to planets adapting, changing, and adjusting; their actions proceed with digressions, ups and downs, and twists and turns before coming to completion.

Table 12. Quadruplicities (Modalities)

QUADRU-PLICITY	FIGURE/ASPECT	SIGNS	SEASON	ELEMENT/GENDER	MODE OF ACTION
Tropical (cardinal)	*Tetragon 4 sides Square*	*Aries Cancer Libra Capricorn*	*Initiates: Spring Summer Autumn Winter*	*Fire (m) Water (f) Air (m) Earth (f)*	*Initiates action, Sudden starts & stops Reversals Shifts*
Solid (fixed)	*Tetragon 4 sides Square*	*Taurus Leo Scorpio Aquarius*	*Stabilizes: Spring Summer Autumn Winter*	*Earth (f) Fire (m) Water (f) Air (m)*	*Stabilizes action, Slow & steady Completes*
Bi-corporeal (mutable)	*Tetragon 4 sides Square*	*Gemini Virgo Sagittarius Pisces*	*Transitions: Spring Summer Autumn Winter*	*Air (m) Earth (f) Fire (m) Water (f)*	*Adapts & changes, Digressive Eventually completes*

For example, Mercury in a tropical sign may initiate action upon an idea, but at some point along the way stops before completing the action and shifts to a different idea. Mercury in a solid sign will stay on course, focusing diligently until the project is done. Mercury in a bi-corporeal sign will consider various options and alternatives, may become distracted by other things that present themselves (which may or may not get incorporated into the original plan), but will eventually end up more or less where it intended.

Hellenistic astrologers were very concerned with the quadruplicity of the signs on the angles of electional charts. Since this category indicates the various modes by which an event comes to completion, it was especially important in all kinds of inceptions (electing times to initiate events). For example, the solid signs on the angles indicate that the event will be permanent, while tropical signs portend reversals.

→ EXAMPLE CHARTS

Let us look at the distribution of planets in the quadruplicities in the example charts and assess the quality of energy shaping each planet. Counting up the number of planets in each category can shed light on the dominant influences in the life.

CHART I contains only one planet—the Moon—in a tropical sign (Aries). The Sun and Mercury (Leo) and the Ascendant (Scorpio) are in solid signs. Venus and Jupiter (Gemini), Mars (Virgo), and Saturn (Sagittarius) are in bi-corporeal signs. This individual may have difficulty in initiating things, but once started, can stay focused on course. However, the mind is always considering other options.

CHART II contains two planets in tropical signs (Mars in Cancer and Venus in Libra), four planets and the Ascendant in solid signs (Sun and Mercury in Scorpio, Jupiter and Saturn in Taurus, Leo Ascendant), and only one planet in a bi-corporeal sign (Moon in Sagittarius). We might conclude that this person can get started, has great focus in staying on course and completing, but little flexibility once the course has been set.

→ EXERCISE 11

Using your own chart, complete exercise 11:
Quadruplicity (Modality) of a Planet's Zodiacal Sign

EXERCISE 11

QUADRUPLICITY (MODALITY) OF A PLANET'S ZODIACAL SIGN

Using your own chart, explore how the quadruplicity of each planet's sign indicates the mode which shapes the planet's actions.

1. *For each quadruplicity, enter the four signs that are members of that modality.*
2. *For each planet, enter its zodiacal sign, then place a check in the box that corresponds to its modality along with a keyword that describes the mode by which the action takes place.*
3. *Tally the numbers for each modality to see if any modality predominates or is lacking.*

Planet	Tropical/ Cardinal Signs	Solid/ Fixed Signs	Bi-corporeal/ Mutable Signs	Keywords
SUN				
JUPITER				
SATURN				
MERCURY				
MOON				
VENUS				
MARS				
ASCENDANT				
TOTAL				

REFLECTION AND ANALYSIS

1. How many planets utilize the initiating energy of tropical signs?
2. How many planets utilize the focused energy of solid signs? How many planets utilize the adaptive energy of bi-corporeal signs?
3. Is there any quadruplicity/modality that predominates or is lacking?
4. Can you recognize these traits described by the quadruplicities in your own ways of proceeding with actions?

THE TRIANGLE: TRIPLICITIES, ELEMENTS, AND WINDS

The three-sided equilateral triangle figure, when inscribed into the zodiacal circle, links together four sets of three signs. These sets of signs were called trigons or triplicities in ancient literature. You may see these two words used interchangeably, but they refer to the same concept.

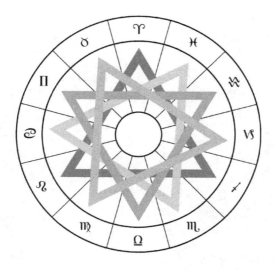

FIGURE 21. TRIPLICITIES (TRIGONS)

FIRE TRIPLICITIES: *Aries, Leo, Sagittarius*
AIR TRIPLICITIES: *Gemini, Libra, Aquarius*
EARTH TRIPLICITIES: *Taurus, Virgo, Capricorn*
WATER TRIPLICITIES: *Cancer, Scorpio, Pisces*

Modern astrologers know this classification as the four elements, consisting of the fire, earth, air, and water signs. However, while these triplicity groupings of certain zodiacal signs are present in the astrological literature from the Babylonian and early Hellenistic eras, originally these sets of signs were not associated with the four elements but rather with the winds from the four directions. Aries, Leo, and Sagittarius were connected with the eastern wind (Eurus); Taurus, Virgo, and Capricorn with the southern wind (Notus); Gemini, Libra, and Aquarius with the western wind (Zephyrus); and Cancer, Scorpio, and Pisces with the northern wind (Boreas).[2]

---

2   Cf. DOROTHEUS, *Carmen* 1.30, trans. DYKES; PTOLEMY, *Tetrabiblos* 1.18; PAULUS, *Introduction* 2.

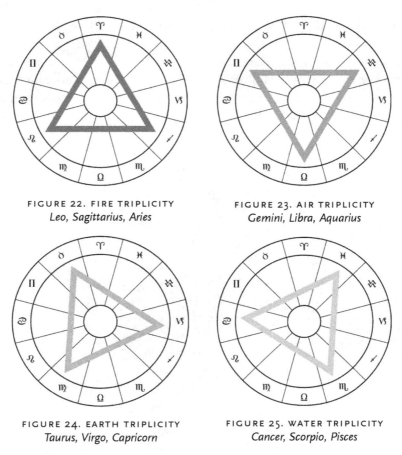

FIGURE 22. FIRE TRIPLICITY
Leo, Sagittarius, Aries

FIGURE 23. AIR TRIPLICITY
Gemini, Libra, Aquarius

FIGURE 24. EARTH TRIPLICITY
Taurus, Virgo, Capricorn

FIGURE 25. WATER TRIPLICITY
Cancer, Scorpio, Pisces

Table 13. Elements and Winds

TRIPLICITY	WIND	ELEMENT	IMAGE
Aries, Leo, Sagittarius	*East wind*	*Fire*	*Bestial*
Taurus, Virgo, Capricorn	*South wind*	*Earth*	*Mixed*
Gemini, Libra, Aquarius	*West wind*	*Air*	*Human*
Cancer, Scorpio, Pisces	*North wind*	*Water*	*Amphibious*

Babylonian astrology focused primarily on mundane events, and the triplicity of the zodiacal sign designated the direction from which the event—such as a battle, plague, flood, or storm—would occur or arrive. The Egyptians believed that the winds carried the celestial bodies in their courses. Early peoples may have thought that the winds from the four directions carried the events signified by planets in those signs to their destination. In Greece, the pre-Socratic natural philosophers sought the primal substance that underlay all matter, and eventually put forth the doctrine that everything was composed of the four elements of fire, earth air, and water. These elements changed into one another through the actions of the four qualities of hot, cold, wet, and dry. Some, but not all, Hellenistic authors seeking to align Greek philosophical ideas with the new astrology assigned each triplicity to one of the elements. Vettius Valens was the first to do so, but not all of the astrologers after him followed suit. Late in the tradition, Rhetorius, after designating each zodiacal sign in accordance with one of the four elements, states: "This was not said heedlessly by the ancients. For since everything in the material realm is composed of the four elements or bodies, it is necessary that man, partaking of the same nature, also has a share in these elements".[3]

The Hellenistic, and then later Arabic and Medieval texts, use the elemental associations of the signs literally when describing such topics as manner of death by water or fire (eighth house sign or sign of its lord) or location of missing objects as high up on a roof or underground (significator in air or earth sign). However, we do not see in the texts the interpretive meanings of how human personality and character operate in the elemental qualities of the signs as pertaining to spiritual (enthusiastic fiery need for autonomy and freedom), physical (practical earthy need for financial and material security), mental (intellectual airy need for communication and human interaction), or emotional (watery need for emotional security and bonding) until the twentieth century. This modern perspective has added much richness to our understanding of the zodiacal signs. We can certainly incorporate this understanding into our interpretations, but should recognize that these insights are a relatively recent addition to the astrological tradition.

In an attempt to bridge this gap, Robert Schmidt offered a view that could lend interpretive meaning to the four elements based upon precepts of grammar in the ancient Greek language used to write the primary source astrological texts. He proposed correspondences between the four triplicities and the four verbal moods of ancient Greek grammar: imperative, indicative, optative, and subjunctive.

Aries, Leo, and Sagittarius—notably masculine and diurnal signs—are associated with the fire element. The brilliant illumination of fire compels the events signified by planets in these signs to be seen, and can be correlated to the imperative mood which is the issuance of commands. Taurus, Virgo, and

3   RHETORIUS, *Compendium* 3.

Capricorn—feminine and nocturnal signs—are those associated with the earth element. Events signified by planets in earth signs are physically tangible, and can be correlated to the declarative mood that gives statements of fact. The signs associated with the air element are Gemini, Libra and Aquarius—the remaining masculine diurnal signs. In the same way that air has a certain transparent and ephemeral nature, events signified by planets in air signs are ripe with potentiality in which only a few of the many imagined possibilities may or may not ultimately occur. The air element is connected to the optative mood—often called wish-fulfilling: "Oh, would that this thing happen". Cancer, Scorpio, and Pisces are associated with the water element, and complete the feminine and nocturnal signs. As water takes the shape of its container, events signified by planets in water signs are contingent and dependent upon the actions of others; thus they can be said to correspond to the subjunctive mood that is used for dependent clauses in sentences.

Thus, planets in fire signs are compelled to take the action they do, while planets in earth signs perform their actions in a matter-of-fact manner. Planets in air signs act on the basis of future possibilities and potentials, while the actions of planets in water signs are dependent upon someone or something else.

→   EXAMPLE CHARTS

Let us look at how the gender, modality, and element of a zodiacal sign shape the mode and manner by which the actions of a planet proceed.

In CHART I, the actions of the Sun in Leo proceed at a faster pace (masculine gender), a focused and steady manner (solid modality), and are urged on by an impulse for freedom and power (fire element). The actions of Jupiter in Gemini proceed at a faster pace (masculine gender), an adaptable manner (bi-corporeal modality), and are urged on by an impulse for mental connection (air element).

In CHART II, the actions of the Sun in Scorpio proceed at a slower pace (feminine gender), a focused and steady manner (solid modality), and are urged on by an impulse for emotional bonding (water element). The actions of Venus in Libra proceed at a faster pace (masculine gender), an initiating manner (tropical modality), and are urged on by an impulse for future possibilities (air element).

→   EXERCISE 12

Using your own chart, complete exercise 12:
Gender, Quadruplicity, and Element of a Planet's Zodiacal Sign

EXERCISE 12

GENDER, QUADRUPLICITY, AND ELEMENT
OF A PLANET'S ZODIACAL SIGN

Using your own chart, consider how the composite characteristics of each planet's zodiacal sign shape the mode and manner of its action.

1. *For each planet in your chart, enter its zodiacal sign, gender, mode, and element.*

2. *Compose a short statement based upon these characteristics of the sign that it occupies that describes how its actions come about. (Look to the main text for examples of how to compose these statements).*

Planet	Sign	Gender	Mode	Element	Action
SUN					
JUPITER					
SATURN					
MERCURY					
MOON					
VENUS					
MARS					

OTHER CLASSIFICATIONS OF THE SIGNS

The zodiacal signs were classified according to various arrangements depending upon astronomical considerations that were derived from their distances from the Aries/Libra equinoctial axis, the Cancer/Capricorn solstitial axis, as well as other axial divisions. These categories were based upon the increasing, decreasing, or equal amounts of hours of daylight and dark as well as the times it took for various signs to fully rise over the eastern horizon. We will not be referring to these factors in our full analysis of each planet's condition, but are including them here for completeness.

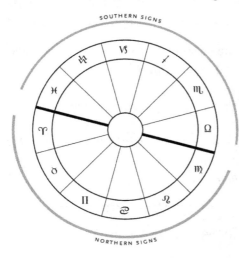

FIGURE 26. NORTHERN & SOUTHERN ZODIACAL SIGNS

NORTHERN AND SOUTHERN ZODIACAL SIGNS are demarcated by the Aries/Libra equinoctial axis and distinguished by those that lie north of the celestial equator and those that lie south of the celestial equator (at least in the northern hemisphere). The northern signs are Aries, Taurus, Gemini, Cancer, Leo and Virgo, and the southern signs are Libra, Scorpio, Sagittarius, Capricorn, Aquarius, and Pisces.

THE COMMANDING AND OBEYING SIGNS derive from the structure of the northern and southern signs, where certain pairs were equidistant from the Aries/Libra equinoctial axis and in opposite hemispheres. The commanding signs were considered more powerful than the obeying signs because they were closer to the earth, and when the Sun was in these signs it made the days longer than the nights. Thus Taurus commands

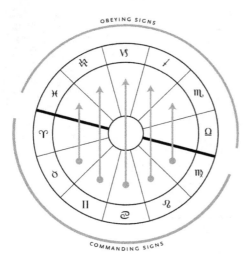

FIGURE 27. COMMANDING & OBEYING ZODIACAL SIGNS

Pisces, and Pisces obeys Taurus. Gemini commands Aquarius which obeys it; Cancer commands Capricorn which obeys it; Leo commands Sagittarius which obeys it; Virgo commands Scorpio which obeys it. Technically Aries and Libra neither command nor obey one another, but some astrologers placed Aries with the commanding signs because the day hours are increasing, and Libra with the obeying signs since the day hours are decreasing.

THE SIGNS OF LONG AND SHORT ASCENSION are demarcated by the Cancer/Capricorn axis. Due to the obliquity of the ecliptic, the signs of long ascension take longer than the signs of short ascension to rise over the eastern horizon. In the northern hemisphere, the signs of long ascension—also called the upright or straight signs—are Cancer, Leo, Virgo, Libra, Scorpio, and Sagittarius; they ascend straight up, requiring more than two hours to rise. In the northern hemisphere, the signs of short ascension—also called slanting or crooked signs—are Capricorn, Aquarius, Pisces, Aries, Taurus, and Gemini; they rise in less than two hours. The reverse is the case for the southern hemisphere. The events signified by the signs of long ascension take longer to fully mature and eventuate than do the events signified by the signs of short ascension.

EQUIPOLLENT SIGNS share the same ascensional rising times and are parallel to each other. Thus Aries and Pisces are equipollent, as are Taurus and Aquarius, Gemini and Capricorn, Cancer and Sagittarius, Leo and Scorpio, and

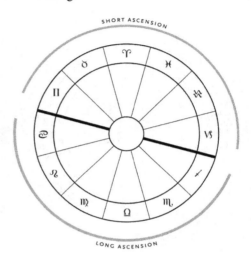

FIGURE 28. SIGNS OF LONG & SHORT ASCENSION

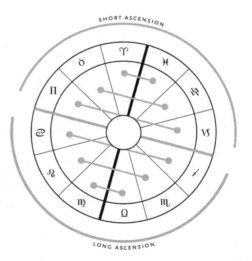

FIGURE 29. EQUIPOLLENT (EQUAL RISING) ZODIACAL SIGNS

Virgo and Libra. The events signified by these pairs of signs ripen and are activated simultaneously, which points to a hidden "reluctant conjunction" between them. These pairs were sometimes said to "agree in journey".

THE SIGNS THAT SEE AND BEHOLD each other are equidistant from the Cancer/Capricorn solstitial axis. These pairs give equal amounts of day and night hours. Each pair rises from the same part of the horizon and sets in the same part. Gemini looks at Leo and Leo beholds Gemini; Taurus looks at Virgo; Aries looks at Libra; Scorpio looks at Pisces. These zodiacal signs contribute towards sympathy, friendship and good-will towards each other.

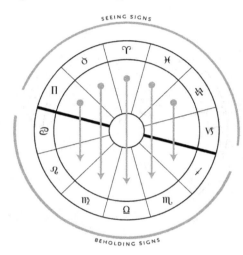

FIGURE 30. ZODIACAL SIGNS
THAT SEE & BEHOLD

SOLAR AND LUNAR SIGNS were demarcated by the Cancer/Leo—Capricorn/Aquarius axis in accordance with the *thema mundi* chart. Both the Sun and Moon in their respective signs of Leo and Cancer started the order of the remaining planets ruling the successive signs according to their mean motions. The solar signs are Leo, Virgo, Libra, Scorpio, Sagittarius and Capricorn. The lunar signs are Cancer, Gemini, Taurus, Aries, Pisces, and Aquarius.

FIGURE 31. SOLAR & LUNAR SIGNS

CHAPTER 12

Signs and Residences

OF THE PLANETS

———

> The seventh zodiacal sign is Libra, masculine, equinoctial, tropical,
> autumnal, domicile of Venus, exaltation of Saturn around 20 degrees,
> fall of the Sun around 19 degrees, triplicity by day of Saturn and by
> night of Mercury. — PAULUS.[1]

IN THE PREVIOUS SECTION WE SAW HOW A ZODIACAL SIGN, AS AN IMAGE,
contributes certain appearances, behaviors, and modes of action to the ways in
which a planet expresses its significations. Now we will learn how a zodiacal sign
also functions as a residence or home for a planet and provides it with various
kinds of resources and powers with which to accomplish its agenda. We have
now arrived at the heart of assessing a planet's condition based upon the zodiacal sign it occupies.

Hellenistic authors used the Greek word *oikos* as well as *zōidion* to refer to
a zodiacal sign. The word *oikos* translates as "house", but in order to avoid confusion with the twelve astrological houses (called "places" by the Greeks), we
are translating the word *oikos* as DOMICILE. An *oikos* referred to the home of a
planetary divinity, who ruled like the lord or lady of a manor. This zodiacal sign
also provided a residence for other planetary gods who dwelled there as guests.

This doctrine reflected one of the most important social customs in the ancient world: the host/guest relationship, by which wealth was exchanged and
power was distributed in society. It is useful to imagine each zodiacal sign as a
different estate or feudal manor that has its own particular natural resources. A
planet might dwell in one of its own estates in which it has access to a certain
kind of power or resource. Or it might find itself residing as a guest in someone
else's estate, where it has to look to its host—the lord of that estate—to provide
the resources it needs to accomplish its intentions on behalf of the individual.
However, some resources are better suited for some planets than for others. This

1   PAULUS, *Introduction* 2.

is the reasoning for why planets can be more effective in some zodiacal signs than others.

As lords of certain signs, planets draw power from those signs in which they have rulership. As guests, planets also benefit from the resources and assistance they are given by their hosts. We are going to look at the four different kinds of rulership systems—DOMICILE, EXALTATION, TRIPLICITY, and BOUND—that ancient astrologers used to determine a planet's ability to bring forth favorable outcomes for the individual. Medieval astrologers added a fifth system, DECANS, which they called "faces". Hellenistic astrologers recognized the importance of decans in their interpretations, but did not consider it a rulership system.

In all of the systems, planets are said to have familiarity—or family connections—in certain zodiacal signs. When the planet occupies these signs, it is in familiar territory because the sign belongs to its family members. Thus it has the authority and permission to access and make use of the kinds of powers available to it when occupying that zodiacal sign. The planet is then called an *oikodespotēs*—a ruler of a household with access to the privileges, influence, and wealth of that estate.

Zodiacal signs can provide different kinds of powers to various planets, based upon the kind of rulership system. For example, the zodiacal sign Cancer is the domicile of the Moon, offering her the power of resources should she live there. Cancer is also the exaltation sign of Jupiter, offering him the power that arises from honors and esteem should he visit there; and it is the triplicity sign of Venus by day, assisting her with support from the members of the community whenever Venus abides in Cancer in a day chart. The Moon, Jupiter, and Venus—when residing in the zodiacal sign Cancer—each have a different kind of rulership and are thus able to draw a certain kind of power.

Each of the four rulership systems are important, but in different ways. And each system, besides conferring different kinds of powers that lead to more effective outcomes of a planet's actions, is also used for various other inquiries. In general, more weight is given to a planet when it occupies its domicile or exaltation than when in the appropriate triplicity or bounds. However, sometimes a strong bound condition can mitigate or counteract the weakness of other indications. Let us more fully discuss each of these four rulership systems in turn.

The first inquiry is to see if the planet occupies one of its own zodiacal signs of rulership, and if not, then to determine the lord of the zodiacal sign in which it resides.

DOMICILE RULERSHIPS

Most modern astrologers are familiar with this first system of rulerships, where the Sun rules Leo, the Moon rules Cancer, Mercury rules Gemini and Virgo, Venus rules Taurus and Libra, and according to traditional astrologers, Mars rules Aries and Scorpio, Jupiter rules Sagittarius and Pisces, and Saturn rules Capricorn and Aquarius. The name "domicile rulership" will be used to refer to this system. In the course of the discussion, you may see the phrase "the Sun is the domicile lord of Leo" used instead of "the Sun rules Leo".

A query that often arises is why certain planets are said to rule certain signs. The obvious response is due to affinity between the nature of the planet and the nature of the zodiacal sign: a planet is like the sign it rules. This is the reasoning behind the assignment of the outer planets to certain signs after their discovery in the eighteenth, nineteenth, and twentieth centuries. The principle of affinity is also the basis of the twelve-letter alphabet system used extensively in modern astrology, in which the meanings of a particular planet, sign, or house are interchangeable. The earliest astrological writings, however, reveal that the correspondence of planetary rulerships to certain zodiacal signs is based upon a geometrical substructure that reflects the astronomy of the solar system. This model was explicated in the *thema mundi*.

THEMA MUNDI:
THE CREATION CHART OF THE WORLD

The *thema mundi* is the name given to an astrological chart that was thought to represent the nativity of the world. It depicted the positions of the planets at the moment of creation. The *thema mundi* originated in Egypt during the Hellenistic era and it was discussed in astrological, philosophical, and literary texts for another 1500 years during the Late Antique, Medieval, and Renaissance periods. Writing in Latin in the fourth century CE, Roman astrologer Firmicus Maternus said that it was derived from Hermes Trismegistus, the legendary founder of Hellenistic astrology, and he provides the details of the nativity itself:

> Petosiris and Nechepso in this doctrine followed Æsculapius and Hanubius. To them, most powerful Mercury (i.e., Hermes Trismegistus) entrusted the secret. They set up the birth chart of the universe as follows: the Sun in the fifteenth degree of Leo, the Moon in the fifteenth

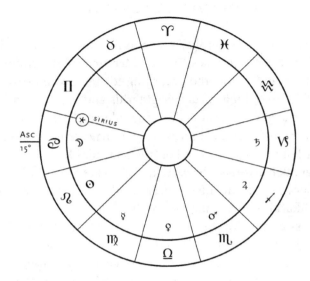

FIGURE 32. THEMA MUNDI:
THE CREATION CHART OF THE WORLD

The placement of the planets at the creation of the world,
according to Hellenistic tradition, with Sirius making its heliacal rising.

degree of Cancer, Saturn in the fifteenth degree of Capricorn, Jupiter
in the fifteenth degree of Sagittarius, Mars in the fifteenth degree of
Scorpio, Venus in the fifteenth degree of Libra, Mercury in the fifteenth degree of Virgo, and the Ascendant in the fifteenth degree of
Cancer.[2]

The *thema mundi* is timed to the Egyptian New Year, which begins in summer with the heliacal rising of the star Sirius that announces the flooding of the
Nile River. In ancient Egypt, the first appearance of the star Sirius coincided
with the Sun's presence in the zodiacal sign of Leo. A heliacal rising star can
only be seen in the pre-dawn hours. During the zodiacal month of Leo, Cancer
by necessity must be the sign rising over the horizon at dawn when Sirius has
its first visibility at this time of year. Thus the *thema mundi* has Cancer as the
Ascendant with the Sun in Leo. Egyptian astro-theology held that the heliacal
rising of a star represented the birth/rebirth of stars and hence the rebirth of
souls who were encased in stars—a fitting moment for the birth of the world.

2   FIRMICUS MATERNUS, *Mathesis* 3.2.1, trans. HOLDEN.

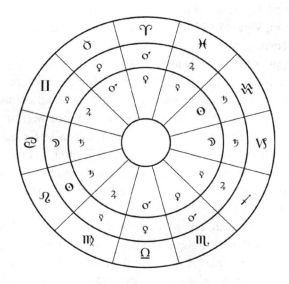

FIGURE 33. DOMICILE RULERSHIPS
& DETRIMENTS (BASED ON THE THEMA MUNDI)

*Planets in the outer ring are in their signs of rulership (domiciles);
planets in the inner ring are in the opposite signs (detriments).*

Table 14. Domicile Rulerships and Detriments

PLANET	DOMICILE	DETRIMENT
Sun	*Leo*	*Aquarius*
Jupiter	*Sagittarius & Pisces*	*Gemini & Virgo*
Saturn	*Capricorn & Aquarius*	*Cancer & Leo*
Mercury	*Gemini & Virgo*	*Sagittarius & Pisces*
Moon	*Cancer*	*Capricorn*
Venus	*Taurus & Libra*	*Scorpio & Aries*
Mars	*Aries & Scorpio*	*Libra & Taurus*

In this archetypal chart, the domicile of Cancer was given to the Moon. Thus the two luminaries, the Sun and the Moon, resided side by side in Cancer and Leo, the zodiacal signs that corresponded to the greatest number of daylight hours in the northern hemisphere. Then each of the remaining planets, in the order of their speed and distance from the Sun, were assigned to each of the successive zodiacal domiciles as they fanned out from the Sun. Mercury took up residence in Virgo, Venus in Libra, Mars in Scorpio, Jupiter in Sagittarius, and Saturn in Capricorn.

A later text, purportedly written by Medieval Persian astrologers and then translated back into Greek, preserves the mythological story regarding the *thema mundi* that God then put the world into motion.[3] As the Sun in Leo moved towards Virgo, the approaching heat of the Sun caused Mercury to flee as far away as it could, and thus it landed in Gemini. Likewise for each of the other planets—Venus fled to Taurus, Mars to Scorpio, Jupiter to Pisces, and then the only domicile left for Saturn was Aquarius. If the *thema mundi* chart is folded in two along the Leo/Cancer axis, each side is a mirror reflection of the other side, reflecting its perfect symmetry.

Popular opinion as related by Macrobius held that the positions of the planets in the *thema mundi* were assigned to the planets by the Demiurge at the beginning of creation.[4] Each planet was thus the lord of the zodiacal sign in which it was believed to have been when the world was born. Hence this zodiacal sign was the planet's most powerful placement in any particular chart.

Firmicus Maternus added that this chart did not represent an actual birthday of the world, but rather that it was a teaching device created by the ancient sages as an "example for astrologers to follow in the charts of men". As a teaching device, the *thema mundi* provides an underlying rationale for many fundamental concepts of the astrological system, including planetary relationships, zodiacal rulerships, aspects, and houses.

When the outer planets Uranus, Neptune, and Pluto were discovered 2000 years later, they were given the domicile rulerships of the zodiacal signs Aquarius, Pisces, and Scorpio, displacing the traditional rulers. This assignment was based upon perceived similarities between planet and sign, but it was not in accordance with the underlying geometrical substructure as understood by Hellenistic astrologers. This is one reason why traditional astrologers do not use the modern rulerships of the outer planets, although these planets have influential roles in the interpretation of the chart.

Planets occupying their own domicile sign of rulership have the greatest power to operate optimally and bring forth favorable events and outcomes. They are powerful because they have full access to and control of the resources of the sign, and have the power to draw upon the wealth of the household in order to accomplish their agenda. They are not dependent upon others to provide for

3   CCAG 5.2, pp. 130–37.
4   MACROBIUS, *Somnium, Commentary on the Dream of Scipio* 1.21, 23–27.

their means. This self-sufficiency enables them to act freely in attending to their business. In addition, the resources of that sign are exactly what are most useful to the planet's nature and intentions. Mercury, the planetary lord of communications, would thrive in his own Gemini home because it is equipped with a state-of-the art business center and drone courier service.

Notice that the Sun and Moon have domicile rulership in one sign each, but the other five planets rule two signs each. A planet will perform better in the domicile it rules when it is of the same sect as the planet. Thus, the diurnal planet, Jupiter rejoices in its diurnal domicile, Sagittarius, rather than its nocturnal domicile, Pisces; and diurnal Saturn rejoices in diurnal Aquarius rather than nocturnal Capricorn. Nocturnal Venus rejoices in nocturnal Taurus rather than diurnal Libra, and nocturnal Mars rejoices in nocturnal Scorpio rather than diurnal Aries. Mercury rejoices in Virgo.[5] When you see a planet that is in its own domicile, you can give it a good evaluation. If, in addition, this is the domicile in which it rejoices by sect, this improves an already positive evaluation.

Planets are in the signs of their detriment when they occupy the zodiacal sign opposite their own domicile. A planet in detriment is in a weakened condition. The *thema mundi* illustrates the sets of planetary pairs that oppose each other as an explanation for the difficulties they face when in the zodiacal signs of their detriment. Rhetorius relates that the domiciles of the Sun and Moon (Leo and Cancer) as the lights of the world oppose the domiciles of Saturn (Aquarius and Capricorn), the lord of darkness.[6] The domiciles of Jupiter (Sagittarius and Pisces), ruler of abundance, opposes the domiciles of Mercury (Gemini and Virgo), the lord of words. The intellectual faculty is contemptuous of desire for possessions, and abundance is contrary to what is intellectual. The domiciles of Mars (Aries and Scorpio) oppose and are contrary to the domiciles of Venus (Taurus and Libra). Venus as the ruler of delight and pleasure is contrary to Mars, the overseer of fear, war, and passion.

Detriments are the zodiacal signs where planets have their least power because of the scarcity or inconsistency of available resources. Here they find themselves in a particularly difficult setting. The Hellenistic astrologers suggested that a planet in detriment "acts badly", and the Medieval astrologers described planets in detriment as being in estrangement or exile.[7] One of the worst punishments in the ancient world was being banished from one's country into a land where the person did not know anyone, could not understand the language, did not have the rights of citizens, and did not have access to any phys-

---

5   DOROTHEUS, *Carmen* 1.1.14, trans. DYKES.
6   RHETORIUS, *Compendia* 8.
7   MORIN, *Astrologica Gallica* 15.4, trans. HOLDEN.

ical or financial support from family, friends, or the government. Imagine the desperate actions of someone who has been exiled from their homeland and is bereft of resources and support.

A planet in detriment is challenged not only because it does not have sufficient resources, but also because these resources are less than optimal or unsuitable for the task trying to be accomplished. A person may bring forth results, but it is often not required, needed, or useful. The planet may be able to manifest its significations, but can run out of energy before bringing them to completion, or has difficulty in sustaining them over time. Thus, a person with a planet in detriment may have to work harder or get less positive, consistent, stable results from their efforts in regards to that planetary function and the topics of the houses in which the planet is located and which it rules.

Detriment has also been interpreted as someone who is antagonistic to themselves regarding that planetary function.[8] There are other factors which can mitigate the difficult outcomes of planets in detriment, enabling them to bring forth successful results, but this is the baseline from which a planet in detriment begins.

Ancient astrologers taught that the astrologer should compare a chart of an individual to that of the *thema mundi* to see how many planets are in the signs of their rulership. The more planets that occupy their own domicile sign (and exaltation sign), the more fortunate the life, and closer to the divine.[9] In general you can assume that a planet in its own domicile indicates that the topics of the house it occupies will turn out well for the individual. That planet has full access to all the resources it needs to bring about its significations successfully. It is the lord of its own castle and it resides there, where it can command all that it desires and needs and receives the bounty of the property and the obedience of the household members. When interpreting a planet in its detriment, first you must try to determine the inherent weakness in how it functions based upon the lack or the instability of what it needs. Does the planet have to use resources that are antithetical to its essential nature? Then how does the person act as a result of the real or perceived deprivation?

---

8   IBN EZRA, *Beginning of Wisdom* 8.86.
9   FIRMICUS MATERNUS, *Mathesis* 2.23.

CHAPTER 13

Planetary Reception

PLANETARY GUEST AND HOST

THE RELATIONSHIP BETWEEN A PLANET AND ANY ONE OF ITS LORDS IS known as the doctrine of reception in Medieval astrology, where one planet is received as a guest into the home of its host. When a planet resides in a zodiacal sign other than its own domicile sign, it is a guest in some other planetary lord's estate. That planet is its domicile lord host. It must look to the host planet who is the lord of that estate to provide the resources it needs to do its business on behalf of the individual. This is where traditional interpretation approaches begin to differ significantly from modern approaches. Instead of saying that a Moon in Gemini has an emotional need to make mental contacts and communicate, the traditional approach would say that the Moon is a guest in the domicile of Mercury, who is its domicile lord host. Mercury provides the Moon with resources from its own basket of Gemini significations—words, reason, intellect, and friends—with which to accomplish its agenda.

When a planet resides in a zodiacal sign other than its own, it lacks its own resources, and is dependent upon its host for its well-being. In crafting an interpretation for a planet, you must think about which other planet is tasked as its host with providing for it, the host's own nature, and what kinds of resources that host has to offer the planet. For instance, should Mercury find himself on the Taurus estate, no matter how beautiful the pastoral setting and delicious the organically grown food, the residence is out of range for phone and internet reception.

If that host is a friend or family member, well-endowed, and generous, the planet has the secondary support and wherewithal to function favorably. However, if it finds itself as a guest in the household of a stranger or enemy, or if the host is impoverished or begrudging, the planet is like a stranger in a strange land. It lacks resources, support, and connections, making it quite difficult to take care of itself and be effective in fulfilling its tasks.

To follow this train of reasoning, let us take the example of Venus in Aries, the sign of her detriment. A typical modern interpretation would suggest that these individuals approach intimate relationships in a direct, daring, feisty, and independent manner. They enjoy the chase and conquest and thrive on adventure and stimulation. This may all be accurate. But the traditional approach recognizes that the nature of Venus is to forge intimate unions that are harmonious, peaceful, and loving. When Venus finds herself on the Aries estate, whose lord is Mars, that environment by nature is full of warriors practicing for battle with their swords, cultivating forcefulness, and competing with each other for dominance. Thus, Venus is challenged in Aries as she finds herself attempting to create intimate loving relationships in a land where her resources entail activities of conflict, competition, power, and independence. This can undermine the loving and harmonious bonding she seeks. On an archetypal level, this is the symbol of the Warrior Queen; but this can be challenging in forming harmonious relationships.

The next step in this process is to determine if the planet is connected to its domicile lord. In the above example of the Moon in Gemini, Mercury as host cannot provide the Moon with resources if Mercury cannot see that his guest is visiting his estate. The host Mercury cannot send orders to his household to take care of his guest, e.g., giving the guest use of a computer, car, library, or whatever the Moon needs from the Gemini domain to accomplish her tasks for the individual.

A connection between host and guest that allows communication is indicated by a whole sign aspect configuration between the two planets. Aspects were understood as the visual rays by which planets could "see" each other and therefore connect. The Hellenistic model recognized only five whole sign aspects: sextile, square, trine, opposition, and conjunction. The semi-square and quincunx/inconjunct were not considered aspects but aversions, i.e. where a blind spot exists.

Whole sign aspects mean that aspects are determined by whole sign rather than by orb of degree, so out-of-sign aspects do not count in this evaluation. For example, a planet at 1° Leo is trine to a planet at 29° Sagittarius, because Leo and Sagittarius share a trine relationship as zodiacal signs. However, a planet at 4° Virgo would not be considered to have an opposition aspect to a planet at 28° Aquarius because the signs do not have a natural opposition between them, even though the orb of separation is only 6° from the exact 180° aspect. The aspect doctrine will be thoroughly discussed in a later chapter.

In the above example (Moon in Gemini), if Mercury is in Leo or Aries (sextile), Virgo or Pisces (square), Libra or Aquarius (trine), or Sagittarius (opposition), there exists an aspect connection between the Moon and her domicile lord host, Mercury. However, if Mercury is in Cancer, Taurus, Scorpio, or Capricorn, there is no aspect connection.

If a planet has an aspect to its domicile lord, then they have a line of communication that enables the planet to request resources, and a conduit to receive them. Even a difficult aspect—such as a square or opposition that entails negotiation—is better than no aspect. The aspect connection significantly improves a planet's condition in terms of its capacity to bring forth its significations. However, the astrologer must also determine the condition of the host planet: does he himself have the resources to give what is asked of him (what is his zodiacal sign), is he generous or harsh (benefic or malefic), and is the aspect connection supportive or begrudging (sextile/trine or square/opposition)? And finally, is the host a friend (sect mate), or is the host a stranger or enemy (member of opposite sect)? As you can see, there are multiple factors involved in judging a planet's condition relative to its domicile zodiacal sign, but with practice this analysis becomes second nature to the astrologer.

When you see a planet that may be in difficult condition, but it has a good aspect to well-endowed domicile lord, that planet will benefit and the good fortune will increase over the lifetime. By contrast, if a planet's domicile lord is in poor condition, there is less possibility of ongoing support and the topics of the planet decrease and suffer over the course of a lifetime.

MUTUAL RECEPTION

Mutual reception occurs when two planets are in each other's domicile signs. For example, if the Sun is in Sagittarius and Jupiter is in Leo, they are in mutual reception. The Sun as host of Leo receives Jupiter into his home while at the same time Jupiter as host of Sagittarius receives the Sun into his domain. If the guest-host relationship is like being an extended guest at someone else's home, mutual reception is like trading homes with them. One is much freer to take advantage of the household's amenities knowing there is reciprocal generosity. Mutual reception allows two planets to share and pool their resources, and facilitates joint endeavors for mutual benefit and gain.

There are gradations in assessing mutual reception, and this topic has spurred debate among astrologers past and present. The Medieval texts specify that the two planets must have an aspect between them for the reception to be valid. In the above example, the Sun in Sagittarius has a trine aspect to Jupiter in Leo, and because the trine is the most favored aspect, this is the best kind of reception. A more challenging situation is when the planets are in aspect, but the aspect is an opposition. An example of this is Jupiter in Virgo and Mercury in Pisces. This challenge of particular combination is compounded by the fact that each of the two planets is in its detriment. So while there is definite benefit and strengthening for each, the amount of good is limited to what each planet has to begin with and there is some tension in reciprocation. The worst situation, according to the ancient astrologers, is when there is no aspect at all between the planets and they are both in detriment, such as Venus in Aries and Mars in Taurus. The detriment of both shows scarcity—there is not much that they can do for each other, and the lack of aspect indicates no line of communication to even discuss helping each other out.

However, not all astrologers agree with the necessity of the aspect. Ibn Ezra gives the term "generosity" to the situation where two planets are in each other's domicile or other rulership, but without an aspect. There is still reception, but apparently not as strong.

The Medieval texts considered mutual receptions between planets to be beneficial in accordance with all rulership systems—domicile and exaltation and some combination of triplicity, bounds, and faces. However, the Hellenistic astrologers limited mutual reception to domicile rulership.

SUMMARY OF IMPORTANT POINTS

1. For all planets, benefics, malefics, and common, the more a planet is in its own signs of zodiacal rulerships, the more favorable the outcomes that it can bring forth for the life of the individual.
2. When a planet occupies its own domicile sign, it has power of resources and self-sufficiency.
3. When a planet is in mutual reception with another planet, it gains a measure of power through the exchange of resources.
4. When a planet is in some other planet's sign as a guest, it must look to that other planet to provide its resources. It is necessary for a whole sign aspect to exist between them, and better yet if their lord and host is also one of their sect mates.
5. When a planet is in its detriment, there is instability or scarcity in terms of accessing the resources needed to accomplish its tasks. If, in addition, the planet does not have an aspect to its domicile lord host, there is no connection to receive resources and the person may feel a lack of support in their life relative to the topics it is charged with bringing about.

→ EXAMPLE CHARTS

Let us now apply all these principles to our example charts. Remember: at this point in our learning process, we are more interested in a planet's condition than in its interpretation. This judgment is preliminary to its more complete delineation in the house it occupies and the houses it rules, which can be done with confidence once all the criteria of condition have been evaluated.

We are determining if a planet is in its own domicile rulership or if it resides as a guest in some other planet's domicile. Is the host planet a friendly and generous provider of the resources that the planetary guest must use to accomplish its agenda? For some lucky planets which reside in their own domiciles, they are not guests beholden to a host (even a generous one), but can provide for themselves. How do these determinations impact a planet's condition?

CHART I: PLANET AND ITS DOMICILE LORD

Planet's sign	Domicile lord	Aspect to lord	Sect mate, benefic, malefic	Mutual reception	Detriment
SUN Leo	Sun*	Own domicile		—	—
JUPITER Gemini	Mercury	Sextile	Sect mate	—	Yes
SATURN Sagittarius	Jupiter	Opposition	Sect mate, benefic	—	—
MERCURY Leo	Sun	Conjunction	Sect mate	—	—
MOON Aries	Mars	Aversion	Sect mate, malefic	—	—
VENUS Gemini	Mercury	Sextile	Contrary sect	—	—
MARS Virgo	Mercury	Aversion	Contrary sect	—	—

ANALYSIS

THE SUN is very powerful because it is in its own domicile of Leo. Its kingly nature has full access to centrality, fame, leadership, nobility, and pride.

MERCURY is a very influential planet because it is the domicile lord host for three of the seven planets (Jupiter, Venus, Mars). Mercury residing on the Leo estate is especially fortunate to be there at the same time as his domicile lord, a powerful Sun, who shares his great bounty with his sect mate, who sits at his table.

JUPITER, who has been looking very good so far in terms of sect and positive sextile aspect with his domicile lord Mercury, shows the first signs of a potential problem because of being in detriment. The detriment confers a certain amount of instability, of loss following gain, and changing circumstances.

SATURN in Sagittarius has the good fortune to have the wise and generous Jupiter as his domicile lord and sect mate, but we might have concern that Jupiter's instability, along with the opposition to Saturn, indicates a tension in the steady and consistent flow required to meet Saturn's needs.

THE MOON in Aries finds that her nurturing instincts have to be sharpened by the blade of her domicile lord, the warrior Mars, in order to protect her young from attack. The Moon is not connected to Mars, so while her lord is her sect-mate ally, he is blind to her presence on his estate.

MARS is not connected to his domicile lord, Mercury. So two out of three of the nocturnal sect members cannot reach their hosts for support.

VENUS does have a good sextile aspect to her host, Mercury, in whose domain good luck, friendship, and literary pursuits abound. Although Mercury is not her sect mate, he is nevertheless likely to take care of her, because she is the lovely (albeit sad: no sect-rejoicing) Venus, because of their sympathetic sextile connection, and also because Mercury is sitting flush at the Sun's table.

CHART II: PLANET AND ITS DOMICILE LORD

Planet's sign	Domicile lord	Aspect to lord	Sect mate, benefic, malefic	Mutual reception	Detriment
SUN Scorpio	Mars	Trine	Contrary sect, malefic	—	—
JUPITER Taurus	Venus	Aversion	Contrary sect, benefic	—	—
SATURN Taurus	Venus	Aversion	Contrary sect, benefic	—	—
MERCURY Scorpio	Mars	Trine	Sect mate, malefic	—	—
MOON Sagittarius	Jupiter	Aversion	Contrary sect, benefic	—	—
VENUS Libra	Venus*	Own domicile	Contrary sect, benefic	—	—
MARS Cancer	Moon	Aversion	Sect mate	—	—

ANALYSIS

A quick scan of domicile lords shows the predominance of Venus and Mars as the main hosts for this nativity. Jupiter and Mercury have one planet each to provide for, but the Sun, Mercury, and Saturn are not responsible for anyone. We also notice that four out of seven planets are not connected to their domicile lord hosts and five out of the seven are in the residences of those planets which are not familiar or friendly relations. The overall impression is one of disconnect and alienation, where the planets reside in the lands of love and strife, unconnected and unseen.

VENUS STANDS OUT as occupying her own domicile (but in the non-rejoicing sign of Taurus); remembering that she also belongs to the sect of the chart, we might, at this stage, expect the best outcomes of this life to be under the auspices of Venus.

THE SUN AND MERCURY in Scorpio find themselves in Mars' other kingdom, where his special forces are trained in stealth and secrecy, with undertones of strong sexual intensity. They are both trine to Mars, who despite being the malefic of the sect in favor and thus potentially beneficial, is situated in the twelfth house of enemies; we may wonder how this will play out. Mars is not a friend to the Sun, but is sect ally to Mercury.

THE DIURNAL PLANETS Jupiter and Saturn both occupy Venus' beautiful Taurean estate where they are immersed in a garden of earthly delights and sensual pleasures. We notice that there is no classical aspect between them, and their domicile lady, Venus, resides at her other palace in Libra. However, we recall the doctrine that if two planets share the same domicile lord (Venus rules both Taurus and Libra), even though there is not an aspect between them, they have a "reluctant conjunction". Thus, they are empowered by receiving Venus' beneficence, even if she is not their sect mate.

THE SAGITTARIAN MOON, who is the sect leader and queen of this nocturnal chart, has a member of the opposite sect, the benefic Jupiter, as her domicile lord, but there is no aspect connection between them. The potential benefactor may not come through with support.

MARS IN CANCER looks to his queen, the Moon in Sagittarius, for recognition of his valor on her behalf, but she does not see him. This may amplify his anger at feeling rejected and unacknowledged.

So far in our analysis, the nocturnal sect planets who rule the life in this nocturnal chart place Venus in the best position to do good, followed by Mercury; both the Moon and Mars are challenged in having access to their resources. The diurnal sect planets have a mediocre leader in the Sun, but Jupiter and Saturn come out okay in spite of themselves.

→   EXERCISE 13

Using your own chart, complete exercise 13:
The Planet and its Domicile Lord

EXERCISE 13

THE PLANET AND ITS DOMICILE LORD

In this exercise, you are assessing the power of resources that a planet might receive from the domicile lord of its zodiacal sign. You are also noting if the planet is its own domicile lord, benefiting from mutual reception, or in the sign of its detriment.

Planet's sign	Domicile lord	Aspect to lord	Sect mate, benefic, malefic	Mutual reception	Detriment
SUN					
JUPITER					
SATURN					
MERCURY					
MOON					
VENUS					
MARS					

1. *Enter the zodiacal sign of each planet.*

2. *Enter the domicile lord of each planet.*

   For example, if the Sun is in Virgo, enter Mercury as the Sun's domicile lord or if the Sun is in Leo, then enter the Sun as its own domicile lord.

3. *If there is a whole sign aspect (sextile, square, trine, opposition, or co-presence) between the planet and its domicile lord, enter the glyph or name of the aspect. If there is no whole sign aspect, enter the word aversion. (Semi-sextile and quincunx are considered aversions).*

4. *If the domicile lord is a sect mate of the planet, enter sect mate. Otherwise enter no. Also enter whether the domicile lord is a benefic or malefic.*

5. *If the planet is in mutual reception with another planet, make a check mark and the name of the planet. Otherwise leave blank.*

6. *If the planet is in the zodiacal sign of its detriment, enter "detriment." Otherwise leave blank.*

7. *Judgment:*

   THE BEST CONDITION is if a planet is its own domicile lord as it has total access to its own resources and they are the optimal kind of resources for it to accomplish its matters.

   THE NEXT BEST CONDITION is if the planet's domicile lord is one of its own sect mates, especially the benefic of the sect, and they are connected by an aspect. This gives a conduit for the flow of resources from the friendly domicile lord host to its guest planet.

   IT IS A PROBLEM if the planet does not aspect its domicile lord. The domicile lord does not see the planet and thus does not know to provide for it.

   A DIFFICULT CONDITION is if the planet has a member of the contrary sect as its domicile lord, and even more difficult if its lord is the malefic of the contrary sect. The resources are given, if at all, begrudgingly or scarcely or are not useful for the accomplishment of the planet's agenda.

   THE WORST CONDITION is if the planet has the malefic of the contrary sect as its domicile and there is no aspect between them. It's like being stuck between a rock and a hard place.

   IF A PLANET IS IN THE SIGN OF ITS DETRIMENT, this is also a problematic situation because the resources are the wrong kind, not useful, or not consistent nor stable. The individual must often work harder for fewer results or the outcomes are inconsistent.

   IF THE PLANET IS IN MUTUAL RECEPTION by domicile with another planet, it may have access to an exchange of resources. A planet's strength in its zodiacal sign and the kind of aspect influence the amount and quality of what can be exchanged for mutual benefit.

REFLECTION AND ANALYSIS

1. Are there any planets that are domicile lords of more than one planet? This planet is like the banker holding the money to dole out to more than one planet and thus has much influence and responsibility.

2. Are there any planets who are not domicile lords of any other planets? They have no responsibility to provide for anyone.

3. Are there any planets in their own domicile? If so, which ones? These are flush with their own resources.

4. Are there any planets in their detriments? If so, which ones? These are needy or perform in unstable or inconsistent ways.

5. Are there any planets in mutual reception? If so, which ones? These are helping each other out.

6. How many planets and which ones are connected to their domicile lords by a whole sign aspect?

7. How many planets and which ones are in the domiciles of their sect-mate friends?

8. How many planets and which ones are in the domiciles of the members of the opposite sect, who may be strangers or foes?

9. Now write a sentence for each planet making a judgment of its capacity to do its job favorably and effectively based upon the planet's zodiacal sign and its relationship with its domicile lord.

CHAPTER 14

Exaltation Lords

———

EXALTATION RULERSHIP IS THE SECOND SYSTEM OF ZODIACAL RULERSHIPS
through which a planet may derive power. When a planet occupies the zodiacal
sign of its exaltation, it receives the power of elevation to great heights of good
fortune where it can receive honor, glory, recognition, and respect. The Greek
term for exaltation is *hupsoma*, which means "elevation" or "height".

Table 15. Domicile and Exaltation Rulerships

PLANET	DOMICILE	DETRIMENT	EXALTATION	FALL
Sun	*Leo*	*Aquarius*	*Aries*	*Libra*
Jupiter	*Sagittarius Pisces*	*Gemini Virgo*	*Cancer*	*Capricorn*
Saturn	*Capricorn Aquarius*	*Cancer Leo*	*Libra*	*Aries*
Mercury	*Gemini Virgo*	*Sagittarius Pisces*	*Virgo*	*Pisces*
Moon	*Cancer*	*Capricorn*	*Taurus*	*Scorpio*
Venus	*Taurus Libra*	*Scorpio Aries*	*Pisces*	*Virgo*
Mars	*Aries Scorpio*	*Libra Taurus*	*Capricorn*	*Cancer*

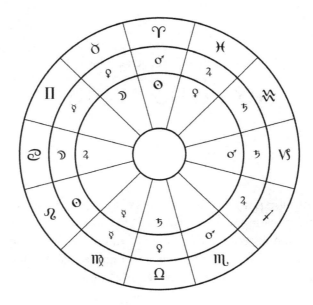

FIGURE 34. DOMICILE
RULERSHIPS & EXALTATIONS

Planets in the outer ring are in their signs of rulership (domicile);
planets in the inner ring are in their signs of exaltation.

The Sun is exalted in Aries, the Moon in Taurus, Mercury in Virgo, Venus in Pisces, Mars in Capricorn, Jupiter in Cancer, and Saturn in Libra. The Hellenistic astrologers gave the specific degrees of each sign for the maximum point of the planet's exaltation, but these exact degrees varied in some cases. According to most ancient astrologers, the Sun is exalted at 19° Aries, the Moon at 3° Taurus, Saturn 19° Libra, Jupiter 15° Cancer, Mars 28° Capricorn, Venus 27° Pisces, and Mercury 15° Virgo.[1]

An exalted planet is held in high esteem and treated as an honored guest relative to the topics of the house it occupies. His or her thoughts, positions, and actions have great influence over the behavior and deeds of others. The closer it is to its exaltation degree, the greater the honor it has. Firmicus Maternus wrote that a planet in exaltation is raised up to the maximum of its own natural force, and those so born are made fortunate and successful.[2] Medieval astrologers likened an exalted planet to a person in his or her own kingdom and glory. Indian

1   FIRMICUS MATERNUS, *Mathesis* 2.3.5, trans. HOLDEN.
2   FIRMICUS MATERNUS, *Mathesis* 2.3.1–2, trans. HOLDEN.

astrologers look to whether the planet is approaching its exact exaltation degree or is separating from it in order to more finely tune their analysis. The power and influence that individuals have with an exalted planet is due partially to the authority or status of their high position, and partially to the respect and esteem in which others hold them.

When a planet occupies the sign opposite its exaltation sign, it is said to be depressed, or in its fall. The Greek term, *tapeinoma*, means a low-lying place, like a depression in the ground. The word carries both the meanings of lower status—humbled, base, low-born—and the corresponding state of melancholy: downcast spirits. Each planet has its fall in the zodiacal sign that is opposite its exaltation sign. The Sun has its fall in Libra, the Moon in Scorpio, Mercury in Pisces, Venus in Virgo, Mars in Cancer, Jupiter in Capricorn, and Saturn in Aries.

A person who has a planet in the sign of its fall may find themselves in situations, in regards to the planet's own nature and house location, where they feel weakened or marginalized due to a lack of authority and respect. Planets in fall can indicate worry and hardship concerning the matter the planet represents. Despite one's best efforts, a person may encounter situations that lead to sorrows and distress and can provoke a sense of being powerless or unfortunate in one's circumstances.

The origins of exaltation rulerships continue to be a matter of scholarly debate. Some argue that they are one of the few Hellenistic doctrines that came from Babylonian astrology, where a cuneiform text relates that each planet had a secret place where it was considered to be auspicious. However, these texts do not specify names for what these secret places were, and we are not even sure that they were zodiacal sign locations. Some Babylonian texts do give the names of the exaltation signs, but their late dating opens the possibility that they may have been influenced by Hellenistic transmission, as other cuneiform texts from this period contain Akkadian language transliterations of Greek astrological terms. Firmicus Maternus conveys a Babylonian tradition that is also held by Vedic astrologers: planets are better positioned in their exaltations than in their domiciles.[3] However, the Arabic/Medieval astrologers reversed this, giving primacy to domicile rulership and second place to exaltation.

In addition to uncertainty about origins, the rationale behind the exaltation signs of planets is also unclear. Ptolemy attempts to give a meteorological explanation based upon the length of day and the heating, cooling, moisturizing, and drying powers of nature, but his arguments are not convincing.[4]

3   FIRMICUS MATERNUS, *Mathesis* 2.3.4, trans. HOLDEN.
4   PTOLEMY, *Tetrabiblos* 1.19.

Returning to the *thema mundi*, we notice that the signs of exaltations of the diurnal planets are trine to one of the signs of their domiciles. The Sun exalted in Aries is trine to its domicile, Leo; Jupiter exalted in Cancer is trine to its domicile, Pisces; Saturn exalted in Libra is trine to its domicile, Aquarius. The signs of the exaltations of the nocturnal planets are sextile to one of the signs of their domicile lords: the Moon exalted in Taurus is sextile to its domicile, Cancer; Venus exalted in Pisces is sextile to its domicile, Taurus; Mars exalted in Capricorn is sextile to its domicile, Scorpio. These geometrical configurations that link the domicile and exaltation signs of each planet with trine aspect relative to the diurnal planets and sextile aspects relative to the nocturnal planets hint at an underlying integrity to the system.

A second pattern that emerges in the *thema mundi* is that the pure masculine planets Jupiter, Sun, Mars, and Saturn (Mercury as common can go either way) occupy the tropical signs of dynamic action and the angular houses of dynamic strength. Both tropical signs and angular houses facilitate the manifestations of planets as outer events.

Note that certain signs do not have exaltation lords. These are Gemini, Aquarius, Sagittarius, Scorpio, and Leo. If a planet occupies one of these signs, there is no resident lord there to raise it up. One might speculate that the diurnal planets do not want some other planet as exaltation lord of the domicile in which they rejoice. Thus the Sun reigns supreme in Leo, Jupiter does not allow an exaltation lord in his rejoicing domicile of Sagittarius, and Saturn does not share power in his rejoicing domicile of Aquarius. The texts tell us that no planet can be exalted in the domicile of Scorpio where the Moon has her fall. Mercury assumes both domicile and exaltation rulership of Virgo. The Arabic astrologers, probably influenced by the Indians who considered the status of the North and South nodes as equal to that of the planets, gave Gemini as the exaltation of the North Node (the head of the dragon) and Sagittarius as the exaltation of the South Node (the dragon's tail).

Rhetorius comments on the causes of these planetary oppositions in the exaltation scheme.[5] The Sun, lord of light, is exalted in Aries, the seasonal sign where the day force begins to increase while Saturn, lord of darkness, is exalted in Libra, the seasonal sign where the dark force begins to increase. Conversely, the Sun has its fall in Libra with shortening daylight, and Saturn has his fall in Aries with increasing daylight.

Jupiter, lord of abundance and life, who signifies children, and whose exaltation is in Cancer, is connected to the increase of the breath of life. Opposing

5   RHETORIUS, *Compendium 7.*

Jupiter is Mars, overseer of death, exalted in Capricorn. Thus Mars, lord of death (Nergal in Babylonian myth), has its fall in Cancer where the life-breath increases; and conversely Jupiter has its fall in Capricorn, where death increases.

The oppositions of the exaltations of Mercury and Venus point to increase in intellectual stimulation (Mercury in Virgo) versus decrease in sexual desire (Venus in Virgo); conversely, the place where longing and pleasure increases (Venus in Pisces) is where the intellectual stimulus falls (Mercury in Pisces).

Rhetorius gives the following explanation for why no planet is exalted in Scorpio:

> Where the Moon is exalted, no planet has its fall, and where the Moon has its fall, no planet is exalted. It is said that the Moon is the Fortune of all, and he whom fortune exalts, no one can bring down, and he whom Fortune brings down, no one is able to exalt.[6]

If a planet is not in the zodiacal sign of its exaltation, investigating its relationship with its exaltation lord can provide additional details. It is the responsibility of its exaltation lord, whichever planet that is, to provide honors to the planet in question. But depending upon the exaltation lord and its relationship to the planet, it may or may not have the capacity or willingness to do so. Again, for a more finely-tuned evaluation, you must investigate whether the planet is connected to its exaltation lord by a whole sign aspect, and whether or not it is a sect mate.

→   EXAMPLE CHARTS

Look at each planet in turn to discover its exaltation lord, and to determine if it is the recipient of any special powers of esteem. This is the formula that you need to repeat in your head in order to get the correct response:

CHART I: THE SUN IS IN LEO. *Which planet is the exaltation lord of Leo? There is no exaltation lord of Leo. Therefore I will put a dash in the blank space for the Sun's exaltation lord.* THE MOON IS IN ARIES. *Which planet is the exaltation lord of Aries? The Sun is the exaltation lord of Aries. Therefore I will put the Sun in the blank space for the exaltation lord for the Moon. Whatever honor the Moon receives is the responsibility of the Sun. If Venus were in Pisces, for instance (which it is not in this chart), the formula would read:* VENUS IS IN PISCES. *Which planet is the exaltation lord of Pisces? Venus. Therefore I will put Venus in the blank space*

---

6   RHETORIUS, *Compendium 7.*

for the exaltation lord of Venus. Venus is its own exaltation lord and thus has great power of esteem.

CHART I: PLANET AND ITS EXALTATION LORD

Planet's sign	Domicile lord	Exaltation lord	Detriment	Fall
SUN Leo	Sun*	—	—	—
JUPITER Gemini	Mercury	—	Yes	—
SATURN Sagittarius	Jupiter	—	—	—
MERCURY Leo	Sun	—	—	—
MOON Aries	Mars	Sun	—	—
VENUS Gemini	Mercury	—	—	—
MARS Virgo	Mercury	Mercury	—	—

ANALYSIS

We can see that there are NO PLANETS EXALTED in this chart, and neither are there any planets in their fall. In fact, most of the planets occupy signs where no exaltation rulership power is available. One might speculate that this native has planets in signs whose natures are not amenable to their power.

CHART II: PLANET AND ITS EXALTATION LORD

Planet's sign	Domicile lord	Exaltation lord	Detriment	Fall
SUN Scorpio	Mars	—	—	—
JUPITER Taurus	Venus	Moon	—	—
SATURN Taurus	Venus	Moon	—	—
MERCURY Scorpio	Mars	—	—	—
MOON Sagittarius	Jupiter	—	—	—
VENUS Libra	Venus*	Saturn	—	—
MARS Cancer	Moon	Jupiter	—	Yes

ANALYSIS

The important piece of information gleaned from this analysis of exaltation and fall is that MARS has its fall in Cancer, and the topics it represents are subject to a certain amount of bad reputation and fall from honor or respect. The MOON is responsible for raising up JUPITER and SATURN, but she is in aversion and cannot notice them.

→ EXERCISE 14

Using your own chart, complete exercise 14:
The Exaltation Lord

EXERCISE 14

THE EXALTATION LORD

In this exercise, you will determine if any planet receives power derived from honors and respect from its presence in a zodiacal sign in which it is exalted, or if it is diminished in the power of respect because it is in the zodiacal sign of its fall. Add this information to the ongoing tabulation of each planet's rulership positions.

Planet's sign	Domicile lord	Exaltation lord	Detriment	Fall
SUN				
JUPITER				
SATURN				
MERCURY				
MOON				
VENUS				
MARS				

1. *Refer to the table of Domicile and Exaltation Rulerships at the beginning of this chapter, and complete the current exercise using your own chart.*

2. *Enter the zodiacal sign for each planet.*

3. *Enter the domicile lord for each planet.*

4. *Enter the planet that is exalted in the sign that the planet occupies.* For example, if Jupiter is in Pisces, Venus is the planet that is exalted in Pisces, so you would enter Venus as Exaltation lord. If Jupiter is in Cancer, since Jupiter is the exaltation lord of Cancer, enter Jupiter in that box. You see that Jupiter is his own exaltation lord and thus has power of esteem.

5. *Place an asterisk next to any planet that is exalted in the zodiacal sign it occupies.* You will know this because the planet that you are inquiring about will be the exaltation lord of that zodiacal sign.

6. *Note if any planet is in a zodiacal sign in which it has its fall (i.e., opposite its exaltation sign).*

REFLECTION AND ANALYSIS

1. Are there any planets in the signs of their exaltations? If so, which ones?

2. Place an asterisk next to them.

3. If you have an exalted planet, can you recognize the ways in which the matters associated with this planet have brought you esteem, honors, recognition, or respect?

4. Are there any planets in the signs of their fall? If so, which ones?

5. Make a notation of this in your table.

6. If you have a planet in its fall, can you recognize the ways in which the matters associated with this planet have brought you worry, distress, lack of appreciation or respect?

CHAPTER 15

Triplicity Rulerships

——

TRIPLICITY (TRIGON) RULERSHIPS ARE THE THIRD TYPE OF ZODIACAL rulership system used in traditional astrology. This rulership system is based primarily upon the four triplicity groupings, now known as the four elements (fire, earth, air, and water, each of which contain three signs) and secondarily upon sect. Each of the four trigons (triplicities) has a set of planetary rulers called its triplicity lords—a day lord that is used for diurnal birth charts, a night lord used for nocturnal birth charts, and a common (or cooperating/ participating) lord that operates in both day and night charts, giving assistance to the other two triplicity lords.

When a planet occupies a zodiacal sign and sect in which it has triplicity rulership, it is supported by its natural elemental environment. It has greater stability, and thus has greater power to bring about its significations in ways that are beneficial to the material well-being of the individual. In terms of interpretation, a planet in its own triplicity has the support of its community in any venture it might undertake. The Medieval astrologers likened this to a person who was among his allies and followers, who follow and obey him, but are not related by kinship.[1]

There is an alternate interpretation for triplicity lords as giving a person "motive power". Robert Schmidt speculates that since the triplicities were originally associated with the winds from the four directions, a planet in its own triplicity, especially if it was its own triplicity lord, indicated that this planet had powerful winds at its back spurring it on to the completion of successful enterprises.

---

1   BONATTI, *Book of Astronomy* 2.2.19, trans. DYKES.

Table 16. Triplicity Lords

Triplicity	Diurnal lord	Nocturnal lord	Cooperating lord
FIRE *Aries, Leo, Sagittarius*	Sun	Jupiter	Saturn
EARTH *Taurus, Virgo, Capricorn*	Venus	Moon	Mars
AIR *Gemini, Libra, Aquarius*	Saturn	Mercury	Jupiter
WATER *Cancer, Scorpio, Pisces*	Venus	Mars	Moon

IN THE FIRE TRIPLICITY (*Aries, Leo, Sagittarius*), the Sun is the triplicity lord in a day chart, Jupiter is the triplicity lord in a night chart; Saturn cooperates with both.

IN THE EARTH TRIPLICITY (*Taurus, Virgo, and Capricorn*), Venus is the triplicity lord in a day chart, the Moon is the triplicity lord in a night chart; Mars cooperates with both.

IN THE AIR TRIPLICITY (*Gemini, Libra, Aquarius*), Saturn is the triplicity lord in a day chart, Mercury in a night chart; Jupiter cooperates with both.

IN THE WATER TRIPLICITY (*Cancer, Scorpio, Pisces*), Venus is the triplicity lord in a day chart, Mars in a night chart, the Moon cooperates.

Taking a closer look at the triplicity lords, you can see that the fire and air triplicities, which are composed of the diurnal masculine signs, have the diurnal planets as their triplicity lords. Likewise, the earth and water triplicities, composed of the nocturnal feminine signs, have the nocturnal planets as their triplicity lords. The air triplicity is comprised of the diurnal planets Saturn and Jupiter, along with Mercury. Thus, in a general sense, the diurnal planets Sun, Jupiter, and Saturn do better in the fire and air triplicities where they have rulership and are supported by their natural elemental environment. If, in addition, they occupy a position in which they also have rulership, this is the best of all possible conditions. The same holds true for the nocturnal planets Moon, Venus, and Mars when located in the signs of the earth and water triplicities.

Let us take several different examples of Jupiter in various signs in both day and night charts to determine a planet's triplicity lord, and make the corresponding judgment of how much power it has in that sign. Go over these examples carefully until you are confident that you can replicate the process. The steps in your analysis that you need to follow are:

1. What is the triplicity of the zodiacal sign the planet occupies? Fire, earth, air, or water?
2. Is the chart a day chart or a night chart?
3. If it is a day chart, which planet is the diurnal ruler of that elemental triplicity?
4. If it is a night chart, which planet is the nocturnal ruler of that elemental triplicity?

JUPITER IN ARIES IN A DAY CHART: Aries belongs to the fire triplicity. The three triplicity lords of fire are the Sun, Jupiter, and Saturn—the three diurnal sect mates. The diurnal triplicity lord (because this is a day chart) of the fire element is the Sun; thus the Sun is Jupiter's triplicity lord. Jupiter has moderate power and support in this sign because he is a member of the fire group in which the Sun, his sect mate, is not only his triplicity lord but also his sect leader.

JUPITER IN LEO IN A NIGHT CHART: Leo belongs to the fire triplicity. The nocturnal lord of fire in a night chart is Jupiter. Jupiter is his own triplicity lord, the most powerful position possible. In this chart, Jupiter rules as triplicity lord and his sect mates, the Sun and Saturn, are both behind him giving support by moving him forward toward completion of his objectives.

JUPITER IN SCORPIO IN A DAY CHART: Scorpio belongs to the water triplicity. Notice that all three triplicity lords of water are the nocturnal sect planets—Venus, Mars, and Moon. The diurnal triplicity lord of water in a day chart is Venus. Thus Venus is Jupiter's triplicity lord. Jupiter does not belong to this group and thus in this sign he has little or no power that comes from community support helping him to move towards his goals. However, Venus is a benefic planet and her role as his triplicity lord does not necessarily hurt him.

JUPITER IN SCORPIO IN A NIGHT CHART: The nocturnal triplicity lord of water is Mars. Thus Mars is Jupiter's triplicity lord. Jupiter has no position among the triplicity lords of the water triplicity. Mars belongs to the contrary sect and is the malefic planet of the contrary sect, relative to diurnal Jupiter. Thus, Jupiter does not receive any supportive help from the community when in Scorpio in a night chart and may even be subject to adversarial opposition from the larger community.

OTHER USES OF THE TRIPLICITY LORDS

The triplicity lords of the sect light (Sun or Moon) was an important technique used by Hellenistic astrologers to determine the overall eminence and fortune of an individual's life. Dorotheus of Sidon, one of the earliest Hellenistic astrologers, used the triplicity lords extensively for many other considerations. He often employed the three triplicity lords of a zodiacal sign (its day lord, night lord, and cooperating lord) rather than the domicile lord for judgments on the various significations of that house. He wrote that "everything which is decided and indicated comes to be from the lords of the triplicities [trigons]".[2]

Dorotheus' work was one of the primary sources for the Arabic astrologers. Al-Andarzaghar said, "the first lord of the triplicity of the house of death [i.e. the eighth] signifies death, and the second one ancient things, and the third inheritance".[3] Thus if a person with a day chart has the zodiacal sign Gemini occupying the eighth house, the first lord Saturn signifies his death; the second lord Mercury signifies ancient things related to him; and the third lord Jupiter signifies his inheritances. Because Dorotheus' work was translated and used by Persian and Arabic astrologers, triplicity lords became an integral part of the astrology that was then passed on into the Medieval era.

The Hellenistic astrologers used the first two triplicity lords, the day lord and night lord, to rule over the first and second parts of life, while the Arabic and Medieval astrologers also took the third cooperating triplicity lord for indications on the third part of life. The condition of each triplicity lord in the natal chart gave indications about the good or bad fortune during the part of life over which it had jurisdiction. In Hellenistic astrology, the changeover from the first to second part of life was timed to the planetary periods of the triplicity lords and the ascensional times of their signs.[4]

RATIONALE FOR TRIPLICITY LORDS AND THE
JOYS OF THE HOUSES

We are going to introduce another seminal chart that is used primarily to illustrate the integrated structure that stands behind the twelve houses. It also serves a secondary purpose in giving hints for the underlying structure of the triplicity

---

2   DOROTHEUS, *Carmen* 1.1.8, trans. DYKES.
3   As cited by AL-QABISI (*Introduction to the Science of Astrology* 1.64) in BONATTI, *Book of Astronomy* 2.3.5, trans. DYKES.
4   VALENS, *Anthology*, 2.2.

lords. Because the triplicity lords were used extensively as rulers of houses in the widespread tradition that followed Dorotheus, this may well have been an alternate or competing doctrine to the influence of the domicile lords as house rulers as illustrated in the *thema mundi*.

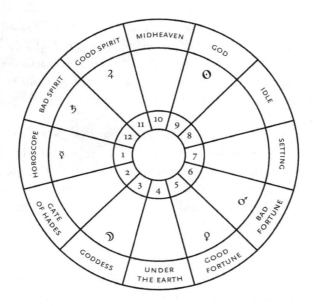

FIGURE 35. TRIPLICITY LORDS &
THE JOYS OF THE HOUSES

Above is a schema that gives the ancient names of the houses and the placements of planets that were said to "have their joy" or "rejoice" in a certain house. In the chapter on houses, we will discover that many significations for the houses were derived from the nature of the planets which had their joy there.

You can see that the Sun has his joy in the ninth house, called God, while the Moon has her joy opposite him in the third house, called Goddess. Benefic Jupiter rejoices in the eleventh house of the Good Daimon/Spirit, while the other benefic, Venus, rejoices opposite him in the fifth house of Good Fortune. Malefic Saturn has his joy in the twelfth house of the Bad Daimon, polarizing malefic Mars in the sixth house of Bad Fortune. Mercury rejoices in the first house.

What stands out is that the Sun, Jupiter, and Saturn—the diurnal triplicity lords of the fire and air elements—all rejoice in houses above the horizon, while the Moon, Venus, and Mars—the nocturnal triplicity lords of the earth and water elements—all rejoice in houses below the horizon. Mercury as common, which can belong to either the diurnal or nocturnal sect, rejoices in the first house, part of which can be above the horizon and part below, depending upon the degree of the Ascendant.

Robert Schmidt first made the observation that the triplicity lords tended to cluster around the four angular houses. The two primary triplicity lords of fire, the Sun and Jupiter, flank the tenth house and their cooperating triplicity lord, Saturn, is adjacent to Jupiter; the two primary triplicity lords of air, Saturn and Mercury, are near the first house and their cooperating triplicity lord, Jupiter, is adjacent to Saturn. The two primary triplicity lords of earth, Venus and the Moon, surround the fourth house and their cooperating triplicity lord Mars is adjacent to Venus; one of the two primary triplicity lords of water, Mars, is next to the seventh house.

Chris Brennan expanded upon these insights, discussing how this scheme informed which of the four elements came to be associated with each triplicity.[5] Looking at Aristotle's doctrine of natural place, fire is the lightest element that rises to the top of the cosmos, while earth is the heaviest element that settles to the lowest regions. Air rises upwards and settles below fire, while water settles downwards and rests upon earth. Once the natural position of each element is linked to its corresponding placement upon the wheel of houses, the assignment of the triplicity lords to their element follows accordingly. The Sun and Jupiter at the top of the chart belong to fire at the heights, while Venus and the Moon at the bottom of the chart belong to earth at the depths. Mercury and Saturn at the Ascendant belong to air that rises up, while Mars belongs to water that sinks downward.[6]

→   EXAMPLE CHARTS

> *Let us now determine whether any planet is its own triplicity lord. Keep in mind that it is not unusual if there are not any planets in their own triplicities, but when they are it is an important indicator that the planet possesses a power of a special nature.*

---

5   BRENNAN, *Hellenistic Astrology*, p. 258.

6   It is important to note that CLAUDIUS PTOLEMY changed the rulers of the water triplicity, and eliminated the cooperating rulers altogether. Some Medieval and classical Renaissance astrology, especially the work of William Lilly, is derived directly from the Ptolemaic tradition and adheres to his convention.

CHART I: TRIPLICITY LORDS, DIURNAL CHART

Planet's sign	Domicile lord	Exaltation lord	Triplicity lord	Detriment, fall, mutual reception
SUN Leo	Sun*	—	Sun*	—
JUPITER Gemini	Mercury	—	Saturn	Detriment
SATURN Sagittarius	Jupiter	—	Sun	—
MERCURY Leo	Sun	—	Sun	—
MOON Aries	Mars	Sun	Sun	—
VENUS Gemini	Mercury	—	Saturn	—
MARS Virgo	Mercury	Mercury	Venus	—

ANALYSIS

The SUN is its own triplicity lord. In addition to its power of resources that is indicated by being its own domicile lord, it has the power that comes from the support of a community whose members go beyond one's kinship system. One might note that the Sun is also the triplicity lord for the planets SATURN, MERCURY, and the MOON. Because the Sun itself is powerful, the support it confers is strong, especially to its sect mates.

CHART II: TRIPLICITY LORDS, NOCTURNAL CHART

Planet's sign	Domicile lord	Exaltation lord	Triplicity lord	Detriment, fall, mutual reception
SUN Scorpio	Mars	—	Mars	—
JUPITER Taurus	Venus	Moon	Moon	—
SATURN Taurus	Venus	Moon	Moon	—
MERCURY Scorpio	Mars	—	Mars	—
MOON Sagittarius	Jupiter	—	Jupiter	—
VENUS Libra	Venus*	Saturn	Mercury	—
MARS Cancer	Moon	Jupiter	Mars*	Fall

ANALYSIS

Because MARS in a night chart is the triplicity lord of the water signs, Mars in Cancer has rulership and power as he is his own triplicity lord in this nocturnal chart. This placement gives him the power of support from his followers and mitigates, to some extent, the difficulties of disrepute that Mars has due to it being in the zodiacal sign of its fall. One might compare the thief and his merry band of followers.

→   EXERCISE 15

   Using your own chart, complete exercise 15:
   The Triplicity Lord

EXERCISE 15

THE TRIPLICITY LORD

In this exercise, you will determine the primary triplicity lord for each planet. You are looking to see if any planet is its own triplicity lord, thus receiving the power of support gained from its community of followers. Add this information to the ongoing tabulation of a planet's rulership positions.

SECT OF CHART (DAY OR NIGHT):

Planet's sign	Domicile lord	Exaltation lord	Triplicity lord	Detriment, fall, mutual reception
SUN				
JUPITER				
SATURN				
MERCURY				
MOON				
VENUS				
MARS				

1.   *Enter the zodiacal sign for each planet.*
2.   *Enter the planet's domicile lord (from the preceding exercise).*
3.   *Enter the planet's exaltation lord (from the preceding exercise).*
4.   *Consult Table 16 (Triplicity Lords) at the beginning of this chapter (page 200). Referring to your own chart, enter each planet's triplicity lord. First note the sect of the chart (diurnal or nocturnal); then note the elemental triplicity of the planet's sign (fire, earth, air, or water). If the chart is diurnal, enter the diurnal lord for that element. If the chart is nocturnal, enter the nocturnal lord for that element.*
5.   *If a planet is its own triplicity lord, mark it with an asterisk.*
6.   *If a planet is not its own triplicity lord, check to see if its triplicity lord is one of its triplicity sect mates.*
7.   *Make a note if the planet is in its detriment, fall, or mutual reception (from the preceding exercises).*

REFLECTION AND ANALYSIS

1.   Do any planets derive power from rulership by triplicity? If so, which ones?
2.   What kind of power do triplicity lords offer?
3.   Which planets are in triplicities of their sect mates?
4.   Which planets are in triplicities of the members of their opposite sect?
5.   Discuss any placement that stands out as significant.
6.   Based upon your analysis of the triplicity lords, can you recognize the presence or lack of support from the community of followers relative to the significations of that planet? Can you gauge the extent of motive power from the followers, or any "wind" spurring the planet on?

CHAPTER 16

Bound Rulerships

——

THE BOUNDS ARE THE FOURTH SYSTEM OF RULERSHIPS THAT WAS USED in Hellenistic astrology. "Bound" comes from the Greek word *horion* (pl. *horia*) which can be translated as the boundaries or limits of a territory. In the various contemporary translations of the ancient texts, you may see this rulership system referred to as the bounds, limits, confines, or in Medieval literature, the terms (which comes from Latin *terminus*, meaning "end limits"). Be aware that all these words are referring to the same concept. In the remainder of this work, we will use the word "bound" as a translation of *horion*.

Each zodiacal sign is subdivided into five unequal sectors. Each sector is called a bound and is under the jurisdiction of one of the five planets—Mercury, Venus, Mars, Jupiter, or Saturn—which is called the bound lord of that portion of the zodiacal sign. The Sun and Moon are not lords of any of the bounds as they—Solar King and Lunar Queen—were thought to rule and have dominion over everything.

While the domicile lord of a zodiacal sign provides the resources available for planets residing in that sign, the bound lord sets the terms, rules, or limits of what is permissible within the particular degrees over which it has authority. The bound lord is also called an *oikodespotēs*, or ruler of the household. When a planet is located within the bounds of another planet, it is subject to the parameters set by its bound lord.

We may compare this to a middle school where the principal is the domicile lord of the sign, and while he governs the school as a whole, is primarily responsible for administrative duties and budget allocations to provide resources. The bound lords are likened to the individual teachers in each classroom, who set the rules for attendance, homework, grading, behavior, etc.

If the bound lord is a benefic planet, its parameters and rules are often lenient and generous, with a wide leeway for transgressions. A Jupiterian bound lord is a teacher who would be easy-going with the rules, allow homework to come in late, give outlines for the exam questions, and accommodate special needs and requests.

Table 17. Bound Lords (Egyptian)

ARIES

1	2	3	4	5	6	7	8	9	10	11	12	13	14	15	16	17	18	19	20	21	22	23	24	25	26	27	28	29	30
♃						♀						☿								♂					♄				

TAURUS

1	2	3	4	5	6	7	8	9	10	11	12	13	14	15	16	17	18	19	20	21	22	23	24	25	26	27	28	29	30
♀								☿						♃								♄						♂	

GEMINI

1	2	3	4	5	6	7	8	9	10	11	12	13	14	15	16	17	18	19	20	21	22	23	24	25	26	27	28	29	30
☿						♃						♀					♂							♄					

CANCER

1	2	3	4	5	6	7	8	9	10	11	12	13	14	15	16	17	18	19	20	21	22	23	24	25	26	27	28	29	30
♂						♀						☿							♃						♄				

LEO

1	2	3	4	5	6	7	8	9	10	11	12	13	14	15	16	17	18	19	20	21	22	23	24	25	26	27	28	29	30
♃						♀					♄							☿						♂					

VIRGO

1	2	3	4	5	6	7	8	9	10	11	12	13	14	15	16	17	18	19	20	21	22	23	24	25	26	27	28	29	30
☿							♀										♃					♂							♄

LIBRA

1	2	3	4	5	6	7	8	9	10	11	12	13	14	15	16	17	18	19	20	21	22	23	24	25	26	27	28	29	30
♄						☿								♃							♀							♂	

SCORPIO

1	2	3	4	5	6	7	8	9	10	11	12	13	14	15	16	17	18	19	20	21	22	23	24	25	26	27	28	29	30
♂						♀						☿							♃						♄				

SAGITTARIUS

1	2	3	4	5	6	7	8	9	10	11	12	13	14	15	16	17	18	19	20	21	22	23	24	25	26	27	28	29	30
		♃										♀					☿				♄					♂			

CAPRICORN

1	2	3	4	5	6	7	8	9	10	11	12	13	14	15	16	17	18	19	20	21	22	23	24	25	26	27	28	29	30
☿							♃						♀								♄				♂				

AQUARIUS

1	2	3	4	5	6	7	8	9	10	11	12	13	14	15	16	17	18	19	20	21	22	23	24	25	26	27	28	29	30
☿							♀						♃							♂					♄				

PISCES

1	2	3	4	5	6	7	8	9	10	11	12	13	14	15	16	17	18	19	20	21	22	23	24	25	26	27	28	29	30
♀											♃				☿				♂								♄		

By contrast, a malefic planet bound lord would have strict and harsh rules, limiting the range of fortunate options and opportunities, or demanding unrealistically high standards of achievement with punishment for incompetency or failure. A Saturnian bound lord teacher would pile on the homework every night, grade down for late submission of work or missed attendance, and consistently grade low with negative remarks about one's performance. However, if Saturn is a functional benefic in a particular natal chart, or is exalted in a zodiacal sector where he has dominion by bound, the enforced hard work can result in the mastery of a difficult skill.

When a planet is in some other planet's bounds, it must abide by the limits set by that bound lord, however generous or harsh. But when a planet has the good fortune to occupy its own bounds, it sets its own rules of operation and is not restricted or subjected to the rules or authority of another. It has autonomy in directing the course of its actions without being constrained by transgressions or repercussions. To extend the example above, a planet in its own bounds may be compared to the student doing an independent study and setting his or her own course, schedule, and structure for evaluation.

Let's now turn to Table 17 (Bound Lords) to examine how it is constructed, and how to determine a planet's bound lord. We will then discuss the finer points of interpretation.

In looking at the table as a whole, you can see that each zodiacal sign is divided into five sectors of unequal length, with a different planet associated with each sector. For example, in the zodiacal sign Aries, the first six degrees are under the governance of Jupiter; Venus oversees the seventh to the twelfth degree, followed by Mercury who rules the thirteenth to the twentieth degree. Mars has jurisdiction from the twenty-first to the twenty-fifth degree, and Saturn governs the twenty-sixth to the thirtieth degree. Each of these planets is the *bound lord* of their particular sector.

To determine the bound lord of a planet in a particular birth chart, locate its sign and degree on the table. See which planet rules the sector in which the degree is located. That planet is the bound lord of the planet under inquiry. When checking each planet, be sure to round up to the next degree for any position that is greater than the whole integer. A planet at 6° Aries 00' is read as 6° Aries. But if that planet were at 6° Aries 01', it would be read as 7° Aries.

Because the Greeks did not have the number zero in their arithmetical system, each zodiacal sign begins with the first degree of that sign. What this means in actuality is that if a planet is at 0° Aries 10', it is in the first degree. Likewise if it is at 6° Aries 03', it is in the seventh degree. Therefore the bounds of Jupiter in Aries begin at 00°00' of the sign and end at 6°00'. In this example, the bounds of Venus in Aries begin at 6° Aries 01' and end at 12° Aries 00', and so on. So if there is a planet at 20° Aries 20', it is read as the twenty-first degree of that sign and located in the bounds of Mars, not Mercury. Read this paragraph over carefully until you thoroughly understand what is being said; otherwise you will make mistakes determining the correct bound lord.

Let us try a few examples. If the planet Jupiter is at 22° Aries, its bound lord is Mars. If it is at 18° Aries, its bound lord is Mercury. If it is at 5° Aries, its bound lord is Jupiter—hence Jupiter is his own bound lord. Similar to the other rulership systems, a planet in its own position of rulership has access to special powers which improve its overall condition.

The Hellenistic texts contain interpretive material describing the qualities of each of the bound sectors in the various zodiacal signs. They describe how planets operate in the various bounds when under the governance of their bound lords. These entries attest to the importance of the bounds in Hellenistic astrology. Vettius Valens delineates each of the bounds, with phrases such as:

> The first six degrees of Aries, those of Jupiter, are well-tempered, robust, prolific, beneficent. The six degrees of Venus are cheerful, skillful, radiant, proper, pure, fair-complexioned [...] The five degrees of Mars are destructive, fiery, unstable due to the wickedness of men, reckless.[1]

Firmicus Maternus wrote that a planet in its own bounds is as powerful as in its own domicile.[2] He approached the delineations from the perspective of the meanings of the Ascendant and planets when occupying the bounds of another planet, or in other words, each planet under the dominion of the various bound lords. He also factored in the ways that sect considerations modified these influences. An abridged excerpt reads:

> If the ASC is found in the bounds of Mercury, it will make literati [...] learned persons always adorned with right judgment [...] but if Mercury is found in those degrees in which the ASC is, it will make astrologers, mathematicians, haruspices, but always decorated with every duty of virtue [...] But if Mars is found in those same degrees [bounds of Mercury], and it is a diurnal nativity, it will make bad, malicious persons [...] defrauders and scoundrels. But if it is a nocturnal nativity, all these things are mitigated to some extent.[3]

---

1   VALENS, *Anthology* 1.3.
2   FIRMICUS MATERNUS, *Mathesis* 2.7, trans. HOLDEN.
3   FIRMICUS MATERNUS, *Mathesis* 5.2.15–18, trans. HOLDEN.

Rhetorius tells us that the actions of the bound lords have an effect upon the fate of the individual. When a planet is found in the domicile of a benefic and in the bounds of a benefic, it benefits the native's fortune; and if found in the domicile of a benefic and the bounds of a malefic, it reduces the good of the fortune. But if it chances to be in a malefic domicile and malefic bound, it afflicts and dims the fate.[4] The Medieval Arabic tradition taught that a planet in its own bounds was likened to a man being among his parents and relatives.[5]

Let's take a closer look at the bound table in order to fine-tune our interpretations. The conditions that a bound lord offers to its resident planets are generally positive and fortunate if the bound lord has domicile or (even more so) exaltation rulership in the portion of the zodiacal sign which it governs. The planet is faced with especially challenging conditions if its bound lord is located in a zodiacal sign in which it has its fall. For example, Valens tells us that the bounds of Jupiter in the sign Cancer (in which Jupiter is exalted) are "kingly, autonomous, esteemed, litigious, high-minded, pertaining to rulers and the good of the whole", while Jupiter's bounds in Capricorn (in which Jupiter has its fall) "make for ups and downs of reputation and disrepute, of wealth and poverty".[6]

A second example is Venus. Despite being a benefic, planets which occupy her bounds in Virgo, the sign of her fall, have a particularly difficult experience; they are "liable to go astray, be blameworthy, erring in matters of marriage and shameful in relation to the passions". By contrast, the bounds of Venus in Pisces, the sign of her exaltation, accord "dedication to enjoyment and living pleasantly".

The bounds of the malefic planets are generally filled with destructive and injurious terrain, with the exception of Saturn's rule of the first part of Libra and Mars' governance of Capricorn, where they are both exalted. The bounds of Saturn in the last degrees of Virgo are "monstrous", but in the first degrees of Libra, its exaltation, are "kingly". As your proficiency with the nuances of this kind of interpretation grows, you will increasingly refine your judgments.

Another point to note is that one of the two malefic planets, either Mars or Saturn, is the bound lord of the last few degrees of each sign. A trace of this technique remains in modern astrology, where the last degrees of each sign are associated with some kind of difficult or fated condition; but most astrologers no longer remember why this is the case. According to Bonatti, if a "malefic did not possess two out of the three rulerships of exaltation, trigon, or domicile in a

---

4   RHETORIUS, *Compendia* 12.
5   AL-QABISI 1.23, as reported by BONATTI, *Book of Astronomy* 2.2.19, trans. DYKES.
6   VALENS, *Anthology* 1.6.

zodiacal sign, as bound lord it was thrown to rule the final degrees of the sign",[7] the hinterlands, the most distant realms of the kingdom where it was unhappy, becoming bitter or mean.

As you check to see who the bound lord of a certain planet is, remember that you are not only looking to see if it is its own bound lord (where, among its kin, it has the most autonomy). You are also looking to see if the bound lord is a benefic or malefic, a sect mate or a member of the contrary sect, and also whether the bound lord is in a zodiacal sign of its own rulership by domicile, exaltation, and even triplicity, or whether it is in its fall or detriment. These considerations add nuance to your interpretations and help you assess the localized terrain in which the planet finds itself, the nature of its rule, and the rules to which it is subject.

The bounds that we are using in this treatment of Hellenistic astrology are known as the *Egyptian Bounds*. Claudius Ptolemy reported that there were two predominant systems of bounds circulating in his time: one attributed to the Egyptians and the other to the Chaldeans. Finding problems with both, he presented his own table of bounds that he claimed to have found in a very old book. Each of these systems gives a different order of bound lord planets and the degrees they rule for the various signs. Ptolemy's system of bounds was recorded by Bonatti and then passed on to the Renaissance tradition of William Lilly and others. If you are using a computer program to generate the bound lords of the planets, be sure to verify which system is being used as a default, and adjust accordingly if needed.

OTHER USES OF THE BOUND LORDS

There is still no clear rationale that has been ascertained for the order of bound lords in each sign and the number of degrees each planet rules. Both Ptolemy and Bonatti's explanations become convoluted and confusing. But what is clear is that the sum of degrees that each planet rules in the bounds table equals the Greater Years of that planet's planetary periods—Saturn: 57 years, Jupiter: 79 years, Mars: 66 years, Venus: 82 years, and Mercury: 76 years. The bound lord of the planet that was chosen as the Ruler of the Nativity was thought to give the expected years of life in accordance with the Greater Years of the planets, as modified by several other factors. The Minor Years of the planets are based upon a planet's synodic recurrence cycle with the Sun, and some variation of this as-

7   BONATTI, *Book of Astronomy* 2.2.14, trans. DYKES.

tronomical cycle may be a likely candidate for the bounds algorithm.

The bounds and bound lords thus had critical roles in timing techniques concerning longevity and vital force. In length of life inquiries, the Hellenistic astrologers searched for a planet that had the authority to be the Ruler of the Nativity (*Oikodespotēs*). Various authors taught that this planet was the bound lord of the Sun, Moon, or Ascendant, or possibly even the Lot of Fortune or Prenatal Lunation. Each of these planets and sensitive points were put through a long and exacting procedure of qualifying criteria, and the bound lord of the most qualified planet was chosen to determine the length of life.

The bounds and the bound lord of the Ruler of the Nativity provide the structure for one of the Hellenistic time-lord procedures called "circumambulations through the bounds". This procedure establishes the general time periods in a person's life by means of primary directions based upon the ascensional times of the zodiacal signs. The Ascendant or some other significator is moved by means of primary directions through the successive sequences of bounds. The duration, ups and downs of a person's life, and the quality of a particular period are indicated by the nature of the bound lord whose terrain the significator is passing through, and its condition in the natal chart.

SUMMARY

The bound lord plays an important role in assessing a planet's condition in terms of its capacity to bring about favorable outcomes. A planet in its own bounds has the power of autonomy, for it is not subject to the rules of others. When a planet is in the bounds of some other planet, it is governed by that bound lord. The bound lord sets the parameters and terms of operation and determines its fate in accordance with its own relative benefic or malefic nature and condition in the natal chart. Under these circumstances, the best bound lord is the benefic planet of the same sect, or better yet, if the bound lord is in the sign of its exaltation. The worst condition is when the bound lord is a malefic planet of the opposite sect, and is especially problematic if that malefic is in the sign of its fall. However, if the malefic planet is in otherwise good overall condition in the natal chart, then some of the difficulties are mitigated and the person has the capacity to transform the difficulties into a source of gain.

→   EXAMPLE CHARTS

Let us now determine the bound lords for each planet in our example charts before repeating the process with our own chart.

CHART I: BOUND LORDS

Planet, sign, and degree	Domicile lord	Exaltation lord	Triplicity lord	Bound lord	Detriment, fall, mutual reception
☉ ♌ 05°09'	Sun*	—	Sun*	Jupiter	—
♃ ♊ 09°34'	Mercury	—	Saturn	Jupiter*	Detriment
♄ ♐ ℞ 24°39'	Jupiter	—	Sun	Saturn*	—
☿ ♌ 02° 24'	Sun	—	Sun	Jupiter	—
☽ ♈ 25°36'	Mars	Sun	Sun	Saturn	—
♀ ♊ 21°46'	Mercury	—	Saturn	Mars	—
♂ ♍ 14°49'	Mercury	Mercury	Venus	Venus	—

ANALYSIS

The important thing to notice here is that both JUPITER and SATURN are in their own bounds, which grants to each of them the power of autonomy. For Jupiter, being its own bound lord mitigates some of the problems of its detriment. If we follow Firmicus Maternus, we could also say that Jupiter has the same power it would have if it were in its own domicile. Furthermore, Jupiter is the bound lord for both its sect mates, the SUN and MERCURY, and here some of its own increased beneficence becomes available to them in regards to the generosity and good fortune of the particular terrain they inhabit.

CHART II: BOUND LORDS

Planet, sign, and degree	Domicile lord	Exaltation lord	Triplicity lord	Bound lord	Detriment, fall, mutual reception
☉ ♏ 02°42'	Mars	—	Mars	Mars	—
♃ ♉ ℞ 23°33'	Venus	Moon	Moon	Saturn	—
♄ ♉ ℞ 09° 27'	Venus	Moon	Moon	Mercury	—
☿ ♏ 24°14'	Mars	—	Mars	Saturn	—
☽ ♐ 08°12'	Jupiter	—	Jupiter	Jupiter	—
♀ ♎ 04°31'	Venus*	Saturn	Mercury	Saturn	—
♂ ♋ 12°21'	Moon	Jupiter	Mars*	Venus	Fall

ANALYSIS

None of the planets are in their own bounds. Thus no planet derives power from operating by its own rules; all are subject to another. SATURN sets the rules for three of the seven planets; as the malefic contrary-to-sect, he is a difficult bound lord for JUPITER and MERCURY, but functions well as a bound lord for VENUS in Libra because he is exalted in Libra. Valens tells us that the first six degrees of Libra, those of Saturn, are kingly, exalted, practical, especially by day, but overly exacting by night. Here, in this nocturnal chart, you can see that while Venus may be subject to overly-exacting rules and expectations, the outcome can result in something that is noble and exalted.

→ EXERCISE 16

Using your own chart, complete exercise 16: The Bound Lord

EXERCISE 16

THE BOUND LORD

In this exercise, you will determine the bound lord for each planet. You are looking to see if any planet is its own bound lord and thus has the power of autonomy. You will add this information to the ongoing tabulation of a planet's rulership positions.

Planet, sign, and degree	Domicile lord	Exaltation lord	Triplicity lord	Bound lord	Detriment, fall, mutual reception
SUN					
JUPITER					
SATURN					
MERCURY					
MOON					
VENUS					
MARS					

1. *Enter the zodiacal sign and exact degree for each planet.*
2. *Enter the planet's domicile lord (from the preceding exercise).*
3. *Enter the planet's exaltation lord (from the preceding exercise).*
4. *Enter the planet's triplicity lord (from the preceding exercise).*
5. *Enter the planet's bound lord.* Remember to round up the degrees of your planetary positions and keep in mind the guidelines about whole integers in the bounds table (i.e., 6° Aries 01' = the seventh degree of Aries).
6. *If a planet is its own bound lord, mark it with an asterisk.*
7. *If a planet is not its own bound lord, check to see if its bound lord is one of its sect mates, a benefic, or a malefic, or if it has any power by domicile or exaltation.*
8. *Make a note if the planet is in its detriment, fall, or mutual reception (from the preceding exercises).*

REFLECTION AND ANALYSIS

1. Are any planets in their own bounds? If so, which ones?
2. What kind of power does a planet in its own bounds have access to?
3. Which planets are in the bounds of their sect mates? Is this bound lord a benefic or malefic?
4. Which planets are in the bounds of planets that belong to the opposite sect? Is this bound lord a benefic or malefic?
5. Check to see if any planet's bound lord is in a sign in which it is exalted or has its fall. If so, does this makes the baseline conditions better or worse?
6. Is any planet the bound lord of several planets? If so, the life as a whole is more subject to that planet's parameters.
7. Discuss the conditions of any planet that stands out in some way.

CHAPTER 17

Decans

——

> Decans are of great divinity and power, and through them all fortu-
> nate and unfortunate things are denoted. —FIRMICUS MATERNUS[1]

THE DECANS ARE THE FIFTH AND FINAL MAJOR DIVISION OF THE ZODIACAL
signs. In Hellenistic astrology the decans have interpretive meaning, but they
are not considered to be a rulership system that influences a planet's good or bad
condition. By contrast, in Medieval astrology where the decans are called "faces",
they are used as a minor rulership system.

The decans divide each zodiacal sign into three ten-degree segments (decan
comes from the Greek word for the number ten), so there are thirty-six decans, and each sign contains three decans. They function as both images whose
characteristics shape human appearance and behavior, and as residences for the
planets. Each ten-degree decanic sector has a planetary ruler that contributes to
the ways that the decan itself, and any planets occupying those zodiacal degrees,
are interpreted.

Firmicus Maternus wrote that the decans are "of unlimited power and license, in that they denote the fates of men through the authority of their own
power".[2] He hinted that the decanic doctrine was one of the secret mystery
teachings of the ancient sages, which they deliberately "entangled in obscurity"
lest these secrets made public become known to profane men.

The decans are the contributions of the ancient Egyptians to the doctrines
of Hellenistic astrology. As early as 2400 BCE, the Egyptians had identified thirty-six stars or star groups that lay in a band south of the ecliptic which rose
heliacally every ten days over the course of the year. These decanic stars were inscribed on the inside of coffin lids to inform the dead of the proper times to say
prayers during their journey through the underworld. By the Middle Kingdom,

---

1   FIRMICUS MATERNUS, *Mathesis* 4.12, 2, trans. HOLDEN.
2   FIRMICUS MATERNUS, *Mathesis* 2.5, 1, trans. HOLDEN.

the thirty-six decan stars had become identified with gods and depicted in their iconography. By the Late Kingdom, the decanic gods were associated with the bringers of disease as well as their cures. Their images were inscribed on amulets for protection. Over the course of this two-thousand-year period, there were a number of different decan families that were identified. At first they were chosen from stars that rose heliacally on the eastern horizon, and then later upon stars that culminated in the mid-heaven overhead.

When Hellenistic astrology developed in Egypt around the second century BCE, the thirty-six decan star system was grafted onto the twelve-sign zodiacal circle, yielding three decans for each zodiacal sign. There are a number of temple facades from Ptolemaic Egypt, such as the Zodiac of Dendera, where we see this confluence of the decans with the zodiacal signs. The Hellenistic astrologers knew that decans were important because of their long and prestigious history in Egyptian astro-theology and healing. However, they were less certain as to how to integrate them into the system of Hellenistic astrology. By the third century BCE, there were five different families of decans in fifty-three lists, not all complete, recorded in the Egyptian texts and monumental iconography. The problem of deciding just which decanic star set with its corresponding deity, and which decanic sector of the zodiac it belonged to, was daunting.

Teucer of Babylon re-imagined each decanic set of stars as the fixed stars of the Babylonian/Greek extra-zodiacal constellations that rise along with the zodiacal signs. These extra-zodiacal constellations are called the *parans* or *paranatellonta*. The early Hellenistic astrologers were also challenged to come up with planetary rulers for each decan, as the Egyptian tradition had the decans' images under the auspices of Egyptian gods that did not have any direct correlations to the Greek gods. One wonders if the Greeks could not understand the material, or if it was a secret doctrine as Firmicus alluded, or simply an awkward fit of an ancient Egyptian doctrine onto the new system of Hellenistic astrology.

Hellenistic astrologers devised a system of assigning planetary rulers to each decan based upon the same order as the *heptazone* (sometimes called the Chaldean order) that puts the planets in the order of their mean motions. This order is Moon, Mercury, Venus, Sun, Mars, Jupiter, and Saturn. Recorded by Teucer of Babylon, this is the most common system in use throughout subsequent traditions. Two other systems recorded in the literature are described at the end of this chapter.

According to this arrangement, the first decan of Aries begins with its own domicile lord Mars; the second decan is under the auspices of the Sun, which precedes Mars in this order; the third decan goes to Venus. Continuing in this order, the first decan of Taurus is ruled by Mercury, the second by the Moon,

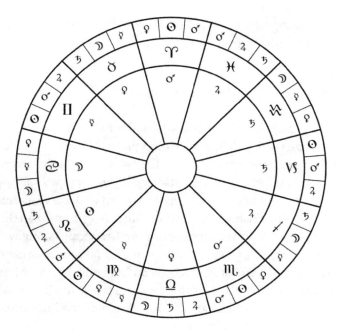

FIGURE 36.
DECAN RULERSHIPS

Table 18. Decan Rulerships I

ZODIACAL SIGN	DECAN I 0°–9°59'	DECAN II 10°–19°59'	DECAN III 20°–29°59'
Aries	Mars	Sun	Venus
Taurus	Mercury	Moon	Saturn
Gemini	Jupiter	Mars	Sun
Cancer	Venus	Mercury	Moon
Leo	Saturn	Jupiter	Mars
Virgo	Sun	Venus	Mercury
Libra	Moon	Saturn	Jupiter
Scorpio	Mars	Sun	Venus
Sagittarius	Mercury	Moon	Saturn
Capricorn	Jupiter	Mars	Sun
Aquarius	Venus	Mercury	Moon
Pisces	Saturn	Jupiter	Mars

and the third, jumping to the end of the list, goes to Saturn. The three decans of Gemini follow with Jupiter, Mars, and the Sun as their faces, and so on.

INTERPRETING THE DECANS

The Greek word *prosōpon*, used in discussion of the decans, means face or mask. The thirty-six decan stars as deities were thought to shine through their portions of the zodiacal signs, where they shaped the faces of the seven stars (planets). In turn, that planet, in sympathy with its decanic god, shaped the appearances, behaviors, ailments, and fate of individuals when that decan was significant in their chart, such as their rising sign, or the residence of some planet.

In Hellenistic astrology, the authors did not list decans along with the other rulerships of domicile, exaltation, triplicity, and bound in terms of giving a planet authority and power. But Paul of Alexandria and Firmicus Maternus both relate the teaching that if a planet is in its own decan (even if it is in the domicile of another star, such as Mars at 26° Leo), it rejoices and performs the same things it denotes when in its own domicile sign.[3]

In Book 5, Firmicus gives the very same delineation for a planet in the domicile or decan of another planet, such as Mercury in the domicile or decan of the Sun. However, the primary use of the decans in Hellenistic astrology was to describe the bodily ailments and fates of individuals, harkening back to their ancient role in Egyptian astral religion.

The Hellenistic astrological literature offers several different sets of interpretive guidelines for the practical use of the decans.[4] Firmicus Maternus wrote that "sudden accidents, pains, illnesses, colds, fevers are denoted by them, and whatever there is that is wont to occur without our wish or knowledge".[5] The decan rising with the Ascendant was said to describe the appearance of the physical body, its health, and illnesses. Both Teucer of Babylon and Hephaistio of Thebes give detailed descriptions for each decan when it is rising on the Ascendant at the moment of birth. Here is a passage about the second decan of Scorpio, which rises along with 17° Scorpio 58' in chart 1. Hephaistio begins the Scorpio section by naming his selection of the Egyptian gods for each of the three decans of this sign: the first is *Stochnene*, the second *Sesme*, the third *Sisieme*. He continues:

3   PAULUS, *Introduction* 4; FIRMICUS MATERNUS, *Mathesis* 2.5.2, trans. HOLDEN.
4   PORPHYRY, *Introduction* 47; RHETORIUS, *Compendium* 10; TEUCER OF BABYLON; PAULUS, *Introduction* 4; ANUBIO, *Carmen*; HEPHAISTIO, *Apotelesmatics* 1.
5   FIRMICUS MATERNUS, *Mathesis* 2.4.5, trans. HOLDEN.

The person who is born upon the second decan [of Scorpio] will be great, wealthy, domineering, educated, pleasant speaking, prudent, having acquired many of his own things, knowledgeable in many things, partakes of many arts, music and wrestling school. Sometimes he can be a ship's captain and at other times a military commander. If this decan is beheld (aspected) by Mars, it produces cuts and burns and ruptures around the extremities. The signs of this decan are medium build, large head, comely eyes, graceful limbs, there will be marks around the bosom and loins. The critical periods are the seventh year, eleventh, twenty-second, thirty-third, forty-second, fifty-seventh, sixty-first, seventy-third, eighty-fourth, and eighty-ninth.[6]

In a very early Hermetic text entitled *From Hermēs to Asclepius on the Thirty-six Sacred Decans*, instructions are given for constructing an amulet for each decan with the advice that if that decan is rising (technically the decan midway between the *Hōroskopos* and the Good Daimon) when a person is born, wearing this amulet will protect them from the illnesses that would otherwise befall them.[7] The amulet is inscribed with the image of an Egyptian god on various kinds of stones, under which is placed a certain herb, before being encased in a certain metal; it is accompanied by a prohibition not to eat a certain food. Here is the description for the same decan as above, the second decan of Scorpio:

> The twenty-third decan. This one has the name *Oustikos*, it has the form of a man who is robed with a *stolus*, standing with his feet bound together on top of the scorpion. This one sends malignant pustules and watery excesses to the genitals of men. Engrave this image in a pyrite stone and place the greater heliotrope plant under it, enclose it in whatever you want and carry it.[8]

Note how the names of the Egyptian gods differ, but that in the first passage there is a black mark upon the loins and in the second, malignant pustules on the genitals. Both of these refer to the ailing parts of the sexual organs that are under the dominion of the sign Scorpio. The first chart example has the Ascendant 17° Scorpio 58' in the second decan. It has been suggested that her difficulties with her lost pregnancies may have been due to venereal disease contracted from her husband. Also note that her second husband owned a shipping empire and her first husband was a military officer.

6   HEPHAISTIO, *Apotelesmatics* 1.
7   Ed. Cardinal PITRA, *Analecta Sacra et Classica*, vol. 5, Paris-Rome 1988, pp. 284–290; ed. C.-E. RUELLE, *Revue de Philologie*, Oct. 1908, pp. 247–277.
8   *From Hermēs to Asclepius on the Thirty-six Sacred Decans.*

Rhetorius passes on a tradition about how to interpret a planet in a certain decan that is ruled by another planet. He gives us an example of the Sun. He relates that since the Sun signifies the matters of the soul, the decan in which the Sun is found describes the nature of his soul. For instance, when the Sun is in the first decan of Aries, which is the face of Mars, the soul of the native is militant; in the second decan of Aries, the face of the Sun, the soul is a lover of fame and honor; in the third decan, the face of Venus, the manly spirit is feminine-souled.[9]

In CHART I, the Sun is in the first decan of Leo, which is ruled by Saturn. This would suggest that the soul of this person is sorrowful. in CHART II, the Sun is found in the first decan of Scorpio, the decan of Mars, which renders the soul militant and delighting in battle.

The full and empty degrees of the zodiac are another way that decans were used in interpretation. This is part of the secret doctrine alluded to by Firmicus Maternus. While there exist three ten-degree segments in each sign, the divinity of the decanic power does not extend uniformly throughout all the degrees of each decan. The exact stellar position of each decan star or star set inhabits certain degrees; these are called the full degrees because they contain a decanic star. The degrees that do not contain a decan star or star set are called empty degrees "to which degrees the divinity of the decans never comes".

The process of judgment involves the examination of whether a person has the Ascendant, Sun, Moon, or any of the five planets in full or empty degrees. The more stars in full degrees, the more fortunate the life; if none, the life will be wretched, deprived, and poor. The Ascendant degree in full or empty degrees is especially important in regards to the strength of the body and power of authority.[10]

Firmicus gives a listing of full and empty degrees, and the names of the Egyptian decan deities residing in the full degrees. Due to precession, this list needs to be adjusted for twenty-first century use by subtracting the differential of the precessional shift. A second problem in the ease of using this procedure is that the names of the decanic star deities as given by Firmicus were corrupted by Medieval scribes transliterating Egyptian to Greek to Latin. This doctrine may be the possible origin of the light and dark degrees of Arabic astrology.

The decans, while being mentioned by most authors, seem to have fallen out of use later in the astrological tradition. Medieval astrology refers to the decans as "faces"; they are used as the fifth and least powerful level of rulership. The Me-

---

9   RHETORIUS, *Compendium* 10.
10   FIRMICUS MATERNUS, *Mathesis* 4.12, trans. HOLDEN.

dieval astrologer Ibn Ezra wrote that a planet in its face is like one in beautiful ornaments and vestments, and ibn-Saul relates that when a planet is in its own face, it is like a person who lives among strangers because of an art, profession, or service he performs.[11]

But the decans continued to have a long, rich, and varied continuity in the Hermetic, Gnostic, and Hindu medical and magical literature that was passed on as the genre of astral magic into the Arabic and Renaissance traditions. The decanic gods took the forms and faces of the daimons and demons invoked in magical rituals and inscribed on talismans. Renaissance frescoes such as the one in Villa Schifanoia in central Italy illustrate how the decan gods became incorporated and reborn as some of the Tarot images.[12]

→ NOTE: *There is no workbook section in this chapter on the decans. If you want to, check to see if any of your planets occupy their own decans, and look at the decan lord of your Sun to reflect upon the nature of your soul.*

In order to give a completeness to this section on decans, we will mention the two other systems described in the astrological literature that assign planetary rulerships to the decans. The second system of decan rulers was based upon the planetary rulers of the zodiacal signs of each triplicity. The Arabic astrologer Abu Ma'shar recorded it from the Indian astrologers. In modern astrology, this system is sometimes called the decanates. Here, each decan of a sign is ruled by a planet that belongs to the same elemental triplicity. They are arranged in the same order as they appear in the zodiac. For the fire triplicity, the first decan of Aries is ruled by Mars, lord of Aries. The second decan is ruled by the Sun, lord of Leo, the next fire sign in the zodiacal order. The third decan of Aries is ruled by Jupiter, the lord of Sagittarius, the final fire sign of this triplicity.

The third system of decan rulers is given by Manilius, based upon the order of the zodiacal signs given to each decan in turn, and was not used by anyone.

---

11 IBN EZRA, *Beginning of Wisdom* 8.82; BONATTI, *Book of Astronomy* 2.2.19, trans. DYKES.
12 Austin COPPOCK offers delineations for the planets in various decans. See *36 Faces: The History, Astrology, and Magic of the Decans* (Three Hands Press, 2014).

Table 19. Decan Rulerships II

FIRE TRIPLICITY	DECAN I 0°–9°59'	DECAN II 10°–19°59'	DECAN III 20°–29°59'
Aries	Mars	Sun	Jupiter
Leo	Sun	Jupiter	Mars
Sagittarius	Jupiter	Mars	Sun

EARTH TRIPLICITY	DECAN I 0°–9°59'	DECAN II 10°–19°59'	DECAN III 20°–29°59'
Taurus	Venus	Mercury	Saturn
Virgo	Mercury	Saturn	Venus
Capricorn	Saturn	Venus	Mercury

AIR TRIPLICITY	DECAN I 0°–9°59'	DECAN II 10°–19°59'	DECAN III 20°–29°59'
Gemini	Mercury	Venus	Saturn
Libra	Venus	Saturn	Mercury
Aquarius	Saturn	Mercury	Venus

WATER TRIPLICITY	DECAN I 0°–9°59'	DECAN II 10°–19°59'	DECAN III 20°–29°59'
Cancer	Moon	Mars	Jupiter
Scorpio	Mars	Jupiter	Moon
Pisces	Jupiter	Moon	Mars

CHAPTER 18

The Judgment

———

> Each planet is a benefic when it is in its house (i.e. domicile), or in its
> trigon/triplicity, or in its exaltation, so that what it indicates of good is
> strong, increasing. A malefic, also, if in its own place [of rulership], its
> evil becomes lighter and decreases. — DOROTHEUS.[1]

WE ARE NOW READY TO MAKE OUR FINAL JUDGMENT CONCERNING THE
condition of each planet based upon its rulership positions in zodiacal signs.
Later we will combine this category with that of sect and the other major criteria, but for now let's ensure we thoroughly understand this category without
mixing it up with other factors. Remember our basic guideline that the more
times a planet occupies a sign where it has rulership according to any of the four
rulership systems, the more powerful it is in its capacity to be effective and to
bring about favorable and beneficial outcomes for the individual. When a planet
occupies two or more positions of its own rulerships, it is said to be in its chariot
or throne, and to rejoice.

Each rulership system—domicile, exaltation, triplicity, and bound—grants
a unique kind of power. When we judge that a planet has power, we must also
specify what kind of power is enhancing its capacity to bring about fortunate
events and outcomes in the houses it occupies and rules. In addition, the domicile, exaltation, triplicity, and bound lords each have their own procedures that
give indications for the life as a whole in accordance with their condition.

The Medieval astrologers attempted to rank and quantify the rulership powers, which they called dignities. They devised a point system, giving five points
for a planet in its own domicile, four points for exaltation, three points for triplicity, two points for bounds, and one point for decan. The planet that had the
most points was judged the strongest—the victor or *almuten* of either a specific
house or the entire chart. A planet that did not have any dignities was called

DOROTHEUS, *Carmen* 1.6, trans. PINGREE.

peregrine, derived from the Latin word *peregrino*, which means "to wander" or "travel": a person without a home or who is outside his homeland. They saw an increase in difficulties and impediments for peregrine planets.

Although there is software for Medieval astrology that reduces all of these calculations to a flat number, all the subtleties and nuances of a planet's assets and deficiencies are lost. I would advise against resorting to this easy approach, because the art of astrology lies in the art of making this judgment.

Let us begin by summarizing our main principles:

1. DOMICILE—power of resources that allows a planet to be effective in its task and to bring forth stable and consistent outcomes
2. EXALTATION—power of honors, respect, and high esteem that enhances a planet's glory and influence
3. TRIPLICITY—power of support from one's community of followers to push one forward to the successful accomplishment of one's task
4. BOUND—power of autonomy to set one's own rules of engagement and not be subject to another's authority

→ EXAMPLE CHARTS

Looking at our example charts, we are examining all of a planet's zodiacal lords—the types of powers and resources that it has available—in order to manifest its beneficial agenda on behalf of the individual. Beginners should consider domicile and exaltation lords; intermediates can add triplicity and bound lords.

CHART I: PLANETARY ZODIACAL RULERSHIP CONDITION

Planet, sign, degree	Domicile lord and aspect	Exalta-tion lord	Triplicity lord	Bound lord	Own ruler-ships	Detri-ment, fall, mutual reception	Judgment grade
☉ ♌ 5°09'	Sun*	—	Sun*	Jupiter	2	—	A+
♃ ♊ 9°34'	Mercury, sextile	—	Saturn	Jupiter*	1	Detri-ment	B+
♄ ♐ ℞ 24°39'	Jupiter, opposi-tion	—	Sun	Saturn*	1	—	A-
☿ ♌ 2° 24'	Sun, conjunc-tion	—	Sun	Jupiter	0	—	B+
☽ ♈ 25°36'	Mars, aversion	Sun	Sun	Saturn	0	—	C-
♀ ♊ 21°46'	Mercury, sextile	—	Saturn	Mars	0	—	C
♂ ♍ 14°49'	Mercury, aversion	Mercury	Venus	Venus	0	—	C

ANALYSIS

THE SUN is in excellent condition. He occupies two places of his own rulership in Leo. The Sun is his own domicile lord in Leo, from where he can draw on all the Leo resources to produce events that are successful, stable, and consistent. In this day chart, the Sun is also his own triplicity lord in Leo, where he can count on the support of a large community of followers to help carry him on towards accomplishment. The Sun has Jupiter for his bound lord, a benefic who is his sect mate, and who sees him via the friendly sextile aspect. This is almost as good as it gets, so I am giving the Sun an A+.

JUPITER presents an interesting challenge to judge. It is a benefic planet in detriment. The general interpretation of a benefic in poor condition is that it is limited in the amount of good it can do. Being in detriment indicates that there is some interruption in the flow and consistency of resources to the individual, leading to a certain amount of instability. However, it is still connected by a friendly aspect to its domicile lord Mercury, also its sect mate, who is sitting flush at the king's table. Its triplicity lord, Saturn, is also his sect mate, and while they have a tense opposition, they are nevertheless still connected. Finally, Jupiter is his own bound lord, where he is free to play by his own rules and is not subject to the constraints of others in order to prime the pump and generate more resources. While I considered giving Jupiter an A-, thinking that the bound rulership almost neutralizes the detriment, I am going with a B+ because of the detriment.

SATURN is a malefic, but even though we are not supposed to be looking at sect considerations now, we can't help but be aware that he belongs to the sect in favor and is thus in a position to do good for the individual (while still being true to his Saturnine nature). Saturn is in the domicile of Jupiter, a benefic who is also his sect mate, and there is an aspect between them. In addition, Saturn has the power of being in his own bounds, bringing up his score. He also has the powerful Sun as his triplicity lord, linked by a supportive trine aspect. I'm in a quandary because I am thinking that Saturn is actually in better condition than Jupiter because he is in one place of his own rulership (like Jupiter), and with all of his sect mates, but he is not in detriment the way Jupiter is. Should I give him a better grade than Jupiter? Yet he is malefic, so maybe not. I'll give Saturn an A-, and will revisit this decision at the end.

MERCURY's condition is overall very good. While not in any of his own places of rulership, he is co-present in the same zodiacal sign as his domicile lord, the powerhouse Sun, who is also his triplicity lord. Mercury's bound lord is the beneficent Jupiter, who also happens to live in one of Mercury's own domiciles, further strengthening their relationship. All of his lords are his sect mates, so Mercury gets a solid B+ in this category.

THE MOON has a succession of considerable problems in terms of zodiacal rulerships. While she occupies Aries, the domicile of her sect mate Mars, there is no aspect connecting her to him. So Mars cannot see her needs and thus there is no check in the mail coming from him. The Moon is in the triplicity of her non-sect mate, the Sun, and in the bounds of a harsh Saturn, who has his fall in Aries and is especially withholding to a non-sect mate. I am trying to decide between a c- or a d+. The factors that would make her situation even more dire would be: to be unaspected in a domicile of a non-sect mate, and to be in signs of her detriment or fall. I think I will go with the c-, because, although considerably challenged, she could be much worse off.

VENUS also has challenges in her condition. She is not in any of her places of rulership. She is in the domicile of Mercury, connected to him by the friendly sextile, but unlike Jupiter, who also has this relationship, Mercury is not her sect mate. But he is a friendly sort of guy who is doing well, so is likely to help her out. Saturn is her triplicity lord, the malefic of the contrary sect, opposing her by aspect and thus not inclined to muster the support of the community on her behalf, and possibly inclined to plot against her. Mars is her bound lord; he is a sect mate, and they are connected by the tense square aspect. I am thinking a c.

MARS' condition involves some thinking. He, like Venus, is also in the domicile of Mercury; but unlike Venus, Mars does not have an aspect with Mercury. So Mercury is blind to his needs (in a similar way that Mars cannot take care of his tenant, the Moon). Mars has some sort of disconnection going on. His triplicity and bound lords are Venus, his sect mate, who as a benefic is more sympathetic to Mars than he is as a malefic to her. And their square aspect points to the tension between team mates.

Here is the dilemma for the astrologer. Venus' main problem is her triplicity lord, Saturn; otherwise she is more or less okay by domicile and bound lord. Mars' principal problem is his disconnection from his domicile lord, but he can probably coax assistance from Venus, his triplicity and bound lord. Which of their two situations is better? We shall call them even and also give Mars a c.

Looking at our evaluations according to zodiacal rulership, we can see that the condition of the diurnal sect planets—Sun, Mercury, Jupiter, and Saturn—is excellent, and the condition of the nocturnal sect planets—Moon, Venus, and Mars—is quite challenged. In the next two chapters, we'll continue to examine planetary condition according to other broad categories, and see how this impacts their capacity to do their best.

CHART II: PLANETARY ZODIACAL RULERSHIP CONDITION

Planet, sign, degree	Domicile lord and aspect	Exalta- tion lord	Triplicity lord	Bound lord	Own ruler- ships	Detri- ment, fall, mutual reception	Judgment grade
☉ ♏ 2°42'	Mars, trine	—	Mars	Mars	o	—	C
♃ ♉ᴿ 23°33'	Venus, aversion	Moon	Moon	Saturn	o	—	B-
♄ ♉ᴿ 9° 27'	Venus, aversion	Moon	Moon	Mercury	o	—	B-
☿ ♏ 24°14'	Mars, trine	—	Mars	Saturn	o	—	C+
☽ ♐ 8°12'	Jupiter, aversion	—	Jupiter	Jupiter	o	—	C+
♀ ♌ 4°31'	Venus*	Saturn	Mercury	Saturn	1	—	A-
♂ ♋ 12°21'	Moon, aversion	Jupiter	Mars *	Venus	1	Fall	B

ANALYSIS

A quick bird's-eye view of this table reveals that two planets, Venus and Mars, have most of the rulership power. However, four of the planets are not connect- ed with their domicile lords. And we see that many planets are not in the signs of their sect mates, which is another cause for concern. Let's evaluate each planet.

THE SUN does not occupy any signs of its own rulership. Its domicile, tri- plicity, and bound lords are under the dominion of the malefic Mars, who is the malefic of the contrary sect and thus especially problematic. While the Sun has a sympathetic and helpful trine relationship with Mars, Mars is not his friend. I am initially giving the Sun a C.

JUPITER AND SATURN for the most part have a similar situation. They are both in the zodiacal sign of Taurus, and thus have Venus as their domicile lord. The quincunx configuration between them is considered a blind spot by the Hellenistic astrologers, but because Venus is in Libra, ruling both Taurus and Libra, there is some connection between them. Venus, while of the contrary sect, is a benefic and well-situated herself, and can thus be expected to provide a moderately helpful amount of resources to Jupiter and Saturn. Their triplicity lord is the Moon, which is of the contrary sect, and unconnected to them. So she is not much help there. Jupiter has his sect mate, Saturn, as his bound lord, whose rules and limits are likely to be harsh, but good for him. Saturn has Mercury as his bound lord, which is of the contrary sect and in opposition. I think I'll give both of them a B or maybe B-.

MERCURY has its sect mate, Mars, as its domicile and triplicity lord, and it is connected by a helpful trine aspect. Mercury is in the bounds of the malefic Saturn, who is not his sect mate, and thus has stringent and restricted parameters of operation. All his lords are malefic planets, and thus I give him a C+. This grade is slightly better than that of the Sun, who also has malefics for all his lords. In the case of Mercury, Mars is at least his sect mate, which is not the case for the Sun.

THE MOON has Jupiter as lord of all three of her possible rulerships—domicile, triplicity, and bound—but there is no aspect between her sign of Sagittarius and Jupiter's sign of Taurus. While Jupiter is a benefic, he is not her sect mate. While the Moon may have had a lot of potential powers with Jupiter as her lords, it might not really work out in actuality. I give her a C+.

VENUS is the strongest planet in this chart. As ruler of her own domicile, she has the power of ample resources for Venus-ruled significations—love, art, beauty, and intimate relationships. Saturn, harsh and exacting, is her exaltation and bound lord. Although Saturn is a malefic planet of the opposite sect, she has a reluctant reciprocal relationship with him as one of her tenants in Taurus. There is a way in which they need to scratch each other's backs, but Saturn doesn't give her too many concessions. Mercury is her triplicity lord, responsible for rousing the community of supporters; and although they are nocturnal sect mates, they are not connected. I am going to give Venus an A- instead of a B+, mainly because she is a benefic belonging to the sect in favor and in her own domicile.

MARS presents a fascinating case. Its domicile lord and sect leader, the Moon, does not see him because of the blind spot (aversion) between them. And furthermore, Mars is in fall in the sign of Cancer, so is both unseen and dismissed with little regard. Jupiter, its benefic exaltation lord, is of the opposite sect and thus will limit what he does to raise Mars up. But Mars is its own triplicity lord, and this indicates that this ruffian of ill repute and little means will have a huge rabble of followers cheering him on. And Venus as his bound lord will probably give him a garden of pleasures in which to indulge, and will continue to make allowances for his bad behavior. I think I will give Mars a B, taking off points for his fall and aversion from his domicile lord, but putting them back on for his triplicity rulership.

→   EXERCISE 17

Using your own chart, complete exercise 17:
Final Judgment of the Planet's Condition
based upon its Zodiacal Sign

EXERCISE 17

FINAL JUDGMENT OF THE PLANET'S CONDITION
BASED UPON ITS ZODIACAL SIGN

In this exercise, you will make a final judgment concerning the condition of each planet based upon its rulership positions in its zodiacal sign.

If you are a beginner and feel overwhelmed by all the factors to synthesize, simply begin with how many times a planet is in its own place of rulership, and look to see if that planet is connected to its domicile lord by a whole sign aspect. As you become comfortable with these steps, you can then add benefic/malefic nature and sect-mate considerations.

When you come to giving each planet its final grade, you may feel uncertain in your evaluation. At the end of all these deliberations, you must use your intuition to make the judgment. Once you have practiced on a dozen or so charts, the process will become easier. Resist trying to completely quantify the results as computer programs do. There are situations in life where all the factors are similar, but a different decision or course of action is called for. This interspace is where our freedom of mind exists, and is the art of judgment.

After you give an initial grade to each planet, review your decisions. If you see that you gave a planet too high or too low a grade relative to other planets' conditions, you may decide to change some.

PLANETARY ZODIACAL RULERSHIP CONDITION

Planet, sign, degree	Domicile lord and aspect	Exalta- tion lord	Triplicity lord	Bound lord	Own ruler- ships	Detri- ment, fall, mutual reception	Judgment grade
☉							
♃							
♄							
☿							
☽							
♀							
♂							

1. *Enter the zodiacal* SIGN AND DEGREE *for each planet.*
2. *Enter each planet's* DOMICILE LORD. *If the planet is its own domicile lord, such as Venus in Taurus, place an asterisk next to it.* This reminds you that it occupies a position where it receives power of resources from its own zodiacal sign. *If the planet is not in its own domicile, then enter the planet which rules and is lord of that domicile. For example, if Venus is in Virgo, her domicile lord is Mercury, the ruler of Virgo. Thus you would enter Mercury in the box.*
3. *Check to see if there is a* WHOLE SIGN ASPECT *between the planet and its lord—is there a conjunction, sextile, square, trine, or opposition between Ve-*

nus and Mercury in this example? If so, there is a supply line for the resources to flow between the host, Mercury, and the guest, Venus. Enter the glyph of the aspect; if there is no aspect, enter a dash—this will remind you that there is a problem with the reception of resources.

4. Enter each planet's EXALTATION LORD. If the planet is its own exaltation lord, such as Saturn in Libra, place an asterisk next to it. This reminds you that it occupies a sign from which it derives the power of being held in esteem. Certain zodiacal signs do not have exaltation lords; in this case enter a dash —.

5. Enter each planet's TRIPLICITY LORD. You will need to determine both the sect of the chart and the element of the sign of the planet in question. Refer to Table 16, Triplicity Lords, on page 200. If the planet is its own triplicity lord, such as the Moon in Capricorn in a night chart, place an asterisk next to it. This reminds you that it occupies a sign from which it derives power of support from its followers.

6. Enter each planet's BOUND LORD (refer to Table 17, Bound Lords, on page 210). If the planet is its own bound lord, such as Mars at 21° Gemini, place an asterisk next to it. This reminds you that it occupies a portion of a zodiacal sign from which it derives power of autonomy. Think about whether the bound lord is a benefic or malefic, and if it has domicile or exaltation rulership in that zodiacal sign. Remember: in determining the bound lord, if a planet is at 6° Aries 00' for example, it is at the sixth degree; but if it is at 6° Aries 01'–7° Aries 00' it is at the seventh degree.

7. Count how many times the planet occupies one of its OWN ZODIACAL RULERSHIPS. This will show up in your table not only with asterisks, but with that planet itself. For example, if Venus is at 6° Taurus in a day chart, it occupies its own domicile, its own triplicity, and its own bounds. You would enter the number "3" in that column. The higher the number, the more powerful the planet is in terms of its zodiacal rulerships, and the better positioned it is to do its best for the person.

8. Check to see if the planet is in MUTUAL RECEPTION with another planet, and if so, if there is a whole sign aspect between them. For example: Mercury in Aquarius has a mutual reception with Saturn in Virgo, but there is no aspect between them since Hellenistic astrology does not recognize the quincunx. However, Jupiter in Scorpio has a mutual reception with Mars in Pisces, and these planets are connected by a trine aspect. If a planet has some kind of mutual reception, it increases the planet's power to effectively do good.

9. If the planet occupies a sign of its DETRIMENT OR FALL, make a notation in the corresponding column. You know it has some handicaps and challenges in being able to do its best for the individual.

10. JUDGMENT: *The more a planet occupies those zodiacal signs in which it has some kind of rulership, the more powerful it is, the better its condition, and thus its predisposition to bring about good outcomes for the individual is improved.*

IN GENERAL, domicile and exaltation rulership (and there is some debate as to which of these two is more powerful) may be more important than triplicity and bound rulerships. Remember to make sure there is an aspect connecting the planet to its lord. However, depending upon the inquiry and the tradition, sometimes triplicity rulership (especially for Arabic/Medieval astrology) and bound rulership (length of life inquiries) take precedence.

A PLANET IN ITS OWN DOMICILE has stable, consistent power, and the most suitable kinds of resources for its own nature with which to accomplish its matters.

A PLANET IN ITS EXALTATION has the power of being held in high esteem and respect.

A PLANET IN ITS OWN TRIPLICITY has the power of support from its community of followers.

A PLANET IN ITS OWN BOUNDS has the power of autonomy.

IF A PLANET IS NOT ITS OWN LORD, then the next best situation is having its sect mates, especially the benefic of its sect, as its lords. The more lords there are that are sect mates, the better it is for the planet.

A PLANET'S GOOD CONDITION DECREASES if its lords are members of the contrary sect, and especially if its lord is the malefic of the contrary sect.

MUTUAL RECEPTION improves a planet's condition, while detriment and fall bring it down.

11. *Grade: Give each planet a grade—A, B, C, D, E, or F—with pluses (+) or minuses (-). You can change your mind later on.*

12. *Compose a judgment for each planet. Factor in as many or as few variables as you feel comfortable with synthesizing at this point. With practice, this process will get easier. ABOVE ALL, BE SURE TO GIVE EACH PLANET A GRADE. You can change your mind later on. Remember, we are learning Hellenistic astrology, where there is a clear-cut difference between good and bad, unlike modern astrology where everything is potentially good. Learning how to make this evaluation and feeling confident about your process is the key to easily and accurately interpreting the planet in its house location.*

REFLECTION AND ANALYSIS

1. Do any planets occupy their own zodiacal signs of rulership?
2. Which planets are these, and how many kinds of rulerships do they have? (This is your most important consideration. Consider how the resources of the zodiacal signs are most suitable and useful for the planet to bring about its significations).
3. Are any planets in the zodiacal signs of their detriment or fall? (This is also an important factor. Consider how the qualities of the zodiacal signs do not provide the optimal kinds of resources for the planet to bring about its significations).
4. Are any planets not aspected to their domicile lord? This is a problem. Do you sense a lack of external support in your life concerning the matters of the planet?
5. The planets that are in the best condition represent the parts of yourself where actions are more likely to result in positive and successful outcomes. The planets that are in poor condition represent the places in your life where you are most challenged.
6. Write a summary for each planet, along with the reasons for the grade that you give.

CHAPTER 19

Summary

AND SOURCE READINGS

———

THE TWELVE ZODIACAL SIGNS ARE IMAGES OF LIVING THINGS. They are based upon the groupings of the fixed stars, which have a higher order of divinity than the planets in the Platonic and Aristotelian cosmologies. These zodiacal images or signs shape the characteristics and behaviors of planets residing in those signs.

The inscription of the hexagon, square, and triangle into the zodiacal circle link certain sets of signs into familial relationships, which in turn determine the speed (gender), mode of completion (modality), and manner of expression (elemental triplicity) by which the significations and events of the planets come about.

The *thema mundi* provides a scheme that gives a rationale for the basic natures of the planets and the assignment of domicile and exaltation rulerships to the zodiacal signs.

Zodiacal signs also function as residences (*oikoi*) for the planets, which in accordance with the four systems of rulership provide a spectrum of powers and resources to the planets in order that they may accomplish their agendas. A planet in its own positions of rulership has greater power and stability to produce its positive significations with consistency.

A planet in its own domicile is self-sufficient and has full command of its own resources. A planet in the sign of its exaltation wields influence from the respect and esteem it is accorded. A planet in its own triplicity is dignified, having the support of its community, and when it is its own triplicity lord, it is more energetic and active. A planet in its own bounds is autonomous and self-determining, and is not subject to another's rules or restrictions.

A planet's placement in some other planet's zodiacal domicile sign is similar to a guest visiting someone else's home, and it must look to the lord of that zodiacal sign as its host to provide for its needs.

There is ambiguity about the decans as a rulership system, but they had an important influence in bodily characteristics and health.

PRIMARY SOURCE READINGS
FOR PART TWO: SIGNS AND RULERSHIPS

CHARACTERISTICS OF THE ZODIACAL SIGNS

TEUCER   The Twelve Signs (*CCAG* 7, pp. 192–213; trans. HOLDEN in *Rhetorius Astrological Compendia*, Appendix 1).

DOROTHEUS   *Carmen Astrologicum* 1.30: Masculine and Feminine Signs, Eastern and Western, Diurnal and Nocturnal.

MANILIUS   *Astronomica* 2. 150–269.

VALENS   *Anthology* 1.2: The Nature of the Twelve Zodiacal Signs.

RHETORIUS   *Compendium* 3: The Nature of the Twelve Zodiacal Signs.

PTOLEMY   *Tetrabiblos* 1.11: Solstitial, Equinoctial, Solid, and Bicorporeal Signs.

PAULUS   *Introduction* 2: The Twelve Zodiacal Signs.

HEPHAISTIO   *Apotelesmatics* 1: The Name and Power of the Twelfth Parts.

FIRMICUS   *Mathesis* 2.16: The Customs, Natures, and Risings of the Signs and the Winds that are Subject to them.

RULERSHIPS OF THE ZODIACAL SIGNS

DOROTHEUS   *Carmen Astrologicum* 1.1: The Triplicities of Zodiacal Signs and their Lords; the Domiciles of the Planets.
              Carmen Astrologicum 1.2: The Exaltations of the Planets.

VALENS   *Anthology* 1.3: The Sixty Bounds.

PORPHYRY   *Introduction* 5: The Domiciles of the Stars which they also call Zones.
              Introduction 6: Exaltations.
              Introduction 7: Co-rulers (Trigons).

FIRMICUS   *Mathesis* 2.2: The Domiciles of the Stars.
              Mathesis 2.3–4 The Exaltations and Falls.
              Mathesis 2.5: The Decans.
              Mathesis 2.7: The Bounds (Terms).

PAULUS   *Introduction* 3: The Bounds that were Allotted to the Five Revolving Stars in the Twelve Zodiacal Signs.
              Introduction 4: The Faces of the Decans in the Twelve Zodiacal Signs.
              Introduction 5: The Single Degrees (*monomoira*) that the Stars Rule in the Signs.

HEPHAISTIO   *Apotelesmatics* 1.6: The Trigons According to Dorotheus.
              Apotelesmatics 1.7: The Zodiacal Signs in which the Stars Rejoice.
              Apotelesmatics 1.8: Exaltations.

RHETORIUS   *Compendium* 7: Exaltations and Falls.
              Compendium 9: The Sect of the Rulers of the Trigons.
              Compendium 10: The 36 Decans and the *Paranatellonta* and the Faces.

THE THEMA MUNDI

ANTIOCHUS	*Summary* 2.1: The Nativity of the Cosmos.
FIRMICUS	*Mathesis* 3.1: The Chart of the World.
PAULUS	*Introduction* 37: Genesis of the Cosmos.

PART THREE

THE SOLAR PHASE CYCLE

CHAPTER 20

Special Solar Considerations

———

ARISTOTELIAN COSMOLOGY PLACED THE EARTH AS THE IMMOVABLE center of the cosmos, with all the celestial bodies revolving in separate nested spheres around its fixed central point. There was no distinction between the two luminaries and the other planets in terms of their orbits relative to the Earth, yet it was clear that the two lights did not behave in the same way as planets. The sphere of the Moon was closest to the Earth, and it was here that the Moon gathered the effluences of the other planets and transmitted them to the terrestrial realm, drawing down the powers of the planets into the physical bodies of animate life. The Sun, while not at the center of the cosmos, held the central position in the order of the planetary spheres surrounding the Earth—Moon, Mercury, Venus, Sun, Mars, Jupiter, and Saturn. Thus, although ancient cosmology was not heliocentric, the Sun still retained the role of central organizing principle in relation to the planets, and in this chapter we will explore this through the synodic cycles.

While the ancient astronomers may not have understood that the planets circled the Sun, their computations concerning the planets' orbital relationship to the Sun in terms of speed, direction, visibility, and phase were accurate. It was from their observations of the fixed stars that early astronomers were able to deduce the movements of the planets relative to the Sun.

The cycle of the appearances and disappearances of the fixed stars was an important part of both early Greek and early Babylonian astronomy, and also hinged on their relationship to the Sun. As they rose and set each night during the various seasons of the year, certain stars would disappear for a period of time when the proximity of the Sun's light obscured their appearances. Some time afterwards, the stars would emerge from their period of invisibility. For the first time in the year, they could be seen rising again in the east a few minutes before dawn.

This re-emergence from invisibility was known as the *heliacal morning rising* of a star. In a similar manner, a star's *heliacal setting* was understood as the time at which a star made its last appearance on the western horizon before entering a period of invisibility for several months. Because each star's unique morning risings and evening settings occurred around the same time each year, they were used to mark the various seasons. Knowledge of these dates was of great practical interest to farmers, sailors, and astrologers, and was collated into early star calendars called *parapegma*.[1]

During the next several centuries, Hellenistic astrologers not only incorporated the risings and settings of the stars into their astrological system, they also adapted the cycle of stellar phases to the planetary phases with accompanying interpretations. Consequently, the activity of a star or planet on the horizon relative to its orbital distance from the Sun commanded special attention for ancient astronomers, astrologers, and priests. Indeed, because it formed the borderline where the heavens touched the Earth and the Earth touched the underworld, the horizon was an especially significant locus of appearances and disappearances.

DIURNAL AND ZODIACAL MOTION

Looking upward at the expanse of sky, ancient peoples watched the daily movements of the Sun, Moon, planets, and stars rising in the east, culminating overhead, and setting in the west. This procession is known as the *diurnal motion* of celestial bodies. Simultaneously with the diurnal motion, the planets, but not the stars, also have a second motion in the opposite direction referred to as *zodiacal motion*. This is the path that the Sun, Moon, and planets take along the ecliptic as they move through the various signs of the zodiac. Plato called these different motions the "circle of the Same" and the "circle of Difference". The Same—the motion of the *constellations*—was more unchanging and self-similar over time, and formed an image of eternity; Difference—the motion of the *planets*—displayed erratic movements and went against the grain of the Same. As such the planets embodied transience rather than eternity, governing the shifting world of fate.[2]

When viewing an astrological chart, diurnal motion depicts the planets moving in a *clockwise* direction, rising at the Ascendant and moving upwards in

---

1   One of the oldest books on Greek mathematical astronomy, *Risings and Settings*, was written by AUTOLYCUS around 320 BCE. He provided a theoretical understanding for the annual cycle of star phases. See James EVANS, *The History and Practice of Ancient Astronomy* (Oxford: Oxford University Press, 1998), 190–97.

2   See PLATO, *Timæus*, 34C–39E.

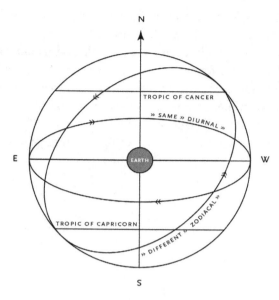

FIGURE 37. DIURNAL ☽
ZODIACAL MOTION

the sky towards culmination at the Midheaven, then setting at the Descendant before moving under the Earth towards the anti-culmination at the Imum Cœli. Zodiacal motion, by contrast, depicts the planets moving from one zodiacal sign to the next in a *counterclockwise* direction. In the course of this chapter, we will be referring to both kinds of motion and both perspectives of viewing the chart.

Because of their erratic and apparently opposite motions, the planets were called "wanderers" by the ancient Greeks. They traveled in both easterly and westerly directions, sometimes faster and other times slower, often direct but occasionally retrograde, making loops in the sky, traveling north and south of the ecliptic, appearing and disappearing. Over time, astronomers and astrologers came to understand all these variables as a factor of a planet's orbital relationship to the Sun, taking it as a central organizing principle.

The Moon also held a special status in the astrological hierarchy, and we will look at this in more detail in the next section of this book. For now, it suffices to say that anyone who looks at the night sky cannot help but notice the Moon's waxing and waning phases. Its alternating cycle of increasing and decreasing light gave early peoples their first intimations about the alternation of life and death; deeply connected to the life cycles of all living things, it was especially synchronized to women's monthly menstrual cycles. Over the millennia, moon gazers have divided this cycle in many ways—by two, three, four, eight, and eleven phases; into twenty-seven *nakshatras*; and twenty-eight lunar mansions. Traditional astrologers look at the Moon as a primary significator of bodily health and illness in humans. The monthly phases of the Moon cycle relative to the Sun, known as the lunation cycle, are easily visible and recognizable.

The other planets also form phase cycles with the Sun, but it takes a more acute eye to notice and track their unique features. There are certain qualities unique to each that influence how a planet's significations are manifested, its condition, and interpretation. This section will focus on the solar phase cycle of the planets. In the next section, we will explore the many factors unique to the Moon and her cycle.

CHAPTER 21

The Synodic Solar

PHASE CYCLE

———

The wandering stars make phases with regards to the Sun when they are morning rising and evening setting and when they are evening rising and morning setting, being borne along their courses towards the first and second stations, from which they decrease in numbers (retrograde motion) and rise at sunset (acronychal) and then they are seen as advancing (direct motion). — PAULUS.[1]

THE CRITICAL TRANSITIONS AND PHASES THAT THE PLANETS MAKE IN relation to their orbital cycle relative to the Sun are depicted in the synodic cycle. The word "synodic" derives from the Greek word *sunodos*, which means a "coming together", a "meeting", and also "sexual union". From one conjunction (*sunodos*) of a planet with the Sun to the time of its next conjunction, the planet's distance from the Sun changes. The different phases that occur at various points during this cycle are relative to a planet's *speed*, *direction*, and *visibility at the horizon*. Each of these visible phenomena affects a planet's condition and plays a role in its interpretation. Another term used for the synodic cycle is the *solar phase cycle*.

The first and broadest division of the planets relative to their location in the solar phase cycle is whether they are *of the morning* or *of the evening*. When planets rise before the Sun in the morning, they are said to be of the morning because they appear in the sky before dawn. When planets rise after the Sun, they are said to be of the evening because they only appear in the sky after the Sun has set at dusk. Let's look at an example to clarify (FIGURE 38).

1   *Introduction* 14.

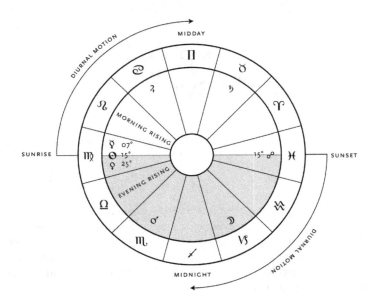

FIGURE 38. MORNING AND EVENING PLANETS

A PLANET OF THE MORNING: *The Sun is at 15° Virgo. A planet at 07°*
Virgo precedes the Sun. A planet in Cancer precedes Virgo and thus the Sun.
A planet in any degree and sign from 15° Virgo to 15° Pisces in the clockwise
direction (towards Leo, diurnal motion) precedes the 15° Virgo Sun and will
therefore rise before the Sun.

A PLANET OF THE EVENING: *The Sun is at 15° Virgo. A planet at 25°*
Virgo follows the Sun. A planet in Scorpio follows Virgo and thus the Sun.
A planet in any degree from 15° Virgo to 15° Pisces in the counterclockwise
direction (towards Libra, zodiacal motion) follows the 15° Virgo Sun, and
will therefore rise after the Sun.

Sometimes you will see a planet of the morning referred to as a "morning
star", "matutine", or "oriental" (from the Latin word for east), because planets
of the morning can potentially be seen rising over the horizon in the eastern
morning sky. Likewise, planets of the evening are often referred to as "evening
stars", "vespertine", or "occidental" (from the Latin word for west), since after the
Sun has set they can be seen upon the western horizon in the evening. But this
nomenclature is not strictly correct. We will define these terms more clearly in
the course of our discussion.

FIGURE 39. SUPERIOR &
INFERIOR PLANETS
(GEOCENTRIC)

THE SYNODIC CYCLES OF THE SUPERIOR PLANETS:
MARS, JUPITER, AND SATURN

The synodic cycle of the superior planets—Mars, Jupiter, and Saturn—differs
from that of the inferior planets, Mercury and Venus. In this context, the words
superior and inferior refer to the order of the planets from the perspective of
the geocentric or Ptolemaic cosmos. The *superior planets* are Mars, Jupiter, and
Saturn because they were thought to be more distant, beyond the orbit of the
Sun, while Venus and Mercury were regarded as *inferior planets* because they
were within the orbit of the Sun relative to the Earth (FIGURE 39). For the superior planets, the major stations or phases of the synodic cycle are as follows
(FIGURE 40):

A. CONJUNCTION (*sunodos*), LYING HIDDEN
The synodic cycle begins when a planet is conjunct the Sun along the
ecliptic. While they rise together over the horizon, the planet is not yet
visible in the sky because its appearance is obscured by the blinding rays
of the Sun. This is point (A) on the diagram (FIGURE 40). This phase
of a planet's (or star's) invisibility is called the "lying hidden phase"; it
extends from a distance of 15° behind the Sun to 15° ahead of the Sun.

B. HELIACAL RISING, FIRST APPEARANCE (*phasis*)

The Sun and the planets travel at different rates. Once a planet separates from the Sun by one degree, it rises over the horizon before the Sun and is said to be *of the morning*. As the arc of separation increases, the planet becomes visible on the eastern horizon after a certain number of days. This is called its *heliacal morning rising* (heliacal is related to *hēlios*, the Greek word for Sun). The exact number of days or degrees of separation varies by planet and by latitude, but for the purposes of interpretation, the Hellenistic astrologers standardized this to 15° (B).

D. MORNING STAR PHASE

A planet was considered to be a *morning star* (or in the morning star phase) between its heliacal morning rising at 15° from the Sun (B) until its retrograde station near the 120° right trine (E).

E. RETROGRADE STATION, ACRONYCHAL PHASE

As the distance between the superior planets and the Sun increases to approximately 120°, they make their first station—standing still—before turning retrograde. At this moment, the morning star phase ends and the *acronychal* phase begins (E). The planets now appear in the eastern sky after the Sun has set in the west. In Greek, *akronuchos* means "at sunset": the phase at the beginning of nightfall.

F. OPPOSITION

The superior planets then move towards an opposition to the Sun (F). If a superior planet is opposite the Sun, it will always be retrograde. Technically, according to the ancient literature, the exact opposition marks their transition from being *of the morning* (oriental) to being *of the evening* (occidental), as their zodiacal longitude is now in the degrees or signs following the Sun. Visually, they still appear in the eastern sky early in the evening, culminate overhead in the south at midnight, and set towards the west before dawn.

G. DIRECT STATION

Continuing their retrograde motion and decreasing their distance from the Sun, the planets form a second trine, but now the planets are behind the Sun. At around 120°, they stand still again, make their second station, and turn direct (G).

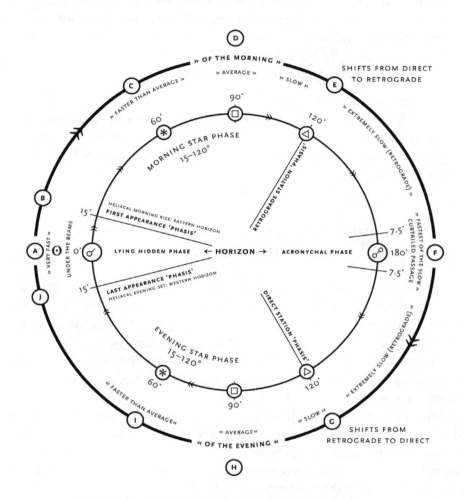

FIGURE 40. SYNODIC CYCLE OF MARS, JUPITER, & SATURN

Solar Phase Cycle of the Superior Planets:
Mars, Jupiter & Saturn

H. EVENING STAR PHASE

They now enter their *evening star phase*. The evening star designation refers to the fact that the planets can now be seen to set in the west rather than rise in the east. A planet was considered to be an evening star during the interval between its direct station near its left-sided trine and its heliacal setting 15° behind the Sun. The planets continue to decrease their distance from the Sun as they re-approach their conjunction.

J. HELIACAL EVENING SET

At 15° from the exact conjunction, the planets make a heliacal *evening set* (J) with their last appearance in the western sky at sunset. After the planet's heliacal set, it is invisible once again, lying hidden until the next heliacal rising.

THE SYNODIC CYCLES OF THE INFERIOR PLANETS: MERCURY AND VENUS

Mercury and Venus follow a somewhat different pattern in their synodic cycle. From the perspective of Earth, these planets never appear more than one or two zodiacal signs apart from the Sun. Mercury's *greatest elongation* (distance) from the Sun is about 28°, and Venus' is about 48°. Thus, Mercury and Venus can never make a square, trine, or opposition to the Sun. Rather, they make a second conjunction with the Sun within one synodic cycle, and two additional phases—a morning setting and an evening rising.

The first conjunction with the Sun, called the *inferior conjunction*, occurs when the planet is retrograde in motion. The planet is *inside* the orbit of the Sun from Earth's perspective. The second conjunction with the Sun, called the *superior conjunction*, takes place when the planet is direct in motion: the planet is *beyond* the orbit of the Sun from Earth's perspective (FIGURES 41–42).

A. INFERIOR CONJUNCTION

The synodic cycle of Mercury and Venus begins at the inferior retrograde conjunction (A); the morning heliacal rise (B), which immediately follows it, symbolizes the rebirth of a star.

B. MORNING RISING, FIRST APPEARANCE (PHASIS)

After the conjunction, as the distance between the planet and the Sun increases, the planet becomes visible in the eastern sky as it makes its heliacal morning rising (B). This begins its *morning star phase*.

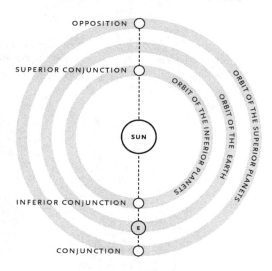

FIGURE 41. CONJUNCTIONS OF
INFERIOR AND SUPERIOR PLANETS
(HELIOCENTRIC)

Superior and inferior conjunctions of the inferi-
or planets (Mercury and Venus) versus conjunc-
tions and oppositions of the superior planets
(Mars, Jupiter, & Saturn).

C. GREATEST ELONGATION, MORNING SKY

Around that time it also stations and turns direct in motion and then moves away from the Sun towards its *greatest elongation* above the horizon (C).

D. MORNING SETTING

Then, as the distance between the planet and the Sun begins to decrease, the planet is seen descending back towards the horizon until, at about 15° from the Sun, it makes its *morning setting* (D) and disappears. This ends its morning star phase.

E. SUPERIOR CONJUNCTION

Still in direct motion, it lies hidden as it makes its next *conjunction* with the Sun (E). Again, as the distance between them increases and reaches 15° from the Sun, it reappears in the western sky making an evening rising (F) shortly after the Sun sets.

F. EVENING RISING

The re-emergence from invisibility begins its *evening star phase*.

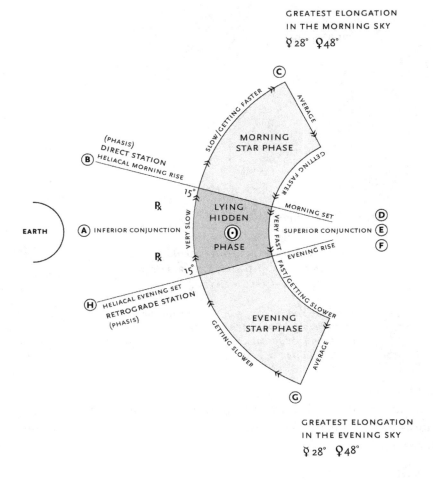

FIGURE 42.
SOLAR PHASE CYCLE OF INFERIOR PLANETS
MERCURY & VENUS

G. GREATEST ELONGATION, EVENING SKY

In the evening star phase, it moves towards its *greatest elongation* above the horizon (G). After peaking at that point, it then descends back towards the horizon.

H. RETROGRADE STATION, HELIACAL SETTING

As the distance between the planet and the Sun decreases to around 15°, it will station, turn retrograde, and begin its *heliacal setting* (H), its last appearance in the western sky before once again disappearing behind the rays of the Sun. This ends its evening star phase. Still in retrograde motion, it lies hidden, and once again conjoins the Sun at the same degree (A).

In most cycles, the retrograde and direct stations of Mercury and Venus are close to their heliacal rise or set. But sometimes there can be a longer interval between the two events. Either the station or the rise/set can occur first and then the other.

CHAPTER 22

Planetary Speed

DIRECTION, AND VISIBILITY

———

TO RECAP, THE KEY MOMENTS IN THE SOLAR PHASE CYCLE OF PLANETS ARE:

1. When planets become visible and invisible at their morning and evening risings and settings
2. When planets make their stations, turning retrograde and direct
3. When planets make their conjunction and opposition to the Sun

Each of these moments signifies an essential shift in a planet's appearance and behavior. The observable phenomena of their speed, direction, and visibility impact the condition of the planet and thus its interpretation. Let us discuss each in turn.

PLANETARY SPEED AND DIRECTION

Each planet has an average rate of speed at which it travels, based in part upon its distance from the Sun and the length of time it takes for one complete revolution. A planet's average daily motion is the average distance it traverses in one day as it travels around the ecliptic (geocentric perspective) as measured in degrees, minutes, and seconds.

However, the planets do not travel at a constant rate of speed throughout their cycle; sometimes they are faster or slower than their average speed. The planet's distance from the Sun along the ecliptic during its synodic cycle determines how fast or slow it is moving. Hellenistic astrologers used speed as an important factor in the assessment of a planet's condition. A planet's direction in terms of forward motion (direct), or backward motion (retrograde) is intimately connected to its speed.

Once again, it should be emphasized that the pattern for Mars, Jupiter, and Saturn differs from that of Venus and Mercury. The Moon is exempt from this pattern because it orbits the Earth, not the Sun; furthermore, the Moon's speed is determined by its proximity to the Earth and is never retrograde.

Table 20. Planetary Speed

Planet	Average Daily Distance in Degrees and Minutes
MOON	13° 10.56″ per day
SUN	0° 59.16″ per day
MERCURY	0° 59″ per day (same as the Sun)
VENUS	0° 59″ per day (same as the Sun)
MARS	0° 31.444″ per day
JUPITER	0° 4.987″ per day
SATURN	0° 2.009″ per day

MARS, JUPITER, AND SATURN

When conjunct with the Sun (A), Mars, Jupiter, and Saturn are each in direct motion and moving at their swiftest speeds (FIGURE 40). Their speeds gradually decrease as their distance from the Sun increases. At around the 60° arc of separation (C), they are slower than the speed at the conjunction, but still moving faster than average. At the 90° arc of separation (D), they are moving at their average rate (with the exception of Mars, which displays anomalies). Beyond that point, they move with slower than average speed. When they are near the right trine, around 120° ahead of the Sun (E), they make their first station, standing still against the background of the fixed stars.

When they turn retrograde, the planets appear to make a backward loop in the sky, and they move at their slowest speeds. The retrograde period lasts from the right trine (E), passing through the opposition (F), until it reaches the left trine (G) 120° behind the Sun. The retrograde period might be considered a case of extreme slowness. However, as the planet approaches the opposition to the Sun, its velocity suddenly increases and, once it passes the opposition, rapidly decreases and resumes its slow motion. The maximum speed of the retrograde period occurs when the planet is in direct opposition to the Sun.

At the second station, near the 120° left trine (G), the planets stand still once again, before resuming direct motion. Still slower than normal, they pick up speed until they reach their average rate near the waning 90° square (H) (note that Mars is an exception to this). By the time they reach the sextile (I), they are traveling faster than average, even faster as they approach the conjunction with the Sun (A), where they are at their swiftest.

Once you are familiar with this pattern, you can look at a chart and approximate a planet's speed by checking its aspect to the Sun. Mars, Jupiter, and Saturn will be moving the *fastest* when near the conjunction with the Sun, *faster than average* around the sextile, *average* near the square, and *slow* near the trines. If these planets are opposite the Sun, they will always be retrograde and extremely slow unless they are very close to the exact opposition.

If the planet is direct at the first trine, it will soon station and turn retrograde. If it is retrograde at the second trine, it will soon station and turn direct.

Mars makes two phases with the Sun which are called "anomalies" because they differ from the pattern of Jupiter and Saturn. When Mars, both as a morning star and as an evening star, approaches the square aspect with the Sun, it abruptly decreases its speed. Reduced to a slower than average rate, Mars thus remains longer than usual in the zodiacal signs that square the Sun.

MERCURY AND VENUS

The synodic cycles of Mercury and Venus begin with their inferior conjunction, when they are retrograde and moving very slowly (A) (FIGURES 41–42). As the distance between the planet and the Sun increases, it slows down to approach its direct station (B). This is one of two points in the cycle during which the planet is motionless. After its direct station, the planet gradually picks up speed, moving towards its greatest elongation ahead of the Sun as a morning star appearing in the eastern sky (C). During its greatest elongation, it travels at its average rate of speed. The planet then begins its descent as a morning star in the east, gradually increasing its speed until it is 15° from the Sun, where it makes its morning set, disappearing from view (D). Moving ever faster, the planet reaches its maximum speed, and forms a superior conjunction with the Sun (E).

Still moving fast, but gradually decreasing their speed, Mercury and Venus pull away from the Sun. At 15° they reappear as evening stars (F). As they approach their greatest elongation from the Sun, their speed normalizes (G). They then begin to move ever slower as they re-approach the Sun. At around 15° before the Sun, they make a heliacal setting in the western sky, turning retrograde near their second station (H). They are now at their slowest speed as evening stars as they move towards the inferior conjunction with the Sun (A). A short burst of speed occurs near the conjunction in this otherwise slow period.

When you look at a chart and see Mercury or Venus conjunct the Sun and in direct motion, you know they are moving at their fastest daily speed. If you see that they are retrograde and conjunct the Sun, you know that they are slower than average. The slowest motion occurs at both station points.

DETERMINING SPEED AND DAILY MOTION

There is software for calculating the speed of each planet on any given date. If you know the average daily motion, you can determine if, on that day, the planet is traveling faster or slower than its daily rate. Some programs will also note if the planet is increasing or decreasing in speed. Historically, this was an important consideration in horary and medical inquiries.[1]

Hellenistic texts used the phrases *additive in numbers* and *subtractive in numbers* when discussing a planet's motion. Generally, *additive in numbers* referred to a planet in direct motion, and *subtractive in numbers* referred to a planet in retrograde motion. However, arguments can also be made for these terms being used to indicate a planet increasing or decreasing its speed. However, this notion is more accurately called *moving towards the greater or lesser extent of a planet's course.*

INTERPRETING SPEED AND DIRECTION

> And if [the stars] occupy the first station and are found to be stepping backwards, the matters that were previously determined, actions, profits, and undertakings are delayed. Likewise, even if the stars rise at sunset (acronychal), they are weak, thwarting, foretelling only illusions and hopes. And if, in any way, they come to the second station, they remove the hindrances, restore the same matters, and they bring stability and successful accomplishment of the livelihood. But if they are carried under the setting phase, they bring hindrances and troubles in what is being accomplished, and also bodily dangers, weaknesses,

---

1   You can also determine the planet's daily motion by looking at an ephemeris. Subtract the longitude of a planet (as given in degrees and minutes) from its position on the day before. This figure tells you the distance it has traveled within a twenty-four hour period. You can then compare this to its average to assess its relative average speed on that day. If you then subtract the longitude of the planet's position on the following day, you can compare the two sums and see whether the figure on the day after is larger or smaller than the figure on the day before. This will tell you if the planet is speeding up or slowing down. If the number is larger than the day before, the planet's speed is increasing. If it is smaller than on the day before, the planet's speed is decreasing.

and afflictions in the secret places. Often holding out the promise of
honors and great expectations, they turn them towards the worse.
— VALENS.[2]

Planetary speed is connected to the planet's level of activity. The faster the planet, the more active and energetic it is. Medieval astrologer Ibn Ezra wrote that
"a planet swift in its motion is like a young man running".[3] A planet that is faster
than average in motion was thought to move more quickly and to accomplish
its agenda sooner, to produce more of its significations, and easily take advantage of opportunities to manifest its significations as outer events. The faster
speeds occur when the planet is direct in motion. The planet proceeds swiftly
and directly towards the accomplishment of its objectives. You may recall
that a planet's presence in a masculine zodiacal sign also indicates moving at
a faster pace.

    The slower the planet's motion, the less active and energetic it was thought
to be. "A planet slowing down", writes Ibn Ezra, "is like a person who is exhausted and has no strength to walk".[4] A planet that is slower than average in motion
was thought to be lethargic, to have low energy, to take longer to accomplish
its objectives, to have fewer events, and to be too hesitant to act (thus missing
advantageous opportunities). The slow speeds occur when the planet is near its
stations and is retrograde in motion. You may recall that a planet's presence in a
feminine zodiacal sign also indicates moving at a slower pace.

INTERPRETING RETROGRADE MOTION

Hellenistic and Medieval astrologers considered a retrograde planet, moving extremely slowly and backwards, to be a problematic condition. Paulus says that
when planets are retracing their paths, their influences are useless, unfavorable
for action, and insignificant; Dorotheus writes that a planet in retrograde motion signifies difficulty and misfortune in the native and others; Ibn Sahl relates
that a retrograde planet signifies disobedience, contradiction, and diversity or
discord.[5] This rebellious quality can be seen in the erratic visual movement of its
retrograde loop, speeding up at the opposition and "pushing the envelope" as it

---

2   VALENS, *Anthology* 4.14.
3   IBN EZRA, *Beginning of Wisdom* 8.95, trans. EPSTEIN.
4   IBN EZRA, *Beginning of Wisdom* 8.94, trans. EPSTEIN.
5   PAULUS, *Introduction* 1.14; DOROTHEUS, *Carmen* 1.6; IBN SAHL, *The Fifty Judgments* 10.

moves beyond the normative boundaries of the ecliptic.[6] The Greek word used for retrograde is *anapodizō*, which means "to step or go back", "to call back", or "to recall". Robert Schmidt suggests that retrograde benefic planets take back what good they have given, and retrograde malefic planets do not give over anything in the first place.[7]

The Medieval term "impedited" had several related meanings. It was used to describe the retrograde predicament as well as an afflicted aspect condition. Impedited comes from Latin *impedire*, roughly translated as "to shackle or snare the feet", i.e., "to impede". It indicates a retarding movement, or progress through obstructions or hindrances.

We might then say that a retrograde planet is not only moving very slowly towards its goals, but it is going backwards or in the opposite direction of accomplishing its objective. There exists some kind of hindrance or obstruction that inhibits the expression of its significations, or which provokes rebelliousness against the norms of consensus behavior.

Modern astrologers have reframed the concept of retrograde planets as an internalization of that planetary function. Mercury retrograde may refer to a mind inwardly turned; Venus retrograde, to the development of one's own values. The rebellious quality ascribed to a retrograde planet by the ancient astrologers is revisioned as the need for a more individualistic expression of that planetary function than that which is the consensus norm for the general population. Vedic astrologers, by contrast, consider the retrograde an auspicious condition because the planet is closest to the Earth and brightest.

Another perspective on the meaning of retrograde planets is that their significations take a longer time to fully mature, bringing forth their objectives at a later age in life. Looking to the timing procedure of secondary progressions, where each day after birth is equated to one year of life, the date at which a natal retrograde planet goes direct after birth corresponds to the age when the planet begins to bring forth its agenda.

When checking to see if a planet is direct or retrograde, it is necessary to investigate *whether the planet made a station within seven days before or after the birth*. You will need to consult an ephemeris to determine this unless your software has a feature that alerts you to this possibility. If this is the case, the planet is imbued with a special significance. When a planet is near its station, it stands still. It is intense, focused, concentrated, and unwavering in its nature. It is also

---

6   For the astronomical and astrological significance of the Mercury retrograde, see especially Gary P. CATON, *Hermetica Triptycha: The Mercury Elemental Year* (Auckland: Rubedo Press, 2017), pp. 21–29.

7   Personal communication/teaching.

at its brightest in the sky because of its proximity to the Earth. This intensity can be beneficial if the planet is a benefic in good condition, but it can also be particularly destructive if the planet is a malefic in bad condition.

Ancient astrologers differentiated between a direct planet which *stations retrograde* (becoming weaker) and a retrograde planet *stationing direct* (becoming stronger). "A planet about to turn retrograde", writes Ibn Ezra, "is like a frightened person, fearing adversities that are coming to him", whereas "a planet in its second [direct] station is like a person hoping for good circumstances".[8] Valens instructs that when a planet is a time lord (an influential planet for a period of time using Hellenistic timing techniques), the first retrograde station indicates the postponement of one's affairs and benefits, but at the second (direct) station, it removes the hindrances and restores the stability and rectification of one's matters.[9]

FAST AND DIRECT VERSUS SLOW AND RETROGRADE

In the analysis of planetary condition, a planet that is *fast and direct in motion* is considered to be more active and better able to accomplish positive outcomes for the individual in a forthright manner. A planet that is *slow and retrograde* is considered less active and is obstructed from bringing about its full potential, or its manifestations are retracted or undone at some point.

We may illustrate this with the example of driving to an appointment. The fast, direct planet is clipping along at a good pace with little traffic along a straight course to its destination. When the planet turns retrograde, it is as if a detour sign appears due to an accident. The retrograde planet must turn off the freeway onto a side road where it becomes snarled in traffic and has to crawl along, heading in the opposite direction to its destination. The first retrograde station corresponds to the moment when the driver realizes that he or she might not make the appointment in time, with all the ensuing consequences. The second direct station corresponds to the moment when the driver is finally back on course, hopeful that all will turn out well.

→ EXAMPLE CHARTS

Let us look to our example charts to see what information can be obtained from the planets' speed and direction.

---

8   IBN EZRA, *Beginning of Wisdom*, 8.91, 93, trans. EPSTEIN.
9   VALENS, *Anthology* 4.14.

CHART I: SPEED, DIRECTION, STATION

Planet	Speed	Direction	Station within 7 days
SUN	N/A	N/A	N/A
JUPITER	Faster than average	Direct	—
SATURN	Very slow	Retrograde	—
MERCURY	Very fast	Direct	—
MOON	N/A	N/A	N/A
VENUS	Average	Direct	—
MARS	Faster than average	Direct	—

ANALYSIS

SATURN stands out as being slow and retrograde, pointing to some difficulties with the ways in which it manifests itself, thus signifying delays and reversals. The other planets are fine in regards to their speed, direction, and motion. No planet makes a station within seven days of the birth.

CHART II: SPEED, DIRECTION, STATION

Planet	Speed	Direction	Station within 7 days
SUN	N/A	N/A	N/A
JUPITER	Very slow	Retrograde	—
SATURN	Very slow	Retrograde	—
MERCURY	Very slow	Direct	Retrograde on 10/29
MOON	N/A	N/A	N/A
VENUS	Faster than average	Direct	—
MARS	Slower than average	Direct	—

ANALYSIS

All the planets except VENUS are moving slowly. JUPITER and SATURN are retrograde. MARS, near the trine aspect to the SUN, is slowing down as it heads towards its retrograde station (not until November 18). MERCURY, while still direct, is very slow in motion as it will make its retrograde station within four days of the birth, on October 29. Thus, MERCURY has the focus and intensity that marks stationary planets, but this part of the cycle also signifies a kind of fear that difficult situations lie ahead.

→   EXERCISE 18

Using your own chart, complete exercise 18:
Speed, Direction, Station

EXERCISE 18

SPEED, DIRECTION, STATION

In this exercise, you will determine each planet's relative speed, direction, and whether it has made a station within seven days before or after the birth. You will need an ephemeris for a thirty-day period around your birth date.

SOLAR PHASE CONDITIONS

Planet	Speed	Direction	Station within 7 days
SUN	N/A	N/A	N/A
JUPITER			
SATURN			
MERCURY			
MOON	N/A	N/A	N/A
VENUS			
MARS			

1. PLANET: *Enter the zodiacal sign and degree of each planet.*

2. SPEED: *for Mars, Jupiter, and Saturn, enter the planet's speed as fast (direct and near the Sun), faster than average (near the sextile to the Sun), average (near the square to the Sun), slower than average (near the trine to the Sun), standing still (at station), or slow (retrograde).*

3. SPEED: *for Venus and Mercury, enter the speed as fast (direct and near conjunction with the Sun), average (near greatest elongation: 28° for Mercury, 48° for Venus), standing still (at station), or slow (retrograde).*

4. DIRECTION: *enter whether the planet is direct (D) or retrograde in motion (RX).*

5. STATION: *Note if the planet has made a station from direct to retrograde or retrograde to direct within seven days before or after the birth.*

REFLECTION AND ANALYSIS

1. Which planets are more active because they are moving faster than their average speeds?

2. Which planets are less active because they are moving slower than their average speeds?

3. Are there any planets that are retrograde?

4. Think about how this is expressed in your life. It may be in ways that are not immediately obvious. For example, my Mercury is retrograde, near its station the day before. My mind is quite active, but I think for a long time before speaking, am a very slow writer, and my reflexes are poor in that it takes a longer time for me to process a visual stimulus before being able to take action. This especially affects driving and certain athletic activities.

5. Are there any planets that will make a retrograde or direct station within seven days before or after the birth? How does this add intensity to the expression of the planet? Do the significations of that planet saturate and overwhelm your life?

CHAPTER 23

Visibility

AT THE HORIZON

——

A PLANET'S VISIBILITY ON THE HORIZON WAS AN IMPORTANT FACTOR IN the determination of its condition. As mentioned previously, while all planets rise, culminate, and set every day, there are times when they are so close to the Sun that they cannot be seen when rising or setting on the horizon due to the glare of the Sun obscuring our vision of the planet. Hellenistic astrologers referred to this condition as a planet "under the beams". Medieval astrologers substituted the word "rays" for beams.

The distance at which a planet cannot be seen because of its position relative to the Sun is highly variable due to the intrinsic brightness of the planet, atmospheric conditions, and geographical latitude. The Hellenistic astrologers standardized this interval in two ways. In the first way, a uniform fifteen degrees on either side of the Sun was assigned to each planet.[1] In the second way, which is more consistent with the intrinsic brightness of the planet, Venus and Mars are assigned eight degrees on either side of the Sun, Jupiter twelve degrees, Saturn fifteen degrees, the Moon fifteen degrees, and Mercury nineteen degrees.[2]

In addition to their proximity to the Sun, the planets Mars, Jupiter, and Saturn have a second period of invisibility near their oppositions to the Sun. When these planets approach their oppositions to the Sun, they are visible in the night sky, but they are not visible when rising over the eastern horizon or setting upon the western horizon. They are first seen in the eastern sky well above the horizon several hours after the Sun sets. They seem to vanish several hours before dawn while still well above the western horizon. The duration of their visibility in the night sky is "docked"—cut off at either end—and they were thus said to be in

---

1   PAULUS, *Introduction* 14; PORPHYRY, *Introduction* 2.

2   FIRMICUS MATERNUS, *Mathesis* 2.15, trans. HOLDEN. The distances from the Sun at which planets could be seen were incorporated by Arabic and Medieval astrologers as the doctrine of moiety, in which the determination of aspects were based upon the intersection of these various orbs of light.

curtailed passage. This interval of invisibility on the horizon was standardized to a planet having a seven-and-a-half degree orb on either side of the opposition to the Sun.[3]

Mercury and Venus are never opposite the Sun, thus they do not have this second period of invisibility on the horizon through curtailed passage, as do Mars, Jupiter, and Saturn. However, since Mercury and Venus have two conjunctions with the Sun during each synodic solar phase cycle, they are invisible not only when they are direct and near conjunction to the Sun, but also when they are retrograde and near conjunction with the Sun.

In summation, all planets are invisible on the horizon when they are under the Sun's beams—within fifteen degrees on either side of the Sun. In addition, Mars, Jupiter, and Saturn are also invisible on the horizon when they are opposite the Sun within seven-and-a-half degrees. Otherwise, all the planets are visible when rising or setting on the horizon.

INTERPRETATION OF VISIBILITY

When planets are visible rising or setting on the horizon, their significations can be made manifest and seen. Valens says that when a planet is rising and visible and the transit comes to an effective house, the power of the planet is aroused and causes its actions to be conspicuous, resulting in significations that are in accordance with its own nature.[4]

Planets that are visible when rising or setting over the horizon have the capacity to bring forth the things they represent and to actualize their agenda for the life of the individual. This improves their condition. When they are invisible, their significations are hidden. This may suggest a secret life, or actions that are hidden from view. Valens wrote that when planets enter a setting phase, interruptions and difficulties are introduced into the planets' objectives.[5] Ancient astrologers also interpreted planets under the beams as weakened or debilitated due to being "burnt in the heat of the Sun", thus losing their power and being unable to manifest their significations and agenda.[6]

To illustrate what debilitation from the Sun's rays feels like, imagine being outside at noon in the scorching sun, carrying your groceries several miles from

3   Be aware that some authors use the term "curtailed passage" to refer to the shortened period of visibility, while others use this term to refer to the orb of invisibility near the horizon. Be sure to ascertain which interval is being referred to when reading various texts.
4   VALENS, *Anthology* 4.14, speaking of a planet as a time-lord.
5   VALENS, *Anthology* 4.14.
6   DOROTHEUS, *Carmen* 1.6, trans. DYKES.

the store to your home. A planet weakened by its proximity to the Sun is in poor condition because it is less able to bring forth its most beneficial outcomes for the individual. The benefic planets lose their ability to do good actions. Some say that the malefic planets also lose their power to do bad, but others hold that the evil happens secretly, just as thieves operate by night when they are less likely to be seen.

The moments when planets first disappear under the rays of the Sun, as well as when they first re-emerge from the beams, were of special interest to ancient astrologers. They gave much commentary on the hidden interval during which the planets were invisible.

When a planet approaches the Sun, it disappears under the beams at about fifteen degrees. This is the beginning of the weakening, when it has "fallen into the burning fire" and encounters distress and diminution.[7] The planet is said to be "combust" when within twelve degrees (Medieval) or nine degrees (Hellenistic). Paulus writes that at this interval, the planets become weak and ineffective, and Bonatti tells us it is like one who begins to grow ill.[8] At extreme combustion, approaching around three degrees, it is like a "sick person when he is in a state of extreme paroxysm, when a fever is upon him".[9]

However, as the planet approaches the *heart of the Sun*, which the Hellenistic astrologers place at one degree on either side of the Sun, the planet is protected from this inactivity, weakening, and irregularity.[10] The Medieval astrologers limit this protective area to seventeen minutes on either side of the Sun, and they compared it to being strong in the Sun's forge, or like sitting with the king in the same seat.[11]

As the planet begins to separate from the conjunction with the Sun, the fever breaks, and the sickness diminishes as it moves out of the nine-degree combustion zone. As the planet begins to emerge from the beams, between twelve and fifteen degrees from the Sun, the person is freed from the illness. Although somewhat weak, recovery is assured and strengthening lies ahead.[12]

A planet is protected from the burning, debilitating power of the Sun when it is in its "chariot" or "throne".[13] This occurs when the planet is strengthened by being in its own domicile, exaltation, or bound (Porphyry adds triplicity to this

7   BONATTI, *Book of Astronomy* 3.2.6; 2.7, trans. DYKES.
8   BONATTI, *Book of Astronomy* 3.2.7, trans. DYKES.
9   BONATTI, *Book of Astronomy* 3.2.7, trans. DYKES.
10   RHETORIUS, *Compendium* 1.
11   BONATTI, *Book of Astronomy* 3.2.7, trans. Dykes; IBN EZRA, *Beginning of Wisdom* 8.98.
12   BONATTI, *Book of Astronomy* 3.2.7.
13   ANTIOCHUS, *Summary* 14; PORPHYRY, *Introduction* 25; RHETORIUS, *Compendium* 43.

list), and it is invested with strength. Robert Schmidt points out that in antiquity, chariots usually had fringed canopies that acted as umbrellas, helping to block the damaging heat of the Sun. When benefic planets are in their chariot, they increase their positive potentials, and malefics change to beneficence.

Ptolemy, in his treatise on the *Phases of the Fixed Stars*, writes that the "period when the stars disappear for a time, we call the times of 'arising and lying hidden'".[14] This statement can lead us to an esoteric mystery interpretation of a planet's union with the Sun under the cloak of darkness. The heliacal setting of a star corresponds to its death and its passage into the underworld. As it proceeds in its course, it unites with the Sun at the conjunction. Remember, the word synodic, or "union", is derived from *sunodos*, and also means "sexual union". The protected space at the heart of the Sun is the *sanctum sanctorum*, the innermost holy chamber of the mystery initiations. Here, the union of a planet or star with the Sun represents the seminal impregnation and regeneration. The rebirth occurs at the heliacal rise, as the planet emerges from the womb of the solar rays.

In the mythology of Mercury, one of Hermēs' epithets was *psuchopompos*, "psychopomp", the guide of souls into and out of the underworld. This aspect of the the god's nature corresponds to the journey undertaken during the Mercury retrograde cycle as he descends into Hadēs, leading the souls of the dead through the hidden realm, where the great mystery of divine sexual union takes place. This is followed by rebirth at the heliacal morning rising.

Venus, in her Sumerian form as Inanna, likewise makes a descent into the underworld to attend the funeral of her brother-in-law, where she dies and is reborn. This epic journey corresponds to Venus' retrograde, where she disappears behind the Sun, transitioning from her heliacal set as evening star to her heliacal rise as morning star, representing regeneration from death.

From the perspective of traditional astrology, the ordinary interpretation of a planet under the beams is one of weakening and debilitating, except when the planet is in its chariot or in the heart. The extraordinary interpretation of this secret obscuration is that of the initiation chamber, where a fundamental death, regeneration, and rebirth occurs relative to that planetary function. For Mercury and Venus, this is during the retrograde conjunction. For Mars, Jupiter, and Saturn, it takes place during the direct conjunction.

In modern astrology, a planet conjunct the Sun is often interpreted in a very positive manner. The archetypal nature of the planet is merged with the basic solar identity and purpose of the individual. A person becomes more Jovian, Mercurial, or Venusian. The traditional perspective is that the Sun takes up and

14   PTOLEMY, *Phaseis* 5.

absorbs the qualities of the planet, so that the Sun is strengthened. The planets' energies are still being expressed, albeit through the agency of the Sun. However, the significations of a planet under the beams have greater difficulty in coming about, or they occur in ways that are ineffectual for the individual in terms of what the planet itself represents. This also extends to its activities in the houses it occupies or rules, as well as its ability to provide for any planets in its domiciles.

SUMMARY

1. If a planet is visible, it is able to manifest its significations and events.

2. If a planet is invisible, its significations and effects do not appear, do not come to anything, or may not be apparent to the external observer.

3. All the planets are invisible if they are within fifteen degrees on either side of the Sun. In addition, Mars, Jupiter, and Saturn are invisible on the horizon if they are within seven-and-a-half degrees on either side of the opposition to the Sun.

4. If a planet is invisible, check to see if it is "in the heart" of the Sun. This orb is one degree on either side of the Sun according to Hellenistic astrologers, and seventeen minutes according to Medieval astrologers. If this is the case, it is protected from being weakened by the Sun's rays.

5. If the planet is in its own domicile, exaltation, triplicity, or bound, it is "in its chariot" and thus protected from the weakening power of the Sun's rays.

→   EXAMPLE CHARTS

Let us now turn to our example charts to determine if any planets are invisible.

CHART I: SOLAR PHASE CONDITIONS

Planet	Speed	Direction	Station within 7 days	Visibility, chariot, heart
☉	N/A	N/A	N/A	N/A
♃	Faster than average	Direct	—	Visible
♄	Very slow	Retrograde	—	Visible
☿	Very fast	Direct	—	Under beams Combust Invisible
☽	N/A	N/A	N/A	N/A
♀	Average	Direct	—	Visible
♂	Faster than average	Direct	—	Visible

ANALYSIS

Our attention is drawn to MERCURY, which is under the beams of the SUN, actually combust within the three-degree orb, and in direct motion. While still of the morning, MERCURY, like Icarus, is moving very fast towards crashing into the SUN. Mental overstimulation and fragmentation, recklessness, and brilliant illumination are all possible expressions of this condition. The house topics that MERCURY rules may not be apparent to the outside observer.

CHART II: SOLAR PHASE CONDITIONS

Planet	Speed	Direction	Station within 7 days	Visibility, chariot, heart
☉	N/A	N/A	N/A	N/A
♃	Very slow	Retrograde	—	Visible
♄	Very slow	Retrograde	—	Invisible, curtailed passage
☿	Very slow	Direct	Rx on 10/29	Visible
☽	N/A	N/A	N/A	N/A
♀	Faster than average	Direct	—	Visible
♂	Slower than average	Direct	—	Visible

ANALYSIS

All the planets are visible, except for SATURN which is in curtailed passage. The seven-and-a-half degree orb of opposition to the SUN lends it an air of mystery and concealment. As ruler of the seventh house of relationships, we may wonder about this topic.

→ EXERCISE 19

Using your own chart, complete exercise 19:
Solar Phase Conditions

EXERCISE 19

SOLAR PHASE CONDITIONS

In this exercise, you will examine whether each planet is visible when rising or setting on the horizon, or if it is invisible under the Sun's beams. If so, you will check to see if it is in its chariot or in the heart of the Sun.

Planet	Speed	Direction	Station within 7 days	Visibility, chariot, heart
☉	N/A	N/A	N/A	N/A
♃				
♄				
☿				
☽	N/A	N/A	N/A	N/A
♀				
♂				

1. VISIBILITY: *If the planet is visible, enter "visible". If the planet is not visible when rising over the horizon, i.e., within fifteen degrees before or after the Sun, enter "USB" (under the Sun's beams), or "CP" ("in curtailed passage") if the planet is within seven-and-a-half degrees on either side of the opposition to the Sun.*

2. CHARIOT: *If a planet is USB or CP, check to see if it is in its chariot (domicile, exaltation, triplicity, bound).*

3. HEART: *If a planet is USB, check to see if it is "in the heart" of the Sun (Hellenistic: one degree on either side of the Sun; Medieval: seventeen minutes on either side of the Sun).*

REFLECTION AND ANALYSIS

1. Which planets, if any, are under the beams of the Sun or in curtailed passage?

2. Do you experience a weakening, secretiveness, or mystery associated with them?

3. Are any of these invisible planets in the heart of the Sun or in their chariots?

CHAPTER 24

Planetary Phases

———

And when the stars happen to be upon their morning risings, they are considered effective and active from the time of youth, bringing forth their own significations. But when they are making their evening risings, they operate after the passage of time in bringing forth their own significations. But when they are making their morning or evening concealments (under the Sun's beams) or retracing their paths (retrograde) or declining, the outcomes of their actions are weak, idle, and insignificant. — PAULUS.[1]

WE HAVE EXPLORED THE SYNODIC CYCLE IN TERMS OF A PLANET'S SPEED, direction, and visibility. We now turn to the phase intervals themselves, as well as the unique moments when the planets make the transitions into these phases. Each phase transition represents a dynamic shift that occurs when a planet either *first appears* at the horizon after a prolonged absence, or when the planet *first disappears* at the horizon after having been visible for a period of time. The retrograde and direct stations in the solar phase cycle also act as pivotal transition points between the phases.

The first and last appearance of a celestial body figured prominently in the astral religions of antiquity. In Egyptian astral theology, the first appearance of a star at its heliacal morning rising on the eastern horizon was seen as the rebirth of the star after its period of invisibility. Later, this appearance was identified as the place of rebirth of pharaohs and then of mortals whose souls were embodied in stars after death. The last appearance of the star sinking into the western horizon was likened to the death of the star and the death of souls who then embarked upon their netherworldly passage.

The star Sirius, personified as the goddess Isis, would disappear for seventy days in each annual cycle. Egyptian religion believed seventy to be the number of days that a soul journeyed through the underworld. The heliacal rising of Sirius

PAULUS, *Introduction* 14.

around the same time each summer heralded the annual flooding of the Nile River, which regenerated the land. Thus, this event also marked the beginning of the Egyptian New Year with great celebrations. Other stars that had the same pattern of visibility at the heliacal rise and invisibility at the heliacal set as Sirius did were codified as the decan stars, which measured the length of the night and the year.

In Babylonian cosmology, the planets were understood as one of the manifestations of the gods. When a planet made a heliacal morning appearance after a time of absence from the skies, it was as if the planetary god was coming out of seclusion to make an announcement to humanity concerning its intentions. This moment can be compared to a yogi coming out of his cave after years of spiritual retreat to give a blessing, the Pope opening the doors of his balcony after a time of intensive prayer to give a benediction, or the King and Queen emerging from their palace to give a dispensation. The power and awe of these ritual moments is the power accorded to the appearance of a planet or star making its heliacal rising.

Phase comes from the Greek word *phasis* which has two distinct meanings. The first refers to an appearance—specifically an appearance of stars above the horizon (from the verb *phainō*, "to appear"). The second meaning has to do with an utterance—something that is said or asserted (from the verb *phēmi*, "to say, declare"). Both of these usages were reflected in ancient Babylonian astrology, where the first appearance of a planet on the horizon was understood as the appearance of that corresponding planetary deity who had emerged to utter a pronouncement about some matter under its jurisdiction. This visual phenomenon was seen as an omen, and marked a significant moment. Robert Schmidt employed the term *phasis* to refer to these critical moments in the solar phase cycle as "an appearance that speaks".[2] Visually, the planet bursts forth as a sudden flash of light on the horizon. This was considered to be an auspicious omen, and any births that took place near this time were invested with a special eminence.

→   REFER TO FIGURE 40

Solar Phase Cycle of the Superior Planets: Mars, Jupiter, and Saturn (chapter 21, page 257)

There are four distinct phases in the synodic cycle for the superior planets Mars, Jupiter, and Saturn. These are the lying hidden phase, the morning star phase, the acronychal phase, and the evening star phase. The transition from

2   Personal communication/teaching.

one phase to the next is a critical *phasis*-like moment, where the dynamic energy of the planet is intensified as it makes its transitional shifts. These transitional *phasis* moments are the *heliacal rise*, when the planet transitions from its lying hidden phase to its morning star phase (B); the *first station*, when the planet turns retrograde and transitions from the morning star phase to the acronychal phase (E); the *second station*, when the planet transitions from the acronychal phase to the evening star phase (G); and the *heliacal set*, when the planet transitions from the evening star phase to the lying hidden phase (J).

→   REFER TO FIGURE 42

Solar Phase Cycle of Inferior Planets Mercury and Venus
(chapter 21, page 260)

Mercury and Venus have three distinct phases—the lying hidden phase (which occurs twice in their synodic cycle); the morning star phase; and the evening star phase. However, in addition to their heliacal rise and heliacal set, they have two additional phase transitions in their cycles. Unlike the superior planets, they also make a morning setting and an evening rising. The transitional shifts in their cycles are thus the *heliacal morning rise*, as they transition from the lying hidden phase to the morning star phase (B); the *morning set*, when they transition from the morning star phase to the lying hidden phase (D); the *evening star rise*, when they transition from the lying hidden phase to the evening star phase (F); and the *heliacal evening set*, when they transition from the evening star phase to the lying hidden phase (H).

INTERPRETING THE PHASES

Let us now turn to our discussion of planetary phases relative to the Sun. Most of what we learn will be focused upon the effects of the planetary phases in this temporal world. However, in order to participate in the greater mystery, keep in mind the deeper spiritual significance associated with a planet's first appearance after having been hidden, and its last appearance before withdrawing into concealment once again.

Paulus of Alexandria tells us that when planets are in their morning star rising phase, they are "effective and active from the time of youth in relation to their specific significations"; and when they are in their evening star rising phase, they are "effective regarding their own significations with the passage of time".[3]

During a planet's passage through its morning or evening star phase, it is visible, direct in motion, and fast in speed. All these factors contribute to its effectiveness in bringing about its significations. To the extent that the heliacal morning rise is equated to the rebirth of a star or planet relative to its solar phase cycle, the activity of morning stars was thought to begin early and continue throughout the life. By contrast, the activity of evening star risings emerged later in life as the person matured.

Paulus adds that when planets are making their morning or evening disappearances or are retracing their path, their influences are useless, unfavorable for action, and insignificant.[4] The main difficulty for planets when passing through the lying hidden phase is that even though they may be fast, they are invisible and their significations cannot be seen and made manifest. There is also a secondary problem of weakening and debilitation that comes from proximity to the heat of the Sun. The acronychal phase slows down and reverses the action of a planet due to the retrograde motion. And for the inferior planets, Mercury and Venus, there is a double indemnity during one of their lying hidden phases when they are not only weakened from the Sun, but also retrograde—moving slowly in reverse direction.

Paulus goes on to say that planets are "weak and ineffective relative to their own matters when they are distant from the Sun within nine degrees or less".[5] While Paulus gives us the fifteen-degree distance from the Sun as one boundary that demarcates a planet's capacity to be effective and active, he also gives us the nine-degree interval from the Sun as demarcating the ineffective and inactive condition. The Medieval authors distinguished between a planet being under the rays at fifteen degrees, but entering into the combust zone at the eighth-to-ninth degree interval. This leaves us with a "grey area" between nine and fifteen degrees from the Sun, where a planet may be weak but not totally ineffective.

This occurs during the lying hidden phase, where a planet may indeed be ineffective at bringing about outer matters because it is in the stage of its cycle where release, regeneration, and the movement toward rebirth occur—the great mystery of transformation from death unto life renewed. However, both Hellenistic and Medieval traditions acknowledge the extremely potent qualities of the planet in exact union with the Sun (*cazimi*) during its lying hidden phase.

3   PAULUS, *Introduction* 14.
4   He is referring here to Mars, Jupiter, and Saturn making a heliacal evening setting into the lying hidden phase; Mercury and Venus making their morning setting into the lying hidden phase; and Mars, Jupiter, and Saturn when retrograding in their acronychal phase.
5   PAULUS, *Introductory Matters* 14

Let us now turn to the moments of the phase transitions themselves, which were imbued with such great potency and significance. These are the intervals in the synodic cycle when the planets make their risings, settings, and stations. On one hand, the Hellenistic astrologers standardized the interval for a planet rising and setting to fifteen degrees from the Sun. But they were aware of the individual variations for each planet due to its intrinsic brightness, as well as geographical latitude and atmospheric conditions. This may be their reasoning for isolating a seven-day interval before and after a heliacal rise or set as conferring an intensified quality to a planet's energy. This situation can also be extended to Mercury and Venus when they make their morning set and evening rise. In these situations, a person's life is saturated with the significations of that planet, for better or worse.

DETERMINING PHASIS

In order to determine the possibility of the *phasis* condition, you must consult an ephemeris.[6] Find the day of the birth. Then count seven days forward and seven days backward. This is the interval you are examining. For *each individual day* of those fifteen days, calculate how many degrees exist between the Sun and the planet being investigated *on that day*. You are looking for a specific day when there are *exactly fifteen degrees* between the planet and the Sun. If you find such a day, then you know that the planet made its rise or set on that day.

While Mars, Jupiter, and Saturn will always be emerging from the Sun's rays when they make their heliacal rise (fifteen degrees ahead of the Sun) and sinking back under the rays at their heliacal set (fifteen degrees behind the Sun), this is not the case for Mercury and Venus. If you find Mercury and Venus at this fifteen-degree interval, you must also determine if they are emerging from under the Sun's beams at their heliacal rise after having recently made the inferior conjunction with the Sun, or whether they are sinking back under the beams at their morning set as they approach the forthcoming superior conjunction with the Sun.

A similar situation exists in distinguishing between their evening rising after their superior conjunction with the Sun, and their heliacal set when they are approaching the inferior conjunction with the Sun. All four possibilities will have a fifteen-degree interval. Each situation has a different interpretation.

---

6   Some astrology software programs, such as Delphic Oracle, tabulate the day when a planet makes its heliacal rise and set, but most of them do not.

INTERPRETING PHASIS

1. If Mercury or Venus are *ahead* of the Sun, and the interval of the daily motion between the Sun and the planet is increasing on several consecutive days, then the planet is moving *away from the Sun* towards its emergence from the beams at its heliacal rise.

2. If Mercury or Venus are *ahead* of the Sun, and the interval of the daily motion between the Sun and the planet is decreasing on several consecutive days, then the planet is moving *towards* the Sun and going *into the beams* at its morning setting.

3. If Mercury or Venus are *behind* the Sun, and the interval of the daily motion between the Sun and the planet is increasing on several consecutive days, then the planet is *moving away from the superior conjunction with the Sun* towards its emergence from under the beams.

4. If Mercury or Venus are *behind* the Sun, and the interval of the daily motion between the Sun and planet is decreasing on several consecutive days, then the planet is *moving towards the inferior conjunction with the Sun*, and sinking under the beams at its heliacal set.

When a planet is at the fifteen-degree rise or set interval, its significations are intensified and saturate the native's life. But depending upon whether it is rising or setting, the intensification is either strengthening or weakening. When a planet is making its rise, it is intense and tends towards strength. When it is making its set, it is still intense, but tends towards weakness.[7]

A *phasis* of Mercury may overwhelm a person's life with piles of books, papers, words, ideas, communications, or business dealings. Venus in this state may bring endless relationship activity, strong sexual drive, and excessive concern with beauty, fashion, or creative endeavors. A *phasis* of Saturn can denote huge and enduring responsibilities, laborious work, and constricting circumstances.

If the planet is in good condition, this intensification can be for the better. However, if the planet is in poor condition, especially if it is a malefic, the potential for difficulty is increased or unrelenting. Given the understanding that

---

7   In order to get a sense of the difference between "intense" and its opposite, "slack", imagine the following contrast. A planet that is intensified is similar to attending a major five-day astrology conference with every moment suffused with classes, networking, meals, parties, and conversations with friends and colleagues. The slack condition consists in lounging and napping by the side of a pool all day and occasionally rolling over into the water or sipping a drink.

the rising of a planet, whether it is a heliacal morning rising for the superiors, or an evening rising for the inferiors, is a condition of strengthening, it follows that a planet is made stronger for effective outcomes. But if the planet is making its heliacal evening setting for the superiors, or the morning setting for the inferiors, the intensification weakens the effectiveness of the planet in accordance with its nature.

In the writings of the Medieval authors, the planets were considered to be especially strong when they first emerged from under the Sun's beams and were in direct motion. They were compared to "someone who has emerged victorious from a battle" and "an ill person who has survived an illness and is restored to full health and vigor".[8] The Medieval astrologers seemed to prefer the evening risings of Mercury and Venus because they were moving fast in direct motion, rather than their morning risings when they were just beginning to gain speed after their retrograde. By contrast, when the planets were moving in direct motion towards the Sun's rays, it was like a person impeded by an illness where they cannot help themselves without the aid of another; for the superior planets, it was likened to a person in flight, tiring, who fears they cannot escape their pursuer.[9]

In summary, when evaluating the condition of a planet in terms of its solar phase, first determine if it is effective as either a morning star or evening star phase, or ineffective as a lying hidden or acronychal phase. This will indicate how effective it is in bringing about its matters. Second, note if the planet is making a heliacal rising or heliacal setting within seven days on either side of the birth. For Mercury and Venus, note if the morning setting or the evening rising occurs within this interval. If the planet is in one of the *phasis* conditions, the intensity of its significations saturate the life for better or worse.

→ EXAMPLE CHARTS: PHASE AND PHASIS

For each planet, we will now examine whether it is a morning star phase, evening star phase, acronychal phase, or lying hidden phase. We will then check the ephemeris to see whether it made its heliacal rise or set, its morning set, or its evening rise, within seven days on either side of the birth. If so, we will enter that notation in the phasis column.

8   BONATTI, *Book of Astronomy* 5.54; 3.2.5, trans. DYKES.
9   BONATTI, *Book of Astronomy* 5.56; 3.2.8, trans. DYKES.

CHART I: PHASE AND PHASIS

Planet	Phase	Phasis within 7 days
SUN	N/A	N/A
JUPITER	Morning star	—
SATURN	Acronychal	—
MERCURY	Lying hidden	—
MOON	N/A	N/A
VENUS	Morning star	—
MARS	Evening star	—

ANALYSIS

JUPITER is strong and effective because it is a morning star and thus rejoices. It is more than 15° ahead of the Sun but not yet within the 120° retrograde station area. It is too far from the Sun to have made a heliacal rise within seven days of the birth.

SATURN is ineffective, due to being in the acronychal phase, where it is retrograde. It is too far from the Sun to have made a rise or set within seven days of the birth. However, because it is of the evening, behind the Sun near its trine, we know that it is heading towards its direct station, which occurs a month later. Even though it is in a weakened condition, it is slowly gaining strength.

MERCURY is of the morning, under the Sun's beams, and thus ineffective in the lying-hidden zone. It does not make a morning set or evening rise at 15° from the Sun during the fifteen-day interval period, so it does not have any additional qualities of intensification.

VENUS is strong and effective as a morning star, although she does not rejoice because she is of the nocturnal sect and ahead of the Sun. She is more than 15° from the Sun; in fact she is 43° distant, near her greatest morning elongation, so she is nowhere near the rising or setting point of her cycle, where a phase transition might occur. An inferior planet is often most effective near its greatest elongation from the Sun.

MARS is strong and effective as it is an evening star. He is more than 15° from the Sun; in fact he is almost forty degrees distant, so is nowhere near the seven-day interval for the setting-point of his cycle, where a phase transition might occur (the heliacal set occurs on October 14).

Thus, Jupiter, Venus, and Mars are all effective by phase. Saturn and Mercury are ineffective and weakened according to solar phase criteria.

CHART II: PHASE AND PHASIS

Planet	Phase	Phasis within 7 days
SUN	N/A	N/A
JUPITER	Acronychal	—
SATURN	Acronychal	—
MERCURY	Evening star	Heliacal set, phase transition
MOON	N/A	N/A
VENUS	Morning star	—
MARS	Morning star	—

ANALYSIS

JUPITER AND SATURN, both retrograde, are in their acronychal phases. Thus, they are ineffective according to the solar phase criteria. Saturn is also in the curtailed passage zone and cannot be seen rising as the Sun sets. This reduces his capacity to make his significations visible and manifest.

VENUS AND MARS are both effective as morning stars, but because they belong to the nocturnal sect, they do not rejoice in this zone. They have cleared the fifteen-degree distance from the Sun, and are nowhere near their stations, so they do not make any phase transition intensifications.

MERCURY is effective in an evening star phase, and he also rejoices in this interval because he belongs to the nocturnal sect. He is 22° from the Sun. However, he will make the heliacal set on November 1, when he will be exactly 15°

from the conjunction with the Sun while he is in retrograde motion (Sun 8°
Scorpio, Mercury 23° Scorpio retrograde). Thus, Mercury has a phase transition intensification condition on the seventh day after the birth. Mercury is effective, intensely saturating the life with mercurial significations, but is rapidly
approaching his weakening, both through retrograde and heliacal set. Mercury
flashes with great intensity, then crashes.

→ EXERCISE 20

Using your own chart, complete exercise 20:
Phase and Phasis

EXERCISE 20

PHASE AND PHASIS

For each planet you will determine if it is in a morning star phase, evening star phase, acronychal phase, or lying-hidden phase. Check the ephemeris to see if it made its heliacal rise or set, its morning set, or its evening rise within seven days on either side of the birth.

Planet	Phase	Phasis within 7 days
SUN	N/A	N/A
JUPITER		
SATURN		
MERCURY		
MOON	N/A	N/A
VENUS		
MARS		

1. *Phase for Mars, Jupiter, Saturn: Enter the phase of the planet as:*

    LYING HIDDEN (within 15° before or after the Sun)
    MORNING STAR (15 – ~120° ahead of the Sun)
    ACRONYCHAL (~120° ahead of Sun/retrograde station – ~120° behind the
    Sun/direct station)
    EVENING STAR (~120° behind the Sun/direct station – 15° behind Sun)

2. *Phase for Mercury and Venus: Enter the phase of the planet as:*

    LYING HIDDEN (within 15° before or after the Sun either at the superior
    direct conjunction of the planet with the Sun or at the inferior retrograde
    conjunction)
    MORNING STAR (15° distant after the retrograde conjunction at the morn-
    ing rising before the Sun through to the greatest elongation to 15° distant
    from the Sun, when it makes its morning setting as it approaches the supe-
    rior direct conjunction)
    EVENING STAR (15° distant from the Sun after the superior direct conjunc-
    tion as it makes its evening rise through to its greatest elongation as an eve-
    ning star until 15° distant from the Sun, when it makes its evening heliacal
    setting on its way towards the retrograde conjunction)

3. *Phasis (intermediate/advanced): Enter whether a planet has made its exact
    rise or set within seven days before or after the birth:*

    ALL PLANETS: Heliacal rise (exact 15° distance between the planet as it
    moves ahead of the Sun, increasing its distance after its conjunction with
    the Sun within seven days before or after the birth)
    MERCURY AND VENUS ONLY: Evening rise (exact 15° distance between the
    planet and the Sun as it moves away from its superior direct conjunction
    towards it greatest evening elongation within seven days before or after the
    birth)
    MERCURY AND VENUS ONLY: Morning set (exact 15° distance between the
    planet and the Sun from its greatest morning elongation as it moves towards
    its superior conjunction within seven days before or after the birth)
    ALL PLANETS: Heliacal set (exact 15° distance between the planet and the
    Sun as it moves from its greatest evening elongation towards the conjunc-
    tion with the Sun within seven days before or after the birth)

REFLECTION AND ANALYSIS

1. Which planets are effective as either morning star or evening star phases?

2. Which planets are ineffective because they are in their acronychal phase or lying-hidden phase?

3. Do you experience *ease* with activating the matters of the planets that are effective as morning or evening stars, or do you *struggle* to get action and external results with planets that are lying hidden or acronychal?

4. Are any planets in a phase transition condition of intensification, making their actual rising or setting within seven days before or seven days after the birth?

5. How does this add intensity to the expression of the planet? Do the significations of that planet saturate and overwhelm your life? Do you experience sudden awakenings or shifts in your understanding concerning the significations of this planet?

CHAPTER 25

Final Overview

OF THE SOLAR PHASE CYCLE

——

LET US GO THROUGH THE VARIOUS STAGES OF THE SYNODIC SOLAR PHASE cycle one more time with the keys for interpretation in order to fix it in our understanding. By now, you should begin to feel comfortable with this material. We will then do our final evaluation for each planet's condition based upon solar phase criteria. Make sure you refer to FIGURE 40 (*Solar Phase Cycle of the Superior Planets: Mars, Jupiter, and Saturn,* page 257) and FIGURE 42 (*Solar Phase Cycle of the Inferior Planets: Mercury and Venus,* page 260) in chapter 21.

SUPERIOR PLANETS: MARS, JUPITER, SATURN

LYING-HIDDEN PHASE: The cycle begins in the middle of the lying-hidden phase at the conjunction of the planet with the Sun. Immediately afterwards, the planet is *of the morning*, although not yet visible. When a planet is within one degree (Hellenistic) or seventeen minutes (Medieval) of the Sun, it is said to be *in the heart of the Sun* and to indicate everything good. As the distance between the planet and the Sun increases to about 8–12° degrees, it is in the combust zone. The planet is moving very fast, making it active, but it is simultaneously being burned up, debilitated, and weakened by the heat. In the glare of the Sun, the planet is lost from sight and thus unable to manifest its significations. From a distance of 12–15° degrees, the planet begins to emerge from under the Sun's beams, still weak, but with recovery in sight. When passing through this lying-hidden phase, with the exception of being in the heart of the Sun, the planet is generally weak, ineffective, and its significations do not eventuate or cannot be seen.

HELIACAL RISE TRANSITION: When a superior planet is 15° from the Sun, it rises heliacally, emerging in the eastern sky as a morning star, and is visible near the horizon. This is its first *phasis* moment, when it transitions from the lying-hidden phase to the morning-star phase. If this occurs within seven days before or after a person's birth, the planet is intensified.

MORNING-STAR PHASE: As this phase begins, the planet is symbolically reborn, regenerated, and filled with vigor and strength. It is moving with faster than average speed, in direct motion, visible, and its greatest strength occurs in the proximity of the 60° sextile aspect with the Sun. Moving with average speed around the square aspect, and hence an average level of activity, it begins to slow down and reduce its efficacy as it approaches the first station near the trine aspect with the Sun. When passing through the morning star phase from 15° ahead of the Sun to the first station at around 120° ahead of the Sun, a planet is very strong and effective in bringing about its significations.

RETROGRADE-STATION TRANSITION: When a superior planet makes its first station, it has experienced its second *phasis* moment. Standing still, its energy is intensified with unwavering focus and concentration. If this station occurs within seven days before or after a person's birth, it is as if it is making its last stand and show of strength before retreating.

ACRONYCHAL PHASE: The planet turns retrograde, weakening and losing its power and strength. It is moving extremely slowly in backwards zodiacal direction and appears to make a loop in the sky. The planet experiences difficulty and reversals in bringing about its agenda. At the same time, the Sun is moving ahead in the zodiacal sequence and comes to oppose the planet. The planet temporarily speeds up when opposite the Sun, indicating confusion and hopes that do not materialize. This disorientation is coincident with it being in curtailed passage when 7½° on either side of the opposition. During curtailed passage, the planet is not visible when rising over the eastern horizon after dusk, or setting on the western horizon as dawn approaches, although it can be seen in the sky during the remaining parts of the night. It is the lack of visibility on the horizon that further undermines the actions of the retrograde superior planet. Once the planet passes the opposition point to the Sun, it is said to be *of the evening*. And after the curtailed passage degree, it can be seen rising and setting again in the evening sky. However, the planet is still retrograde and remains weak, ineffective, and powerless in the acronychal phase until its direct station, when it is around 120° behind the Sun.

DIRECT-STATION TRANSITION: The planet once again stands still at its second station as it is about to turn direct. This is its third *phasis* moment, and if this station occurs within seven days before or after a person's birth, it brings a focused, concentrated intensity to the planet's matters. This is its "comeback" moment.

EVENING-STAR PHASE: As it resumes its direct motion, the planet begins to gain speed and its power returns. The superior planets are generally active and effective during their evening star phase, because they are increasing in speed, direct in motion, and visible. However, the Medieval authors point out that they are not truly strong, but simply less weak than during their acronychal phase. The best indications for the superior planets are said to occur during their morning-star phase. The planet in the evening-star phase slowly diminishes in strength after the 90° square with the Sun. Even though it is moving very fast as it approaches the 60° sextile aspect, it progressively sinks closer to the western horizon on each successive night and becomes dimmer in appearance. Hence it is interpreted as moving towards weakening in its ability to bring about its effects.

HELIACAL-SET TRANSITION: When a superior planet is 15° behind the Sun, it sets heliacally, disappearing at sunset in the western sky near the horizon for a number of days. This is its fourth and final *phasis* moment, when it transitions from the evening-star phase to the lying-hidden phase. Check to see if this occurs within seven days before or after the birth.

LYING-HIDDEN PHASE: The superior planet is now in the segment of its cycle that corresponds to the death and dissolution stage of the lying-hidden phase, when none of its power remains. Moving with increasing speed, it is nevertheless obscured from sight. Hence, it is weak and ineffective in bringing about its external events, but hurtling into the womb of renewal as it approaches the throne, where it will conjoin the Sun to be revivified in the mystery chamber.

INFERIOR PLANETS: MERCURY AND VENUS

LYING-HIDDEN PHASE: This conjunction is the moment of the great mystery. Once the distance between the planet and the Sun extends beyond this interval, the planet finds itself in the fiery crucible of the combust zone, both moving slower and burning up, where it is ineffective, weak, and unable to manifest its significations. From 12°–15° degrees ahead of the Sun, the inferior planet begins to emerge from under the Sun's beams and comes to a standstill.

HELIACAL-RISE TRANSITION: The first phasis moment is an auspicious omen announcing the planet's rebirth and increase in strength. Here the planet's significations are intensified in the life if the heliacal rise occurs within seven days before or after the birth.

MORNING-STAR PHASE: The morning star designation for Mercury and Venus is limited to the duration from their heliacal morning rise to their morning set. During this time, they are visible, direct in motion, and gaining in speed and thus generally effective in bring about their significations, strongest around their greatest elongation.

MORNING-SETTING TRANSITION: The second *phasis* moment occurs when an inferior planet makes its last appearance as morning star in the eastern sky, and begins to sink under the Sun's rays. It is always in direct motion when making its morning setting. The planet's significations are intensified, but now tending towards weakening.

LYING-HIDDEN PHASE: The inferior planet is now entering into its second lying hidden phase. It is invisible, but this time moving extremely fast and direct in motion as contrasted to the first lying-hidden phase, when it is slow and retrograde. Invisible and debilitated, the inferior planet has difficulty bringing forth its agendas.

EVENING-RISING TRANSITION: The evening rising near the western horizon just after sunset is the third *phasis* moment. It is once again intensified, but now moving into the strongest segment of its cycle.

EVENING-STAR PHASE: The evening-star phase in general supports a planet's effectiveness in bringing about its matters with the first part of it better than the second part. This phase ends at the heliacal set.

HELIACAL-SET TRANSITION: This is its fourth and final *phasis* moment. The combination of heliacal set and retrograde station gives a double intensification to its significations, but now the tendency is toward its ultimate weakness.

LYING-HIDDEN PHASE: The planet now descends into the lying-hidden phase; it is very slow, and retrograde in motion. This segment closes its cycle as it is the dissolution stage of the cyclic process. On the ordinary level, it is inactive, ineffective, and powerless, as it is devoid of vital life-force in actualizing its significations. However, on the extraordinary level, it is bringing its matters to closure and completion, and distilling the essence into the seed that will be fertilized at the inferior conjunction and reborn at the heliacal rising.

IN SUMMARY, when evaluating the condition of a planet relative to its solar phase, the *best condition* is for a planet to be fast in speed, direct in motion, visible, and in the morning or evening star interval, preferably in accordance with its sect. The *worst condition* is for a planet to be slow in speed, retrograde in motion, and invisible in the lying-hidden or acronychal phase. If a planet is in its chariot (occupying the sign of domicile, exaltation, triplicity, or bound), it is protected from the debilitating effect of excessive proximity to the Sun. A planet is also protected when "in the heart" of the Sun, within a one-degree orb on either side (or seventeen minutes, depending on your preference for Medieval or Hellenistic interpretation). When a planet makes a station, or makes an appearance or disappearance (exact rise or set within seven days before and after the birth), it adds an intensifying quality to the planet's energy and moves it towards strengthening or weakening.

→ EXAMPLE CHARTS

Looking to the example charts, let us make our final judgment for each planet relative to its solar phase conditions, and give the planet a grade.

CHART I: FINAL JUDGMENT OF SOLAR PHASE CONDITIONS

Planet	Speed	Direction	Station within 7 days	Visibility, chariot, heart	Phase	Phasis within 7 days	Judgment grade
☉	N/A	N/A	N/A	N/A	N/A	N/A	N/A
♃	Faster than average	Direct	—	Visible	Morning	—	A
♄	Very slow	Retrograde	—	Visible	Acronychal	—	C-
☿	Very fast	Direct	—	Under beams Combust Invisible	Lying hidden	—	D+/B
☽	N/A	N/A	N/A	N/A	N/A	N/A	N/A
♀	Average	Direct	—	Visible	Morning	—	B+
♂	Faster than average	Direct	—	Visible	Evening	—	A

ANALYSIS

JUPITER is faster than average, direct in motion, and is visible rising over the eastern horizon; he rejoices as a morning star at the most potent part of his cycle around the sextile aspect to the Sun. He is active and effective. Grade: A.

SATURN, of the evening, is very slow, retrograde in motion, but is visible setting on the western horizon. He is ineffective in the acronychal phase, and too far away from his direct station (which occurs a month later) for any intensification or significant tendency towards strengthening. Grade: C-.

MERCURY is of the morning, under the Sun's beams, and very close to the Sun in the combust zone. It is direct in motion and moving very fast. In a few days (July 31) it will make the exact conjunction with the Sun. It is debilitated and weakened by proximity with the Sun, and its invisibility obstructs its significations from becoming manifest, or they may occur hidden from the view of others. It does not make a morning set or evening rise during the fifteen-day interval period, so it does not have an additional intensification quality. Grade: D+. Some Medieval astrologers held that Mercury does not suffer from debilitation when conjunct the Sun in Leo or Aries—the signs of the Sun's domicile and exaltation; this consideration would raise Mercury's grade to perhaps a B.

VENUS is moving at average speed, direct in motion, and is visible as a morning star. While she is strong and effective in the morning-star phase, she does not rejoice because she is a nocturnal planet ahead of the Sun. She is 43° from the Sun in the region of her greatest morning elongation, so is full of potency. Venus is nowhere near the rising or setting point of her cycle, where a phase transition intensification might occur. Grade: B+.

MARS is traveling with faster-than-average speed, direct in motion, and is visible as an evening star. As a nocturnal-sect planet, he rejoices in this evening-star phase, where he is active and effective. Mars is nowhere near any *phasis* conditions, stations, or heliacal risings/settings, which would intensify his significations. Grade: A.

Jupiter, Venus, and Mars are all effective by phase. Saturn is ineffective, and Mercury has the greatest weakness.

CHART II: FINAL JUDGMENT OF SOLAR PHASE CONDITIONS

Planet	Speed	Direction	Station within 7 days	Visibility, chariot, heart	Phase	Phasis within 7 days	Judgment grade
☉	N/A	N/A	N/A	N/A	N/A	N/A	N/A
♃	Very slow	Retrograde	—	Visible	Achronychal	—	C-
♄	Very slow	Retrograde	—	Invisible, curtailed passage	Achronycal	—	D+
☿	Very slow	Direct	Rx on 10/29	Visible	Evening	Heliacal set, phase transition	B-
☽	N/A	N/A	N/A	N/A	N/A	N/A	N/A
♀	Average	Direct	—	Visible	Morning	—	B+
♂	Slower than average	Direct	—	Visible	Morning	—	B

ANALYSIS

JUPITER, of the morning, is extremely slow, retrograde, but visible in his acronychal phase. Thus, he is ineffective according to the solar phase criteria. C-.

SATURN, of the evening, is within 7½° of the opposition to the Sun. Thus, even though retrograde, he is moving faster than usual for a retrograde planet, but is also invisible in the curtailed-passage zone, unable to be seen rising in the east or setting in the west. He carries rebellious and unruly qualities, and is judged as active, but ineffective in the acronychal phase. Grade: D+.

MERCURY, of the evening, is moving quite slowly in direct motion, as he approaches his retrograde station in a few days. He is still visible, but will make his heliacal set on the seventh day after birth, placing him in double *phasis* conditions. Mercury remains mildly effective in this evening-star phase, intensely saturating the life with mercurial significations, but he is rapidly approaching weakening, through both retrograde and heliacal set. Grade: B-.

VENUS, of the morning, is moving at average speed, is direct in motion, and stretching towards her greatest elongation. While she is effective in the morning star phase, as a nocturnal sect planet, she does not rejoice. Grade: B+.

MARS, of the morning, is moving with slower-than-average speed, direct in motion, and is visible as a morning star. While effective in the morning star phase, as a nocturnal sect planet, Mars does not rejoice. Grade: B.

→   EXERCISE 21

Using your own chart, complete exercise 21:
Final Evaluations for Solar Phase Conditions

EXERCISE 21

FINAL EVALUATIONS FOR SOLAR PHASE CONDITIONS

In this exercise, review the previous entries and make a final evaluation for each planet based upon all of the solar phase criteria—speed, direction, visibility, and phase. Each of these factors influences the planet's condition and has an interpretive meaning. Use the following guidelines to help you arrive at your judgment.

Planet	Speed	Direction	Station within 7 days	Visibility, chariot, heart	Phase	Phasis within 7 days	Judgment grade
☉	N/A	N/A	N/A	N/A	N/A	N/A	N/A
♃							
♄							
☿							
☽	N/A	N/A	N/A	N/A	N/A	N/A	N/A
♀							
♂							

1. *Judgment:*

    A planet that is fast (active), direct (moving towards its goal), and visible (able to manifest its agenda) is in the best condition.
    A planet making a direct station, a heliacal rise or evening rise (becoming stronger after being weaker) increases its intensity in a positive manner.
    A planet that is slow (inactive), retrograde (moving in the opposite direction from its goal), and which is invisible under the Sun's beams (unable to manifest its agenda) predisposes it towards ineffective or weak outcomes.
    A planet that is in its chariot or in the heart of the Sun is protected from being weakened under the Sun's beams.
    A planet making a retrograde station, a heliacal set, or morning set also increases its intensity (in the direction of weakening), but towards more problematic outcomes.
    A planet that is in a morning or evening-star phase is more effective than in the lying-hidden or acronychal phases.

2. *Grade: Give each planet a grade:* A, B, C, D, *or* F, *with pluses or minuses.*

REFLECTION AND ANALYSIS

    1. Write a few sentences for each of the five planets, describing their solar phase and how it affects their condition and their capacity to bring about beneficial outcomes.

CHAPTER 26

The Synodic Cycle

AND THE MINOR YEARS OF THE PLANETS

———

THE SYNODIC CYCLE IS ALSO THE BASIS FOR THE HELLENISTIC TIMING procedure called the minor years of the planets. This is a subdivision of timing by planetary periods which includes the minor, mean, and greater years of the planets. Timing by the minor years was the most basic timing method used by almost every ancient astrologer. The minor years of the planets are derived from the confluence of a planet's tropical cycle with its synodic cycle.

As we mentioned earlier in this section, a planet's tropical period is the amount of time that it takes—as seen from Earth—for it to go all the way around the ecliptic (i.e., the circle of zodiacal signs). The synodic or solar phase cycle is the average amount of time between a planet's successive conjunctions with the Sun as seen from Earth, as well as its phases.

A Sun-planet conjunction occurs at a specific degree and sign of the zodiac. At the completion of its synodic cycle, the next conjunction will occur at a later sign and degree of the zodiac. A planet's minor years are the number of years it takes for the Sun-planet conjunction to progress in successive synodic cycles all the way around the ecliptic and then to return and reoccur at the very same degree of the zodiac as it did previously. For instance, if you look at the position of Venus in your solar return chart, it will be within several degrees of its natal position every eight years.

The minor years of each planet, sometimes called the "least" years, are as follows:

MERCURY	20 years
VENUS	8 years
MARS	15 years
JUPITER	12 years
SATURN	30 years
SUN	19 years
MOON	25 years

The minor years of the Sun and Moon are not based upon a synodic interval because the Sun itself is the reference point for the synodic cycle, and the Moon does not revolve around the Sun, but rather around the Earth. The Sun's minor years are based upon the nineteen-year Metonic eclipse cycle, when an eclipse recurs at the same degree of the zodiac. One speculation concerning the Moon's minor years are that they are the interval of time it takes for its phases to occur on the same days of the year.[1] These recurrences of the planets were first observed by the Babylonians and then imported into Hellenistic astrology as an important astrological timing device.

As a stand-alone method called "timing by planetary periods", the minor years indicate the times at which the significations of planets would fully mature, become busy, and bring forth their events. Moreover, Valens informs us that the planets become activated not only at the completion of their minor years, but also at one-third, halfway, and two-thirds through these periods. Remember, the critical points of the solar phase cycle are at the first station—one third of the way around the synodic cycle; the opposition—halfway through the cycle; and the second station—two-thirds of the way through the cycle.

The minor years of the planets also form a component of various time-lord procedures. Valens gives a brilliant exposition concerning the minor years of the planets in combination with the ascensional times of the zodiacal signs to discover the times at which planets becomes activated and bring about their events.[2] The minor years of the planets are also used in the time-lord system of zodiacal releasing from the Lots of Fortune and Spirit. As the process of releasing moves from one zodiacal sign to the next, the planet that is the domicile lord of each successive sign becomes a time lord, governing the affairs of the life for the duration of the period of its minor years.

The minor years of the planets are part of a larger system entailing the greater years and the mean years. The greater and mean years were used for inquiries concerning longer periods of time. The greater periods of the planets come from the total number of degrees allocated to each planet in the system of bounds or terms. We suspect that the greater years are also derived from longer successive cycles of the synodic cycle, but the mathematical algorithms have not yet been uncovered. The mean periods are an average derived from the minor and greater years.

1   Robert HAND, "Predictive Periods in Vettius Valens", in *Introduction* to Vettius VALENS, *Anthology* 2, translated by Robert SCHMIDT (Berkeley Springs, WV: Golden Hind Press, 1994).
2   VALENS, *Anthology* 7.

Table 21. Minor, Mean, and Greater Planetary Periods

	Moon	Mercury	Venus	Sun	Mars	Jupiter	Saturn
MINOR	25	20	8	19	15	12	30
MEAN	66.5	48	45	69.5	40.5	45.5	43.3
GREATER	108	76	82	120	66	79	57

CHAPTER 27

Summary

AND SOURCE READINGS

———

A PLANET'S SPEED, DIRECTION, VISIBILITY, AND PHASE ARE ALL factors of its synodic cycle with the Sun.

A planet is effective in bringing about its significations when it is fast, direct, visible, and in a morning or evening star phase. It is intensified, and growing stronger, when it is making a morning or evening rising, or stationing direct within seven days either side of the birth.

A planet is less effective when it is slow, retrograde, invisible, and in the lying-hidden or acronychal phase. It is intensified, and growing weaker, when it makes an evening or morning set and a retrograde station within seven days either side of the birth.

The minor years of the planets are derived from their recurrence synodic cycle with the Sun.

PRIMARY SOURCE READINGS
FOR PART THREE: THE SOLAR PHASE CYCLE

DOROTHEUS	*Carmen* 1.29.7 (trans. Dykes): (Excerpt on retrograde).
PTOLEMY	*Phaseis* (trans. Schmidt): The Phases of the Fixed Stars (Berkeley Springs, WV: Golden Hind Press, 1993).
ANTIOCHUS	*Summary* 15: Rising and Setting.
PORPHYRY	*Introduction* 2: Changes Produced by the Transfers of the Sun, Moon, and Stars.
FIRMICUS	*Mathesis* 2.12–15 (trans. Holden): When the Stars are Matutine and when Vespertine.
PAULUS	*Introduction* 14: The Phases which the Five Stars make with the Sun. *Introduction* 15: Stations.

RHETORIUS   *Compendium* 25 (trans. Holden): Stars under the Sun's Beams.
               Compendium 43: Chariots.
IBN EZRA   *Beginning of Wisdom* 6; 8.89–98 (trans. Epstein).
BONATTI   *Book of Astronomy* 3.2.5 (trans Dykes): When the Planets are said to
               be Oriental, and when Occidental.
               Book of Astronomy 3.2.6: Of the Two Inferiors, when they are Oriental
               and when Occidental.
               Book of Astronomy 5: Considerations 52–54.

PART FOUR

THE LUNAR PHASE CYCLE

CHAPTER 28

Special Lunar Considerations

———

All the substance of the human body is ruled by the power of this divinity [i.e., the Moon] and by her courses, she sustains the form of the body. — FIRMICUS MATERNUS.[1]

THE MOON WAS ELEVATED AS QUEEN OF THE HEAVENS WHO ILLUMINATED the night sky with her waxing and waning light. However, the Moon was also the planet that was closest to the Earth, and as such, she presided over everything in the sublunary realm—including both the atmosphere, and all life on Earth. According to the Hellenistic astrologers, the Sun governed the seasons of the year, but the Moon arranged the four weeks of the month and the hours of the day.

In their search to identify the primal substance of the cosmos, ancient Greek philosophers posited that the heavenly realm was made of a divine substance called *aithēr*, while the terrestrial realm was composed of the four elements of fire, earth, air, and water. These four *elements* were in a continual state of transformation, changing into one another due to the four *qualities* of hot, cold, wet, and dry. It was the heating and cooling activity of the Sun and Moon that caused the elemental changes on Earth. Because humans were also composed of these same four elements, the Moon, being the closer of the two lights, had a direct role in the changes affecting the health and illness of human bodies. Ancient physicians held that a balance of the elements and qualities within the human body led to the state of optimal health, while imbalance predisposed one toward illness.

The Moon was intimately connected to all vegetative and human life and its cyclical processes of birth, growth, decay, and renewal, which were mirrored in her phases. Porphyry wrote how the Moon's wetness was thought to cause the swelling and ripening of plants. The Moon regulated the flows of women's monthly menses and that of rivers, springs, and seas, as well as maritime

1   FIRMICUS MATERNUS, *Mathesis* 4.1, trans. HOLDEN.

creatures, which all change with the increasing and decreasing nature of the Moon.[2] Above all, she was the main significator of conception and the health and illnesses of the human body. More than that, all prosperity and fortune related to the creature comforts of life were also under her dominion.

Many spiritual teachings hold that the body is the temple of the soul, pointing to the union of the lunar and solar principles within human life. Eastern philosophies speak of the "precious human rebirth", in that it is only while being alive within a body that humans have the possibility of spiritual realization. In the Hellenistic astrological texts, the Moon is one of the five "places of life". She represents both the physical body itself, as well as the necessary matrix in which the process of spiritual transcendence can take place.

There are a number of special concepts related to the Moon that we shall discuss in the following section. Some of them influence the condition of the Moon herself in the nativity, and others impact the condition of the planets to which she is joined in various ways.

LUNAR APPLICATIONS AND SEPARATIONS

> Without the matter of separation and application [of the Moon], neither longevity, nor brevity of life, nor sickness, nor injury, nor wealth, nor misfortune, nor fame, nor obscurity, nor manliness, nor weakness is established in the nativity. — PAULUS.[3]

The Moon is the planet that is closest to the Earth. Due to her swift motion, she circles the entire zodiac every month. Along her course she is able to make applying aspects with each of the other planets. As she does so, she was thought to gather up their effluences and transmit them to Earth. It follows that if the Moon applies to a planet, she is able to help bring down and make manifest the significations of that planet into the terrestrial realm. Thus, an application (applying aspect) from the Moon improves the planet's condition by bringing its matters to fruition.

An applying aspect from the Moon occurs when the Moon is moving towards a planet, either bodily by conjunction or by aspect ray. In this case, the Moon will be in a lesser degree than the planet. A separating aspect occurs when the Moon has already made contact with the planet and is now moving away from it. In this case, the Moon will be in a greater degree than the planet. For

2   PORPHYRY, *Introduction* 2.
3   PAULUS, *Introduction* 17.

example, the Moon at 6° Libra is applying to a conjunction with Jupiter at 10° Libra or to a trine with Venus at 10° Aquarius (6° is less than 10°), but it is separating from a conjunction with Mars at 2° Libra or from a trine with Saturn at 2° Aquarius (6° is greater than 2°).

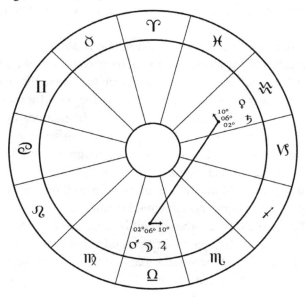

FIGURE 43. APPLYING & SEPARATING LUNAR ASPECTS

The Moon at 6° Libra is separating from a bodily conjunction with Mars at 2° Libra, and applying towards a bodily conjunction with Jupiter at 10° Libra. The same Moon at 6° Libra is also separating from a trine with Saturn at 2° Aquarius, and applying to a trine with Venus at 10° Aquarius.

Paulus makes a distinction between the allowable orbs in the Moon's applications and separations to other planets, giving a wide orb for conjunctions and a small orb for the other aspects.[4] For the conjunction, Paulus states that if the planets are found in the zodiacal sign before or after that of the Moon, within an orb of 30°, they are also considered in this topic of lunar applications and separations. He further elaborates that the specific range of degrees between the Moon and the planet which she conjoins indicates the stage in a person's life when the effects of this aspect will occur. If the distance between them is less than three degrees, the aspect will manifest in youth; 3°–7°, prime of life; 7°–15°, later years; 15°–30°, old age.

4   *Introduction 17.*

However, when determining the allowable range for the Moon's application to the planets by means of the aspects (sextile, square, trine, opposition), he gives an orb of 3°.[5] To anticipate our discussion of the Hellenistic view of aspects in the next section, we should note that the Moon is given a range of 13° for her application to the other planets when assessing the conditions of bonification and maltreatment.

Hellenistic texts contain extensive delineations about the Moon's applications and separations in the interpretation of natal charts, as well as in katarchic, inceptional, or electional charts for commencing various activities.

Firmicus Maternus provides interpretations for the Moon's application to each of the planets by conjunction.[6] Similar to his distinctions between planets belonging to the day or night sect, he draws out the differences in interpretive meaning between the Moon when she is waxing in light or waning in light as she makes applying aspects to each planet.

For the most part, a Moon that is increasing in light when applying to a planet is interpreted as giving more favorable indications than when decreasing in light. He follows this with another set of delineations regarding which planet the Moon has most recently separated from, and towards which planet it is next applying. In general, if the Moon had separated from a malefic and was applying towards a benefic, the situation would move towards improvement, but if the Moon had separated from a benefic and was moving towards a malefic, the situation would worsen.

When this doctrine was incorporated into horary astrology, particularly in the Arabic and Medieval traditions, the Moon's separations indicated what had already taken place in the past, while her applications pointed to what would come about in the future. The Arabic/Medieval traditions developed many more considerations regarding the Moon's motion that were expressed in terms of the collection and transfer of the Moon's light from one planet to another.

Because the Moon is so connected to the physical earth, there exist many texts detailing the applications of the Moon regarding auspicious times to commence events such as farming, sailing, marrying, building, buying, selling, and legal actions. Antiochus gives delineations for the Moon's applications to the various planets, both bodily by conjunction, and by aspect ray, giving recommendations for engaging in specific kinds of activities. For example:

5   PAULUS, *Introduction* 17.
6   FIRMICUS MATERNUS, *Mathesis* 4.

When the Moon is conjoining Saturn, opposition is encountered in all matters. But the conjunction of the Moon to Saturn is fine for planting and bloodletting.... When the Moon is sextile to Saturn it is fine for building, planting trees, and sowing pulses.... When the Moon squares Saturn, the person traveling abroad will be taken captive, the one building a house will not finish it and the building will fall, and the person who is engaged in business will be fined.[7]

MOON VOID IN COURSE

Many modern astrologers are familiar with the void of course moon as an interlude that is slack and inactive, where "nothing will come of the matter". The void of course phenomenon occurs when the Moon is not making any applications by conjunction or aspect ray to another planet for a certain interval of degrees. The Hellenistic astrologers defined the Moon as void in course when she did not make any applying aspects within a range of thirty degrees, and clearly articulated that this interval could cross sign boundaries. This stands in contrast to Medieval and modern astrologers, who limit the range of the interval to that of the time between the Moon's last aspect to a planet within a certain zodiacal sign until she leaves that sign.

Void in course comes from the Greek word *kenodromia*, which literally means "empty course". It is sometimes translated as "emptiness of course", "moving toward nothingness", or "without attendant planets". If one of the Moon's primary functions is to draw down the significations of the other planets into the terrestrial realm, while she is void in course there is no one for her to connect with and nothing for her to do. If this is the case, and there is no benefic on an angle, Firmicus Maternus writes that these individuals are denied the supports of daily life, face poverty and need, and suffer from weakened and tired bodies.[8] He may be alluding to the idea that when something has "run its course", it is depleted of vital energy and finished.

Firmicus also looks at the last planet the Moon conjoined before she moves towards nothingness. In accordance with the nature of each planet, he associates this condition with loss of inheritance and parents, orphans, illness, sluggishness, captivity, poverty, and wandering travelers.[9] The Arabic astrologer Ibn Sahl wrote that the Moon void in course—that is, joined to none of the planets—signifies

---

7 ANTIOCHUS, *Thesaurus* (CCAG 7, pp. 107–08).
8 FIRMICUS MATERNUS, *Mathesis* 4.2.3, trans. HOLDEN.
9 FIRMICUS MATERNUS, *Mathesis* 4.3G, trans. HOLDEN.

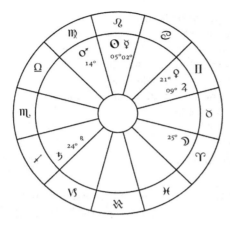

FIGURE 44. VOID IN COURSE MOON
(MEDIEVAL & MODERN)

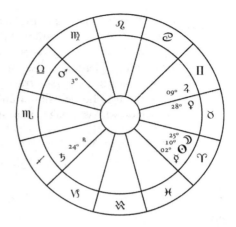

FIGURE 45. VOID IN COURSE MOON
(HELLENISTIC)

The Moon will not make any applying aspects before it leaves its sign (Aries). The Moon at 25° Aries made its last aspect to Saturn at 24° Sagittarius. Because it will not make any more aspects while it is in Aries, it is considered to be void in course according to Medieval and modern definitions. The Hellenistic definition, however, allows the Moon to cross sign boundaries for an interval of up to 30°. Thus, in the above chart, when the Moon enters Taurus, it will make a square to Mercury at 2° Leo; therefore it would not be considered void in course according to the Hellenistic definition.

The Moon will not make any applying aspects for the next 30°. The Moon's last aspect while in Aries was a trine to Saturn at 24° Sagittarius. Once it enters the next sign, it has until 25° Taurus to make an applying aspect to another planet. While in Taurus, it will be in aversion to planets in Sagittarius (Saturn), Libra (Mars), Gemini (Jupiter), and it has already separated from its conjunction to the Sun and Mercury in Aries. Its allowable interval expires at 25° Taurus, and so the conjunction to Venus at 28° Taurus is beyond the allowable orb. Thus, this Moon is void in course according to the Hellenistic definition.

futility and annulment, and turning back from that same purpose, and the impediments of that same purpose.[10]

The Hellenistic void in course condition is relatively rare, since the Moon has the opportunity to make contact with another planet for a 30° range that can cross sign boundaries. One of the most fundamental interpretative meanings for a void in course Moon is the lack of connection and subsequent alienation or isolation that a person can experience as the predominant feature of their emo-

10   IBN SAHL, *The Fifty Judgments* 6.

tional landscape. It can also point to challenges in being able to take effective actions in regards to bringing anything to pass. So it can point to experiences of failure, a sense of futility resulting in lack of motivation, or aimlessness. Some texts call the person with a void in course moon a traveler and vagabond, with reluctance to putting down roots.

From a spiritual perspective, the void in course interval is a kind of *bardo* interlude, the liminal space between two states of consciousness, such as the interval between waking and sleeping, or between death and life. It is the interludes of transition when the Moon pauses between her activities in regulating earthly and human affairs. As such, it can be an optimal time for meditative reflection on concepts such as emptiness, as well as a period of deep rest and regeneration following the exertion of energy. During void in course intervals, the Moon can turn her focus to the inner and non-manifest realms of being.

INTERPRETING LUNAR APPLICATIONS
AND THE VOID IN COURSE MOON

Looking to the planet from which the Moon has most recently separated, and then to the planet to which she next applies, can deepen our understanding of the Moon's influence in a person's life. This provides insight into whether circumstances will improve, decline, or remain the same. In this determination, you can extend the interval of the Moon's motion across sign boundaries until you reach the next planet to which the Moon applies—unless it first becomes void in course. Keep in mind that the condition of this planet is not necessarily improved by an application from the Moon unless it has a valid, applying whole-sign configuration. We shall not detail these kinds of interpretations, however. The focus of this chapter is on determining the condition of the Moon herself, as well as how she impacts the condition of the other planets in their capacity to bring about their agenda for the best interests of the individual.

When the Moon is applying to planets, especially when she is waxing in light, she is an active and purposeful Moon helping to manifest the other planets' significations. It is almost as if the Moon draws her energy from her associations with other planets. In turn, if a planet has an applying aspect from the Moon, this contact improves the planet's condition.

When the Moon is void, she herself is inactive and aimless in terms of ordinary, everyday life-matters, which can result in loss, decrease, and emptiness. However, in terms of non-ordinary states of awareness, the void Moon has the capacity to travel in the subtle realms of consciousness and survey the mysteries.

→   EXAMPLE CHARTS

Let us now turn to our example charts to determine if the Moon is void
in course. If not, then we will identify the planets to which she is making
an applying aspect. These planets are assisted by the Moon, who helps
draw down their significations into the terrestrial realm and life of the
individual. Their condition is thus improved.

CHART I: MOON'S CONDITION: VOID, SEPARATING, APPLYING

Moon sign and degree	Void in course?	Separating from/ Applying to
25° ARIES 36'	No	Trine Saturn Square Mercury

LUNAR INFLUENCES ON PLANETS

Planet	Application from Moon
SUN 5° LEO	Yes
JUPITER 9° GEMINI	—
SATURN 24° SAG. RX	—
MERCURY 2° LEO	Yes
MOON 25° ARIES	N/A
VENUS 21° GEMINI	—
MARS 14° VIRGO	Yes

ANALYSIS

The WANING MOON at 25° Aries has just separated from a trine to SATURN.
She does not make any other applying aspects while she is in the sign of Aries. Modern astrologers would consider this to be a moon void in course.
However, the Hellenistic guideline extends her range of applications for
the next 30°, and the Moon could cross the sign boundaries in this interval. Thus the Moon has until 25° Taurus in which to make applying aspects.

After the Moon enters Taurus, she will apply to a square with MERCURY at 2° Leo.

From an *interpretive* perspective, the Moon is moving *away* from past conditions of hardship (SATURN) concerning money (2nd house), and moving *towards* future conditions regarding literary creativity (MERCURY in Leo) expressed through the profession (10th house). In fact, it was through a career as an editor in a publishing house later in life that this person earned a livelihood for the first time from her own efforts.

From a *condition* perspective, the Moon is active because she is not void in course. The planets MERCURY, SUN, and MARS all benefit from her application, and have her assistance in manifesting their matters in the life of the individual. However, because this a waning Moon, and even more so a waning moon in a diurnal chart, the potential for benefit is somewhat lessened.

CHART II: MOON'S CONDITION: VOID, SEPARATING, APPLYING

Moon sign and degree	Void in course?	Separating from/ Applying to
8° SAG 12'	No	Sextile Venus Sextile Sun

LUNAR INFLUENCES ON PLANETS

Planet	Application from Moon
SUN 2° SCORPIO	Yes
JUPITER 23° TAURUS RX	—
SATURN 9° TAURUS RX	—
MERCURY 24° SCORPIO	—
MOON 8° SAG.	N/A
VENUS 4° LIBRA	—
MARS 12° CANCER	—

ANALYSIS

The MOON at 8° Sagittarius has separated from a sextile with VENUS at 4° Libra. It does not make any other conjunction, sextile, square, or trine aspects to any other planet while in Sagittarius. Again, modern astrologers might consider the moon void in course (unless they allow the quincunx aspect, which Hellenistic astrologers did not consider to be an aspect). However, once the Moon enters Capricorn, it will sextile the SUN at 2° Scorpio before exceeding its 30° range, which ends at 8° Capricorn.

From an *interpretive* point of view, the Moon is separating from Venusian entanglements of love affairs and moving towards the SUN. With the passage of time, it gives increase in personal wealth and fulfillment of desires.[11]

From a *condition* perspective, the Moon is active because she is not void in course. While the SUN is the next planet to which the Moon applies, preventing the Moon from being void in course, the Sun's condition is not necessarily improved by this application, because the Moon at 8° Sagittarius does not have a valid aspect configuration to the Sun at 2° Scorpio in the natal figure.

→   EXERCISE 22

   Using your own chart, complete exercise 22:
   Active or Void Moon

---

11   FIRMICUS MATERNUS, *Mathesis* 4.3F, trans. HOLDEN.

EXERCISE 22

ACTIVE OR VOID MOON

In this exercise, you will investigate whether your Moon is void in course and inactive, or if it is active, making applying aspects to other planets.

CRITERIA OF THE MOON'S CONDITION

Moon sign and degree	*Void in course?*	*Separating from/ Applying to*

LUNAR INFLUENCES ON PLANETS

Planet	*Application from Moon*
SUN:	
JUPITER:	
SATURN:	
MERCURY:	
MOON:	N/A
VENUS:	
MARS:	

1. *Enter the sign and degree of your Moon.*
2. *Determine if your Moon is void in course. It will be so if it does not make any applying aspects to any planet within the next 30°, including crossing zodiacal sign boundaries. (Compare this to the modern definition of a void in course moon, where the interval for application is limited to the zodiacal sign*

in which the Moon is located.)

3. *Determine the planet from which your Moon has last separated. Then determine the planet to which it next applies (within a 30° range that can cross sign boundaries).*

4. *If your Moon is not void in course, note which other planets the Moon is making an application to within the next 30°, and enter the kind of aspect configuration (conjunction, sextile, square, trine, opposition).*

QUESTIONS FOR REFLECTION

1. Is my Moon void in course? (Y/N) Thus, is it active or inactive?
2. If it is void, do you experience a sense of aimlessness or difficulty in bringing things to completion?
3. If it is void, can you easily enter into meditative or psychic states of awareness?
4. Which planet has the Moon last separated from?
5. Which planet will the Moon next apply to?
6. Based upon your understanding of the planets and houses, what kinds of circumstances are part of your past, and what kinds of circumstances are you moving towards?
7. Which planets (if any) benefit from the Moon's application? The Moon assists these planets in bringing forth and grounding their significations in your life.

CHAPTER 29

The Lunar Phases

———

THE MOON'S INCREASE AND DECREASE IN LIGHT IS DISPLAYED IN HER monthly cycle of waxing and waning phases, which were thought to affect all living things. As the Moon circles the Earth each month, she continually changes her relationship to the Sun. The arc of the distance between them increases as she approaches the Full Moon. The arc then decreases as she moves towards reunion with the Sun at the New Moon. Each night in her dance with the Sun, the queen of the night displays yet another phase of her multi-faceted nature through her changing luminosity. Her cycle can be divided in several different ways.

THE TWOFOLD DIVISION gives rise to a *waxing hemisphere,* where the Moon *increases* in light from the New Moon to the Full Moon, and a *waning hemisphere,* where the Moon *decreases* in light from the Full Moon back to the New Moon. The increasing and decreasing light of the Moon was used in natal interpretation, in lunar guides to planting, and in medical diagnosis and treatment.

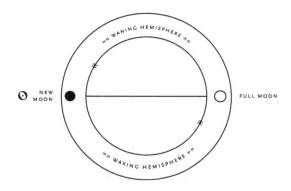

FIGURE 46. TWOFOLD DIVISION OF THE LUNAR CYCLE
Upper hemisphere: Waning Moon decreasing in light from full to new; lower hemisphere: Waxing Moon increasing in light from new to full.

THE THREEFOLD DIVISION of the lunar cycle—New, Full, and Dark—was personified as the Triple Moon Goddess. The most well-known faces of the trinity are personified in Artemis, Selēnē, and Hekatē. These three phases represented the three stages of a woman's life—maiden, mother, and crone—and their initiation rites were timed in accordance with women's blood mysteries: menstruation, lactation, and menopause.

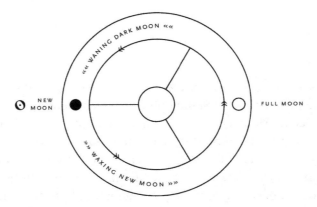

FIGURE 47. THREEFOLD DIVISION OF THE LUNAR CYCLE
Waxing Moon, Full Moon, Waning Moon, representing the Triple Goddess: Artemis, Selēnē, & Hekatē.

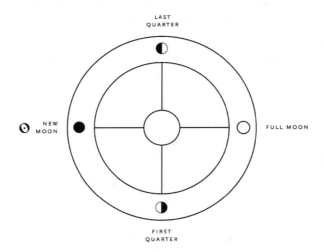

FIGURE 48. FOURFOLD DIVISION OF THE LUNAR CYCLE
The four quarters of the lunar cycle, and the pivotal turning points where light increases and decreases, reflect the four quarters of the solar cycle: first quarter (spring), second quarter (summer), third quarter (autumn), and fourth quarter (winter).

THE FOURFOLD DIVISION mirrors the solar cycle, where the critical turning points of increasing and decreasing light at the four quarters of the Moon correspond to the increase and decrease of solar light marked by the equinoxes and solstices. Ptolemy explains how the Moon is more productive of moisture in its waxing from New Moon to First Quarter; of heat in its passage from First Quarter to Full; of dryness from Full to Last Quarter; and of cold from Last Quarter to occultation (New Moon).[1] Porphyry relates how the Moon's first appearance until the First Quarter is like spring; and thence to the Full Moon like summer; from there to the Second Quarter like autumn; and next down to its disappearance (at New Moon) like winter.[2] The quarters of the Moon were very important in the timing of the critical days during the course of an illness. It is also the basis of a Hellenistic time-lord technique called "Quarters of the Moon".

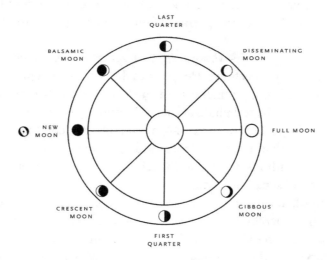

FIGURE 49. EIGHTFOLD DIVISION OF THE LUNAR CYCLE
The eight quarters of the lunar cycle add the halfway points between solstices and equinoxes.

When these four quarters are subdivided once again, THE EIGHTFOLD DIVISION corresponds to the addition of the cross quarter days which stand midway between each solstice and equinox. This was ritualized in the pagan holiday celebratory rites of the wheel of the year—Winter Solstice, Candlemas, Spring Equinox, Beltane (May Day), Summer Solstice, Lammas, Autumn Equinox, and Hallomas (Halloween).

1   PTOLEMY, *Tetrabiblos* 1.8.
2   PORPHYRY, *Introduction* 2.

The eightfold division of the lunar cycle, based upon increments of 45° (New, Crescent, First Quarter, Gibbous, Full, Disseminating, Last Quarter, and Balsamic), is the most frequently used in modern western astrology. It was revisioned by Dane Rudhyar in his seminal 1936 work, *The Lunation Cycle*. Rudhyar uses the phases of plant growth as a metaphor for the cyclic development of all life processes. The New Moon thus corresponds to the germination of a seed, while the successive phases correspond to the first shoots above ground (Crescent), the root and stems systems (First Quarter), the bud (Gibbous), flower (Full), fruit (Disseminating), harvest (Last Quarter), and finally the decomposition of the old plant (Balsamic); in the final Dark Moon phase, the seed is released and buried underground to await germination at the onset of the next cycle.[3]

Ancient astrologers such as Porphyry identified seven phases.[4] But Valens, Paulus, and Rhetorius set out several additional phases, bringing the total to eleven.[5]

Porphyry distinguishes seven phases that generally correspond to the arcs of the seven planetary aspect rays. He specifies the two crescent phases at the 60° sextiles, the two half/quarter phases at the 90° squares, the two gibbous phases at 120/110° trine, and the full phase at the 180° opposition.

Paulus specifies three more phases—the conjunction, coming forth, and rising—and mentions that some astrologers add an eleventh phase, the nearly full, at 150°. He agrees with Porphyry that the crescent and gibbous phases have the 60° and 120° arcs of separation with the Sun.

Valens and Rhetorius agree with Paulus on the eleven lunar phases, but they differ on the arc separations of the crescent and gibbous phases, stating that the crescent phases have a 45° separation rather than 60°, and that the gibbous phases are marked by the 135° separations rather than 120°. They specify a setting phase that begins 15° before the Moon re-conjoins the Sun.

The lunar phases were not given interpretation as to personality typing as they are in modern astrology, but they were used in other ways, some of which have been mentioned above.

---

3   See Demetra GEORGE, *Finding Your Way through the Dark* (Tempe, AZ: American Federation of Astrologers, 1994), chapter 1.
4   PORPHYRY, *Introduction* 2.
5   VALENS, *Anthology* 2.36; PAULUS, *Introduction* 16; RHETORIUS, *Compendium* 79.

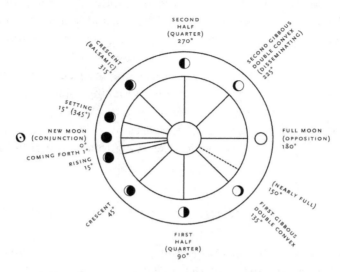

FIGURE 50. ELEVENFOLD DIVISION OF THE LUNAR CYCLE
Following Porphyry, Valens, Paulus, & Rhetorius

Table 22. Elevenfold Division of the Lunar Cycle.

1. CONJUNCTION. Moon is in the same degree as the Sun.

2. COMING FORTH. Moon is 1° past the Sun; it begins to appear in the cosmos, though is not visible from Earth.

3. RISING. Moon is 15° past the Sun; first appearance as a thin streak of light (2°–15°).

4. WAXING CRESCENT. Moon is 45° from the Sun (Rhetorius, Valens) or 60° (Porphyry, Paulus); name in accordance with shape (15°–45°/60°).

5. FIRST HALF (QUARTER). Moon is 90° from the Sun; grown to half its full amount (90°–120°/135°).

6. FIRST GIBBOUS (DOUBLE CONVEX). Moon is 135° past the Sun (Valens); 120° (Paulus); 110° (Porphyry); both sides appear to be humped.

7. WHOLE (FULL) MOON. Moon is 180° from the Sun; completely filled with the Sun's light.

8. SECOND GIBBOUS (DOUBLE CONVEX). Moon 225° (135°) from the Sun (Valens); 240°/120° (Paulus).

9. SECOND HALF (LAST QUARTER). Moon is 270°/90° from the Sun.

10. WANING CRESCENT. Moon is 300°/60° or 315°/45° from the Sun.

11. SETTING. Moon is 345°/15° degrees from the Sun; lessening of light.

Valens discusses how each lunar phase gives indications for various inquiries.[6] For instance, the conjunction phase of the Sun and Moon gives indications for reputation and power, while the rising phase gives determinations for the length of life. Both he and Rhetorius instruct how the astrologer must look to the house of the phase as well as the planet that is the ruler of the sign of the phase.[7] Rhetorius then presents a method for making a judgment as to how well-born, renowned, and fortunate the life will be. Valens gives associations for various planetary gods who assist the lords of the phases. However, both their explanations prove cryptic when attempting to apply them to particular birth charts.[8]

DETERMINING THE LUNAR PHASE

Let us first determine if the Moon is waxing or waning, and then find its specific phase. In some cases you may have to decide which system of division (Porphyry/Paulus or Valens/Rhetorius) you are going to employ.

A WAXING MOON is increasing in light; it is moving away from the New Moon conjunction with the Sun and heading towards the Full Moon opposition to the Sun. It will be located from 0° to 180° ahead of the Sun (between the New Moon and Full Moon).

A WANING MOON is decreasing in light; it is separating from the Full Moon opposition to the Sun, and heading back towards the New Moon solar conjunction. It will be located from 180° to 0° behind the Sun.

If you are not sure how to see this in the chart, draw a line from the Sun across to its opposition point. Then, move from the Sun in the natural order of the zodiac; if you find the Moon before you come to the opposition point, it is a waxing Moon. If you cross the opposition point to get to the Moon, it is a waning Moon.

In order to determine the phase of the Moon more specifically, count how many degrees there are between the Sun and the Moon. Refer to the above table of phases to obtain the correct lunar phase based upon its arc of separation (number of degrees) between the Moon and the Sun. If you have a waning Moon, it might be easier to count in the other direction to see how many degrees the Moon is behind the Sun.

---

6   VALENS, *Anthology* 2.36.
7   RHETORIUS, *Compendium* 79.
8   For personality profiles for each of the phases, you can refer to modern astrological books such as *The Lunation Cycle* by Dane RUDHYAR, or my book *Finding Your Way through the Dark*. However, keep in mind that this was not a feature of the traditional texts.

LUNAR REJOICING

Because the Moon does not revolve around the Sun, the sect rejoicing by solar phase does not apply to the Moon as it does for the other planets. However, the Moon's phase is the key to her rejoicing by sect.

A WAXING MOON (increasing in light from New Moon to Full Moon) *rejoices in a diurnal* chart. A Moon that is filling up with light resonates with the energies of *day*.

A WANING MOON (decreasing in light from Full Moon to New Moon) *rejoices in a nocturnal* chart. A Moon that is emptying herself of light is more in accordance with the energies of *night*.[9]

→   EXAMPLE CHARTS

Let us look at the example charts in order to determine the lunar phase and whether the Moon rejoices by phase and sect.

9   SERAPIO, 229, 11–12.

CHART I: MOON'S CONDITION: PHASE, SECT-REJOICING

Moon sign and degree	Waxing or waning phase	Rejoicing by sect
25° ARIES 36'	Waning Gibbous (Disseminating)	No

ANALYSIS

The Moon's phase is WANING GIBBOUS, as it is 260° ahead of the Sun (or 100° behind Sun). In contemporary astrology, this phase is called the disseminating phase. The chart is diurnal, and thus a waning Moon, decreasing in light, does not rejoice in a diurnal chart where the light abounds.

CHART II: MOON'S CONDITION: PHASE, SECT-REJOICING

Moon sign and degree	Waxing or waning phase	Rejoicing by sect
8° SAG 12'	Waxing Rising (New)	No

ANALYSIS

The Moon's phase is WAXING RISING, as it is almost 36° ahead of the Sun in zodiacal motion (more than 15°, but less than 45° or 60°, which begins the crescent phase). In contemporary astrology, this is called the New Moon phase. The chart is nocturnal, and thus a waxing Moon, increasing in light, does not rejoice in a nocturnal chart, where the dark prevails.

→   EXERCISE 23

   Using your own chart, complete exercise 23:
   Lunar Phase and Rejoicing by Sect

EXERCISE 23

LUNAR PHASE AND REJOICING BY SECT

In this exercise, you will determine the phase of your Moon, and whether it rejoices by phase and sect.

Moon sign and degree	Waxing or waning phase	Rejoicing by sect

1. *Using the Sun as your point of reference, determine if the Moon is moving away from the Sun in accordance with the natural order of the zodiac (counterclockwise) up to the opposition degree of the Sun. If so, the Moon is waxing, increasing in light. If the Moon has passed the opposition degree of the Sun, it is waning, decreasing in light.*

2. *Count the number of degrees between the Sun and Moon, again using the Sun as the point of reference. Referring to table 22 (page 335), locate your Moon phase based upon the arc of separation between the two lights. In some cases, you may need to make a choice between two different phases depending on which astrological author you want to follow.*

3. *Waxing or waning phase: In the above table, enter whether the Moon is waxing or waning, as well as its phase.*

4. *Determine if your Moon rejoices. A waxing moon rejoices in a diurnal chart. A waning moon rejoices in a nocturnal chart. (Is your Moon waxing or waning? Is the sect of your chart diurnal or nocturnal? In your chart, does the Moon rejoice?). Enter yes or no in the table above.*

REFLECTION AND ANALYSIS

1. Depending upon whether or not your Moon is in a rejoicing condition by sect, do you feel comfortable in your body?

2. Does your body feel in sync with the usual activities that take place during day and night hours?

CHAPTER 30

Bonding

AND THE MOON UNDER THE BONDS

———

THE ASTROLOGICAL TERM "BONDING" COMES FROM THE GREEK WORD *sundesmos*, which means "union", "fastened", or "that which is bonded together". It is sometimes used to refer to the conjunction aspect. Rhetorius tells us that the Moon is carried under the bond when it comes to 15° approaching the conjunction with the Sun.[1] It escapes or loosens the bond when it has separated from the Sun by 15°. The same is true for the Full Moon when it is approaching the opposition by 15° and separating from it by 15°. Paulus adds all the other aspects as well (sextile, square, trine), but reduces the orb to 5° on either side of the exact aspect.[2]

The Moon under the bond of the Sun is conceptually similar to a planet that is under the beams of the Sun. When the Moon is under the bonds, there is a sense in which she is held captive and her significations are constrained. From the traditional perspective, it is a condition of debilitation and weakening. It is unclear from the texts whether the 1° orb on either side gives her the protection of being "in the heart", although the ancient astrologers recognized the exact conjunction of the Moon with the Sun within the same degree as a distinct phase in their cycle, signifying their union.

Firmicus Maternus indicates dangers and illnesses when the Moon is too close to the Sun. The Medieval astrologers said that the Moon signifies secrets and hidden things when under the bond at the conjunction, and especially those things that we want hidden and concealed. When she moves under the bond at the Full Moon opposition, she signifies contrariety and its cause.[3] Looking at the placement of the Moon's domicile lord may give further information concerning what topics are being hidden, concealed, or are the cause of rebellion.

---

1   RHETORIUS, *Compendium* 38.
2   PAULUS, *Introduction* 35.
3   BONATTI, *Book of Astronomy* 3.7, trans. DYKES.

The Hellenistic astrologers paid careful attention to the arrangement of the planets when the Moon loosened herself from her bonds. This happened when she moved 15° past the conjunction or opposition. Exiting from hiddenness and captivity, she was in a weakened state and especially vulnerable to the first planet she encountered, bodily or by aspect. If the planet was benefic, she would benefit and be assisted. However, if it was a malefic, she would be harmed. The situation was especially dangerous if she encountered Mars after loosening the bond at the conjunction with the Sun (excessive heat with a waxing Moon), or had an encounter with Saturn after the opposition to the Sun (excessive cold with a waning Moon). This was a basic guideline in the analysis of the course of an illness employed in medical katarchic charts.

LOOSENING THE BOND

The notion of "loosening the bond" is also used in the time-lord technique of zodiacal releasing from the Lots of Fortune and Spirit, where sudden reversals and changes in the life often occur. This term derives from the Roman religious ritual of Saturnalia. For the majority of the year, the feet of Saturn's cult statue in his temple were tied with rope. During his festival days, the bonds constraining his feet were loosened, and the restrictions governing society were temporarily undone, turning the world topsy-turvy. Roles were reversed: masters became slaves and slaves became masters. "Loosening the bond" is thus a release from previous circumstances where one was confined by law or regulated by custom.

INTERPRETING MOON UNDER THE BOND

When looking at a chart, you should note if the Moon is within 15° on either side of the conjunction with, or opposition to, the Sun. If so, the significations of the Moon are being restricted in some way and there may be an air of secrecy, concealment or sedition regarding the topics of the Moon. The Moon's seclusion within the fortress of the Sun may also suggest a kind of protection. This may especially be the case with a new Moon, which is still young and vulnerable.

Check the planet that is the domicile lord of the Moon and its house location for more information on what may be concealed. Look ahead and see what planet the Moon first aspects when she is released from the bonds at 15° past the conjunction or opposition. Then make a judgment as to the kind of influence to which the Moon is most subject, according to the nature of the planet (and the nature of the aspect).

→ EXAMPLE CHARTS

The Moon is not under the bond in either of our example charts, as the distance between the Sun and Moon is more than 15° on either side of the New Moon conjunction or Full Moon opposition.

CHART I: MOON'S CONDITION: UNDER THE BOND

Moon sign and degree	Under the bond?
25° ARIES 36'	No

CHART II: MOON'S CONDITION: UNDER THE BOND

Moon sign and degree	Under the bond?
8° SAG 12'	No

→ EXERCISE 24

Using your own chart, complete exercise 24:
Moon Under the Bond

EXERCISE 24

MOON UNDER THE BOND

In this exercise you will determine if your Moon is under the bond.

Moon sign and degree   Under the bond?

1.   *Was I born within a day before or after the New Moon conjunction, with the Moon within 15° on either side of the Sun?*
2.   *Was I born within a day before or after the Full Moon, with the Moon within 15° before or after the opposition point of the Sun?*
3.   *If you answered no to both questions, enter* NO *in the box above.*
4.   *If the answer to either question is yes, your Moon is under the bond. Enter* YES *above and reflect upon the following questions.*

REFLECTION AND ANALYSIS

1.   Do you experience a sense of constraint, restriction, or secrecy concerning the significations of your Moon?
2.   Is this an area of vulnerability where you feel the need to protect yourself, or where others attempt to protect you in accordance with or against your wishes?
3.   If your Moon is under the bond, project it forward until it is loosened from the bond (15° past the conjunction or opposition points with the Sun). What is the first planet it encounters by either bodily conjunction or aspect (sextile, square, trine, opposition)?
4.   Is that planet a benefic or malefic?
5.   What is the aspect?
6.   Does this strengthen or weaken the condition of the Moon?
7.   What house does the Moon rule in your natal chart and what topics

does that house signify? These topics indicate the originating cause of the restriction that the Moon experiences. (The houses will be dealt with in detail in volume two).

8. Which planet is the domicile lord of the Moon, and which house is that planet located in?

9. What information does this give concerning the nature of the constrictions or secrets to which the Moon is subject?

CHAPTER 31

Phases and Illnesses

OF THE MOON

———

THE MOON IS CONSIDERED TO BE THE PRIMARY SIGNIFICATOR OF THE body. According to the doctrine of *melothesia*, the zodiacal signs correspond to the various parts of the body, as follows:

1. ARIES, *head*
2. TAURUS, *throat and neck*
3. GEMINI, *shoulders, arms, lungs*
4. CANCER, *breast, stomach*
5. LEO, *heart*
6. VIRGO, *intestines*
7. LIBRA, *kidneys*
8. SCORPIO, *private parts (reproductive and sexual)*
9. SAGITTARIUS, *hips and thighs*
10. CAPRICORN, *knees*
11. AQUARIUS, *ankles*
12. PISCES, *feet*

The zodiacal sign of the Moon at birth shows the part of the body that is predisposed to illness, especially if the Moon is configured to Mars or Saturn by a "harsh destructive" aspect (conjunction, square, opposition).

The Moon played a primary role in many methods of katarchic medical astrology (known as *iatromathēmatika* to the Greeks). *Iatros* comes from the Greek word for "physician" or "doctor", and *mathēmatikoi* referred to "astronomers" and "astrologers", who were always calculating numbers. Several texts describe the role of the Moon in the diagnosis and prognosis of illnesses.[1]

---

1   *Iatromathematika: From Hermes to Ammun to Egyptian,* in J. L. IDELER, *Physici et Medici gracci minores* (Berlin 1841), vol. 1, pp. 387–396; 430–440; *Prognostications from the Astrological Science,* in *Galenus Opera* (ed. Kuhn), vol. 19, pp. 529–573; *Concerning Taking to*

One popular method investigates the state of the Moon at the time a person becomes ill. The Moon's speed, waxing or waning light, and configuration to the benefic and malefic planets are taken into consideration and provide the basis for a diagnosis as to the origin, cause, course, critical days, and prognosis of the illness.

The Moon has an average motion of 13° per day, but in the course of the lunar month, its motion varies from as little as 11° per day near apogee (when the Moon is farthest from the Earth), to as much as 15° per day near perigee (when the Moon is nearest to the Earth). In general, when the Moon is fast ("additive in numbers") or increases in speed, the illness is active and increases, but when the Moon is slow ("subtractive in numbers") or decreases in speed, the illness is less active and slows down.

In the analysis of a chart at the moment a person takes to bed ill, a Moon that is fast, waxing, and conjunct/square/opposed to Mars indicates a severe illness due to overheating (such as inflammations and fevers), while a Moon that is slow, waning, and conjunct/square/opposed to Saturn points to cold and constrictive diseases (such as bronchitis and paralysis). If the Moon is also witnessed by Venus or Jupiter, especially by conjunction, sextile, or trine, recovery is indicated.

If, at the time of the onset of the illness, the Moon was under the bond, it was carefully observed as to its increasing or decreasing speed after it was loosened from the bond. If it was released after the New Moon conjunction, and it traveled toward the greater extent of its course (i.e., towards its fastest speed), the illness would become severely acute as it reached the opposition, and could be destructive. But if after leaving the bond, the Moon traveled toward the lesser extent of its course (i.e., towards its slowest speed), the patient would recover, as the crisis of the opposition was behind them.[2]

The lunar phases were an essential component of another system of medical diagnosis known as the *doctrine of critical days*. First suggested by Hippocrates in the fifth century BCE, it was based upon the idea that diseases reach critical turning points, for better or worse, after a certain interval of days from the onset of the illness. Galen, the second-century Roman physician, attempted to provide a rational explanation for the critical days theory. The Moon was thought to govern changes in the atmosphere, which in turn affected changes on Earth and thus in the human body, which was composed of the same elements. The strongest changes occur at the New Moon, followed by the Full Moon (14th

  One's Bed and Illnesses (Peri katakleison kai noson), in CCAG 1, pp. 122–124.

2 *Iatromathematika: From Hermes to Ammun to Egyptian*, in J. L. IDELER, *Physici et Medici gracci minores* (Berlin 1841), vol. 1, pp. 387–396; 430–440.

day), lesser changes at quarters (waxing 7th day; waning 20th–21st day), weak changes at crescent (4th day) and gibbous (11th day). Each consecutive lunar phase correlated to the critical days when there were thought to be changes in the course of an illness.

Astrologers adapted this model and superimposed it upon the lunar phase cycle. They posited that the cycle began in whatever sign the Moon was located in at the onset of illness, regardless of the Moon's actual objective phase in the sky. The patient was thought to undergo critical changes in the course of their illness on the days when the Moon made phase aspects to her position at the inception of the illness. On these critical days, the Moon would be investigated as to its contacts with the benefic or malefic planets in order to judge if the illness would worsen or improve, and suggestions were made as to appropriate treatments.[3]

Dorotheus of Sidon (circa 75 CE) made a direct analogy between the critical days and the days of the lunar cycle, and spoke to the role of the Moon's phases in tracking the course of the disease:

> Note the position of the Moon at the time of becoming ill. Look in the daily ephemerides to where the Moon has moved after 7 days to the square aspect figure, after 9 days it goes to the trine figure in the inception chart, after 14 days it will clearly oppose its own position, after 19 days it will go to the right trine figure, and after 21 days it will have come to its own right square figure. It is necessary to accurately examine these five figures of the Moon, and which of the stars, after the inception chart, the Moon is about to conjoin. For if [the Moon] conjoins a benefic, health comes to pass, but if a malefic, illness and harm.[4]

3   Glen M. COOPER, *Galen, De diebus decretoriis, from Greek into Arabic: A Critical Edition, with Translation and Commentary, of Hunayn ibn Ishāq, Kitāb ayyām al-buhrān* (Surrey: Ashgate, 2011); DOROTHEUS, *Carmen* 5.42; HEPHAISTIO, *Apotelesmatics* 3.3.31; DOROTHEUS, *Fragment* 5.41; Nicholas CULPEPPER, *Astrological Judgment of Diseases from the Decumbiture of the Sick* (Astrology Classics, 2005).

4   DOROTHEUS, *Fragment* 5.41, 12–14 (CCAG 1, p. 123), in HEPHAISTIO, *Apotelesmatics* 3, Appendix F, trans. GRAMAGLIA, ed. DYKES

CHAPTER 32

Nodes, Bendings, Eclipses

———

THE LUNAR NODES DEFINE TWO POINTS IN SPACE WHERE THE PLANE OF
the Moon's orbit around the Earth intersects with that of the ecliptic (the apparent path of the Sun). The North or Ascending Node (the dragon's head, *caput
draconis*) marks the point where the path of the Moon crosses the ecliptic from
the south to the north latitude; the South or Descending Node of the Moon (the
dragon's tail, *cauda draconis*) is where the path of the Moon crosses the ecliptic
from the north to the south latitude. When the Moon or any other planet is conjunct the nodes, it has 0° latitude relative to the ecliptic.

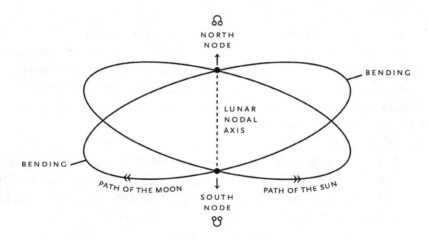

FIGURE 51. THE LUNAR NODES

*The North Node (Ascending Node, Head of the
Dragon) and the South Node (Descending Node,
Tail of the Dragon) on the intersecting paths of Sun
and Moon.*

Whenever a New Moon (Sun and Moon conjunct) or a Full Moon (Sun and Moon opposed) occurs at the nodes, an eclipse will occur. Because these bodies of light are located at the same latitude, the shadow of one is capable of obscuring the light of the other. This is why ancient astrologers referred to the nodes as the "eclipsing places". The ominous quality associated with eclipses was also carried by the nodes as the places where eclipses could take place. Imagine a mountain pass where at certain times of the year the dragon might come out of its cave and devour you. Even if you were passing through at a time when the dragon did not ordinarily come out, it would still be a frightening place because of its associations. For this reason, ancient astrologers regarded the nodes with trepidation.

The lunar nodes were mentioned by the Hellenistic and Medieval astrologers, but not given the importance with which they are invested in Vedic and some modern western astrologies. There is no indication in the Hellenistic texts that they had anything to do with karma, reincarnation, evolution, or past lives. These associations were imported from Vedic astrology during the late nineteenth century, when there were cross-cultural transmissions of metaphysical doctrines between east and west by astrologers such as Alan Leo, who spent time in India under the influence of the Theosophical Society.

Valens relates that if the benefic planets are with the North Ascending Node, the life will be successful and practical. However if the Ascending Node is with the malefic planets, the life will be marked with loss and accusations.[1] Rhetorius begins with the instruction that all planets are problematic when with the Ascending Node, but qualifies this by saying that "the Ascending Node is good with benefics and the Descending Node is good with the malefics".[2] This statement is echoed in the writings of the Arabic astrologers.

The Medieval Arabic astrologer Abu Ma'shar explained that the nature of the North Ascending Node is toward increase, and it increases the good with benefics and also increases the bad with malefics.[3] Conversely, the nature of the South Node is toward decrease; it decreases the good of the benefics and the bad of the malefics. In summary:

NORTH NODE conjunct benefics *increases the good of benefics.*
NORTH NODE conjunct malefics *increases the bad of malefics.*
SOUTH NODE conjunct benefics *decreases the good of benefics.*
SOUTH NODE conjunct malefics *decreases the bad of malefics.*

---

1   VALENS, *Anthology* 1.15.
2   RHETORIUS, *Compendium* 80.
3   ABU MA'SHAR, *The Abbreviation of the Introduction to Astrology* 4.19–20.

The meanings behind the North and South Nodes reflect a worldview in which up equates to good and down to bad. This bias is embedded in common phrases and gestures: life can "look up" or it can "bring one down". In modern astrology, the North Node is often given a positive slant and interpreted as our future path of growth and integration, while the South Node is considered to be less desirable and infused with a sense of weaknesses and vulnerability to unconscious, destructive behavioral patterns. In Vedic astrology, the North Node (Rahu) signifies desire for increase and material acquisition, while the South Node (Ketu) is associated with release and surrender to emptiness.

It is thus important to distinguish between the eastern views and the traditional western interpretation, in which increase (of both good and bad) is associated with the North Node, and decrease (of both good and bad) is associated with the South Node.

In a general sense, the house location of the North Node of the Moon indicates an area of life that is directed towards increase, while the house of the South Node tends towards decrease. That being said, the focus of this chapter is not to interpret the meanings of the Nodes in the various signs and houses, but rather to investigate how a planet's contact with the Nodes impacts its condition and capacity to bring forth fortunate outcomes for the individual.

A traditional astrologer would see Jupiter conjunct the North Node as the increase of prosperity, while Jupiter conjunct the South Node would indicate a decrease of prosperity. In the same way, Mars with the North Node was understood as an increase of conflict, while Mars with the South Node was seen as a decrease in conflict. It is thus important to take especial note of any planets located in the same sign and house as the Nodes, and to judge their significations of increase/decrease together with the benefic/malefic nature of the planet.

Abu Ma'shar considers it a great misfortune if the Moon is within 12° of the head or tail of the dragon. When the Moon is conjunct the Nodes, it is experiencing a kind of phase change, for it is passing from the north latitude, the "great above", to the south latitude, the "great below" (or vice versa). These times of transition can be fraught with great instability and danger, for we are passing the dragon's lair.

When the Moon is conjunct the Nodes, her significations are infused with a similar kind of intensity as when the planets shift between their appearances and disappearances at their rising and setting phases. A Moon that is conjunct the Nodes is filled with a sense of urgency and need for mindfulness as she navigates the powerful shifts and great divides encountered on her journey.

BENDINGS OF THE MOON

While the Nodes represent the points on the Moon's orbital path that intersect with the ecliptic, the *bendings* of the Moon are located in the degrees of the zodiacal signs that are *square* to the Nodes (see FIGURE 51). Here at the bendings, the orbit of the Moon's plane reaches her greatest northern and southern latitudes, which mark the farthest distance of the plane of the lunar orbit from that of the Sun's path on the ecliptic. The Moon at the bendings suggests both a state of objective awareness between the lunar body and solar soul, but can also indicate the potential for disassociation and lack of connection. Planets that are square the Nodes are an important feature in the doctrines of modern evolutionary astrology, where they represent parts of the personality that are not fully integrated into the psyche.

Valens explains how the Nodes break down the power of the signs they occupy. In a discussion about inception charts (electing a time to commence an event), he relates that when the Moon is in the same sign as either Node or in a sign squaring the Node, one must guard against beginning anything, for the matter will not be stable or easily brought to completion; instead, it will be inconstant, incomplete, or painful.[4]

By contrast, Ptolemy presented a more positive view of the Moon at the Nodes and bendings. He states that if the Moon is at the bendings of its northern or southern limits, it helps with the character of the soul in the direction of greater versatility, resourcefulness, and capacity for change. The Moon at the Nodes inclines the character towards greater keenness, activity, and excitability.[5]

While many modern astrologers look to planets at the bendings of the Moon, it should be recognized that, strictly speaking, each planet also has its own nodal path, where the plane of its orbit intersects that of the Sun's solar path. Therefore, it could be argued that a planet should be investigated relative to its location at the bendings of its *own* nodal orbital path rather than that relative to the Moon.

ECLIPSES

When the Sun or Moon are conjunct with either of the Nodes, and it is a New Moon (Sun and Moon conjunct), a *solar eclipse* occurs. A *lunar eclipse* takes

---

4   VALENS, *Anthology* 5.2.
5   PTOLEMY, *Tetrabiblos* 3.13.

place at the Full Moon, when the Sun and Moon are opposed and conjunct the Nodes. Photographs of solar eclipses that are taken from above the earth show a large dark smudge over the sky that looks like black smoke. This is the shadow that blocks the life-giving energies of the Sun from reaching the Earth below. Imagine standing underneath a great plume of dark smoke, which engulfs you and obscures your vision.

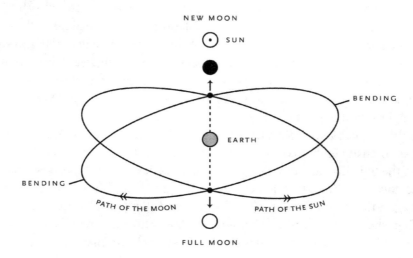

FIGURE 52. ECLIPSES AT THE NODES

A New Moon (conjunction of Sun and Moon) occurring at either the South Node or North Node produces a Solar Eclipse. A Full Moon (opposition of Sun and Moon) occurring at either the South Node or North Node produces a Lunar Eclipse.

In the interpretation of eclipses, the significations of the Sun and Moon are intensified, which adds a "fated" quality to the life of the native. Historically, eclipses were used as one of the main techniques in mundane or general astrology to investigate collective matters such as earthquakes, floods, nations, and their leaders. Under eclipses, there can be sudden, dramatic events, reversals, or the revelation of hidden information. If someone is born near an eclipse, the personal events of their life are "fated" in so far as the person plays a role that impacts or participates in collective destinies.

ECLIPSE INTERPRETATION GUIDELINES

The condition of the Moon, as well as other planets, are impacted when they are connected to the lunar nodal cycle and the eclipses. If the MOON IS CONJUNCT

THE NORTH NODE within a 10–12° degree orb on either side, she is in transition from the south latitude below the plane of the ecliptic to the north latitude above the plane of the ecliptic. She is moving towards an increase of her significations, but has just navigated—or is about to navigate—a precipitous pass in her course. This can be exciting, adventurous, and dangerous; in any case it requires a keenness of attention when walking along the razor's edge.

If the MOON IS CONJUNCT THE SOUTH NODE within a 10–12° orb on either side, she is in transition from the north latitude above the plane of the ecliptic to the south latitude below the plane of the ecliptic. She is moving towards a decrease of her significations; likewise, she has just navigated—or is about to navigate—a precarious pass in her course that will take her down and under into unknown terrain. Some may surrender to the unknown and others may use their night vision to guide their way.

If the MOON IS SQUARE THE NODES, she is at the bendings. This is another point of intensity on her course, where her path has taken her the farthest from that of the Sun. The distance can give both objectivity as well as disassociation. At the north bending, she is at her greatest height in the "above", but has turned and begun the descent towards the "below" and the South Node. At the south bending, she is at the depths of her journey, but is turning towards the ascent at the North Node. The Moon at her bendings can make dramatic reversals in her directions.

If PLANETS ARE CONJUNCT THE NORTH NODE, their significations are subject to increase in accordance with their benefic or malefic natures. If PLANETS ARE CONJUNCT THE SOUTH NODE, their significations are subject to decrease in accordance with their benefic or malefic natures.

If A PERSON IS BORN NEAR AN ECLIPSE—the Sun and Moon are conjunct on either the North Node or the South Node (New Moon); or the Sun is conjunct one Node and the Moon the other (Full Moon)—the Sun (and any planet within a 3° orb of the Nodes) and the Moon (within a 13° orb of the Nodes) are intensified and have a fated quality to their significations.

→   EXAMPLE CHARTS

Let us determine if any planets are subject to increase or decrease of their benefic and malefic significations as a result of their conjunction with the lunar Nodes, or if the Moon is at the bendings. Pay special attention to the occurrence of an eclipse.

CHART I: MOON'S CONDITION; NODES, BENDINGS, ECLIPSES

In chart I, the Moon is not at the nodes, not at the bendings, and there is no eclipse pattern in the chart. Nor are there any planets conjunct the Nodes. Let us move on to chart II.

CHART II: MOON'S CONDITION; NODES, BENDINGS, ECLIPSES

Moon sign and degree	Conjunct node, bending, or eclipse?
8° SAG 12'	Moon conjunct North Node

ANALYSIS

The Moon is CONJUNCT THE NORTH NODE. Thus the Moon is in a precarious condition. The latitude of the Moon is 0.06° south. Its conjunction to the North Node indicates that it is about to transition from the south latitude, below the plane of the ecliptic, to the north latitude, above the plane of the ecliptic, moving towards an increase of her significations. This improves the future condition of the Moon, but also gives an undertone of risk and danger associated with the Moon's actions.

→   EXERCISE 25

Using your own chart, complete exercise 25:
The Moon's Nodes and Eclipses

EXERCISE 25

THE MOON'S NODES AND ECLIPSES

1. *Is the Moon conjunct either the North or South Node within a 10–12° degree orb?*
2. *Is the Moon at the bendings (square the lunar nodal axis) within a 10–12° orb?*
3. *Were you born near an eclipse?*
   If the Moon was conjunct the Sun at either of the Nodes (within 10–12°), you were born on the day of a solar eclipse. If the Moon was conjunct one of the nodes and also opposite the Sun (within 10–12°), you were born on the day of a lunar eclipse.
4. *Conjunct Node, Bending, or Eclipse: If you answered yes to any of these questions, enter the appropriate information in the table below.*

THE MOON'S CONDITION: NODES, BENDINGS, ECLIPSES

Moon sign and degree	*Conjunct node, bending, or eclipse?*

REFLECTION AND ANALYSIS

1. If your Moon is conjunct one of the Nodes, have you seen an increase in lunar significations (North Node conjunction) or a decrease (South Node conjunction)? Some people may experience the North Node conjunction as an increase in desire to manifest more, and the South Node conjunction as a decrease in desire—a willingness to surrender matters associated with the Moon's significations.
2. If your Moon is conjunct one of the Nodes, do you feel that certain aspects of your life are precarious, presenting you with risky, dangerous, but exciting situations?
3. If your Moon is at the bendings (square the nodal axis), do you feel a sense of disassociation or lack of integration with your body, health, or emotions? Or do you experience the reverse: a greater capacity for objectivity and change?

4. If you were born within a day of an eclipse, have you experienced a "fated" quality to your life? Do you perceive that you have played a role impacting the larger collective events of your world?

LUNAR INFLUENCES ON PLANETS: NODES

Planet	Conjunct Nodes?	Conjunct Bendings? (Square Nodes)
SUN		
JUPITER		
SATURN		
MERCURY		
MOON		
VENUS		
MARS		

1. *Are any planets conjunct or square the Nodes?*
    If so, enter them in the table above.

REFLECTION AND ANALYSIS

1. Which planet(s) are conjunct which Node?
2. How do you experience the increase or decrease of the significations of that planet?
3. When the North Node is conjunct the benefics, it is said to increase the good, and when conjunct the malefics, to increase the bad. Does this apply to your chart, and if so, how?
4. When the South Node is conjunct the benefics it is said to decrease the good, and when conjunct the malefics, to decrease the bad. Does this apply to your chart, and if so, how?

CHAPTER 33

The Lot of Fortune

THE SPECIAL LOT OF THE MOON

———

HELLENISTIC ASTROLOGY EMPLOYS THE USE OF VARIOUS "LOTS", WHICH are better known today as the Arabic Parts. The notion of Lots comes from Greek words related to the concept of fate as one's allotted portion in life. The Lots are mathematical analogs of the arc interval between various planets or sensitive points, which are then projected from the Ascendant. The ancient astrologers constructed special Lots for each planet, as well as several Lots for the various topics of each house. The Lots are ways to differentiate among the various topics associated with each house as well as the significations of its lord. The conjunction of a planet with a Lot can impact its condition, and the presence of a Lot in a house changes the relative dynamic quality of the house.

In Hellenistic astrology, each planet had its own special Lot. As a group, these were called the Hermetic Lots. The Lot of Fortune is the special Lot of the Moon, and it speaks to matters of the body, health, and wealth. The Lot of Fortune is one of the five places of life, standing alongside (and equal in rank to) the Sun, the Moon, the Ascendant, and the Prenatal Lunation. It is often interpreted as indicating an area of life where accidental good fortune and happiness of a material nature may come to a person by means of luck or chance, rather than by actions and intent.

While the basic underlying foundation of Hellenistic astrology was oriented towards fate personified as the goddess Moira, there was an accompanying belief in the possibility of the power of chance personified by the goddess Tychē (Fortuna). The ancient astrologers attempted to acknowledge the role of chance and the amount of accidental good luck a person could expect.

The Lot of Fortune is calculated differently for day and night births.[1] For diurnal charts, the distance is taken from the Sun to the Moon in the order of the zodiac signs. This distance is then projected from the Ascendant. In nocturnal

---

1   Ptolemy was the only Hellenistic astrologer who used the diurnal formula for both day and night charts.

births, the order of the luminaries is reversed. The distance is taken from the Moon to the Sun, in the order of the zodiac signs, and then projected from the Ascendant. The sign and degree where this falls in the chart is the location of the Lot of Fortune.

The analysis of the Lot of Fortune is based upon the relative angularity and favorability of the house in which it falls (angular, succedent, cadent, fortunate, or unfortunate), how it is witnessed by the benefic and malefic planets, and the location and condition of its lord. The focus of this chapter is not an exposition on how to interpret Fortune in a chart, but more on how a planet's condition is impacted by its association with Fortune as derived from the Moon. Simply stated, a planet that is conjunct Fortune is made more fortunate. The house that contains Fortune is also made more active.

LOT OF FORTUNE AND ILLNESS

Valens presents a method that looks to the zodiacal sign of the Lot of Fortune (and its lord) for indications concerning the parts of the body that are liable to injury, and to the Lot of Spirit (and its lord) for indications of ailments. He lists the kinds of physical afflictions that are associated with each zodiacal sign. The injuries are more active when the malefic planets are upon the place of Fortune or its lord, or are witnessing them by aspect; and likewise the ailments for the Lot of Spirit or its lord. Lack of injuries in the body parts are indicated when the zodiacal places of the Lot of Fortune and its lord are well situated and the rulers not afflicted.[2]

→   EXAMPLE CHARTS

Let us examine the calculation and interpretation of the Lot of Fortune.

CHART I

This is a DAY CHART. To calculate the Lot of Fortune, the distance is taken between the Sun at 5° Leo, counting the number of degrees in the natural order of the signs to the Moon at 25° Aries (25° remaining in Leo + 30° of Virgo + 30° of Libra + 30° of Scorpio + 30° of Sagittarius + 30° of Capricorn + 30° of Aquarius

---

2   VALENS, *Anthology* 2.37. See our discussion in chapter 31, *Phases and Illnesses of the Moon*, for the correspondences of zodiacal signs and body parts. Valens includes an expanded listing of limbs, organs, and ailments.

+ 30° of Pisces + 25° of Aries = 260° total. This total (260°) is then projected from the Ascendant at 17° Scorpio, and comes to 08° Leo. The Lot of Fortune is located at 08° Leo.

CHART I: MOON'S CONDITION: LOT OF FORTUNE

Moon sign and degree	Lot of Fortune
25° ARIES 36'	08° Leo 24'

ANALYSIS

The LOT OF FORTUNE is located in the dynamically strong and favorable tenth house, and is witnessed by both benefics. The lord of the Lot is the Sun, very powerful in its own zodiacal sign of Leo, and co-present with the Lot. The tenth house is made more fortunate, active, busy, and advantageous for doing the business of reputation and profession. The Lot of Fortune is in the sign of Leo, which rules the heart. Neither of the malefics witness the house of Fortune, and both of the benefics see it by sextile. Thus, there is not much concern about heart issues.

CHART I: LUNAR INFLUENCES ON PLANETS: LOT OF FORTUNE

Planet	Conjunct Lot of Fortune
SUN	Yes
JUPITER	—
SATURN	—
MERCURY	Yes
MOON	—
VENUS	—
MARS	—

ANALYSIS

The LOT OF FORTUNE at 08° Leo falls in the tenth house. The Sun and Mercury, which are co-present with Fortune, likewise participate in the accidental good luck and material well-being that accompanies Fortune.

CHART II

This is a NIGHT CHART. Count from the Moon at 8° Sagittarius to the Sun at 2° Scorpio in the order of the signs, giving 324°. Project 324° from the Ascendant at 5° Leo and arrive at 0° Cancer. The Lot of Fortune is in the twelfth house in Cancer.

CHART II: MOON'S CONDITION: LOT OF FORTUNE

Moon sign and degree	*Lot of Fortune sign and degree*
8° SAG 12'	0° Cancer 07'

ANALYSIS

The LOT OF FORTUNE is located in the cadent, weak, and unfavorable twelfth house. While the amount of accidental good luck is slight, the house itself is improved and made more active due to the presence of the Lot. The lord of the Lot is the Moon, which is in aversion to the Lot, decreasing its effectiveness. Fortune is in the sign of Cancer, which rules the breast and stomach. The presence of Mars in the same house may point to injuries in this part of the body. And in fact, this person had an ulcer operation.

CHART II: LUNAR INFLUENCES ON PLANETS: LOT OF FORTUNE

Planet	Conjunct Lot of Fortune
SUN	—
JUPITER	—
SATURN	—
MERCURY	—
MOON	—
VENUS	—
MARS	Yes

ANALYSIS

The LOT OF FORTUNE is co-present with Mars. Thus the condition of Mars is made more fortunate, but not by much, as the Lot itself and its lord are relatively weak.

→ EXERCISE 26

Using your own chart, complete exercise 26:
The Lot of Fortune

EXERCISE 26

LOT OF FORTUNE

Calculate the Lot of Fortune and enter its position in the table below.

MOON'S CONDITION: LOT OF FORTUNE

Moon: sign and degree   *Lot of Fortune: sign and degree*

LUNAR INFLUENCES ON PLANETS: LOT OF FORTUNE

Planet	*Conjunct Lot of Fortune?*
SUN	
JUPITER	
SATURN	
MERCURY	
MOON	
VENUS	
MARS	

REFLECTION AND ANALYSIS

1. In what sign and degree is my Lot of Fortune located?
2. What house does it fall in? What are the topics associated with this house? This house is made more active regarding matters of the body, health, and wealth, increasing the fortunate outcomes of the favorable

houses, decreasing the unfortunate outcomes of the unfavorable houses, and making the cadent houses busier.

3. Which part of the body is associated with the sign of the Lot of Fortune? See the *melothesia* listing at the beginning of chapter 31 for correspondences; consider how it may be more sensitized?

4. What planet is the lord of the Lot of Fortune? What zodiacal sign is the lord in? If Mars or Saturn is in the same sign as Fortune, or in the same sign as the lord of Fortune (or making a square or opposition aspect), this part of the body may be vulnerable to injury or ailment.

5. Which planets, if any, are in the same sign and house as the Lot of Fortune? These planets partake of the accidental good fortune concerning matters of the body, health, and wealth accorded to them by the Lot of Fortune.

CHAPTER 34

Zodiacal Releasing

FROM THE LOT OF FORTUNE

———

ZODIACAL RELEASING FROM THE LOT OF FORTUNE IS A TIME-LORD procedure that investigates the matters of the body, health, and prosperity over the course of life. Beginning with the sign and ruler of the Lot of Fortune, it demarcates the favorable and unfavorable periods over the entire life. The lord of Fortune rules the first part of life for the duration of the period of its minor years. The zodiacal sign that follows that of Fortune marks the second period of the life, and it is under the jurisdiction of the lord of that sign for the duration of its minor years, and so on. The "loosening of the bonds" is part of this time-lord technique, and it indicates when dramatic reversals in fortune, health, and wealth can occur.

A complete teaching upon this time-lord method is beyond the scope of this book. However, I will present a very simple short form of the procedure so that you can see how the Lot of Fortune, the special lot of the Moon, was used, along with the minor years of the planets, in order to time issues related to the body. We will illustrate this method using chart 1.

CHART 1: ZODIACAL RELEASING TIMELINE

AGE 0–19
At birth, the Lot of Fortune is in the sign of Leo. The lord of Leo is the Sun. The minor years of the Sun are 19. Thus the first 19 years of life are under the jurisdiction of the Sun, and are influenced by the other planets in the zodiacal sign of Leo, which are the Sun and Mercury.
AGE 19–39
The next sign is Virgo, whose lord is Mercury. The minor years of Mercury are 20. Thus the next 20 years are under the jurisdiction of Mercury and are influenced by any planets in the sign of Virgo, which in this chart is Mars.
AGE 39–47
The next sign is Libra, whose lord is Venus. The minor years of Venus are 8.

Thus the next 8 years are under the jurisdiction of Venus and influenced by any planets in the sign of Libra, which are none.

AGE 47–62

The next sign is Scorpio, whose lord is Mars. The minor years of Mars are 15. Thus the next 15 years are under the jurisdiction of Mars, and are influenced by any planets in the sign of Scorpio (there are none).

AGE 62–74

The next sign is Sagittarius, whose lord is Jupiter. The minor years of Jupiter are 12. Thus the next 12 years are under the jurisdiction of Jupiter, and are influenced by any planets in the sign of Sagittarius, which in this chart is Saturn. This native died when she was 63.

Each period can be further subdivided three more times into increments of months, weeks, and hours. Any specific date will have a hierarchy of four levels of time lords operating at a given time, which shape the events of the life in terms of health, wealth, general happiness, and well-being.

For example, with our example chart, this person's first child was born when she was 28 years old on November 27, 1957, after two failed pregnancies. According to Zodiacal Releasing from Fortune, which governs matters of the body, the time lords for levels 1, 2, 3, and 4 are Mercury, Jupiter, the Moon, and Mercury, respectively.

LEVEL 1	Virgo/Mercury	4/19/48–1/5/68
LEVEL 2	Pisces/Jupiter	7/1/57–6/26/58
LEVEL 3	Cancer/Moon	11/16/57, 6:30 a.m.–1/17/58, 6:30 p.m.
LEVEL 4	Virgo/Mercury	11/25/57, 10:30 a.m.–11/29/57, 2:30 p.m.

Note that in this chart, Jupiter in Gemini is the lord of the fifth house (Pisces) of children, Mercury is the domicile lord of Jupiter, and the Moon is a general significator of conception. These three planets are favorably connected in the natal chart with trine and sextile aspects. The relevance of these planets to the topics of conception, birth, and children, and their generally benefic nature and harmonious interaction, provided favorable conditions for a successful birth.

THE DAYS OF THE MOON

This special timing procedure is based upon the position and condition of the Moon on the 3rd, 7th, and 40th days after birth. The Moon at birth describes the life as a whole, but its position on the 3rd day gives specialized information concerning the quality of the person's upbringing and the general fortunate, unfortunate, or mediocre circumstances of their life. Firmicus explains that it is on this day that nourishing food is first given to the infant and so the configurations of stars relative to the Moon on this day likewise show the cosmic nurturance, for better or worse.

Valens explains that if a person has the Moon at 7° Scorpio at birth, on the third day, the Moon will be at 7° Sagittarius. Remember that the Hellenistic astrologers are counting without the use of zero, so the third day is actually two days later. The Moon on this day is examined as to its location by sign and house, its aspects to the benefic or malefic planets, and for determinations as to a prosperous or miserable upbringing. Dorotheus points out the problems of a void Moon indicating hardship in the pursuit of one's needs, as well as the difficulties concerning livelihood of a waxing Moon configured by conjunction, square, or opposition with Mars, or a waning Moon configured in these ways with Saturn.

The seventh day of the Moon is found by the zodiacal sign that is square to the natal Moon, which in the above example would be 7° Aquarius. It is evaluated in the same way, but aside from it being an important day, there is no interpretive material in the texts giving indications as to the specific meanings.

However, the fortieth day is mentioned by a number of astrologers as shedding light on the quality of the death, and particularly the possibility of violent death.[1] According to Rhetorius, "Saturn, Mercury, and Mars lying on the place of the Moon on the fortieth day make those dying violently".[2]

---

1   FIRMICUS MATERNUS, *Mathesis* 3.14.10; 4.1.7, trans. HOLDEN; DOROTHEUS, *Carmen* 1.12.1, trans. DYKES; VALENS, *Anthology* 1.14.

2   RHETORIUS, *Compendium* 77.

The Prenatal Lunation

———

HELLENISTIC ASTROLOGERS PAID SPECIAL ATTENTION TO THE PRENATAL lunation—the degree of the New or Full Moon before birth. These are sometimes referred to as the conjunction (New Moon) and Whole Moon (Full Moon) in the texts. The prenatal lunation was considered to be one of the five "places of life", along with the Sun, Moon, Ascendant, and Lot of Fortune. It was considered to be equal in importance to these more well-known significators.

If a person is born during the waxing part of the lunar cycle, between the New Moon and the Full Moon, the prenatal lunation is the zodiacal degree of the New Moon before the birth. If a person is born during the waning part of the lunar cycle, between the Full Moon and the New Moon, the prenatal lunation is the zodiacal degree of the Full Moon before birth.

Valens tells us that if the zodiacal sign of the prenatal lunation or its lord marks the hour (first house) or culminates (tenth house), the person will be fortunate.[1] The prenatal lunation was also examined in relation to which of the parents might die first, or the possibility of one's own violent death.[2]

The prenatal lunation is considered to be one of the five possible candidates chosen to play a key role in a Hellenistic time-lord procedure called "circumambulations through the bounds", a form of primary directions.[3] In this context, the prenatal lunation has the potential power to determine the broadest divisions of life, particularly the assessment of longevity and vital force.

The prenatal lunation was used in conjunction with the Nodes in another technique that investigated the length of life in the event that the chart does not have a predominator or ruler (which can happen in some instances). The interval between the degrees of the prenatal lunation up to either the ascending or descending node, proceeding in the order of the zodiacal signs, is then projected

---

1   VALENS, *Anthology* 2.23.
2   VALENS, *Anthology* 2.34; 2.41.
3   DOROTHEUS, *Carmen* 3.1–2, trans. DYKES; HEPHAISTIO, *Apotelesmatics* 2.26.

from the degree of the Ascendant towards the Midheaven. One then calculates the number of years between this point and the Ascendant in accordance with the ascensional times of each of the zodiacal signs for the latitude of the birth. This technique may be beyond the scope of the beginning student, but we have included it for the advanced student, who is referred to Valens for a full discussion and exposition.[4]

The prenatal lunation degree marks the syzygy between the Sun and Moon, when they are either united at the conjunction or diametrically polarized at the opposition. To the extent that the Sun and Moon signify the soul and body respectively, on a spiritual level this syzygy of the lights may speak to the moment when the soul is fully united with the body. Everyone born within a two-week period shares this moment of the unification of the soul and body as they will have the very same prenatal lunation degree and lord of that degree. Of course, the prenatal lunation and its lord will vary by house location for each person. However, on a broader, soul level, the prenatal lunation may address concepts regarding the incarnation of individuals who, in addition to their individual path, also share a collective intention and destiny.

→   EXAMPLE CHARTS

Let us determine the PNL (prenatal lunation) for each of our charts, and note if its sign is either in the Ascending sign (first house) or the Midheaven sign (tenth house).

CHART I: MOON'S CONDITION: PRENATAL LUNATION

Moon sign and degree	Prenatal lunation
25° ARIES 36'	28° Capricorn

ANALYSIS

Chart I has a WANING MOON at 25° Aries. Therefore, we search for the previous Full Moon just before birth, which occurred on July 21 at 28° Capricorn. The PNL thus falls in the third house, and the lord, Saturn, falls in the second.

4   VALENS, *Anthology* 3.9–10.

CHART II: MOON'S CONDITION: PRENATAL LUNATION

Moon sign and degree   *Prenatal lunation*

08° SAGITTARIUS 12'   29° Libra

ANALYSIS

Chart II has a WAXING MOON. The previous New Moon before birth occurred on October 23 at 29° Libra. The PNL thus falls in the third house, and the lord, Venus, is also in the third house.

→   EXERCISE 27

Using your own chart, complete exercise 27:
The Prenatal Lunation

EXERCISE 27

THE PRENATAL LUNATION

Calculate the prenatal lunation. Enter its zodiacal sign and degree in the table below.

CHART I: MOON'S CONDITION: PRENATAL LUNATION

Moon sign and degree   *Prenatal lunation*

REFLECTION AND ANALYSIS

1. Does your PNL or its lord fall in the first or tenth houses?
2. If so, in what ways does this connote a measure of good fortune to the life as a whole?

CHAPTER 36

Final Judgment

ON THE INFLUENCE OF LUNAR CONCEPTS

———

WE ARE NOW READY TO MAKE OUR FINAL JUDGMENTS CONCERNING THE special concepts associated with the Moon outlined in the last several chapters. In most charts, there may not be any special factors that stand out. However, if there are, it is important to pay attention to them. First, look to see if the Moon herself stands out in any particular way.

1. Does the Moon rejoice by waxing or waning phase in accordance with sect?
2. Is the Moon active or slack (void in course)?
3. Is the Moon free or captive under the bond?
4. Is the Moon precarious, conjunct either Node, or unintegrated at the bendings?
5. Is the Moon intensified as part of a solar or lunar eclipse?
6. Are the Moon's Lot (Fortune) and its ruler in strong and favorable houses?
7. Is the prenatal lunation and its ruler fortunate in the first or tenth houses?
8. Next look at how the Moon impacts the other planets, affecting their condition.
9. Does the Moon make an applying aspect to a planet, helping to manifest that planet's significations?
10. Does the conjunction of a planet with the Moon's North Node contribute towards the qualities of increase for benefics and malefics?
11. Does the conjunction of a planet with the Moon's South Node contribute towards the qualities of decrease for benefics and malefics?
12. Finally, does the Moon's Lot of Fortune bring some measure of good luck to a planet by means of conjunction?

CHART I: FINAL JUDGMENT

Chart I has a waning gibbous moon that does not rejoice, but is active (not void), and free (not captive). The Moon is not captive under the bond; it is not in a precarious position crossing the Nodes; and is not intensified due to an eclipse. The Moon's Lot, Fortune, is located in a strong and favorable house and brings good luck concerning reputation and profession. The Moon, as the ruler of the body, points to both the head (Moon in Aries) and heart (Fortune in Leo) as the sensitive areas of injury and illness. Fortune in Leo, and its lord the Sun, are both strong and protected—and the native did not suffer from heart problems. However, the Moon in Aries in the sixth house, and in aversion to its lord Mars, points to some difficulty regarding the head. It was speculated that the native's prolonged use of black hair dye was a contributing cause to the cancer which led to her death.

The Sun, Mercury, and Mars are improved in regards to their condition because they are receiving an applying aspect from the Moon. In addition, the Sun and Mercury benefit from being in the same sign as the Lot of Fortune. None of the planets are conjunct the Nodes.

CHART II: FINAL JUDGMENT

Chart II has a waxing rising Moon that does not rejoice in a nocturnal chart. The Moon is active (not void), and free (not captive). It is precarious as it crosses a Node, and it is not intensified as part of an eclipse. The Moon's Lot, Fortune, is located in a weak and unfavorable house, which on one hand lessens the amount of accidental good luck, but on the other hand saves one from disasters. The Moon as the ruler of bodily matters points to both the hips and thigh area (Moon in Sagittarius), as well as to the stomach (Fortune in Cancer) as sensitive areas of injury and illness, which is exacerbated by the co-presence of Mars with Fortune.

The condition of the Sun is improved by the Moon's applying aspect as she helps to manifest his significations in the physical world. The condition of Mars is improved by the accidental good luck that brushes off on him due to his conjunction by sign with the Lot of Fortune. The influence on the Moon via her conjunction with the North Node has already been discussed above.

→   EXERCISE 28

   Using your own chart, complete exercise 28:
   Final Judgment on Lunar Concepts

EXERCISE 28

FINAL JUDGMENT ON LUNAR CONCEPTS

Review the previous exercises and compile them in the following table.

MOON SIGN AND DEGREE	
WAXING/WANING	
ACTIVE/SLACK (VOID IN COURSE)	
FREE/CAPTIVE (UNDER THE BOND)	
PRECARIOUS (NODES, BENDINGS)	
ECLIPSES	
LOT OF FORTUNE	
PRENATAL LUNATION	

1. *Compose a brief summary describing the special lunar considerations regarding the condition of your Moon. Include whether the Moon is active or void, its phase and whether it rejoices by sect, if it is under the bond, conjunct a Node, or involved in an eclipse. Think about the extent to which the Moon's condition is improved in its ability to be beneficial or if it is challenged.*
2. *Discuss how the Moon's special Hermetic Lot, the Lot of Fortune, impacts the good fortune of the house in which it is located, and how it affects your bodily health. Check to see if your prenatal lunation (PNL) gives an added boost to good fortune in your life if it is located in the 1st or 10th houses.*

3. *Next, evaluate the extent to which each planet benefits from its contact with the Moon, based upon whether it receives an applying aspect (within 30° crossing sign boundaries), is conjunct the appropriate Node in accordance with its own nature, and whether it is in the same sign as the Lot of Fortune.*

SUN

JUPITER

SATURN

MERCURY

VENUS

MARS

REFLECTION AND ANALYSIS

1. Which planets are made fortunate by one of these connections with the Moon or a lunar factor? (You will incorporate this judgment in your final evaluation of each planet at the end of this volume).

CHAPTER 37

Summary

AND SOURCE READINGS

────

THIS CONCLUDES OUR SECTION ON THE SPECIAL LUNAR CONCEPTS THAT were employed in Hellenistic astrology. We have focused on those that have an impact upon how the Moon functions on her own, in terms of her motion, speed, phases, light, and her relation to the Nodes and eclipses. We have also seen some of the ways in which the Moon was used in the analysis of bodily matters regarding health, injury, and illness. In addition, we have set out the ways in which the Moon impacts the other planets in the chart. The general principles may be summarised as follows:

A planet that receives an *applying aspect* from the Moon is assisted in manifesting its significations.

The Moon is ineffective when it is *void in course* and does not conjoin to a planet or its ray for an interval of 30° (including crossing sign boundaries). This is a rare condition.

The Moon is *under the bond* when it is within 15° on either side of the conjunction or opposition with the Sun.

The North Node of the Moon is a principle of *increase*: it magnifies the good of the benefics and also the bad of the malefics. The South Node of the Moon is a principle of *decrease*: it diminishes the good of the benefics as well as the bad of the malefics.

PRIMARY SOURCE READINGS
FOR PART FOUR: THE LUNAR PHASE CYCLE

ANTIOCHUS   *Thesaurus*: Applications of the Moon to the Seven Planets
                 (CCAG 7, pp. 107–11; trans. Schmidt in *Antiochus of Athens,*
                 Thesaurus, Berkeley Springs: WV, Golden Hind Press, 1993).

PAULUS   *Introduction* 17: The Separations and Applications that the Moon
                 Makes with the Revolving Stars.

PORPHYRY   *Introduction* 2: Changes Produced by the Transfers of the Sun, Moon,
                 and Stars (Phases).

PAULUS   *Introduction* 16: The Configurations that the Moon Makes with
                 the Sun (Phases).

VALENS   *Anthology* 2.36: The Eleven Figures of the Moon (Phases).

FIRMICUS   *Mathesis* 1–3; 14 (trans. Holden): Applications and Separations
                 of the Moon.

ANTIOCHUS   *Summary* 11: Void of Course.

PORPHYRY   *Introduction* 23: Void of Course.

RHETORIUS   *Compendium* 39: Void of Course.

PAULUS   *Introduction* 35: Configuration of the Moon with the Sun (Bonding).

RHETORIUS   *Compendium* 38: Bonding.

VALENS   *Anthology* 1.14: Concerning the Third, Seventh, and Fortieth Days
                 of the Moon.

                 Anthology 2.23: Excerpt on the Prenatal Lunation.

                 Anthology 5.2: Lunar Nodes and Prenatal Lunation.

PART FIVE

ASPECTS

CHAPTER 38

Aspects

THE COSMIC DANCE OF THE PLANETS

——

IN THE CELESTIAL COSMOLOGY, PLANETARY GODS ARE THE MEDIATORS between the zodiacal signs and the houses. Their function is to bring the life of the individual—whom they serve—to its natural conclusion, which is the person's destiny. Planets stand midway between the divine energies flowing down through the zodiacal images of the stars and the terrestrial realm here on Earth.

The terrestrial realm is divided into twelve sectors that describe the range of human experiences. The planets move along their courses in nested spheres at different rates of speed, ever passing by each other in a continual dynamic dance. Their first relationships are to the two luminaries, the Sun and Moon, the king and queen of the heavens, which we explored in the previous sections. Next, the planets relate to each other.

In this section we turn to the aspects, which are one of the fundamental components of astrological interpretation, alongside planet, sign, and house. Aspects depict the wide variety of interactions that take place between the planets. Planets have harmonious and unharmonious relationships which move them to help, harm, or even be indifferent to each other. As a result of the supportive or antagonistic interactions between the planets, the aspects also contribute to shaping and modifying the behavior of planets individually as well as in combination. Sometimes their two natures blend together in accordance with their aspect, and sometimes one planet takes the active role in impacting the outcomes of the other planet.

Since our focus with this book is the determination of planetary condition, many teachings in this section will be directed to how planetary aspects improve a planet's condition, assisting it to bring forth its positive significations for the benefit of the individual. The correlate to this is the exploration of the ways in which planets can block or oppose one another, preventing the matters from being realized in ways that serve the best interests of the individual. In some aspect situations, one planet can actively harm and injure another to the extent that it is unable to bring forth its significations, or does so in ways that can be destructive for the well-being of the person.

The Hellenistic aspect doctrine in its entirety is a complex and sophisticated vision of the cosmic dance of the planets. This aspect doctrine has been one of the most challenging parts of the Hellenistic astrological system to translate, understand, and integrate into the reconstruction of the practice. The basic components are contained in a series of definitions found in the texts of Antiochus and Porphyry (which may have originated from some other common but unknown source), and then repeated by Hephaistio and Rhetorius.[1]

While many of the definitions are broadly similar in each of the texts, the various versions reveal disagreements over some critical details. Some manuscripts even by the same author differ, and some manuscripts have different lines of transmission. The definitions have names that seem strange and exotic to our contemporary ears. It has been extremely challenging for those of us translating and reconstructing the aspect doctrine to find translations for these words that aptly convey their meanings, which have been a struggle to fully understand in the first place. So be aware that in your studies you may encounter different words used by different contemporary authors to refer to the same original concept. In some cases, I will use the Greek technical term because so far, as a community, we cannot settle upon a satisfactory English translation for the concept. Here is a short list of various aspect terms described in the Hellenistic texts. The term in Greek is followed by the term I'll use throughout this manual.

EPIMARTURIA	Witnessing
DEXIOS & EUŌNUMOS	Right and Left Figures
PARALLAGĒ	Passing Beyond
SUNAPHĒ	Connecting
KOLLĒSIS	Adherence
SUNODOS	Meeting
APORROIA	Separation
PERISCHESIS	Containment
EMPERISCHESIS	Enclosure
MESEMBOLĒSIS	Intervention

---

1 ANTIOCHUS, *Summary*, CCAG 7.3, pp. 111–119. PORPHYRY, *Introduction to Ptolemy's Tetrabiblos*, CCAG 5.4, pp. 187–228. HEPHAISTIO OF THEBES, *Apotelesmatics* (Leipzig: Teubner, 1973). RHETORIUS OF EGYPT, *Compendium*, CCAG 1, pp. 140–64; CCAG 8.4, pp. 115–24. For translations and commentary, see Robert SCHMIDT, *Definitions and Foundations* (Cumberland, MD: The Golden Hind Press, 2009); HOLDEN, *Introduction to the Tetrabiblos* (Tempe, AZ: American Federation of Astrologers, 2009); SCHMIDT, *Apotelesmatics* 1 and 2; GRAMAGLIA, *Apotelesmatics* 3, ed. DYKES (Minneapolis, MN: Cazimi Press, 2013); GEORGE (in the present volume).

EPIDEKATĒSIS	Domination
KATHUPERTERĒSIS	Overcoming
HOMORĒSIS	Neighboring
KENODROMIA	Traveling Alone (Void)
AKTINOBOLIA	Hurling a Ray
LAMPANĒ	Chariots
ANATOLĒ & DUSIS	Rising & Setting
METOCHĒ	Joint Possession
ANTANALUSIS	Counteraction
KAKŌSIS	Maltreatment
DORUPHORIA	Spear-bearing Bodyguard

In the study of the Hellenistic aspect doctrine it becomes evident that the understanding of aspects changed many times as the doctrines were translated and transmitted through the Persian, Arabic, Medieval, Renaissance, and modern cultures. On one hand, all of the approaches to the interpretation of aspects are similar in that aspects show the ease or difficulty that the planets have in their interactions with one another. However, there is great divergence when it comes to which aspects are valid, which orbs to use, whether the orbs go with the planet or the aspect, the use of whole sign aspects or degree-based aspects, and the validity of out-of-sign aspects. The underlying view concerning how aspects operate differs as well.

Before engaging more deeply in the Hellenistic view, take a moment to look over the following brief historical summary of how the various astrological traditions approached their understanding of aspects.

HISTORICAL OVERVIEW OF ASPECT DOCTRINES

Hellenistic astrologers recognize only four aspects, which they called "configurations"—the 60° sextile, the 90° square, the 120° trine, and the 180° opposition. The conjunction was not technically an aspect, although it was treated like one in most instances. The quincunx and semi-sextile were not considered aspects, but called "aversions". The trine and sextile configurations are harmonious, the square and opposition unharmonious, and the conjunction variable. Aspects are primarily determined by whole sign, rather than by an orb of exact degree. Thus, for the most part, no out-of-sign aspects are acknowledged as aspects. However, there are a number of specific and quite important situations where orbs of degrees are important.

Similar to modern astrology, the individual meanings of planets are blended together by means of their easy or challenging aspect. However, what differs is the additional distinction that one planet can *do something* to the other planet, either helping or harming it, which impacts its condition. This is the difference between the modern interpretation of Mercury square Mars indicating aggressive speech as part of one's personality characteristics and the Hellenistic view that Mercury is being harmed and injured by Mars in regards to the faculty of speech, with the result that the individual experiences slander, accusations, and betrayals.

The Arabic/Medieval tradition assigned orbs in the determination of aspects. The orbs were not associated with the individual aspects, but rather with each of the planets based upon the distance of the orbs of light that emanated from each planet. The Sun has an orb of 15°, the Moon 12°, Mercury 7°, Venus 7°, Mars 8°, Jupiter 9°, and Saturn 9°.[2] Known as the doctrine of moiety, an aspect between two planets becomes effective when the two orbs are added together, and then halved to obtain a mean value that applies to both. This moiety sets the range that the planets' actual distance can deviate from the exact aspect whereby the planets have a valid interaction. Therefore, each set of planets has its own orb of connection.

During the Renaissance, Kepler added many more aspects, including the quintile, septile, and novile. Modern astrology includes a multitude of aspects, and some modern astrologers consider the quincunx a major aspect. There are descriptions and interpretations of many aspect patterns such as the T-square, the grand trine, and the yod. The orbs are assigned to the aspects themselves, rather than to the planets. The practice of using orbs varies among modern astrologers. There is dissent about whether to use narrower or wider orbs, how to apply the orbs in different circumstances, as well as which aspects and aspect patterns are significant.

In Hellenistic astrology, aspects and their interpretation are primarily determined by the nature and relationship of the zodiacal signs the planets occupy, regardless of orb or degree. So for the most part, the concept of out-of-sign aspects doesn't exist in the source material.

In Medieval astrology, aspects are determined by the orbs of the planets, regardless of their zodiacal signs. In modern astrology, aspects are determined by the orb of degrees of the aspect itself, regardless of zodiacal sign. In Medieval and modern astrology, this range of degrees can cross sign boundaries, allowing for out-of-sign aspects.

2   IBN SAHL, *Introduction* 5.3.

THE SEVEN VISUAL RAYS

The broad vision that stands behind the Hellenistic aspect doctrine is that of visual rays. Porphyry wrote that "each star sends forth seven rays, three upwards and three downwards, and one towards the diameter".[3]

These seven visual rays emanate from the planets and are the means by which planets can see each other's sig-nifications and see into the affairs of the various houses. All of the Greek words that refer to aspects have visual mean-ings such as "to see", "to look upon", "to gaze at", "to scrutinize", or "to behold". The English word "aspect" derives from the Latin *adspicere*, which translates as "to look at". The Vedic astrologers, when discussing aspects, use the Hindu word *drishti*, meaning "to glance".

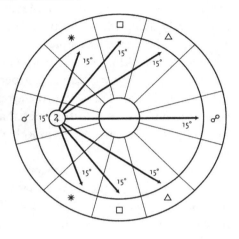

FIGURE 53.
PLANET CASTING
SEVEN VISUAL PARTILE RAYS

The ray cast from Jupiter at 15° of a Whole Sign goes to the fifteenth degree of its sextile, square, trine, and opposition aspects.

To visualize the aspect doctrine, you might imagine that a planet is like a flashlight. The beam of light that it sends forth is refracted into seven primary directions (aspects) that il-luminate the spaces where they land. That beam enables the planet to "see" what is going on in certain sectors of the chart. To determine whether there is a helpful or harmful impact upon the outcomes of the house topics and planetary significations, we take into account the planet's own essential benef-ic or malefic nature, as well as the kind of "look" (sympathetic or unsympa-thetic) that emanates from the angle of a visual ray. And we add to our con-sideration the significations of the house and planet where those looks land. Imagine the difference in how you might be affected by receiving a loving gaze from a parent versus a glaring stare from a frightening stranger. This notion of a "bad look" is related to the fear of the "evil eye", an archetypal symbol in ancient cultures.

In Hellenistic astrology, aspects operate both by whole sign and by specific degree. We can think of planets that "observe" each other by whole sign as-

3 PORPHYRY, *Introduction* 9.

pect as influencing one another through the process of witnessing each other
and then giving friendly or hostile testimony about what they have seen. In this
way, planets have an influence upon one another, for good or for ill, as a result
of what they see and say. Planets that observe each other in a closer manner, according to degree-based aspects, have more intense interactions, and for better
or for worse, they engage with one another and have a stronger impact. They
can actively change the ways in which each other's significations come about, or
even block them from eventuating.

Special conditions of maltreatment, bonification, and protection fall under
the category of the more complex aspect relations based upon degrees and spatial considerations. As a whole, the aspect doctrine describes the many kinds of
beneficial and harmful testimonies that planets present about one another as
they "negotiate" (in the words of Robert Schmidt) "about the fate of the native"
whose life they oversee.[4]

This is a very different conception of the workings of aspects than that of
modern astrology, which poses that when planets move into a certain angular
relationship, regardless of sign, it is as if their gears lock, they connect, and they
have an interaction based upon the nature of the aspect, which blends their individual significations into a hybrid expression. Hellenistic astrology definitely
contains the delineations of hybrid expressions of the various planetary aspect
combinations. But it also goes a step further to show how the significations of
certain planets can become better—or others become worse—as one planet
takes the initiative to actively help or harm the other.

Within the context of each planet sending forth seven visual rays, the movement of the planets in their orbits is dynamic. One might imagine strobe lights
flashing from dancers as the circular stage on which they are performing spins
around. The planets are in continual motion, ever-changing in their relationships towards one another. Planets unite at conjunctions and then move apart as
they travel at different rates of speed: now faster, now slower, sometimes moving
towards each other and then separating away, stepping forwards and backwards,
the one leading the moves of the dance and the other following. Their view of
each other is in constant flux as they find themselves in sextile, square, trine, and
opposite formations. At times they even disappear from each other's sight, before reuniting at their next union. In many ways, the cycles of relative planetary
motion have similarities to the lunar and solar phase cycles, where at critical
points in the cyclic dance, special kinds of interactions take place.

The music temporarily stops when a child is born, and the cosmic dancers

4   Robert SCHMIDT, personal communication.

freeze in place. The arrangement of the planets' positions defines their relationships to one another at that moment in time. In this way, the aspects formed in this dynamic planetary dance contribute to shaping the experiences of the life of the native.

Because aspects are relationships, their interpretation speaks to the ways planets (and the people they serve) come together, feel connected, loved, supported, or helped. Others point to ways in which they break up, disconnect, and move apart; how they suffer, feel hurt, are harmed, or become alienated. The relationships of the planets at the moment of birth prefigures the internal dynamic in the psyche and its relation to others, which individuals then act out externally in their dance with the other.

We will now begin our study of the Hellenistic aspect doctrine. We will start with whole sign aspects, then move on to degree-based aspects and spatial directions, and finally, discuss some other ways planets relate to one another based upon zodiacal signs, rather than aspects.

CHAPTER 39

Whole Sign Aspects

WITNESS AND TESTIMONY

———

THE FIRST DEFINITION IN OUR LIST CONCERNING ASPECTS REFERS TO *Epimarturia*, a Greek word meaning "to bear witness or give testimony". The doctrine teaches that each planet sends forth seven rays, understood as beams of light that enable planets to see into other parts of the sky, where the activities of other planets are taking place in their respective house locations. The planets then give a report or testimony about what they have witnessed.

The ideas of witnessing and testimony were very important concepts in the Hellenistic world generally. They appear frequently in the religious literature of the *New Testament*, in which people affirmed their belief in Jesus because they had *witnessed* a miracle, either directly or through a vision. They then gave their eye-witness *testimony*, which helped to convince others of the authority of this new dispensation.

Robert Schmidt first pointed out the legal paradigm that works as a metaphor for understanding the aspect doctrine.[1] Similar to a court of law, the planets are called to the witness stand in order to offer their affirmative or negating testimony about what they have seen regarding the actions of some other planet or house. After all the testimony is taken into account, a judgment is rendered. The issues that are up for judgment are not only the specific agendas of each planet, but also the topics designated by the twelve houses, such as marriage, children, or wealth. The operative question is if the various topics of life will eventuate for the individual, and if so, whether those topics will be a source of happiness or suffering.

Two popular titles used for astrology books in the ancient periods were *Apotelesmatica* (Hellenistic) and the *Judgment of Nativities* (Arabic). The art of astrology is making the judgment as to how something will turn out in the end (*apoteleō*) after taking all the various factors into consideration. And the testimony of the planets via their aspects is a major factor influencing one's final decision.

---

1   Robert SCHMIDT, personal communication.

It is useful to compare the similarities and differences in the definitions of witnessing provided by Antiochus and Porphyry. These definitions provide an overview of the entire aspect doctrine. We will unpack each of the concepts in the discussion that follows.

> ANTIOCHUS: [Antiochus told] How the stars are said to bear witness to one another whenever they are tetragons or triplicities or diameters or hexagons of one another, and at how many intervals (zodiacal signs) each one of these foresaid [figures] is configured. And how the trigonal figure is sympathetic and helpful, even if one of the stars is a destroyer, for it is less harmful; the tetragon is the opposite, even if the star is benefic; the diameter is adversarial, but worse when a malefic star is present; the hexagon is less effective than the others. The aforementioned figures are brought about according to two different ways, either simply by zodiacal sign or by degree. Wherefore many times the stars that are triangular to each other according to zodiacal signs are not triangular according to the degrees; so it is with the other figures.[2]

> PORPHYRY: They call the configurations of the stars towards each other bearing witness. There are the following figures: the trigon is through five [intervals] whenever there are three zodiacal signs between the two; the tetragon is through four [intervals] whenever there are two zodiacal signs between them; the diameter is through seven [intervals] whenever there are five in the middle; and the hexagon is through three [intervals] whenever there is one between them. And the trigon is sympathetic and helpful, and even if a destructive star is there, it is less damaging. The tetragon is harsh and unsympathetic and capable of causing pain if a destructive star is present. The diameter is adversarial, but worse if a malefic star is present. The hexagon is less efficacious. It is necessary to consider if the figures are perfect by degree and not only according to zodiacal sign. The triangular figure is at an interval of 120°, the tetragon at an interval of 90°, the hexagon at an interval of 60°, the diameter at an interval of 180°. For often [stars] are configured according to zodiacal sign, but not further according to degree.[3]

---

2   ANTIOCHUS, *Summary* 6.
3   PORPHYRY, *Introduction* 8.

THE CONFIGURATIONS

So, under what circumstances can planets see each other for the purpose of giving testimony? Our authors tell us that planets bear witness towards each other when they stand in certain configurations (*schēmatismos*) towards one another. These configurations are the *tetragon* (square), *trigon* (triangle or trine), *diameter* (opposition), and *hexagon* (sextile). The Greek word *schema* means "a form, shape, or figure", and can be used to refer to a geometrical figure. When the geometrical figures of regular polygons are inscribed into the zodiacal circle, they connect certain sets of signs. When planets stand in the zodiacal signs that

FIGURE 54. WHOLE SIGN ASPECTS:
TRIGONS, TETRAGONS, DIAMETERS, HEXAGONS

are connected by these polygonal figures, they are configured, and are thus able to bear witness and give testimony. The visual rays emitted by planets travel along the pathways designated by the angular slopes of the sides of these regular polygons, which establish the connection between the planets in their respective zodiacal signs.

As we saw in section two, the *tetragon* (four-sided figure, square, 90°) configures zodiacal signs of the same modality (tropical/cardinal, solid/fixed, and bi-corporeal/mutable). The trigon (three-sided figure, triangle, 90°) configures signs of the same triplicity or element (fire, air, water, earth). The *diameter* (line, opposition, 180°) configures signs that are opposite each other. The *hexagon* (six-sided figure, sextile, 60°) configures signs of the same gender (male, female).

Here we see that Hellenistic astrologers understood the zodiacal signs to form the configurations. Certain sets of zodiacal signs have a coherent and intrinsic relationship with one another due to the geometrical figures that connect them. Planets that stand in these signs are thus likewise configured—not due to the orb of degrees, but rather by the pre-existing connection of the signs. Any planet in those signs partakes of the relationships that those signs already have between them.

This is the rationale for the use of whole sign aspects. A planet in any degree of Leo (even 2° Leo) is trine to a planet in any degree of Sagittarius (even 28° Sagittarius), because the zodiacal signs of Leo and Sagittarius are connected by the sides of the trigon. The same is true for planets in square, opposition, or sextile configurations. The sympathy or antipathy that shapes the relationship between planets is prefigured by the sympathies or antipathies of the signs they occupy.

Imagine the animosity during the Wars of the Roses, a series of wars for control of the throne of England between the Houses of Lancaster and York. A member of one of these families was likely to have an adversarial attitude toward a member of the other family, not because of any particular individual interaction—the two might never have even met. Rather, their interaction was based upon their belonging to families that had pre-existing relations with each other. In whole sign aspect configurations involving witnessing and testimony, it is the zodiacal signs that the planets occupy which determine the harmonious or unharmonious relationships between them—not the number of degrees in their angular arcs of separation.

What about the conjunction, quincunx, and semi-sextile? The conjunction was not technically an aspect, but it was treated as an aspect. Planets in the same sign could not see each other, but they were nevertheless connected through a kind of commingling or cohesion of their significations. Planets in the same sign were said to be co-present.

The 30° semi-sextile and the 150° quincunx were not considered aspects. They were called aversions, from the word *apostrophē* meaning "to turn away from, be estranged, or alienated". It is not possible to see something right next to you in an adjacent sign (semi-sextile), and there is a blind spot in the vision at the 150° angle (quincunx). When learning to drive, you learn to use the mirror rather than turning your head to look behind when getting ready to pass. That particular angle is the 150° blind spot.

Because planets in aversion could not see each other, they could not give testimony. However, there were other means of interaction available to them not determined by configurations. These will be discussed later in this section.

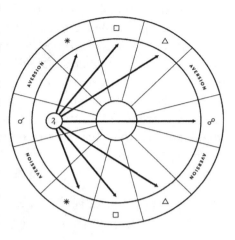

FIGURE 55.
AVERSION

When planets occupy the geometrically configured signs (square, trine, opposition, and sextile aspects) they have the potential to act as witnesses to each other's significations and provide testimony regarding certain matters or topics. This is a very different way of looking at planetary aspects than the approach of blending together the individual significations of each planet in accordance with easy or difficult modes of interaction.

THE NATURE OF THE ASPECT CONFIGURATIONS

The Greek word *schēmatismos* translates as "configuration", and suggests a certain attitude that is conveyed by a "posture". Think of approaching someone who has their arms crossed in front and then another whose arms are opened wide. The first posture suggests that person is resistant, blocking, and keeping you away. The second posture is welcoming, inviting you in.

Both Antiochus and Porphyry describe the nature of each of the aspect configurations. The trigon (trine aspect) is sympathetic and helpful. Even when one of the stars is a malefic, it is less harmful when in a trine configuration. The tetragon (square aspect) is harsh and unsympathetic. It is capable of causing pain if one of the stars is a malefic. Antiochus holds that the tetragon is harmful, even if one star is a benefic. The diameter (opposition aspect) is adversarial, but even worse if one of the stars is a malefic. The hexagon (sextile aspect) is weak and ineffective.

The notion that the trine aspect is harmonious and the square and opposition aspects are challenging has remained consistent throughout the tradition from ancient to modern times. In the Hellenistic view, the trine is a helpful aspect, and especially beneficial when Jupiter is involved. The square and opposition aspects are unsympathetic, and harmful, injurious, inflicting damage or pain when Mars or Saturn is involved. The sextile was acknowledged as an aspect, and while not destructive, it was nevertheless weak and ineffective. One might interpret that the sextile was mildly sympathetic, but could not be counted on to give much help.

RATIONALES FOR THE NATURE OF THE ASPECT CONFIGURATIONS

Several rationales have been proposed to explain the relative natures—friendly or antagonistic—of each of the aspects. Ptolemy and Manilius approached the explanations in terms of the affinities and aversions between the configurations of the zodiacal signs themselves.[4] The sextile aspect is called harmonious because it configures signs that are of the same gender, either entirely feminine or entirely masculine. The implication is that signs of the same gender are harmonious because they move at a similar pace. Likewise, the trine configures signs that are the same element—fire, earth, air, water—so their manner of operation is in sympathetic accord. The lack of harmony in the square aspect is due to it linking signs that are composed of different genders and different elements, though they are of the same modality. And the opposition is adversarial because it is composed of signs that are of opposite kinds, according to Ptolemy. This lack of common orientation coming from different zodiacal signs can create a sense of otherness, engendering challenge and conflict. Thus there is an enmity or rivalry between planets occupying signs that are linked by the sides of a square or opposition. The quincunx is an aversion because the signs are of a different gender, different element, and different modality. Zodiacal signs in aversion thus have no connection with one another, and share no common ground.

The inherent meaning of each aspect can also be approached through the symbolic significance of the number that is used to divide the zodiacal circle in order to create the regular polygons:

---

4   PTOLEMY, *Tetrabiblos* 1.13; MANILIUS, *Astronomica* 2.446–692.

THE CONJUNCTION, which unites, relates to the number *one*, a symbol of unity.

THE OPPOSITION, which is divisive, relates to the number *two*, a symbol of duality.

THE TRINE, which is harmonious, relates to the number *three*, a symbol of synthesis.

THE SQUARE, which is challenging, relates to the number *four*, a symbol of conflict.

THE SEXTILE, which is mildly easy, relates to the number *six*, a symbol of harmony.

THE THEMA MUNDI

An elegant view into the intrinsic benefic or malefic nature of each type of configuration is revealed by the construction of the *thema mundi*. As we have seen in section two, the "nativity of the world" provides the underlying structure for the assignment of the domiciles and exaltations of the planets. The *thema mundi* also shows that the natures of the planets and their configurations to the Sun and Moon play a role in the nature of the aspect.

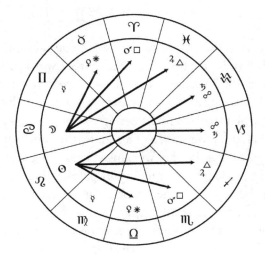

FIGURE 56. ASPECT RELATIONS
DERIVED FROM THE THEMA MUNDI

The two luminaries, the Sun and the Moon, are the domicile lords of the zodiacal signs Leo and Cancer. Fanning out to one side, Libra, the domicile of Venus, is the zodiacal sign that is configured to Leo by the side of the hexagon. Fanning out to the other side, Taurus, also the domicile of Venus, is the zodiacal sign that is configured to Cancer by the side of a hexagon. Therefore, the mildly harmonious nature of the sextile aspect partakes of the nature of the benefic planet Venus (sometimes referred to as the lesser benefic). In a similar manner, Scorpio, the domicile of Mars, is in a square configuration to Leo, just as Aries, the domicile of Mars, is in a square configuration to Cancer. Thus, the destructive and harsh nature of the square aspect partakes of the nature of the malefic planet Mars. Proceeding with this pattern, the zodiacal signs of Sagittarius and Pisces, both domiciles of Jupiter, are configured by the sides of a trigon to Leo and Cancer, placing the sympathetic and supportive trine aspect under the auspices of Jupiter. Finally, Capricorn and Aquarius, both the domiciles of Saturn, are opposed to the signs Leo and Cancer. Thus, the adversarial and conflictual opposition aspect is under the influence of the malefic planet Saturn. In this way, the *thema mundi* gives an insight into the harmonious and unharmonious natures of the four major aspects by means of their intrinsic associations with the benefic and malefic planets.

ANOTHER VIEW

Yet one more view into the nature of the aspect configurations has been proposed by Robert Schmidt.[5] He begins with the Greek word *schema* as a geometrical figure whose additional meanings include "posture, stance, gesture, and attitude". He then looks at the physical stances accompanied by certain attitudes that planets adopt when they assume a configuration with one another.

When planets assume the stance of a square, the right angle that is formed between them suggests that they are working at cross purposes. The oppositional stance suggests the planets are moving in parallel, but opposite directions. Planets assuming the stance in the trigonal figures have an acute inclination towards one another, and the sextile depicts a smaller angle which gives a lesser inclination. It follows that the blockage, frustration, and tensions that are associated with square aspects can be derived from the stance of being at cross purposes. The disagreement, open conflict, and contrariness associated with the opposition can be seen as a pull toward opposite directions. The sharply slop-

5   SCHMIDT, *Definitions and Foundations*, pp. 134–135.

ing inclination of one planet towards another via the trine aspect gives rise to sympathetic attitudes and supportive, helpful actions. A sympathetic feeling but with less actual support behind the sentiment is in line with the more gradual inclination of the sextile aspect. In these ways we can see how the natures of the aspects can be derived from the stances taken by the planets in the angles formed by their configurations.

PERFECTION

The final section of the opening definition pertains to the notion of perfection, and it addresses the use of both whole sign aspects and degree-based aspects. Antiochus writes that "these figures are brought about and completed according to two different ways, either simply by zodiacal sign or by degree". The important Greek term in the original sentence is the verb *apoteleō*, whose definitions include "to bring to an end", "to complete", and "to accomplish". Many of the ancient astrology books, such as those by Ptolemy and Hephaistio, are entitled *Apotelesmatica*, which suggests that the inquiry of ancient astrologers was to foresee the final outcome of the combinations of planetary factors.

The root verb *teleō* suggests the final outcome or result of an action that has been brought to fulfillment or perfection. In the Hellenistic world, the study of astrology was understood as the final outcomes of planetary actions when they have been completed or perfected. In the *New Testament*, *teleō* (*tetelestai*) was the final word of Jesus (John 19:30) when he said, "It is finished", meaning that the purpose for which his life was intended had been fulfilled, perfected, and brought to a successful end.

Given the usage of this word during the era when these astrological texts were written, we can see a deeper meaning here. The planets in their configurations witness and testify about each other's significations, impacting how another planet will be judged. The final outcome of these actions, as the purpose for which they were intended, is brought to completion, fulfilled, and made perfect according to zodiacal sign as well as according to degree. This establishes that the matters of the planets in aspect configuration can be accomplished by the considerations of whole sign aspects. Through these aspects, a planet in any degree of a sign that is configured to a planet in any degree of another sign can bear witness and give testimony.

Porphyry gives the intervals at which each aspect is exact—120° for the triangular (trine) figure, 90° for the square, 180° for the diameter (opposition), and 60° for the hexagon (sextile). Both he and Antiochus instruct that, "often the stars are configured according to zodiacal sign, but not further according to degree". They are preparing the reader for the number of other instances when the consideration of exact degrees is important and necessary. Many of the following aspect definitions pertain to these situations.

The Arabic and Medieval authors pick up on the notion of perfection, especially when addressing horary questions, where they enumerate a number of ways to determine when the matters of the planets are perfected, confirmed, and brought to a successful completion. The later understanding of perfection by aspect necessitates that the faster-moving planet makes the exact aspect to the slower-moving planet before either planet leaves the zodiacal signs of the configuration. However, a reading of the Hellenistic texts illustrates that most examples of the witnessing and testifying of planets operate by whole sign aspects and do not necessitate the more precise definition of perfection that develops later in the tradition.

Because whole sign aspects were used extensively in Hellenistic astrology, a quick perusal of a chart involved looking to see if a planet, house, or sensitive point was witnessed by benefics or malefics. This affirming or negating testimony then impacted the astrologer's judgment concerning the final outcomes of the various matters under the auspices of a planet as well as the topics of life. A planet that received positive testimony would be enhanced in the judgment of its final outcome, while one receiving negating testimony would raise concern as to its ability to bring about fortunate events for the individual, as well as disappointments regarding the matters it represented.

CHAPTER 40

Interpretation

OF WHOLE SIGN CONFIGURATIONS

———

ALL ASPECT CONFIGURATIONS HAVE AN INTERPRETIVE MEANING. VALENS and Firmicus Maternus both give "cookbook" interpretations for the planets commingling in the same sign (conjunction) and in aspect configuration (sextile, square, trine, opposition).[1] In spirit, these are similar to modern interpretations in which the significations of the planets blend together, forming hybrid characteristics as a result of the harmony or lack of harmony of the aspect rays. Here is an excerpt from Valens:

> Mercury trine with Jupiter is indicative of great achievements, especially when it is at morning rising. For these individuals become scribes or administrators of kings, cities, or the populace. And if the star of Mercury should be in altogether good condition and provide results, it will bring about high reputation and acquisition of livelihood, especially when it occupies the profitable zodiacal signs. And if the stars are sextile, they will effect the same things, but to a lesser degree. If they should be well-positioned and square, they bring forth to some extent reputation and acquisitions, but with envy. But if they are poorly situated, they bring ruin together with hatred and opposition from those more powerful. If the stars are in opposition, they bring greater slanders and those who are inconstant and contrary. And if the stars are in opposition in the house of the Bad Daimon, these individuals will be oppressed by great authorities, experience the insurrection of the masses, and they will have few siblings or hatred towards brothers, children, or relatives.[2]

Looking carefully at the above delineation you will notice that both planets contribute their significations—as a scribe (Mercury) of kings (Jupiter). The best indications are for the trine, and somewhat less auspicious for the sextile

---

1   VALENS, *Anthology* 1. 19–20; 2.17; FIRMICUS MATERNUS, *Mathesis* 6.3–27, trans. HOLDEN.
2   VALENS, *Anthology* 2.17.

(hexagon), but still good. A well-figured square indicates some beneficial re-sults, but with envy, while a poorly situated square is much more difficult. And the delineation for the opposition aspect is quite dire. These delineations are in accordance with the essential meanings of the aspect configurations.

Aspects not only contribute to the shaping of one's own personality charac-teristics, but also have independent injurious or beneficial impacts upon other people in one's life. In the following examples, we see how one planet affects the significations of the other planet.

Valens writes that Saturn square the Sun on the left impedes the father's income even while he is alive, especially in feminine zodiacal signs, while Venus sextile the Sun when she is rising in the morning signifies that the father and child are charming and notable.[3] Firmicus Maternus explains that when Mars is on the right side of a square aspect to the Sun, it impugns all opportunities for advancement, but when on the left side, a miserable demise is prepared for both the father and for the native.[4] The Sun signifies the father, and the nature of the aspects in one's own chart also describes the good or bad that happens to the parents.

Embedded within the delineations are a host of other factors that contribute to the final judgment of the configuration, such as a planet's sect status, the gen-der of its zodiacal sign, whether a planet is in its own signs of rulership, whether it is morning or evening rising, if the planet is in a fortunate or unfortunate house, if the aspects are on the right or left hand sides. In our final summary for each planet, we will consider each of these factors.

However, for the purposes of this chapter, we will keep our focus upon the aspect configuration criteria, and in particular, how each planet's condition is improved or weakened as a result of its configuration with the benefic or malefic planets. The actual interpretation of the meaning of an aspect is the final step, after all the factors that contribute to the condition of that planet are thoroughly understood and integrated.

GUIDELINES FOR INTERPRETING WITNESSING AND WHOLE SIGN TESTIMONY CONFIGURATIONS

1. Being witnessed by a benefic gives positive testimony on behalf of the planet and is supportive. The basic nature of a benefic is affirmative, and

---

3   VALENS, *Anthology*, 2.17.
4   FIRMICUS MATERNUS, *Mathesis* 4.11, trans. HOLDEN.

it says "yes" to the other planet's significations.

2. Being witnessed by a malefic gives negative testimony on behalf of the planet and is obstructive. The basic nature of a malefic is negating, and it says "no" to the other planet's significations.

3. Being witnessed by trine is supportive to a planet, helping to bring forth its positive significations.

4. A benefic witnessing by trine enhances the best and most positive qualities a planet has to offer.

5. A malefic witnessing by trine is less harmful than would otherwise be the case.

6. Being witnessed by square or opposition is not supportive to a planet being able to bring forth its positive significations.

7. A benefic witnessing by square or opposition does not harm (and in some special cases may help).[5]

8. A malefic witnessing by square or opposition is destructive and harmful for a planet's positive significations, and in some cases may amplify the planet's negative significations.

9. Being witnessed by sextile, though mildly beneficial, does not have a particularly strong impact. While sympathetic, its beneficial support may be limited.

10. Co-presence (conjunct in the same sign) with a benefic is beneficial for a planet, and co-presence with a malefic is not beneficial for a planet.

11. Planets in their own signs of rulership will bring forth better outcomes, even when in square and opposition configurations. In some cases they are considered "functional benefics".

12. If a planet is witnessed by both benefics and malefics, they do not cancel each other out. Rather, the expression and experiences that pertain to that planet's significations will be a mixture of good and bad regarding the events and outcomes in a person's life.

13. A benefic that receives good testimony is enhanced in being able to bring about its best.

14. A benefic that receives bad testimony is limited in the amount of good it can do.

15. A malefic that receives good testimony is supported in bringing about better outcomes for the individual, albeit at the expense or loss of others.

16. A malefic that receives bad testimony has its own malefic tendencies

5   Note, however, that according to Antiochus, a benefic in square aspect *could* harm.

amplified and activated.

17. The semi-sextile and quincunx/inconjunct are called aversions. They are not considered aspect configurations and are not used in the assessment of a planet's condition, although they do have an interpretive meaning of being associated with enmities and factionalisms.[6]

→ EXAMPLE CHARTS

Let us assess each planet's condition based upon the positive and negative whole sign testimony it receives from the benefic and malefic planets. Keep in mind that whole sign testimony impacts the outcomes of the houses as well, even if there are no resident planets in a particular house. This will be covered in volume 2.

For each planet, we will note if it is co-present, sextile, or trine with Venus or Jupiter. These aspect configurations will improve the planet's condition and enhance the planet's ability to bring forth its more beneficial significations. If the planet is co-present, square, or opposed to Mars or Saturn, this weakens a planet's condition and supports the planet's more problematic expressions. We will enter a plus (+) mark for each positive testimony from a benefic and a minus (-) mark for each negative testimony from a malefic. We will then give a preliminary grade to each planet based only upon whole sign testimony.

6   PAULUS, *Introduction* 11.

CHART I: WHOLE SIGN TESTIMONY FROM BENEFICS AND MALEFICS

Zodiacal sign	Conjunction, sextile, or trine from benefics	Conjunction, square, or opposition from malefics	Adjustment	Grade
SUN Leo	Venus sextiles Jupiter sextiles	—	+ +	A
JUPITER Gemini	Venus conjoins	Mars squares Saturn opposes	+ - -	C
SATURN Sagittarius	—	Mars squares	-	D
MERCURY Leo	Venus sextiles Jupiter sextiles	—	+ +	A
MOON Aries	Venus sextiles Jupiter sextiles	—	+ +	A
VENUS Gemini	Jupiter conjoins	Mars squares Saturn opposes	+ - -	C
MARS Virgo	—	Saturn squares	-	D

ANALYSIS

THE SUN AND MERCURY in Leo receive mildly helpful assistance (sextile) from the two benefics, Venus and Jupiter in Gemini, enhancing their capacity to bring forth their best outcomes. There is no negative testimony from the malefics. Therefore I give both of them a grade of A. VENUS AND JUPITER are each strengthened by the mutual commingling of their benefic natures in the same zodiacal sign. However, the square from Mars and the opposition from Saturn both pose severe difficulties as regards their beneficial outcomes along with the good for these two benefics. The double negative testimony leads me to give them a grade of C. THE MOON in Aries receives mildly helpful testimony from the two benefics, Venus and Jupiter in Gemini, which can ease some of the problems she may encounter in the sixth house. There is no negative testimony. Therefore I give her a grade of A, similar to Sun and Mercury. SATURN AND MARS are both suffering from the square configuration between them, and each is made more malefic and problematic because of the other. There is no positive testimony from either benefic (although we will modify this statement later). I give them both a D grade.

CHART II: WHOLE SIGN TESTIMONY FROM BENEFICS AND MALEFICS

Zodiacal sign	Conjunction, sextile, or trine from benefics	Conjunction, square, or opposition from malefics	Adjustment	Grade
SUN Scorpio	—	Saturn opposes	-	C
JUPITER Taurus	—	Saturn conjoins	-	C
SATURN Taurus	Jupiter conjoins		+	B+
MERCURY Scorpio	—	Saturn opposes	-	C
MOON Sagittarius	Venus sextiles		+	B+
VENUS Libra	—	Mars squares	-	C
MARS Cancer	Jupiter sextiles		+	B+

ANALYSIS

THE SUN AND MERCURY receive negating testimony by the opposition from Saturn and are hampered in bringing about their best for the individual. There is no positive testimony from the benefics. I give them a grade of C. JUPITER is harmed by its conjunction with SATURN in the same sign; however, Saturn is helped by Jupiter's presence. This commingling is good for Saturn but bad for Jupiter. Thus I am giving Saturn a B+, but Jupiter a C. VENUS is harmed by the negative testimony square from Mars and is obstructed from manifesting her best outcomes. She is in aversion to both Jupiter and Saturn. I am giving her a C. MARS is mildly helped by its sextile from Jupiter, able to do better on behalf of the individual. The Venus square does not help and the Saturn sextile does not harm. I am giving Mars a B+.

→   EXERCISE 29

   Using your own chart, complete exercise 29:
   Whole Sign Testimony by Benefics and Malefics

EXERCISE 29

WHOLE SIGN TESTIMONY BY BENEFICS AND MALEFICS

Preparing Your Chart

It will be easier for you to follow the discussions in this chapter if you have a visual map in your mind concerning how and where the planets cast rays. If you have studied modern astrology, it will be necessary to retrain your mind as to how aspects operate according to Hellenistic understanding of this doctrine. So first, let's prepare your chart that you will use for all of the remaining exercises in this section.

Print out a copy of your chart, using whole sign houses, the seven visible planets, the lunar Nodes and the Lot of Fortune. For each planet in the chart, draw the seven rays that emit from it (two sextiles at 60°, two squares at 90°, two trines at 120°, and one opposition at 180°) into the appropriate signs/houses at approximately the same degree as that of the planet emitting the ray. In Example Chart 1, the two sextile rays from the Sun will land at 5° Gemini and 5° Libra, the two square rays will land at 5° Taurus and 5° Scorpio, the two trine rays will land at 5° Aries and 5° Sagittarius, and the opposition ray will land at 5° Aquarius.

Be sure that the ray falls in front of or behind any planet that is in that house, based upon their respective degrees. In Example Chart 1, one of the square rays from Jupiter at 9° Gemini falls into the 11th house at 9° Virgo. Make sure that ray falls in front of Mars, which is at 14° Virgo.

I suggest that you use a different color pen or pencil for each of the various aspects—green for sextile, blue for trine, red for square, and purple or orange for opposition. You can choose your own colors for each aspect, but think about the differences between colors that suggest harmony and those that suggest conflict. Based upon the colors, you immediately can see to what extent a house is filled with harmonious light rays or unharmonious light rays. It may be less frustrating if you first draw the ray in pencil that can be erased. Once you are satisfied that the line of the ray is correctly placed, you can draw over it in color.

In this exercise, you are going to look at the whole sign affirming and negating testimony that each planet receives from the benefics and malefics and how that impacts its ability to express its positive significations. Then you are going to make a judgment and give each planet a preliminary grade based upon testimonial relations.

WHOLE SIGN TESTIMONY FROM BENEFICS AND MALEFICS

Zodiacal sign	Conjunction, sextile, or trine from benefics	Conjunction, square, or opposition from malefics	Adjustment	Grade
SUN				
JUPITER				
SATURN				
MERCURY				
MOON				
VENUS				
MARS				

1. *Zodiacal sign: Enter the zodiacal sign for each planet. Since we are looking at whole sign testimony, degrees are not important.*

2. *Conjunction, sextile, or trine from Venus or Jupiter: If the planet receives a whole sign conjunction, trine, or sextile from Venus or Jupiter, enter the planet and the aspect. In the score column, enter a plus sign for each affirming testimony.*

3. *Conjunction, square, or opposition from Mars or Saturn: If the planet receives a whole sign conjunction, square, or opposition from Mars or Saturn, enter the planet and the aspect. Then, in the score column, enter a minus sign for each negating testimony.*

4. *Remember: Whole sign aspects, no out of sign aspects, no orbs.*

5. *Judgment:*

   A planet's condition is *improved* by benefic testimony from the benefic planets that affirm its significations. This positive testimony helps the planet to bring about its most positive significations for the benefit of the individual.

   A planet's condition is *worsened* by malefic testimony from the malefic planets which negate its significations. This negative testimony blocks the planet from bringing about its most positive significations for the benefit of the individual, or activates the more problematic expressions.

   A *mixture* of benefic and malefic testimonies do not cancel each other out, but result in some good outcomes and some bad outcomes. Like a court of law, this testimony influences the final judgment made by the judge or jury (or astrologer) concerning the planet's relative condition that enables it to bring forth its best significations on behalf of the individual.

6. *Give each planet a grade—A, B, C, D, or F—with pluses or minuses.*

REFLECTION AND ANALYSIS

1. Which planets are being helped by the benefics to bring forth their best significations?

2. Which planets are being harmed by malefics that hinder or prevent their most positive significations?

3. Which planets receive a mixture of both help and harm, resulting in both good and bad things arising?

4. Overall, is there more witnessing by benefics or malefics, or is there an even mix?

5. Write a sentence for each planet, detailing which planets help it, which planets harm it, and which are neutral or indifferent.

6. Which planet is in the best condition due to whole sign testimony configurations?
7. Which planet is most handicapped due to whole sign testimony configurations?
8. Which sect of planets, the day or night, is doing better overall?

CHAPTER 41

Aspect Relations

———

IN THE HELLENISTIC TEXTS, THE DOCTRINE OF BENEFIC AND MALEFIC planets witnessing and testifying by whole sign configuration is the primary mode of evaluating a planet's condition according to aspect criteria. This approach views the planetary interactions as relatively static in their configurations to their respective zodiacal signs.

Hellenistic astrology also contains another more complex view, where the ever-changing relationship formed by planets in their moving cycles with one another presents a dynamic range of interactions that dramatically impact the interpretation of aspect relations between planets. Here, specific degrees are important, along with certain spatial considerations.

THE CYCLE OF ASPECT RELATIONS:
AN OVERVIEW

The cycle of any two planets begins at the conjunction, where they come together at the same degree and merge their essences in a seminal inception. Due to the different rates of speed and the direction of their courses, the faster-moving planet pulls away from the slower-moving planet and increases the distance between them until it reaches the opposition. At the opposition, the two planets stand at their maximum polarity from one another and a fundamental directional shift occurs. The faster-moving planet then begins to re-approach the slower-moving planet, decreasing the distance between them until they unite at the next conjunction. In the course of this cycle there are critical interactions that occur near the places where the seven rays of one planet more closely encounter the seven rays of the other planet. These planetary encounters occur near the 60° sextiles, the 90° squares, the 120° trines, and the 180° opposition. As in the solar phase cycle, these critical points have special interpretive meanings.

The Hellenistic aspect doctrine superimposes two different conceptual overlays upon this cycle. One is based upon the relative speed of each planet, and employs the notions of *application* and *separation*. The other is based upon the planet's *right* and *left-sided* directions. The left/right direction establishes which of the two planets holds the *superior* and which holds the *inferior* position in their relationship. Each system has its own specific effects that occur at the critical junctures of a planet's rays, and in some instances exact degrees are important. Further details of the aspect doctrine take the zodiacal sign and house location of a planet into account.

There are various kinds of relationships formed between planets as they move through their courses relative to one another. When examining these, it is important to note that the direction in which the planets move as they form aspects with one another is based upon the *counterclockwise* or secondary motion as they travel along the ecliptic through the natural order of the zodiacal signs. This stands in contrast to the solar phase cycle, discussed in the previous chapter, which is based upon the clockwise, diurnal motion due to the Earth's rotation on its axis. Before we discuss each aspect in greater depth, we will first give an overview of the cycle as a whole.

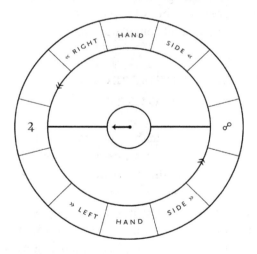

FIGURE 57. LEFT-HAND SIDE
AND RIGHT-HAND SIDE OF A PLANET

Like all cycles, the major axis of division is the *diameter* between the *conjunction*, when the two bodies are united, and the *opposition*, when they are at their furthest distance apart. The first cut, so to speak, is to distinguish between a planet's RIGHT SIDE (*dexios*) and its LEFT SIDE (*euōnumos*). The right side of a planet is defined as the arc containing those zodiacal signs from which it has recently departed, as far back as its opposition point. The left side of a planet is defined as those zodiacal signs towards which it is being carried upon its course, up to the opposition point. When it passes by the OPPOSITION (*parallagē*), it makes a transitional shift from the left side to the right side. A good way to conceive this division is to imagine a line extending from the *center* of a chart towards the planet in question: the left and right-hand sides are relative to the direction that you "face" when looking at the planet from this center.

The CONJUNCTION is multi-layered, and there are many incremental divisions based on the interval between the individual planets in question. Planets in the same whole sign did not "see" each other by means of rays. And so, while the conjunction was not considered an aspect (like the sextile, square, trine, and opposition), it was still treated like one. Regardless of their specific degrees, planets in conjunction were still connected by their CO-PRESENCE (*sumparousia*) in the same sign, and thus commingled their significations.

Within the range of the whole sign conjunction, further levels of intimacy were distinguished. ASSEMBLY (*sunodos*) occurs when a faster-moving planet comes within a 15° interval of a slower-moving planet. We will remember that the 15° interval was a very important marker in the solar phase doctrine, as it represented the full extension of the Sun's orb of light that encompassed another planet. ADHERENCE (*kollēsis*) occurs when the planets adhere to one another within a 3° interval. They remain bonded until one planet has begun to flow apart (*aporroia*) from the other.

A similar process of COMING TOGETHER in connection (*sunaphē*) and FLOWING APART (*aporroia*) occurs at each of the other aspect configurations at both right and left-sided sextiles, squares, and trines, as well as at the opposition, when the planets are within the range of 3° (applying) and 1° (separating). On the left side of the cycle, one planet is increasing its distance from the other, which pursues it, while on the right side it is closing back in and bearing down on the other planet as the distance between them shrinks.

With square and trine aspects, there are special instances in which a planet can HURL RAYS BACKWARDS and STRIKE (*aktinoboleō*) a planet at the left square, and OVERCOME (*kathuperterēsis*) and DOMINATE (*epidekateia*) a planet at the right square. Recall the solar phase cycle, in which Mars made its anomalies around the squares and the superior planets made their stations around the trines.

As rays are being cast about by the planets, some manage to ENCLOSE (*emperischesis*) and CONTAIN (*perischesis*) a planet, holding it captive or protecting it, unless some other planet INTERVENES (*mesembolēsis*) by interposing its own ray as a shield. Planets can travel together as NEIGHBORS (*homorēsis*), RULE TOGETHER (*metochē*) in a certain domicile, or TRAVEL ALONE (*kenodromia*). At many points in this cycle, a planet can receive tremendous assistance in realizing its best potential through BONIFICATION, or be injured by MALTREATMENT (*kakōsis*) by another planet. Sometimes bodyguards BEARING SPEARS (*doruphoria*) stand in certain formations to offer protection to those who are sufficiently eminent to warrant this extra attention.

CHAPTER 42

Bonification

AND MALTREATMENT

———

CONCERNING INJURY (*kakōsis*). It is called maltreatment (*kakōsis*) whenever some [star/planet] is struck with a ray (*aktinoboleō*) by malefic destroyers, or it is enclosed or if it is in a connection (*sunaphē*) with a destructive star or an adherence (*kollēsis*), or if it is opposed (*diametreō*) or overcome (*kathupertereō*) or ruled (*oikodespoteō*) by an evil doer which is badly situated, and when it itself declines in the ineffective places. — PORPHYRY.[1]

AFTER THE OPENING PARAGRAPH IN THE ANTIOCHUS AND PORPHYRY texts concerning witnessing and testimony, many of the subsequent definitions in the series are simply statements of the various aspect formations without any interpretive commentary. A few definitions include a phrase concerning the effects when either the malefic or benefic planets are involved in the formation. However, the aspect section culminates with the articulation of the seven conditions of maltreatment (*kakōsis*), whereby a planet (i.e., its significations) can be severely injured and destroyed when certain aspect formations involve a malefic planet. In short, maltreatment is a condition in which a planet finds itself in extremely unfortunate circumstances due to especially harsh aspects with malefic planets.

MALTREATMENT AND ITS MODERN APPLICATION

Kakōsis translates as "ill treatment, oppression, suffering, and distress". We are going to use the word "maltreatment" as the preferred convention. When a plan-

---

1   PORPHYRY, *Introduction* 28. In similar definitions, Antiochus omits "opposed by a malefic", Rhetorius omits "overcome by a malefic" and rewrites that it is only when the domicile lord of the malefic is in unadvantageous/ineffective houses. Note that the next section of the text tells us that the unadvantageous places are the 2nd, 3rd, 6th, 8th, and 12th houses; and that declining in unadvantageous/ineffective places are the cadent houses (6th, 12th).

et is maltreated by certain kinds of aspect relations, it can be abused, severely injured, and sometimes even disabled in its capacity to bring forth its positive significations. A very close encounter with a visual ray from a malefic planet in a harsh configuration may be connected to the widespread belief in the power of the "evil eye". This results in extremely difficult life experiences that lead to suffering and pain. This distress impacts the life and can have a lasting effect on the individual.

In the Hellenistic texts, references to maltreatment conditions often show up in discussions of accusations, betrayals, dishonor, deformities, illness, longevity, and violent death. From a modern perspective, the level of injury indicated by these aspect patterns can be associated with trauma. This trauma may be karmic, prenatal or perinatal,[2] or it may derive from repressed or vividly conscious memories of traumatic experiences from the current life. These sources of pain become a nexus of malfunction on the physical, emotional, mental, or spiritual level. They are the wounds that do not heal.

Most charts have whole sign aspects through which the malefics witness, and therefore bring disharmonious influences, to other planets. Although bad things happen, they are not necessarily catastrophic. Life is a mix of good and bad; people deal with their difficulties, recover, and move on. However, the conditions of maltreatment, because they are so specific and precise, occur with much less frequency.

It is useful for the counseling astrologer to be able to identify serious problems that are unlikely to go away on their own or after the transit is over. Recognizing maltreatment conditions enables the astrologer to give appropriate guidance. In some instances, mitigating factors can be seen in a chart that point to the possibilities of remediation and healing. Other cases indicate a level of damage that may leave lifelong scars. In such cases, the client should be referred to professional help. It is important for the astrologer to understand this difference, and to recognize further help is needed. It is for this reason that we will give some deeper attention to the conditions of maltreatment.

BONIFICATION

The conceptual correlate to maltreatment is bonification, whereby a planet finds itself in extremely fortunate circumstances due to certain aspect relations with the benefic planets. The bonified planet is not only protected from harm, usually

---

2   That is, things that happened while in the womb or during the birth; see Stanislav GROF, *The Adventure of Self-Discovery* (New York: State University of New York Press, 1988), p. 5.

by the agency of the benefic planets, but also enhanced in its capacity to bring forth the best of fortunate outcomes for the individual. The texts often discuss bonification conditions as a signature of notable nativities. Some of these special bonification aspect patterns are sprinkled through the series of definitions, but they are not explicitly enumerated as are the maltreatment conditions. In the absence of explicit explanations of such conditions, we can propose they are the same structural patterns as the maltreatment conditions, but involving the benefic planets instead of the malefic planets. We will list the conditions of bonification as the corresponding correlates of maltreatment, but keep in mind that in some cases this is not supported by direct textual evidence.

Table 23. Maltreatment and Bonification Conditions

MALTREATMENT	BONIFICATION
Struck with a ray by malefics	*Struck with ray by benefics (stated by Valens)*
Enclosed or contained by malefics	*Enclosed or contained by benefics (stated)*
Connection with malefic	*Connection with benefic (implied)*
Adherence with malefic	*Adherence with benefic (implied)*
Opposed by badly situated malefic	*Opposed by benefic (stated by Petosiris)*
Overcome by badly situated malefic	*Overcome by well-placed benefic (stated)*
Has a badly situated malefic as its domicile lord	*Has well situated benefic as domicile lord (implied)*
In sixth or twelfth house	

We are now going to proceed into the more complex interactions of the planets. When planets stand in whole sign configurations, they are involved in certain kinds of relationships with one another. The degree-based aspects and directional-spatial relations point to even closer relationships. Instead of going through all the aspect definitions in the order given in the Hellenistic texts, the ones that are relevant to our discussion will be presented in thematic groups. However, they will be taught within the context of the larger view of the workings of the aspects in the Hellenistic approach. In the course of this discussion we will itemize the specific conditions of maltreatment and bonification, which are the main considerations in this evaluation of a planet's condition concerning its ability to do good for the person.

CHAPTER 43

Coming Together

ADHERENCE, CONNECTION, FLOWING APART

———

And they say that connection (*sunaphē*) and adherence (*kollēsis*) is whenever the stars join together by degree according to any figure whatsoever or are about to join within three degrees. And it may also be said this way. Adherence (*kollēsis*) is whenever the faster star approaches the slower star, being yet distant no more than three degrees. In regards to the Moon, some say that within thirteen degrees—that is the course of a day and night—that the Moon is observing the connection towards which she is conjoining. — PORPHYRY.[1]

PLANETS CHANGE THEIR ASPECTUAL RELATIONSHIPS TO ONE ANOTHER as they move through their courses. At various points in their cycles relative to one another, good and bad interactions can take place between them. This chapter will discuss the two primary ways in which planets come together: where they *connect* or *adhere*, intermingling their natures, and then *flow apart*. We will make a distinction between the process that takes place when planets are in the same sign and when they are configured by aspect.

The first form of close union that we will examine is *bodily conjunction*, where planets come together in the same zodiacal sign. This is called *kollēsis* in Greek, which we translate as "adherence". The second way that planets make a close union is connecting by means of their rays. This is called *sunaphē* in Greek, which we translate as "connection".

At certain moments during these processes, both bonification and maltreatment can occur. The closest kinds of interactions between planets, either by AD-HERENCE (*kollēsis*) or by CONNECTION (*sunaphē*), are based upon a narrow degree range where the faster-moving planet is moving towards and applying to the slower-moving planet, either bodily or by ray, at critical points of their cycle.

1   PORPHYRY, *Introduction* 11.

COMING TOGETHER BODILY: CO-PRESENCE, ASSEMBLY, ADHERENCE, AND NEIGHBORING

The CONJUNCTION, often referred to as a *bodily conjunction,* is defined by the physical proximity of the planets in the same whole sign. ADHERENCE occurs when two planets come together by conjunction within 3°. When planets are in the same whole sign, regardless of degree, they are said to be CO-PRESENT (*sumparousia* (FIGURE 58). Planets that are co-present mix their significations, and the result is often a combination of the two separate natures. Depending upon the benefic or malefic nature of each planet, their relationship can be harmonious or unharmonious, or a mixture: sometimes better, sometimes worse. Valens devotes two chapters to the commixture of two and three planets in the same sign.[2] To the extent that the planets support or negate each other's significations, each planet in the commingling may have a different experience. For example, a Venus-Mars whole sign co-presence can be good for Mars but bad for Venus. When two or more planets are in the same sign regardless of degree, they have already begun to mingle their significations (imagine two roommates in the same house, or two co-workers in the same office space).

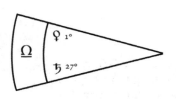

FIGURE 58.
CO-PRESENCE (*SUMPAROUSIA*)
Planets co-present in the same whole sign, regardless of degree.

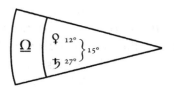

FIGURE 59.
ASSEMBLY (*SUNODOS*)
Planets within a 15° interval of one another.

The closer stages of relating within the whole sign conjunction require the faster-moving planet to be moving towards (i.e., applying to) the slower-moving planet. When the faster planet moves within 15° of the slower planet, they are said to be "coming together" for a meeting, gathering, or ASSEMBLY (*sunodos*) (FIGURE 59). In contemporary parlance, one might say they are meeting up. By now, the 15° interval should be a familiar number to you. It is the orb of the Sun and an important number that determines when a planet is under the beams of the Sun, or of the Moon coming under the bonds of the Sun. The 15° range is a sensitive boundary marker that brings two planets into a more binding relationship.

2   VALENS, *Anthology* 1.19–20.

In Paulus' discussion concerning the applications of the Moon, he writes that the number of degrees between the Moon's application to a planet corresponds to the age in life (0–3 youth, 3–7 prime, 7–15 maturity) when the significations of the aspect manifest in the life. This may suggest that when planets have entered into this 15° range, the inherent potential of what they represent in commixture does in fact emerge during the course of the life. This interval of assembly extends up to the 3° interval before exact conjunction. At this point another stage ensues.

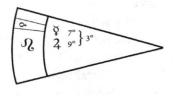

FIGURE 60.

ADHERENCE (*KOLLĒSIS*)

Faster planet applying to slower planet within a 3° interval. (If the Moon is applying, it is a 13° interval).

FIGURE 61.

NEIGHBORING (*HOMORĒSIS*)

Faster planet applying to slower planet within a 3° interval (kollēsis), and both planets are in the same bounds (in this case, the bounds of Venus: 7°–9° Leo).

When a faster-moving planet approaches a slower planet within 3° in a bodily conjunction, there is said to be a "gluing", "bonding", or ADHERENCE (*kollēsis*) between them (FIGURE 60). The range for the Moon's adherence to another planet is within 13° of approach (i.e., the course of a day and night, in which the Moon anticipates the approaching conjunction). For example, the Sun at 18° Scorpio adheres to Jupiter at 20° Scorpio. The Moon at 15° Aquarius adheres to Mercury at 25° Aquarius.

Generally speaking, adherence is the closest kind of relationship. It points to the deepest kind of intimacy between planets; the two merge into one, as if in sexual union. Adherence begins when the faster planet approaches the slower within the 3° range. The cohesion between the two planets exists uniformly throughout the 3° applying interval. The texts do not state that the closer the planets are to their exact conjunction, the more connected they are in adherence.

An even closer relationship is called "juxtaposition" or NEIGHBORING (*homorēsis*). It occurs when two planets are in an adherence (3° applying bodily conjunction) and they are also in the same *bounds*. For example, in addition to adherence, Mercury at 7° Leo neighbors (or is juxtaposed upon) Jupiter at 9° Leo, because both are in the bounds of Venus. However, if Mercury were at 5° Leo (which is in the bounds of Mars) it would not neighbor Jupiter at 7° Leo (which is in the bounds of Venus), although they are still in adherence. So planets can be in adherence and neighboring, or they can be in adherence and not neighboring (FIGURE 61).

If an adherence has occurred, it stays in effect until the faster planet has passed beyond the slower planet, when it departs and is borne away. There is no exact degree range of separation given in the texts for the adherence condition. We will consider this topic further in the section on separating. Planets in a separating bodily conjunction still commingle while in the same zodiacal sign, but they are not in adherence.

MALTREATMENT AND BONIFICATION
BY ADHERENCE

The most important thing to note about adherence is that if one of the planets involved is a malefic, maltreatment occurs. As you look at a chart, take note of any planets within a 3° applying conjunction. If one of the planets is Mars or Saturn, the faster planet is maltreated and suffers some sort of injury in its capacity to bring forth its positive significations for the individual (FIGURE 62). As we will see when we look at *hurling rays*, there are mitigating factors to take into account (for instance, a ray from the Sun can block the maltreatment). We will deal with those factors separately.

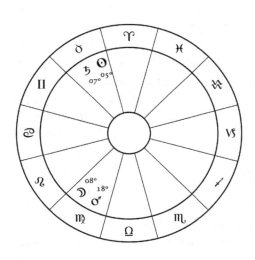

FIGURE 62.

MALTREATMENT BY ADHERENCE

Faster planet applies to malefic within a 3°
interval (or for the Moon, a 13° interval).

Because adherence requires a faster-moving planet applying towards a slower-moving planet, the Moon, Mercury, Venus, and the Sun all can be maltreated by adhering to Mars or Saturn. Jupiter normally cannot be maltreated by Mars. This is because Jupiter is slower and cannot apply to Mars, unless it is retrograde; but Jupiter can adhere to Saturn. Saturn in direct motion cannot be maltreated by any other planet. However, when it is retrograde, it can back into Mars (should Mars be within 3° behind it).

If the planet being adhered to by bodily conjunction is a benefic, it is considered to be a most fortunate circumstance and is one of the implied conditions of bonification. The Moon, Mercury, and the Sun can all potentially adhere to

Venus; but be sure to check the relative speed of Mercury and Venus in each situation. The Moon, Mercury, Venus, the Sun, and Mars can all adhere to Jupiter. However, Saturn cannot apply to Jupiter and become bonified, unless it happens to be retrograde.

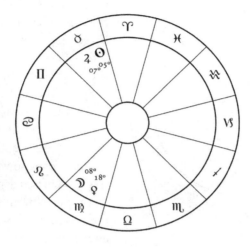

FIGURE 63.
BONIFICATION BY ADHERENCE
*Faster planet applies to benefic within a 3°
interval (or for the Moon, a 13° interval).*

MALTREATMENT AND BONIFICATION
BY ASPECT RAYS

In addition to adherence by bodily conjunction, the close connection of two planets can also occur by *aspect* configuration. This was referred to as a CONNECTION (*sunaphē*) by the Hellenistic authors. It occurs whenever the planets are about to join via an aspect configuration within a range of 3°. Like adherence, connection (*sunaphē*) entails an *applying* aspect of the faster-moving planet to the slower-moving planet, with the exception of the Moon, which applies within a 13° range.

This is practically the same definition as given for adherence, but rather than bodily merging in the same sign, *connection* occurs when one planet encounters the *aspect ray* of another planet. Thus, planets *adhere* in bodily conjunction, but *connect* by means of their rays.

As with adherence, MALTREATMENT can occur if one of the planets involved in a connection is a malefic. A planet can be severely injured by coming into contact with the harsh rays of Mars or Saturn. Unlike the trine and sextile, which are supportive aspects, it is only the square and opposition rays from Mars or Saturn that can maltreat another planet.

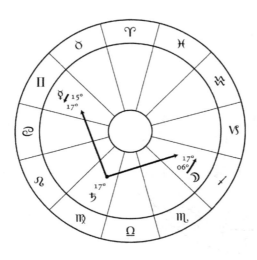

FIGURE 64.

MALTREATMENT BY CONNECTION

A faster planet applies to a square or opposition ray of a malefic within a 3° interval (or for the Moon, a 13° interval).

To illustrate MALTREATMENT via "casting rays", imagine Mercury at 15° Gemini and Saturn at 17° Virgo. Like an archer shooting an arrow, Saturn casts one of its square rays to 17° Gemini. Like a bird, Mercury (the faster-moving planet) will fly into the ray of Saturn, and thus be maltreated. The two planets will *connect* because the faster-moving planet moves towards and encounters a projected aspect ray sent forth from the slower planet. Similarly, the Moon at 6° Sagittarius will also encounter Saturn's square ray from 17°Virgo (within the 13° range), and thus be maltreated (FIGURE 64).

To illustrate BONIFICATION via "casting rays", imagine Mars at 15° Sagittarius connecting to a trine ray cast from Jupiter at 18° Leo and directed to 18° Sagittarius. Mars is bonified by Jupiter. The Moon at 5° Pisces connects with a sextile ray cast from Venus at 12° Taurus directed to 12° Pisces. The Moon is bonified by Venus (FIGURE 65).

NEIGHBORING, or juxtaposition (*homorēsis*) while forming a connection (*sunaphē*) can also occur in an aspect connection. As we saw with adherence, this is a closer form of interaction that takes place when two planets form an aspect figure within a 3° applying interval *while also* being in the bounds of the same planet.

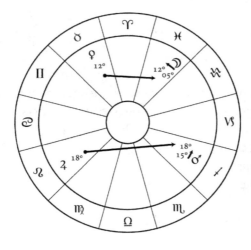

FIGURE 65.

BONIFICATION BY CONNECTION

A faster planet applies to a sextile or trine ray of a benefic within a 3° interval (13° for the Moon).

For example, Venus at 5° Gemini (in the bounds of Mercury) connecting to a trine (within a 3° interval) sent from Mars at 6° Aquarius (also in the bounds of Mercury) are said to be "neighboring" (FIGURE 66). Note that in this example, there is no maltreatment from Mars because, while malefic, it is making a trine aspect and not a square or opposition. Instead, a bonification occurs, because Venus is a benefic and is casting a trine aspect.

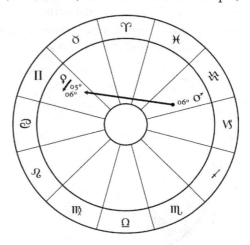

Finally, although it is not altogether clear from the texts, we could speculate that neighboring also applies to whole sign configurations. For instance, if Venus at 5° Gemini (within the bounds of Mercury) is configured by sextile to Mars at 23° Leo (within the bounds of Mercury), their interaction could be stronger due to juxtaposition because they are both in the bounds of Mercury: i.e., both are subject to the same rules of operation that are set by their shared bound ruler, Mercury.

FIGURE 66.

NEIGHBORING BY ASPECT CONFIGURATION

The faster planet applies to another planet within a 3° interval (or for the Moon, a 13° interval), while both planets are in the bounds of the same planet. (Mercury rules the first six degrees of Gemini, and the first seven degrees of Aquarius).

FLOWING FORTH AND SEPARATING (*APORROIA*):
EMANATION, EFFLUENCE

And Antiochus told how separation (*aporroia*) is whenever a slower star departs from a connection with a faster star after having been adhered or whenever a star withdrawing from the connection begins to have more degrees than belong to the figure.
— ANTIOCHUS.[3]

After the planets make a connection, the faster planet withdraws from the union as it begins to separate from the slower planet. The Greek term for this separation is *aporroia*, which literally means "flowing away" or "effluence". Like the tides which cause the waters to flow out of a bay, the faster planet slowly with-draws its essence and flows away.

Human relationships provide a good symbolic paradigm for the aspect inter-actions between planets. Just as two people become aware of one another (*sump-arousia*), make comments expressing interest (whole sign testimony), meet up and spend personal time together (*sunodos*), enter into an intimate connection (*sunaphē*), or merge bodily (*kollēsis*), so too do the planets. Their connection can turn out either good or bad, leaving a positive afterglow, or a residual shock. They then withdraw and separate (*aporroia*).

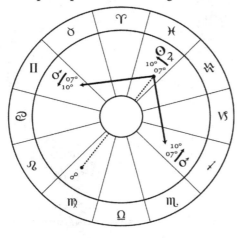

FIGURE 67.

PLANETARY SEPARATION

Faster planets separate from a bodily conjunction or aspect connection with slower planets: the Sun separates from its adherence (kollēsis) to Jupiter; Mars separates from its connection (sunaphē) to Jupiter. Note how Mars in Gemini separates from the connection by moving towards opposition with Jupiter, while Mars in Sagittarius separates from the connection by moving towards conjunction with Jupiter.

Due to ambiguities in the texts, it is hard to know exactly when this separation begins to occur. What is certain is that, as long as the two planets remain within the same degree as one another (whether bodily or by aspect), they are locked in their embrace and are not yet separated. *Partile* is the term given by Medieval astrologers to planetary aspects that are exact by whole integer degree.

Some authors place the interval of separation at 1° past this point. One can also look to the definition of *parallagē*—a passage that has been vexing to translators. One in-terpretation may suggest that sepa-ration occurs when planets or their rays pass by another planet by degree of an equal-sided figure (or the exact number of degrees in an exact partile aspect).[4] Other authors place the interval of separation at 3°.[5]

Antiochus and Porphyry offer an alternative definition of *aporroia* in which the planets require more intervening degrees than are necessary for the aspect figure.[6] This pertains to the "waxing" half of the cycle, when a faster planet separates from a slower planet by *increasing* the distance between them. This

4   PORPHYRY, *Introduction* 10; ANTIOCHUS, *Summary* 8.
5   HEPHAISTIO, *Apotelesmatics* 1.14.
6   PORPHYRY, *Introduction* 13; ANTIOCHUS, *Summary* 9.

stands in contrast to the "waning" aspect, where the faster planet separates from its connection to the slower planet by *decreasing* the distance between them (FIGURE 67).

When examining the close union of a planet (by connection or adherence), the main thing to observe is whether it involves a malefic planet. If so, it forms two of the conditions of maltreatment. This is a red flag indicating a potentially serious problem in the healthy functioning of that planet. Careful attention should be given to a planet that is maltreated in order to assess the nature of the injury and the resulting damage in the life. If the connection is with a benefic planet, the planet may meet the conditions of bonification (when it is especially enhanced and supported in its efforts to bring about the positive range of its significations).

→   EXAMPLE CHARTS

Let us look at the example charts to see if any planets are maltreated or bonified by adherence or connection. Unlike testimony, which is by whole sign aspect, maltreatment and bonification by connection and adherence involve exact degree ranges. For maltreatment we are looking only to a 3° applying conjunction (13° for the Moon), square, or opposition to Mars or Saturn. For bonification we are looking for a 3° applying conjunction, sextile, or trine to Venus and Jupiter (13° for the Moon).

Note that there are two options for proceeding with this analysis. One is from the perspective of each planet; the other is from the perspective of each of the benefics and malefics.

CHART I: MALTREATMENT/BONIFICATION BY ADHERENCE OR CONNECTION

	Adhering to planets	Connecting to planets	Sextile, square, trine, opposition?	Is the planet bonified or maltreated?
MOON	—	—	—	—
SUN	—	—	—	—
MERCURY	—	—	—	—
VENUS	—	Saturn	Opposition	Maltreated
MARS	—	—	—	—
JUPITER	—	—	—	—
SATURN	—	Venus	Opposition	No

FROM THE PERSPECTIVE OF EACH PLANET

THE SUN at 5° Leo is not conjunct, square, or opposed to either Mars or Saturn. Thus there is no possibility of maltreatment by connection or adherence from the malefics. The Sun at 5° Leo sextiles Jupiter at 9° Gemini and Venus at 21° Gemini, but these planets are outside of the 3° applying interval. *There is no bonification by connection or adherence from the benefics.*

JUPITER at 9° Gemini is square to Mars at 14° Virgo and opposed to Saturn at 24° Sagittarius. It cannot apply to Mars because it is slower than Mars. It does apply to Saturn, but is too far away from the 3° interval for maltreatment to occur. While Jupiter is co-present with Venus at 21° Gemini, Jupiter is the slower of the two and cannot apply to Venus. *There is no maltreatment or bonification by connection or adherence.*

SATURN is the slowest-moving planet and cannot apply to any other planet unless it is retrograde. It is retrograde in this chart, but is too far away from the square to Mars for maltreatment to occur; it is not trine or sextile to Venus or Jupiter for the possibility of bonification. *There is no maltreatment or bonification by connection or adherence.*

MERCURY at 2° Leo is not conjunct, square, or opposed to either Mars or Saturn. *Thus there is no possibility of maltreatment by connection or adherence from the malefics.* Mercury at 2° Leo sextiles Jupiter at 9° Gemini and Venus at 21° Gemini, but these planets are outside of the 3° applying interval. *There is no bonification by connection or adherence from the benefics.*

THE MOON is not conjunct, square, or opposed to either Mars or Saturn. *Thus there is no possibility of maltreatment by connection or adherence from the malefics.* The Moon at 25° Aries is sextile to both Venus and Jupiter, but it is the faster-moving planet and separating from both. *There is no bonification by connection or adherence.*

VENUS at 21° Gemini is co-present with Jupiter. However, she is faster-moving, separating, and too far away to consider bonification. Venus is square to Mars at 14° Virgo, but separating and so no maltreatment occurs. Venus is applying to the opposition with Saturn at 24° Sagittarius. *Since this aspect is within the 3° interval, Venus encounters the ray of Saturn projected to 24° Gemini and is maltreated.*

MARS at 14° Virgo is not conjunct, trine, or sextile to Venus or Jupiter. Thus there is *no possibility of bonification by connection or adherence* within the 3° range. Mars is applying to a square with Saturn at 24° Sagittarius, but it is *too far away for maltreatment by connection or adherence.*

In sum: none of the planets are bonified by a connection or adherence. However, Venus is maltreated by a connection to Saturn.

FROM THE PERSPECTIVE OF THE BENEFICS AND MALEFICS

MARS at 14° Virgo. There are no other planets in Virgo, so Mars is not maltreating any planets by adherence. Mars casts a square ray to 14° Gemini, a square ray to 14° Sagittarius, and an opposition ray to 14° Pisces. Venus, at 21° Gemini, moves faster than Mars, is flowing away and escaping from Mars' ray. Jupiter, at 9° Gemini, moves slower than Mars and is behind his ray; it is not possible for Jupiter to run into Mars' ray. The square ray from Mars at 14° Sagittarius falls behind slower-moving Saturn at 24° Sagittarius, but Mars is too far away from the 3° interval. There are no planets in Pisces. Mars does not maltreat any planets by connection or adherence conditions.

SATURN at 24° Sagittarius casts square rays to 24° Virgo and 24° Pisces, and an opposition ray to 24° Gemini. There are no other planets in Sagittarius, so adherence is not a consideration. While Mars at 14° Virgo is moving faster than Saturn, and is approaching Saturn's ray at 24° Virgo, Mars is too far away from the 3° interval to suffer maltreatment. There are no planets in Pisces. However, Saturn's opposition ray, falling at 24° Gemini, is within the 3° interval of Venus' faster-moving approach at 21° Gemini. Venus will hit Saturn's malefic ray and become injured. Saturn thus maltreats Venus by connection.

VENUS casts a sextile ray to 21° Leo, but it is too far away for either the Sun or Mercury to engage with it within the 3° interval. Venus' other sextile ray falls at 21° Aries, but the fast-moving Moon at 25° Aries has already passed it. There are no planets in Libra or Aquarius where the trine rays fall. Venus at 21° Gemini is faster and separating from Jupiter at 9° Gemini, so no bonification by adherence can occur.

JUPITER casts one of his sextile rays to 9° Leo. While it is tempting to think that the Sun at 5° Leo might be bonified, the 4° interval between the Sun and Jupiter's ray is just out of range. There are no planets in Aries (the Moon is too far and separating), Libra, or Aquarius to engage with Jupiter's rays there. Venus at 21° Gemini is faster and moving away from Jupiter at 9° Gemini, so no bonification by adherence can occur.

CHART II: MALTREATMENT/BONIFICATION BY ADHERENCE OR CONNECTION

	Adhering to planets	Connecting to planets	Sextile, square, trine, opposition?	Is the planet bonified or maltreated?
MOON	—	—	—	—
SUN	—	—	—	—
MERCURY	—	—	—	—
VENUS	—	—	—	—
MARS	—	—	—	—
JUPITER	—	—	—	—
SATURN	—	—	—	—

FROM THE PERSPECTIVE OF EACH PLANET

THE SUN at 2° Scorpio is not conjunct, sextile, or trine to Venus or Jupiter. Thus there is no possibility of bonification by connection or adherence within the given degree interval. The Sun applies to an opposition with Saturn at 9° Taurus, but is too far away for maltreatment. And the Sun is not conjunct, square, or opposite Mars. *The Sun is not bonified or maltreated by connection or adherence with the benefics or malefics.*

JUPITER at 23° Taurus can only be maltreated by Saturn, but it is separating from Saturn. *Jupiter is not bonified or maltreated by connection or adherence with the benefics or malefics.*

SATURN is the slowest-moving planet and cannot apply to any other planet unless it is retrograde. It is retrograde in this chart, but separating from Jupiter and in aversion to Venus. It is not conjunct, square, or opposed to Mars. *Saturn is not bonified or maltreated by connection or adherence with the benefics or malefics.*

MERCURY at 24° Scorpio is not conjunct, sextile, or trine to Venus or Jupiter. It is opposite Saturn at 9° Taurus, but separating. It is not conjunct or square

Mars. *Mercury is not bonified or maltreated by connection or adherence with the benefics or malefics.*

THE MOON at 8° Sagittarius is sextile to Venus at 4° Libra, but separating. It is in aversion to Jupiter and Saturn, and not square to Mars. *The Moon is not bonified or maltreated by connection or adherence with the benefics or malefics.*

VENUS at 4° Libra is not conjunct, sextile, or trine to Jupiter. Venus is not conjunct, square, or opposite Saturn. However, Venus is square to Mars at 12° Libra and applying to him, but she is outside the 3° interval of application. *Venus is not bonified or maltreated by connection or adherence with the benefics or malefics.*

MARS at 12° Cancer is not conjunct or trine to Jupiter. Mars is applying to a sextile with Jupiter at 23° Taurus, but not within the 3° interval. *Mars is not bonified or maltreated by connection or adherence with the benefics or malefics.*

FROM THE PERSPECTIVE OF THE BENEFICS AND MALEFICS

MARS is at 12° Cancer. There are no other planets in Cancer, so Mars is not maltreating any planets by adherence. Mars casts its square rays to 12° Aries and 12° Libra. There are no planets in Aries. Venus is at 4° Libra, and while faster-moving, she is too far away from the 3° interval for maltreatment by connection to occur. Mars casts an opposition ray to 12° Capricorn, but there are no planets in Capricorn to maltreat.

SATURN is at 9° Taurus, and retrograde. There are no planets in earlier degrees that could apply to Saturn. Jupiter at 23° Taurus, retrograde, while moving towards Saturn is too far away from the 3° interval to be maltreated. Saturn casts its square rays to 9° Leo and 9° Aquarius, but there are no planets in those zodiacal signs that could be maltreated.

VENUS is at 4° Libra. There are no other planets in Libra, so Venus cannot bonify any planets by adherence. Venus casts sextile rays to 4° Leo and 4° Sagittarius. The Moon at 8° Sagittarius is separating from the ray of Venus and hence there is no bonification by connection. There are no planets in Leo, but if one was inquiring into vitality, the Venus ray falling close to the Ascendant degree would enhance or protect the life force. Venus' trine rays are cast to 4° Gemini and 4° Aquarius. Since there are no planets in these signs, there is no possibility of bonification.

JUPITER is at 23° Taurus, and retrograde. Saturn at 9° Taurus is slower, too far away, and moving backwards. Jupiter casts its sextile rays to 23° Cancer and 23° Pisces. There are no planets in Pisces. Mars at 12° Cancer is too far away to apply to the ray of Jupiter within 3°. Jupiter casts its trine rays to 23° Virgo and 23° Capricorn. Since there are no planets in these zodiacal signs, there is no possibility of bonification by connection. *Overall, there are no instances of mal-treatment or bonification by connection or adherence.*

→   EXERCISE 30
         Using your own chart, complete exercise 30:
         Maltreatment or Bonification by Connection or Adherence

EXERCISE 30

MALTREATMENT OR BONIFICATION BY CONNECTION OR ADHERENCE

In order to do this exercise, you must know the relative speed of the planets and the difference between applying and separating aspects. The average speeds of the planets from fastest to slowest are:

Moon, Sun, Mercury, Venus, Mars, Jupiter, and Saturn

Note, however, that when planets are about to station, their motion is extremely slow. When they are direct and conjunct the Sun, their motion is faster than average. As you become more familiar with the basics, you will begin to recognize this and factor it into your analysis.

In the previous exercise, you have already determined the whole sign aspect configurations that are operative regardless of degree. In this exercise, you will isolate the configurations that are degree-based. Specifically, you will look for a faster-moving planet making an application (whether bodily or by aspect figure) to a slower-moving planet. You will then ascertain whether it is within a 3° applying range, or in the case of the Moon, a 13° applying range. If the aspect is partile—exact at the same whole integer degree—it is considered effective even if the faster planet has passed beyond the slower planet by mere minutes. However, once the planet has moved beyond the partile point by whole integer degree, it is considered to be separating, even if the difference is less than 60 minutes.

1. *Begin by looking at the seven rays emanating from the Moon—the fastest-moving planet.* Will the Moon or one of its rays approach any other planet within the next 13° of its motion? If so, write that down in the table below.

2. *Next, check Mercury, Venus, the Sun, Mars, Jupiter, and Saturn, moving from the faster-moving planets to the slower, and list any adherences (bodily conjunctions) and connections (aspect configurations: sextiles, squares, trines, oppositions) within 3° applications.* If two planets are in the same whole integer, you should consider that to be a connection or adherence, even if there is no application by minutes. If you are already familiar with recognizing aspects

by degree, you can certainly just look at the degree numbers and signs, and proceed accordingly. However, the visual approach allows you to better understand the concept of a planet encountering the ray of another planet within a certain range of application.

3. *Finally, determine if any of these close adherences or connections is by a faster-moving planet applying to a malefic (Mars or Saturn) or to a benefic (Venus or Jupiter) within the 3° interval range (13° for the Moon).*

	Adhering to planets	Connecting to planets	Sextile/trine, or square/opposition?	Bonified or maltreated?
MOON				
SUN				
MERCURY				
VENUS				
MARS				
JUPITER				
SATURN				

REFLECTION AND ANALYSIS

1. Are any planets bonified or maltreated?
2. If so, how do these conditions influence your judgment concerning each planet's capacity to do its best for you?

CHAPTER 44

Superior Aspects

LEFT- AND RIGHT-SIDED FIGURATIONS

WE NOW TURN TO OVERCOMING AND HURLING RAYS, THE NEXT SET OF paired concepts in interplanetary relations. Although we are still looking at the cycle of two planets in relation to one another, we are now considering the spatial directions of a planet's motion along its course, rather than its relative speed and applying aspects. These directional relationships determine which planet is *dominant* in any interaction, and what recourse is available to a planet that is being overpowered by another planet. In some instances of overcoming and hurling rays, planets can be maltreated as well as bonified.

The first step in understanding the doctrines of overcoming and hurling rays is to differentiate between the *right and the left sides* of aspect figures. We must then say a few words about the *directions* in which planets cast their rays.

RIGHT AND LEFT FIGURES

> They say that the trigon, tetragon, and hexagon from which a star has come are on the right side, but those [figures] towards which the star is going towards are on the left side . . . For each star sends forth seven rays, three upwards and three downwards, and one towards the diameter, of which the upward ones are on the right side, but the downward ones are on the left side.—PORPHYRY.[1]

The right and left side of a planet are determined by its motion along the ecliptic through the natural order of the zodiacal signs (counterclockwise). The aspects on the right side of a planet are those zodiacal signs from which the planet has recently departed as it follows the natural order of the zodiac. For example, if the

---

1   PORPHYRY, *Introduction* 9. See also ANTIOCHUS, *Summary* 7; FIRMICUS MATERNUS, *Mathesis* 2.24, trans. HOLDEN.

Sun is in Leo, its trine configuration with Aries is on its *right* side. A planet in Aries would be said to be making a *right-sided trine* with the Sun.

In Medieval astrology, the Latin terms *dexter* (right) and *sinister* (left) are used to refer to right and left aspect formations. You may come across phrases such as "when Jupiter is making a *dexter* trine to the Sun, such and such will occur".

Porphyry gives an example with the Sun in Leo as the point of reference. The aspect made by Aries and Leo is a right-sided (*dexter*) trine, but the aspect made by Sagittarius is a left-sided (*sinister*) trine. The aspect of Taurus and Leo is a right-sided (*dexter*) square, but Scorpio is a left-sided (*sinister*) square. The aspect of Gemini and Leo is a right-sided (*dexter*) hexagon, but that of Libra is left-sided (*sinister*) hexagon (FIGURE 68).

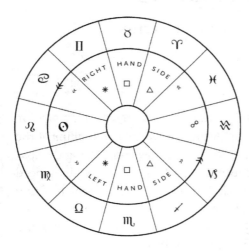

FIGURE 68.
RIGHT- AND LEFT-SIDED ASPECT FIGURES

The aspects on the left side of a planet are the zodiacal signs which it is moving towards in its course along the ecliptic. The aspects on the right side are the signs it is moving away from. In this example, a planet in Leo has recently departed from aspects on its right side in Gemini, Taurus, & Aries—all signs that precede it in the zodiacal order (relative to its current position). By contrast, the aspects towards which it is moving are those on the left side of the planet: Libra, Scorpio, & Sagittarius.

Note that the only aspects mentioned are the sextile, the square, and the trine. The conjunction is not technically a configuration, and it is not possible for the opposition to be on the left or right side of a planet.

Right-sided aspects were considered more powerful because they rise and culminate *before* the planets that they aspect on their left; planets on the left were considered inferior because they rise and culminate *after* the planets that aspect them from the right. Thus, each planet is *superior* to those planets on its left and *inferior* to those planets on its right.[2]

Aspects between planets were given very different interpretations depending upon which planet was in a superior (right-sided) position, because the benefic or malefic natures of the superior planet would prevail over the significations

2   Note that the terms *superior* and *inferior* are used here in the context of aspect relations, and are conceptually different than the solar phase terminology, where the superior planets are Mars, Jupiter and Saturn and the inferior planets are Mercury and Venus.

of the inferior-positioned planet (in accordance with the nature of the aspect).

For example, Valens writes that Mars, in a nocturnal birth and in feminine zodiacal signs, in a right trine to the Sun, signifies those who are great, estimable, and have the power of life and death.[3]

Here we see how sect conditions combine with right and left side interpretations to form a delineation. In this example, the nocturnal sect planet Mars in a feminine nocturnal zodiacal sign brings about benefic outcomes when combined with the power of the right-sided supportive trine aspect, indicating an estimable individual. We will return to this theme in our discussion of overcoming. However, before we can discuss the next two aspect relations—*overcoming and hurling rays*—we must first ascertain whether the directions of the seven rays that emanate from each planet are being cast "forward" or "backward". As we will see, this distinction is a logical extension of the left- and right-sided aspects we have just been looking at.

THE DIRECTIONS OF THE RAYS

After discussing the left- and right-sided figures, Porphyry tells us that "each of the stars sends forth seven rays, three upwards and three downwards, and one towards the diameter, of which the upward ones are on the right side, but the downward ones are on the left side".[4] Antiochus informs us that "the visual sight of every beam is carried forwards (to the front), but the ray is carried backwards (to the back)"; this distinction between a planet's forward *sight* and its backward *rays* is confirmed by Porphyry: "for every celestial light in the sky, the sight is borne towards the star ahead, but the ray to the star behind".[5]

Thus, when a planet is on the right side of its aspect figure (i.e., in the superior position relative to another planet), it is emitting its rays *forward* in the natural order of the zodiac. The Greek word for the casting of forward rays is *horeō*, which means "to see". A planet casting forward rays *sees* what is ahead of it. When a planet is on the left side of its aspect figure (i.e., in the inferior position relative to another planet), its rays are cast *backwards* towards the planet that is behind it. This is referred to as the *hurling of rays* (FIGURE 69).

It is likely that Hellenistic aspect theory was based in part upon ancient Greek optical theory. One school of thought, called emission theory, maintained that vision occurs when rays emanate from the eyes and fall upon objects, which

---

3   VALENS, *Anthology* 2.17.
4   PORPHYRY, *Introduction* 9.
5   ANTIOCHUS, *Summary* 13; PORPHYRY, *Introduction* 24.

are then seen. Things that the rays do not fall upon cannot be seen. This process could also happen by refraction, where a single ray could be split into multiple directions, and objects could be seen as the rays emanate from the eye (Euclid and Ptolemy). The other school, known as the intromission theory (advocated by Aristotle and Galen) believed rays emanated from the object and entered the eyes. Modern physics confirms that light is transmitted from a light source, such as the Sun, to visible objects, and is received by a detector such as a human eye or camera.

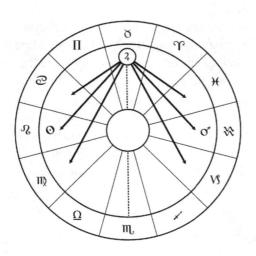

FIGURE 69.

FORWARD AND BACKWARD RAYS

A planet in superior position casts forward rays to a planet in inferior position (Jupiter casts forward rays to the Sun). A planet in inferior position hurls backward rays to a planet in superior position (Jupiter casts backward rays to Mars).

Contemporary beliefs concerning light, rays, and vision were incorporated by Hellenistic astrologers into the aspect theory. Thus, planetary gods were understood to both emanate rays that fell upon objects (e.g., other planets), which were thereby seen; at the same time, the planets themselves cast rays back to the observer. Arabic astrologers added many innovations in the aspect doctrine, including concepts such as the collection and transfer of light from one body to another. They may have been influenced by the Zoroastrian religious teaching concerning the twin forces of light and dark.[6]

→   EXAMPLE CHARTS

Let us look at our example charts to see which planets hold the superior position in their aspect configurations. Remember, with this exercise we are not taking exact degrees or applying and separating aspects into account. This is strictly a spatial consideration based upon the right and left sides of each planet.

6   For more on this subject, see *On the Stellar Rays*, by the ninth-century Arabic philosopher, AL KINDI (translated by Robert Zoller, WV: Berkeley Springs, The Golden Hind Press, 1993).

CHART I: SUPERIOR ASPECTS

Planet	Superior Aspects
SUN	Trine to Saturn
JUPITER	Sextile to Sun
	Sextile to Mercury
	Square to Mars
SATURN	Trine to Moon
MERCURY	Trine to Saturn
MOON	Sextile to Jupiter
	Trine to Mercury
	Trine to Sun
VENUS	Sextile to Sun
	Sextile to Mercury
	Square to Mars
MARS	Square to Saturn

THE SUN will be in a superior right-sided position relative to any planets on its left side to which it is configured. Mars in Virgo is on its left, but Leo and Virgo are not configured, so there is no aspect. Saturn in Sagittarius is on its left side, and these signs are configured by the trine. Thus, the Sun is in a superior right-sided trine to Saturn. The converse statement is that Saturn is in an inferior left-sided trine relative to the Sun.

JUPITER in Gemini is on the right side of the Sun and Mercury in Leo, and thus holds the superior sextile to both of them. From the point of view of the Sun and Mercury, Jupiter is on their left side, and they are inferior relative to Jupiter. Jupiter is on the right side of Mars in Virgo and thus has a superior square to Mars. Remember that the co-presence of Jupiter with Venus in Gemini, and the opposition to Saturn in Sagittarius, do not figure in this determination of superior and inferior aspects.

SATURN in Sagittarius holds a superior trine to the Moon in Aries. That is its only superior aspect.

MERCURY in Leo has the same configuration as the Sun. Mercury holds the superior right-sided trine to Saturn.

THE MOON in Aries holds the superior right-sided sextiles to Venus and Jupiter in Gemini, and the superior right-sided trines to Mercury and the Sun in Leo.

VENUS in Gemini is similar to Jupiter. Venus holds the superior right-sided sextiles to Mercury and the Sun, and the superior right-sided square to Mars.

MARS in Virgo holds the superior right-sided square to Saturn in Sagittarius.

CHART II: SUPERIOR ASPECTS

Planet	Superior Aspects
SUN	—
JUPITER	Sextile to Mars
SATURN	Sextile to Mars
MERCURY	—
MOON	—
VENUS	Sextile to Moon
MARS	Square to Venus

THE SUN and MERCURY in Scorpio are not configured to Sagittarius, and there are no planets on their right side in Capricorn, Aquarius, or Pisces to which they might be configured.

JUPITER and SATURN in Taurus are in superior sextiles to Mars on their right side. There are no planets in Leo or Virgo to which they might be configured by right-sided squares or trines.

THE MOON in Sagittarius is not in a superior position to any planet. There are no planets on its right side in the zodiacal signs of Aquarius, Pisces, or Aries to which it might be configured.

VENUS in Libra is in a superior sextile to the Moon in Sagittarius on its right side.

MARS in Cancer is in a superior position to Venus, making a right-sided square. It is also in a superior position to the Sun and Mercury with right-sided trines.

→ EXERCISE 31

Using your own chart, complete exercise 31:
Right-sided Superior and Left-sided Inferior Aspects

EXERCISE 31

RIGHT-SIDED SUPERIOR AND LEFT-SIDED INFERIOR ASPECTS

Determine which planet holds the superior/dominant position in each aspect in the chart. This planet has more influence in the interpretation of the aspect.

1. *Enter the zodiacal sign of each planet.* The sign that the planet is in, and the sign that is opposite that planet, form the zodiacal "axis" that divides the left side from the right side of the planet in question. (It sometimes helps to view the planet from the center of the chart to see the left and right sides).

2. *Investigate each planet from its own reference point in order to determine its right and left sides.* Observing the axis between the sign and its opposition, note which planets are to its left (i.e., ahead of it in zodiacal order), and which planets are to its right (i.e., behind it in zodiacal order).

3. *Look at the aspects that the planet makes, and determine if it is in a superior position or an inferior position.* A superior planet makes a right-sided sextile, square, or trine to planets on its left side. An inferior planet makes a left-sided sextile, square, or trine to planets on its right side. (Do not consider co-presence or opposition in this exercise).

4. *Enter the superior aspects that a planet makes.* A planet will be superior to those planets that follow it in zodiacal order (up to its opposition sign). A planet will be inferior to those planets that precede it in zodiacal order (up to its opposition sign).

5. *Have patience with this exercise and do it diligently.* Although it may be challenging to grasp at first, identifying superior aspects is in fact simple and will soon become second nature. If you are having difficulty, refer to FIGURES 57, 68, and 69 to help visualize the spatial and directional relationships between planets. Repeat the exercise with other charts if necessary.

Planet	Sign	Superior Aspects
SUN		
JUPITER		
SATURN		
MERCURY		
MOON		
VENUS		
MARS		

REFLECTION AND ANALYSIS

Planets in a superior position have more influence on the interpretation of the aspect. They have the power to impress their own significations, for better or worse, in accordance with their natures and condition, on the planet in the inferior position.

1. How might you begin to interpret each aspect based upon the dominance of the planet in the superior position?
2. Who has the upper hand in the aspect relation?
3. Are there any planets which only make superior aspects?
4. Are there any planets which only find themselves in the inferior position? How do you experience this in your life relative to the planetary significations of each aspect?
5. Are there situations in which part of you dominates, and takes the initiative to push its agenda onto another part, or situations where part of you feels dominated and controlled by stronger forces?
6. Does this inner pattern have any relation to the external interactions that you have with others?

CHAPTER 45

Overcoming

AND HURLING RAYS

———

OVERCOMING

Every star, the one which is lying on the right triangle or square or hexagon overcomes the one on the left, for it is going towards it. Thus, some star which is in Capricorn prevails, overcoming one in Taurus by trigon figure and one in Aries by tetragon figure and one in Pisces by hexagon figure.—PORPHYRY.[1]

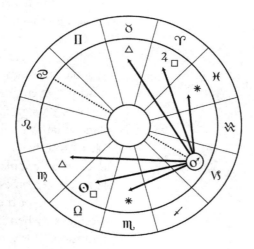

FIGURE 70. OVERCOMING AND HURLING RAYS

A planet in superior position casts forward rays to a planet in inferior position, overcoming any planets in a right-sided sextile, square, or trine (Mars in Capricorn overcomes Jupiter in Aries). A planet in inferior position hurls backward rays to a planet in superior position (Mars in Capricorn casts backward rays to the Sun in Libra, but does not overcome it; instead, the Sun overcomes Mars).

1   PORPHYRY, *Introduction* 21.

"Overcoming" is a translation of the Greek word *kathuperterēsis*, which also means "prevail", "overcome", "have the upper hand", or "superior". When a planet is in the superior position in a right-sided figure, it is casting its rays in a *forward*

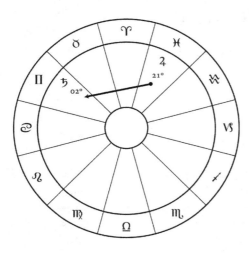

FIGURE 71.

JUPITER OVERCOMES SATURN

direction, *looking* upon the other planet. Its significations prevail and overcome those of the planet in the inferior position. With the concept of overcoming, it is important to note that we are not considering the relative speeds of the faster and slower-moving planets as we do in adherence by conjunction (*kollēsis*) and connection by aspect configuration (*sunaphē*). Nor are we looking at exact degrees. Rather, we are observing the *order of the zodiacal signs* that are on the *right side of a planet* or the *left side of a planet*, by whole sign aspect.

Overcoming is more powerful when the planets are either in trine or square configurations. The planet which overcomes is stronger: it imposes its significations upon the planet that is inferior to it, regardless of whether it is benefic, malefic, or in an angular house. When a benefic overcomes another planet, the outcome of the configuration is good, even when it is a square configuration. This was said to be a sign of an eminent nativity, where an individual is overcome with a surplus of beneficial forces.

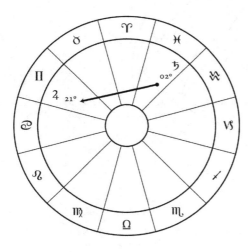

FIGURE 72.

SATURN OVERCOMES JUPITER

When a malefic overcomes another planet, the outcome is problematic. The commentaries enumerate many kinds of adversities, suggesting a life beset by misfortune and the lack of eminence.[2]

The potential difficulties of overcoming are specific to the square, and in particular to the superior right-sided square. Indeed, a special term, *epidekatesis*, was used to describe one planet overcoming another planet by means of the square. In this case, the overcoming planet is positioned in the tenth sign relative to the planet being overcome. *Epidekatesis* literally means "lying upon the tenth" (from the word for the number ten); it was used in the Hellenistic world when extracting a ten-percent tithing, or the execution of every tenth captive during the frequent wars. *Epidekatesis* is thus translated sometimes as "decimate" (or alternatively, "dominate").

This does not mean that one planet must occupy the tenth house and the other the first house, but rather that the planet is located in a sign that is ten signs away from the other planet (following the natural order of the zodiac). Thus, a planet in the fifth house is overcome by a square aspect from a planet in the second house, because (in the natural order of the zodiac) there are ten whole signs between the fifth house and the second house. By definition, this is the superior square.

Firmicus Maternus delineated the differences in meanings between Saturn and Jupiter, when each was in the tenth sign relative to the other. He observes that if Saturn and Jupiter are joined in a square aspect, and if Saturn is in the superior position (a right-sided square), it denotes dangers to the native's life and a diminishment of wealth. But, if Jupiter holds the superior (i.e., right-sided) position, the parents are famous and some measure of wealth is bestowed upon them.[3]

Here we see that Saturn, in the superior position, imposes his negative significations upon Jupiter: danger to the life and loss of wealth. When Jupiter overcomes Saturn, by contrast, its beneficence is more powerful than Saturn's maleficence. Jupiter suppresses the negative manifestations of Saturn, transforming them into positive ones (FIGURES 71–72).

2 PORPHYRY, *Introduction* 21
3 FIRMICUS MATERNUS, *Mathesis* 5.9.2–3, trans. HOLDEN.

HURLING RAYS

> A star that is leading hurls a ray at a star that is following according to
> figure. For example, a star in Aries hurls a ray at a star in Capricorn,
> and in similar manner. The star following looks upon the star leading
> and prevails by overcoming it, being carried towards it, but it does not
> hurl a ray. For, the visual sight of every beam is carried forwards (to
> the front), but the ray is carried backwards (to the back). It is said that
> hurling a ray occurs both zodiacally and by degree.—ANTIOCHUS.[4]

A planet on the left side of an aspect figure stands in the inferior position to
a planet overcoming it from behind. The planet on the left side of the aspect
figure—the one who is pursued—is leading (moving ahead of the planet that is
trying to overcome it). The inferior planet on the left responds by hurling rays
behind it at the superior planet, like an outlaw shooting its pursuer in an old
Western.

The details concerning the hurling of rays have been especially challenging
to decipher. The ancients themselves mention several schools of thought on this
matter, and the fine points vary among four different authors. What seems to
be clear is that hurling rays is destructive according to the square and opposition figure, but according to the trine figure can be protective. Note that planets
can hurl backward rays from the opposition figure, even though they cannot be
overcome by the opposition.

Thus the right-sided superior planet in a configuration holds the dominant
position as it casts forward rays, overcoming and imposing its good or bad significations upon the left-sided inferior planet. The inferior planet in response
hurls backward rays. In some instances, the forward rays can maltreat a planet
in front of it, while the backward rays strike and destroy a planet behind it.
Our specific concerns are with how overcoming and hurling rays can maltreat
a planet.

4   ANTIOCHUS, *Summary* 13.

CHAPTER 46

Maltreatment

BY OVERCOMING

———

IN THE CYCLE OF ASPECT RELATIONSHIPS, CONDITIONS OF MALTREATMENT by overcoming and the hurling of rays occur at the critical points of the two squares, and at the opposition. Maltreatment by overcoming occurs at the superior square of a figure. Maltreatment by hurling rays occurs at the inferior square.

In the course of its synodic cycle, at each of its squares to the Sun, Mars makes two unique phases called "anomalies". At the first square, Mars begins to slow down as it approaches the first station (near the trine), instead of speeding up like Jupiter and Saturn do. From its first square with the Sun, Mars travels very slowly through the retrograde period as it moves through the first trine, the opposition point, to the second trine. Unlike the other planets that begin to increase speed after the direct station, Mars continues in slow motion until he clears the final square with the Sun. In contrast to his average speed (one sign per two months), Mars can spend up to nine months in one or two signs during this passage.

As the *thema mundi* shows us, the square aspect is of the nature of Mars. And there is something very Mars-like in the conditions of maltreatment that occur at the superior and inferior squares. As an archetypal war god, Mars embodies aggression, dominance, menace, and retaliation. These malefic qualities are expressed when planets are maltreated by overcoming or by hurled rays.

MALTREATMENT AND BONIFICATION
BY OVERCOMING

Maltreatment by overcoming is based upon the planets' relative right or left directional sides and house location. Unlike maltreatment by connection (*sunaphē*) and adherence (*kollēsis*), maltreatment by overcoming is not based upon the planet's speed and applying aspect by degree.

In overcoming, the superior planet on the right is dominant. But this is only problematic at the square (*epidekatesis*), when the superior planet is a malefic. And while the Hellenistic authors give troublesome interpretations concerning a malefic in a superior position, this in and of itself is not a case of maltreatment. Maltreatment by overcoming necessitates an additional requirement. The texts explain that a planet is maltreated when it is overcome by a "badly positioned" destructive star. Both Antiochus and Porphyry define the "badly positioned" or "disadvantageous" houses as the second, third, sixth, eighth, and twelfth houses. These were considered ineffective or disadvantageous for conducting profitable business. Later, Medieval authors called these the "unfortunate" houses. The topics of these places encompass the bad things that can happen in life. We will discuss the reasoning behind house significations in more detail in volume two. For now, the following working descriptions will suffice:

SECOND HOUSE	Excessive greed or debt
THIRD HOUSE	Rivalry and fratricide between brothers over primogenitor inheritance
SIXTH HOUSE	Illness, accidents, injuries, slavery
EIGHTH HOUSE	Death, anguish of the mind
TWELFTH HOUSE	Suffering, losses, enemies, incarceration

While a malefic in a whole sign superior square aspect is already harsh, this in and of itself is not as catastrophic as maltreatment by overcoming. The malefic planet must be located in the houses where unfortunate activities occur. Only then are they capable of inducing events that are destructive to the well-being of the individual. For MALTREATMENT BY OVERCOMING to occur, the following conditions have to be met:

1. A malefic planet (Mars or Saturn)
2. located in a "bad house" (second, third, sixth, eighth, or twelfth)
3. configured in a whole sign superior square (*epidekatesis*)
4. overcomes another planet in the inferior position

An example of maltreatment by overcoming is Mars in Cancer in the twelfth house squaring Jupiter in Libra in the third house (FIGURE 73). Here, the malefic is in a house that represents the difficult conditions of life, and is also in a superior position to another planet through a whole sign square. Note that degree-based speed considerations (e.g., faster planet applying to slower planet) are not necessary here. In regards to bonification by overcoming, although it is not articulated in the ancient texts, we can extrapolate the following conditions:

1. A benefic planet (Venus or Jupiter)
2. located in a "fortunate house" (first, fourth, fifth, seventh, ninth, tenth, or eleventh)
3. configured in a whole sign superior sextile or trine
4. overcomes another planet in the inferior position

FIGURE 73.
MALTREATMENT &
BONIFICATION BY OVERCOMING

Venus bonifies Mars by overcoming (superior sextile). Mars maltreats Jupiter by overcoming (superior square).

An example of bonification by overcoming is Venus in Taurus in the tenth house sextiling Mars in Cancer in the twelfth. The benefic is in a strong, positive house, and is in a superior position (sextile) (FIGURE 73). Although bonification would logically apply to sextiles and trines, it may also be applied to the square configurations. Here we follow Firmicus Maternus, who gives very positive interpretations for Jupiter in the superior square to another planet:

> If Jupiter and the Sun are conjoined in the square aspect, and Jupiter possessing the superior part of a *dexter* (right) square aspects the Sun posited in a sinister (left) square with a menacing aspect, that configuration denotes the insignia of dignity through either his own merit or that of his father, but it also bestows increases and promotions to good and great honors.[1]

→ EXAMPLE CHARTS

Let us now look at our example charts for any conditions of maltreatment or bonification by overcoming.

---

1 FIRMICUS MATERNUS, *Mathesis* 6.10.4, trans. HOLDEN.

For maltreatment, Mars or Saturn must be in a superior square to another planet and also in an unfortunate house (second, third, sixth, eighth, or twelfth). For bonification, Venus or Jupiter must be in the superior position by sextile, trine, or square to another planet, and also in a fortunate house (first, fourth, fifth, seventh, ninth, tenth, or eleventh).

CHART 1: MALTREATMENT AND BONIFICATION BY OVERCOMING

Malefic	*Bad house*	*Superior square*	*Maltreatment by overcoming*
SATURN	Yes (second)	No	No
MARS	No	Yes	No

Benefic	*Good house*	*Superior sextile, trine, or square*	*Bonification by overcoming*
JUPITER	No	Superior sextile to Sun and Mercury; superior square to Mars	No
VENUS	No	Superior sextile to Sun and Mercury; superior square to Mars	No

SATURN is located in the second house. However, it does not hold the superior position in any square configuration. In its square to Mars, it holds the inferior position, so there is no maltreatment by Saturn. While MARS in the superior position does overcome Saturn by a whole sign square, Mars is not located in any of the unfortunate houses. Again, there is no maltreatment by overcoming. Since VENUS and JUPITER are both in the unfortunate eighth house, they are not capable of bonifying any planet by overcoming.

CHART II: MALTREATMENT AND BONIFICATION BY OVERCOMING

Malefic	Bad house	Superior square	Maltreatment by overcoming
SATURN	No	No	No
MARS	Yes (twelfth)	Yes	Mars maltreats Venus

Benefic	Good house	Superior sextile, trine, or square	Bonification by overcoming
JUPITER	Yes (tenth)	Superior sextile to Mars	Jupiter bonifies Mars
VENUS	Yes (third)	Superior sextile to the Moon	Venus bonifies the Moon

SATURN is located in the tenth house, so it cannot maltreat by overcoming. MARS in Cancer is in the twelfth house. It holds the superior position in a whole sign square, overcoming Venus at 4° Libra. Thus, Venus is maltreated by Mars. JUPITER in Taurus is located in the tenth house and holds the superior position in the sextile with Mars. Jupiter overcomes Mars with its benefic influences, albeit somewhat weakly due to the sextile. VENUS is in a good house (third), and forms a superior sextile to the Moon, thus bonifying her (albeit weakly). Note that Jupiter's bonifying influence over Mars helps to mitigate the destructive actions of Mars upon Venus to some extent; as a result, Venus' ability to bonify the Moon (which is already weak due to the sextile) is also affected by Mars' condition.

→ EXERCISE 32

Using your own chart, complete exercise 32:
Maltreatment and Bonification by Overcoming

EXERCISE 32

MALTREATMENT AND BONIFICATION BY OVERCOMING

In this exercise, you are going to investigate whether any of your planets are maltreated or bonified due to overcoming.

MALTREATMENT CONDITIONS

1. *Look to see if Mars or Saturn is located in the second, third, sixth, eighth, or twelfth houses.* If not, move on to bonification conditions.
2. *If a malefic is located in one of these houses, see if it occupies the superior position in a whole sign square to any planet that is in the inferior position.* If so, the inferior planet is maltreated.

BONIFICATION CONDITIONS

Keep in mind that these are *implied* conditions of bonification, i.e., they are not explicitly articulated in the texts.

1. *Look to see if Venus or Jupiter is located in the first, fourth, fifth, seventh, ninth, tenth, or eleventh houses.* If not, there is no bonification.
2. *If a benefic is located in one of these houses, see if it occupies the superior position in a whole sign trine, sextile, or square to any planet that is in the inferior position. If so, the inferior-positioned planet is bonified.*

Remember that the benefic influences of the trine aspect are stronger than those of the sextile. Also, this is one instance when a square aspect from a planet is actively beneficial, enhancing the positive outcomes of the inferior planet.

MALTREATMENT AND BONIFICATION BY OVERCOMING

Malefic	Bad house	Superior square	Maltreatment by overcoming
SATURN			
MARS			

Benefic	Good house	Superior sextile, trine, or square	Bonification by overcoming
JUPITER			
VENUS			

REFLECTION AND ANALYSIS

1. Which planets, if any, are maltreated or bonified by overcoming?
2. How are the planetary significations made better or worse by the power of the overcoming planet?

CHAPTER 47

Maltreatment

BY STRIKING WITH A RAY

———

IN THE MYTH OF THE LOVERS ORPHEUS AND EURYDICE, EURYDICE IS bitten by a snake, dies, and descends into the underworld. Orpheus, a sublime musician, enchants Pluto and Persephone—the King and Queen of Hades— with his lyre, and convinces them to release Eurydice. He is given permission to lead her up to the world of the living, on the condition that he doesn't look back to ensure she is following him. At the last moment, he can no longer stand the suspense and as he turns his head, his eyes briefly connect with her wisp-like figure before she vanishes out of his sight. Astrologically speaking, it is almost as if he struck her with the glance of a backwards-hurled ray.

The guidelines for maltreatment by hurling rays are less clearly defined than they are for overcoming. There is no requirement that the malefic planet be located in the badly positioned houses, so other factors must be required for maltreatment to occur. We know that hurling a ray occurs both zodiacally and by degree, but no specific degree ranges are given in the Antiochus or Porphyry definitions. So we must reconstruct the underlying reasoning from clues scattered throughout the texts in order to arrive at working definitions.

I have spent countless hours discussing hurling and striking with rays with colleagues. I have consulted several translations, have translated these passages myself, and read them over and over again. Based upon the texts we have available, however, definitive guidelines still remain inconclusive. I encourage you to think about these matters as you look at charts, and to experiment with the various options. You are invited to keep an open mind and to participate in the ongoing reconstruction of Hellenistic astrology.

The Antiochus and Porphyry texts state that "a planet is maltreated when struck with a ray by malefics". There are four ways to interpret this:

1. A planet must be struck by both malefics, necessitating that both Mars and Saturn be in the same zodiacal sign, hurling backward rays at a planet. If this is the case, does maltreatment occur by whole sign hurled rays only, if both

malefics are in collusion? For example, Mars and Saturn at any degree of Sagittarius, both hurling square rays at Venus at any degree of Virgo, would qualify as maltreatment by hurling rays.

2.   A single malefic in an inferior square can maltreat another planet by hurling a whole sign ray, regardless of degree. That is exceptional power. If this were the case, it redefines whole sign testimony as well as obfuscating the power of maltreatment by connection (*sunaphē*). And it throws into doubt the strength of the superior overcoming planet.

3.   The inferior planet must not only hurl a backwards ray by whole sign, it must also strike the other planet by degree. We could safely assume a 3° applying orb, so the planet being maltreated runs into the malefic ray hurled slightly ahead of it, much like a bird flying into an arrow shot by a hunter just ahead of its flight path. This necessitates that the planet hurling the ray is the slower planet, striking the faster planet running into its hurled ray. However, this equates to maltreatment by connection (*sunaphē*), which is a separate condition; it also involves planetary speed, which is not part of the right and left distinctions with which we are working.

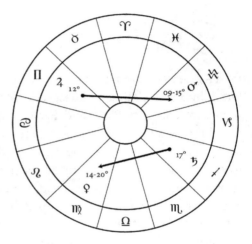

FIGURE 74.
MALTREATMENT & BONIFICATION
BY STRIKING WITH A RAY
Jupiter bonifies Mars by hurling a trine ray.
Saturn maltreats Venus by hurling a square ray.

4.   According to Valens, there is a 3° range on either side of the planet that is vulnerable to destruction when being struck by a backward hurled ray.[1] If this is the case, a malefic planet can hurl a backward square ray at another planet, and maltreatment would occur if that ray should strike the planet within a 3° orb on either side (thus a 7° range altogether). Saturn at 17° Sagittarius, for example, would hurl a square ray at Venus in Virgo (who could be located from 14–20°). This interpretation of maltreatment by striking with

---

1   VALENS, Anthology 3.3. Valens also instructs that benefics that hurl rays within this 3° interval on either side become "preventers of destruction".

a ray has the benefit of maintaining the left/right distinction, and does not necessitate a faster and slower planet with an applying aspect.

The working definition used in this book follows a reconstruction of the earliest Hellenistic authors.[2] *Maltreatment by striking with a ray occurs by a malefic planet in any house, hurling backward rays and striking the maltreated planet within an interval of 3° on either side of it.*

→ EXAMPLE CHARTS

Let us see if any planets are maltreated by being struck by a backward-hurled ray from an inferior planet to a superior planet.

CHART I

SATURN at 24° Sagittarius hurls a backward ray at Mars at 14° Virgo. This 10° interval between the ray of Saturn and Mars is beyond the 3° range on either side, so there is no maltreatment. MARS at 14° Virgo hurls a backward square ray at Venus at 21° Gemini, and at Jupiter at 9° Gemini. Mars' ray falls between them at 14° Gemini, but it is too far away from either planet to strike and maltreat them.

JUPITER and VENUS' backward-hurled sextile rays into Aries are too far away from the Moon at 25° Aries. Their backward-hurled trine rays fall in Aquarius, where there are no planets.

CHART II

The backward-hurled square rays of MARS and SATURN do not strike any planets in the signs that are configured to Aries (for Mars) or Aquarius (for Saturn). Hence, no maltreatment.

JUPITER in Taurus hurls a backward sextile ray into Pisces that does not encounter any planets; neither does its backward-hurled trine ray into Capricorn. VENUS at 4° Libra hurls a backward sextile ray offering protection and bonification to the Ascendant at 5° Leo. There are no planets in Gemini where her backward trine rays fall.

---

2   In August 2010, Chris Brennan, Benjamin Dykes, and I settled upon this reconstruction after a week-long re-translation, analysis, and discussion of the relevant texts, especially the definitions given by Antiochus and Porphyry.

→ EXERCISE 33

Using your own chart, complete exercise 33:
Maltreatment and Bonification by Striking with a Ray

EXERCISE 33

MALTREATMENT AND BONIFICATION
BY STRIKING WITH A RAY

In this exercise, you are going to determine if any of your planets are maltreated or bonified due to the hurling of backward rays.

MALTREATMENT

1. *Look to see if Saturn or Mars is hurling a backward square ray to any planet that is in a superior position to them.* (The malefic can be located in any house). In the first column of the following table, list any planets that are in a superior square to a malefic.
2. *Does the ray from the malefic fall within a 3° orb on either side of the planet (7° altogether)?* In the second column, list any planets that receive a backward ray from Mars or Saturn, within a 7° range. (It is not necessary that one planet be faster- or slower-moving).
3. *In the third column, list any planets that are maltreated by striking with a ray.*

BONIFICATION

1. *Look to see if Venus or Jupiter is hurling a backward sextile, square, or trine ray to any planet in a superior position relative to them.* List any planets that are in a superior sextile, square, or trine to a benefic. (The benefics can be located in any house).
2. *Does this ray fall within a 3° orb on either side of the planet (7° altogether)?* List any planets that receive a backward ray from Jupiter or Venus, within a 7° range. (It is not necessary that one planet be faster- or slower-moving).
3. *List any planets that are bonified by striking with a ray.*

MALTREATMENT AND BONIFICATION BY STRIKING WITH A RAY

Malefic	*Backward square to a superior planet*	*Ray strikes within a 7° range*	*Maltreatment by striking with a ray*
SATURN			
MARS			

Benefic	*Backward square to a superior planet*	*Ray strikes within a 7° range*	*Bonification by striking with a ray*
JUPITER			
VENUS			

REFLECTION AND ANALYSIS

1. Are any planets struck by a ray from a malefic or benefic? If so, what are their significations?
2. Are these planets improved or compromised in regards to the outcomes that they signify in your life?

CHAPTER 48

The Opposition

———

WE HAVE EXAMINED THE CIRCUMSTANCES OF SPECIAL ASPECT relationships around the conjunction and around both squares. Now we turn to the opposition. At the opposition, two planets stand diametrically opposed to one another. According to Firmicus Maternus, it is a hostile aspect in which the two planets mutually attack each other; like the square, it is a malign aspect. It is important to note that, with the square, one planet *dominates* the other, but in the opposition, the rivals are of *potentially equal power*. There is a strong tension, and the outcome could go either way.

According to Porphyry, planets can both overcome and hurl rays at the opposition, depending on whether they stand on the right or left side of the aspect figure.[1] This assertion has generated much confusion, because elsewhere in the same text we are told that overcoming can only occur by sextile, square, or trine. The planet on the right side of a figure overcomes, but on the left side hurls rays. However, the opposition is the very point where a planet changes sides, from left to right. Thus, a planet can be to the left or right in an opposition, but whole sign aspects are too imprecise to determine this. We must use a degree-based assessment to ascertain which side the planet is on.

We must also take speed into account. The exact line of the diameter is taken from the degree of the *slower* planet, while the *faster* planet changes sides. Up to that point, the faster planet has been on the left side, in the inferior position, increasing its distance from its earlier union with the slower planet. It hurls rays behind itself as it is pursued. At the opposition, however, the adversaries stand face to face across the great divide. "They strike each other in turn with the distant power of their own forces", remarks Firmicus.[2] In the span of a degree, a fundamental shift takes place, as the faster planet turns and begins the long journey back. It is now on the right side, in the superior position. The hunter

1   PORPHYRY, *Introduction* 24.
2   FIRMICUS MATERNUS, *Mathesis* 6.15; Holden translation.

becomes the hunted, and begins to overcome the slower planet.

Other qualities also shift at the opposition. In the solar phase cycle, when Mars, Jupiter, and Saturn are opposite the Sun, they go through a fundamental phase transition from being "of the morning" to being "of the evening". There is also a rebellious quality to a retrograde planet at the opposition to the Sun. The opposition, therefore, is not only an archetypal exchange of hostilities by adversaries; it also harbors the inherent risk of sudden change.

The dynamics of this change are closely bound up with the concept of *parallagē*, which is presented by Porphyry directly after the definition of right and left figures:

> They call it a passing beyond (*parallagē*) whenever stars pass beyond
> a configuration by degree of an equal-sided figure.[3]

The simplest translation of the word *parallagē* is to "pass beyond" or "pass by". It is a change of position or movement, which is certainly what happens when a planet shifts from left to right, or from morning to evening. But as Robert Schmidt has pointed out, there is an inherent destabilization to the shift that occurs at the opposition, which can throw both planets off balance. Indeed, he discusses *parallagē* in terms of the perturbation—the madness or frenzy of the soul—that occurs when planets abruptly exchange their relative positions, throwing one or both into confusion.[4]

MALTREATMENT BY OPPOSITION

Maltreatment by opposition follows the same guidelines as maltreatment by overcoming. A planet can be maltreated by a whole sign opposition from Mars or Saturn, through overcoming or hurling rays, *if* Mars or Saturn are in one of the disadvantageous houses (second, third, sixth, eighth, or twelfth).

In the more specific condition of maltreatment by connection (*sunaphē*), where the faster planet applies within 3° to an opposition with a slower planet, the malefic can be in any house. However, maltreatment by whole sign opposition requires the malefic to be located in an unfortunate house, regardless of the relative speed of the planets (FIGURE 75).

---

3   PORPHYRY, *Introduction* 10; ANTIOCHUS, *Summary* 8.
4   SCHMIDT, *Definitions and Foundations*, p. 149.

There are no specific instructions given for bonification by opposition. In his delineations of the opposition aspect, Firmicus does not give positive outcomes for either Venus or Jupiter opposed to another planet.[5] In several instances, the outcomes of planets in opposition are not as severe if they belong to the same sect. However, in the case of spear-bearing bodyguards, there are certain circumstances where benefic planets can cast opposition rays that act as protective forces in the charts of eminent figures. A fragment from Petosiris states that "in diameters, benefics are never bad, neither with each other nor with the lights".[6]

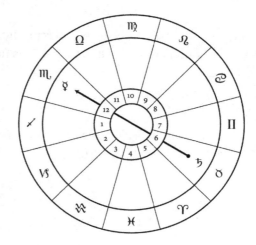

FIGURE 75.
MALTREATMENT BY OPPOSITION
Saturn maltreats Mercury by opposition from a bad house (sixth house).

→ EXAMPLE CHARTS

Let us investigate whether any planets are maltreated by an opposition from a malefic located in an unfortunate house.

CHART I

SATURN is located in the unfortunate second house and casts opposition rays into the eighth house, where both benefics are located. VENUS and JUPITER are both maltreated by the opposition from Saturn. Furthermore, because Saturn's ray falls at 24° Gemini, Venus at 21° Gemini runs into it, and we have already seen that this is maltreatment by connection (*sunaphē*). Note that Saturn is not bonified by Jupiter. It is unlikely that this would be the case even if Jupiter were in a more fortunate house. MARS is not in an unfortunate house and does not oppose any planets.

---

5   *Mathesis* 6, 15–19.
6   CCAG 6, p. 62, trans. Robert SCHMIDT in *The Astrological Record of the Early Greek Sages* (Berkeley Springs, WV: The Golden Hind Press, 1995), p. 18.

CHART II

SATURN opposes the Sun and Mercury by sign. However, he is not in an unfortunate house, and so maltreatment does not occur. MARS does not oppose any planets.

→   EXERCISE 34

Using your own chart, complete exercise 34:
Maltreatment by Opposition

EXERCISE 34

MALTREATMENT BY OPPOSITION FROM A MALEFIC

In this exercise, you will ascertain whether any of your planets are maltreated due to being opposed by a badly-placed malefic.

1. *Look to see if Mars or Saturn is located in the second, third, sixth, eighth, or twelfth houses.* (If they are not, then the conditions aren't met). List the house in the first column of the table below.
2. *Look to see if Mars or Saturn make a whole sign opposition to any other planets.* No orbs are necessary if the malefic is in a bad house. Write yes or no in the second column.
3. *List any planets that are thus maltreated in the final column.* This will be the planet that is opposed by the malefic. Due to the structure of the houses, it will also be in a bad house (i.e., the second and eighth houses oppose each other, as do the sixth and twelfth).

MALTREATMENT BY OPPOSITION FROM A MALEFIC IN A BAD HOUSE

Malefic	Located in a bad house	Whole sign opposition	Planet maltreated
SATURN			
MARS			

REFLECTION AND ANALYSIS

1. Are any planets opposed by a malefic from a bad place? If so, what are their significations?
2. Are they compromised in regards to their significations or outcomes?

CHAPTER 49

Enclosure

———

Enclosure (*emperischesis*) is whenever two planets enclose one planet with no other star casting its ray between the two of them, and certainly not whenever another star casts its ray according to figure within 7°, either upon the degrees [the enclosed star] has passed by or the 7° upon which the enclosed planet is going. This kind of enclosure is good when done by benefic planets, but bad when done by malefic planets.—ANTIOCHUS.[1]

EMPERISCHESIS IS RELATED TO THE VERB MEANING TO "ENCOMPASS", "surround", or "enclose". As a noun, it has a specific astronomical meaning in the Greek lexicon: "the hemming in of a planet by two others". The Vedic astrologers call this "scissoring". Planets can be enclosed by other planets *bodily*, by physical proximity, as well as by *rays*. Benefic rays encompassing a planet offer protection and assist the planet in prospering. Malefic rays enclosing a planet surround it with a host of difficult and sometimes dangerous circumstances; they block or prevent a planet's positive potential from coming about. However, another planet can intervene, interposing its own ray that acts as a "shield", preventing either the good or bad from enveloping the planet in question.

Maltreatment by enclosure occurs when the planet is enclosed by both malefics with no interposing ray from another planet blocking the enclosure. This can occur *bodily*, when the malefics are in physical proximity surrounding the planet, or *by ray*, when the rays from malefic planets fall on either side of the planet in question. It can also occur by a combination of bodily proximity and ray, where one malefic is in physical proximity to the enclosed planet, and a ray from the other malefic falls on the other side of the planet. The Medieval astrologers referred to this condition as *besiegement*. Let us illustrate with some examples.

1 ANTIOCHUS, *Summary* 12.

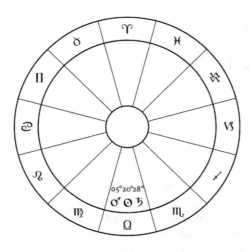

FIGURE 76.
BODILY ENCLOSURE

Mars and Saturn bodily enclose the Sun through physical proximity.

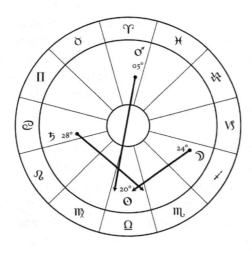

FIGURE 77.
ENCLOSURE BY RAYS, INTERVENTION

Saturn and Mars enclose the Sun by rays: Saturn via a square ray, and Mars by opposition. The Moon intervenes with a sextile.

BODILY ENCLOSURE would occur with Mars at 5° Libra, the Sun at 20° Libra, and Saturn at 28° Libra. The Sun is physically enclosed by the bodily presence of Mars on one side and Saturn on the other—as long as no other planet casts a ray into the interval of 7° on either side of the Sun, i.e., between 13–27° Libra (FIGURE 76).

ENCLOSURE BY RAYS: The Sun is at 20° Libra. Mars in Aries sends an opposition ray to 5° Libra, and Saturn in Cancer sends a square ray to 28° Libra, again with no intervention. If the Moon at 24° Sagittarius sent a sextile ray to 24° Libra, it would intervene and prevent the enclosure (FIGURE 77).

There is some ambiguity as to whether the rays from malefics that enclose planets have to be from square or opposition figures, or if they can also be from sextile and trine figures. Porphyry gives an example in which a ray from a trine is part of a "containment" (a variation of enclosure). We can thus assume that rays from any of the figures carry, at least in part, the nature of the planet emitting them. Enclosure by rays is by whole sign aspect, but intervention necessitates the 7° orb range.

ENCLOSURE BY BODILY PRE-
SENCE AND A RAY: Saturn at 23°
Cancer is *enclosed by benefics* when
Venus, at 25° Cancer (bodily proximity), and the square ray of Jupiter,
at 17° Libra, falls at 17° Cancer. We
might surmise that in this example,
Saturn is overcoming Jupiter by the
superior square, which it is; but nevertheless, Jupiter still protects Saturn. There are some circumstances
in life where the victim is moved or
forced to protect the abuser (FIG-
URE 78).

CONTAINMENT (*perischesis*) is
a variation on enclosure. It occurs
when a single planet sends two of
its rays onto either side of another
planet. The example given by Porphyry has the Moon in Virgo and
Mars in Aries.[2] Mars sends a trine
ray into Leo, the sign to the right
of the Moon, and an opposition ray
into Libra, the sign to the left of the
Moon. He concludes that the Moon
is encompassed by destructive rays
(FIGURE 79).

This example tells us several
things. The first is that containment,
like enclosure, can operate by whole
sign configurations. In the above example, Mars in Aries is in aversion
to the Moon in Virgo, and while it
cannot impact it directly, its rays can
still contain it (assuming there are
no interventions) by means of the
signs to which it is configured (Leo

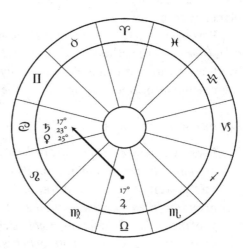

FIGURE 78.
ENCLOSURE BY BODILY PRESENCE AND RAY
*Saturn is enclosed between Venus (physical
proximity) and Jupiter (square ray).*

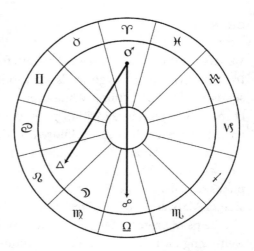

FIGURE 79.
ENCLOSURE BY CONTAINMENT
*Mars contains the Moon by two rays: a trine to
Leo, and an opposition to Libra. The two
signs that receive the rays flank Virgo.*

2 PORPHYRY, *Introduction* 14.

and Libra). Containment is also an example of how a malefic can harm another planet by means of a trine ray.

Porphyry also tells us that if malefic stars surround the Moon or the Ascendant (*hōroskopos*) without any benefic stars intervening, the child will be short-lived. Maltreatment is therefore not only about painful life circumstances and trauma, but also about the viability of life itself.

→   EXAMPLE CHARTS

Looking at our example charts, let us see if we can find any conditions of maltreatment or bonification by enclosure or containment. For MAL-TREATMENT BY ENCLOSURE, *both malefics must enclose a planet bodily and/or by ray; however, another planet with an intervening ray within 7° of the enclosed planet can break or shield the enclosure. For* BONIFICA-TION BY ENCLOSURE, *both benefics must enclose a planet bodily and/or by ray; another planet outside the enclosure can intervene with a ray falling within 7°of the enclosed planet. For* CONTAINMENT, *the various rays of one single malefic or benefic planet must surround and contain the planet under investigation, with no intervention by the ray of another planet falling within a 7° orb on either side of the enclosed planet.*

CHART I

VENUS at 21° Gemini is *enclosed* by rays from Mars and Saturn, and is thus *maltreated.* MARS at 14° Virgo sends a ray to 14° Gemini. SATURN at 24° Sagittarius sends a ray to 24° Gemini. Venus is enclosed between them, and no other planet interposes with a ray within 7° on either side of Venus to block the malefic enclosure. Venus is severely injured by this maltreatment, which damages the beneficial outcomes of her significations.

MARS at 14° Virgo is *enclosed* by both of the benefics and thus *bonified.* Jupiter's ray falls on one side of Mars at 9° Virgo, and Venus' ray falls on the other side of Mars at 21° Virgo. Here Mars is the cause of harm to Venus, but Venus also helps to protect Mars. The actions of Mars are protected from harming the well-being of the native, and the condition of Mars is substantially improved to bring forth better outcomes.

ASCERTAINING ENCLOSURE BY DEGREE RANGE

A useful shortcut for ascertaining enclosure (but not containment) is to first determine the *degree range* of the malefics, and then see if any planets fall within this range, regardless of sign. For example, in CHART I, the degree range formed between the malefics is 14°–24° (Mars 14° Virgo, Saturn 24° Sagittarius). It doesn't matter what signs they are in. Simply ascertain the *range*, and see if any other planets fall within that same range. *Only the planets that fall within this range will have the possibility of being enclosed* (also, only the planets that fall within this range will have the possibility of *intervening* in an enclosure). You will still have to check the conditions of bodily presence and rays, but if a planet is *outside* this range, it cannot be maltreated by enclosure by rays. The same shortcut applies to benefics and bonification.

CHART I: ENCLOSURE, CONTAINMENT, INTERVENTION

	Degree range	Enclosed	Contained	Intervention
MALEFICS	14°–24°	Venus	None	No intervention; Venus is maltreated
BENEFICS	9–21°	Mars	None	No intervention; Mars is bonified

CHART II

There are no instances of enclosure by malefics. A shortcut to making this determination is to note that SATURN is at 9° Taurus and MARS is at 12° Cancer. Thus, only a planet between 9° and 12° degrees of any sign can be enclosed. The Moon at 8° Sagittarius might be such a candidate. However, both Cancer and Taurus are in aversion to Sagittarius. Thus they do not see the Moon and cannot enclose her with their malefic rays. All other planets fall outside of the 9-12° range.

MARS at 12° Cancer *could* be enclosed by the square ray from Venus cast to 4° Cancer and the sextile ray from Jupiter cast to 23° Cancer. However, SATURN at 9° Taurus casts his sextile ray to 9° Cancer and blocks the benefic ray from Venus at 4° Cancer. This is an instance of *intervention*.

CHART II: ENCLOSURE, CONTAINMENT, INTERVENTION

	Degree range	Enclosed	Contained	Intervention
MALEFICS	9°–12°	None	None	None
BENEFICS	4–23°	Mars	None	Saturn intervenes. Mars is not bonified.

→ EXERCISE 35

Using your own chart, complete exercise 35:
Maltreatment and Bonification by Enclosure or Containment

EXERCISE 35

MALTREATMENT AND BONIFICATION BY ENCLOSURE
OR CONTAINMENT

**In this exercise, look for any planet that may be enclosed or contained by the
malefics and thus maltreated; repeat for the benefics and bonification.**

1. *Look at the degrees of Mars and Saturn in your chart and determine the range
    that they enclose.* Enter them into the first column of the table overleaf. If no
    planets fall within this range, then proceed to step 3 (containment).

2. *If another planet falls within the degree range of the malefics, look at the rays
    cast by Mars and Saturn to see if they enclose that planet.* In addition to rays,
    look also for *bodily proximity*. Enter any enclosed planets in column two of
    the table.

3. *Check for containment.* Do you see two rays from a single malefic surround-
    ing another planet? Note that the rays must hit the two signs immediately
    flanking the sign that the planet is in. Check to see if any other planetary ray
    intervenes within 7° on either side of the contained planet.

4. *Finally, check for intervention.* If a planet is enclosed or contained by malef-
    ics, look to see if another planet in the degree range intervenes. Specifically,
    look for a ray cast within 7° on either side of the enclosed planet. If there is
    intervention, the planet under investigation is not maltreated. If there is no
    intervention, the planet is maltreated. Enter these details in column 4.

    *Repeat these steps, substituting the benefics for the malefics, in order to check
    for bonification.*

ENCLOSURE, CONTAINMENT, INTERVENTION

	Degree range	Enclosed	Contained	Intervention
MALEFICS				
BENEFICS				

REFLECTION AND ANALYSIS

1. Are any planets enclosed or contained by malefics, with no intervention? If so, what are their significations?
2. Are these planets compromised in regards to their significations or outcomes?
3. Are any planets enclosed or contained by benefics, with no intervention? If so, what are their significations?
4. Are these planets supported in regards to their significations or outcomes?

CHAPTER 50

Maltreatment

BY DOMICILE LORDS AND HOUSE LOCATIONS

———

> It is called counteraction [...] whenever stars that lie upon zodiacal
> signs operate effectively, but the rulers of those signs are in a state of
> maltreatment, rendering them ineffective.—PORPHYRY.[1]

THERE ARE TWO MORE CONDITIONS OF MALTREATMENT ARTICULATED
by Porphyry and Antiochus that pertain to a planet's domicile lord and house
location: counteraction (*antanalusis*), and disadvantageous declining places
(*achrēmatistos apoklino*).

COUNTERACTION is one of the definitions in the series about aspect relations that both Antiochus and Porphyry include in their texts.[2] Counteraction
comes from the Greek word *antanalusis*, which carries the notion of "undoing
something that has been done". It addresses the importance of a planet's domicile lord (which we have discussed in previous chapters). The definition states
that:

> *If a planet occupies a zodiacal sign that operates effectively, but its lord is
> unfavorably situated, the good of the planet is counteracted or undone.*

The following list of maltreatment conditions specifies that a planet is maltreated if it occupies the domicile of a malefic *and* that malefic is located in one
of the unfortunate houses. Generally speaking, and as we have seen, the ongoing
support and stability that a planet receives is due to the good or bad condition
of its domicile lord. Thus, when that domicile lord happens to be a malefic, *and*
it is also situated within influence of a difficult house, it sends injurious matters
to its guest planet. This injurious influence damages the ability of the guest to do
good for the native.

If a planet occupies the zodiacal signs of Aries or Scorpio, its domicile lord

---

1   PORPHYRY, *Introduction* 27.
2   ANTIOCHUS, *Summary* 16; PORPHYRY, *Introduction* 27.

is Mars. If it occupies the signs of Capricorn or Aquarius, its domicile lord is Saturn. For maltreatment to occur, Mars or Saturn must be located in the second, third, sixth, eighth, or twelfth houses. The malefic planets, when located in these houses, can activate difficult experiences connected with the topics of these houses: i.e., finances, siblings, illness, death, or enemies. This in turn impacts the guest planet and the life of the individual.

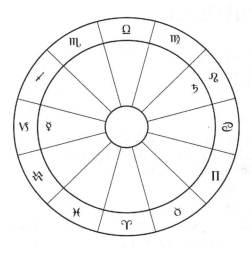

FIGURE 80.

MALTREATMENT BY BADLY-PLACED DOMICILE LORD

A planet can be maltreated if it occupies the domicile of a malefic that is located in an unfortunate house. No aspect between the two planets is necessary. Here, Mercury is in Capricorn, the domicile of Saturn; the domicile lord, Saturn, is located in the eighth house (one of the unfortunate places).

In the hierarchy of planetary beneficence, a planet's residency in the zodiacal signs of Taurus, Libra, Sagittarius, or Pisces, the domiciles of Venus and Jupiter, seem to put the planet at an automatic advantage; it is "ahead of the game" from the start, so to speak. One could argue that a planet occupying the domicile of a benefic, while that benefic is well-placed in a fortunate house, could be considered a condition of bonification. Once again, this is implied, but is not explicitly stated in the texts.

The final condition of maltreatment is a planet's presence in one of the DISADVANTAGEOUS DE-CLINING PLACES (or more simply: one of the unfortunate houses). The Antiochus text lists the second, third, sixth, eighth, or twelfth houses, but the Porphyry text limits it to the sixth and twelfth only. I am more inclined to accept Porphyry's rendering of this condition. We will discuss the significations of these houses—and the difficult topics contained in these sectors of human experience—in volume two.

→   EXAMPLE CHARTS

Let us see if any planets are maltreated due to their domicile lord or house location. We can also explore the possible corresponding bonification conditions.

CHART I

THE MOON is in Aries, the domicile of Mars. However, Mars is located in the eleventh, a fortunate house. Thus there is no maltreatment, according to this rule. However, the Moon itself is located in the sixth, a house associated with illness, accidents, and injuries. This itself is a maltreatment concern.

There are no planets in Scorpio, Capricorn, or Aquarius, so no planets are maltreated by the lords of these signs according to the rules of this condition.

SATURN is in Sagittarius, the domicile of a benefic. However, JUPITER is in the eighth, an unfortunate house, so there is no possible bonification according to this criterion. There are no planets in Pisces, Taurus, or Libra.

CHART II

Both THE SUN and MERCURY occupy the zodiacal sign of Scorpio, the domicile of Mars. And Mars is located in the most unfortunate house, the twelfth. Thus, the Sun and Mercury are both maltreated in accordance with this condition.

MARS, a malefic, is located in the twelfth house, and this brings more concern to the destructive nature of this planet.

THE MOON is in Sagittarius, and her domicile lord is the benefic JUPITER in the angular tenth house. This is a potential instance of bonification according to the implied condition, but with the following caveat: the aversion between the Moon and Jupiter might divert some of the full beneficence. There are no planets in Pisces, Jupiter's other domicile.

While Jupiter and Saturn are in Taurus, the domicile of Venus, Venus herself is located in the disadvantageous third house. Thus there is no bonification for these planets.

→ EXERCISE 36

Using your own chart, complete exercise 36:
Maltreatment and Bonification by Domicile Lord and
House Location

EXERCISE 36

MALTREATMENT AND BONIFICATION BY DOMICILE LORD
AND HOUSE LOCATION

In this exercise you are looking for any planet that might be (1) maltreated due to being located in the domicile of a malefic planet that is badly situated, or in an unfortunate house; and (2) bonified due to being located in the domicile of a benefic planet that is favorably situated, or in a fortunate house.

MALTREATMENT

1. *Are any of your planets in the signs of Aries, Scorpio, Capricorn, or Aquarius?*
2. *If so, check to see if their domicile lord—either Mars or Saturn—is in any of the unfortunate house locations: the second, third, sixth, eighth, or twelfth.*
3. *Are any of your planets in the sixth or twelfth houses?* If so, the planet is maltreated.

BONIFICATION

4. *Are any of your planets in the signs of Taurus, Libra, Sagittarius, or Pisces?* If not, they are not bonified.
5. *If so, check to see if their domicile lord—either Venus or Jupiter—is in any of the fortunate house locations: the first, fourth, fifth, seventh, ninth, tenth, or eleventh.*

MALTREATMENT

	In Aries, Scorpio, Capricorn, or Aquarius	*Domicile lord in an unfortunate house*	*In 6th or 12th house*
SUN			
JUPITER			
SATURN			
MERCURY			
MOON			
VENUS			
MARS			

BONIFICATION

	Planet in Taurus, Libra, Sagittarius, or Pisces	*Domicile lord in a fortunate house*
SUN		
JUPITER		
SATURN		
MERCURY		
MOON		
VENUS		
MARS		

REFLECTION AND ANALYSIS

Before you complete the final summary for your own chart, take a little more
time to understand the impact that the maltreatment and bonification of planets
has for your chart. In particular, consider the correlations that they have in your
life.

CHAPTER 51

Final Judgment of a Planet

BASED ON ASPECT CONDITIONS

———

WE ARE NOW READY TO MAKE OUR FINAL JUDGMENTS ON HOW A planet's condition is impacted by its aspect relationships with other planets. The broad strokes of our analysis are based upon the whole sign testimony given to the planets by the benefics and malefics (Venus, Jupiter; Mars, Saturn) through their harmonious and inharmonious configurations. All charts will contain a mixture of supporting and negating testimonies.

The finer details are provided by the more specific instances of maltreatment and bonification. Although less frequent, they are extremely important factors, and therefore receive more weight in the final judgment.

Always keep in mind that we are evaluating the *propensity of a planet*, based upon its condition, *to bring about actions and events that lead to positive outcomes that are in the best long-term interests of the individual.* It is important to emphasize that, just because a person's planets are in a bad condition, it does not necessarily mean that the person is bad, or even that the person's actions are bad; rather, it indicates that those actions may lead to less positive outcomes for the individual in question.

→ EXAMPLE CHARTS

In the tables below we will compile all of our previous exercises. Using these tabulations, we will attempt to make a final judgment.

CHART ONE: ONASSIS

SUMMARY OF MALTREATMENT CONDITIONS

ASPECT/ CONDITION	SUN 5° LEO	JUPITER 9° GEM	SATURN 24° SAG	MERCURY 2° LEO	MOON 25°ARIES	VENUS 21° GEM	MARS 14°VIRG
Struck by a ray from a malefic	—	—	—	—	—	—	—
Enclosed or contained by malefics	—	—	—	—	—	Enclosed by rays	—
Connection (sunaphē) with a malefic	—	—	—	—	—	Sunaphē to Saturn by opposition	—
Adherence to a malefic	—	—	—	—	—	—	—
Overcome by a malefic in a bad house	—	—	—	—	—	—	—
Opposed by a malefic in a bad house	—	Opposed by Sat. from 2nd house	—	—	—	Opposed by Sat. from 2nd house	—
Domicile lord is a malefic in a bad house	—	—	—	—	—	—	—
Located in sixth or twelfth house	—	—	—	—	6th house	—	—

SUMMARY OF BONIFICATION CONDITIONS

ASPECT/ CONDITION	SUN 5° LEO	JUPITER 9° GEM	SATURN 24° SAG	MERCURY 2° LEO	MOON 25°ARIES	VENUS 21° GEM	MARS 14°VIRG
Struck by a ray from a benefic	—	—	—	—	—	—	—
Enclosed or contained by benefics	—	—	—	—	—	—	Enclosed by rays
Connection (sunaphē) with a benefic	—	—	—	—	—	—	—
Adherence to a benefic	—	—	—	—	—	—	—
Overcome by a benefic in a good house	—	—	—	—	—	—	—
Opposed by a benefic in a good house	—	—	—	—	—	—	—
Domicile lord is a benefic in a good house	—	—	—	—	—	—	—

SUMMARY OF ASPECT RELATIONSHIPS

Planet and sign	Positive testimony	Negative testimony	Maltreatment	Bonification	Grade
SUN 5° LEO	Sup. sextile from Venus; sup. sextile from Jupiter	—	—	—	A–
JUPITER 9° GEM	Co-presence with Venus	Inf. square from Mars; opposition from Saturn	Opposition from Saturn in 2nd house	—	C–
SATURN 24° SAG RX	—	Overcome by sup. square from Mars	—	—	C
MERCURY 2° LEO	Sup. sextile from Venus; sup. sextile from Jupiter	—	—	—	A–
MOON 25° ARIES	Inf. sextile from Venus; inf. sextile from Jupiter	—	In 6th house	—	B
VENUS 21° GEM	Co-presence with Jupiter	Inf. square from Mars; Opposition from Saturn	*Sunaphē* by opposition from Saturn in 2nd house; enclosed by malefics	—	D–
MARS 14° VIRGO	Sup. squares from Venus and Jupiter	Inf. square from Saturn	—	Enclosed by rays from benefics	B–

ASSESSMENT

THE SUN and MERCURY in Leo receive positive testimony from the two benefics, Venus and Jupiter in Gemini. VENUS and JUPITER are in a superior sextile overcoming the Sun and Mercury with their beneficent significations. However, this is not a case of complete bonification because Venus and Jupiter are in the unfortunate eighth house, which limits their effectiveness. While the sextile in and of itself is not a powerful aspect, the superior sextile is stronger than the inferior sextile. Furthermore, Gemini and Leo, equidistant from the solstice axis, are signs that see and perceive each other and contribute towards sympathy, friendship, and goodwill. Mars is in aversion to the Sun and Mercury, and does not impact it; Saturn holds the inferior trine and does not harm them. There is no maltreatment of any kind. I give both the Sun and Mercury an A–.

JUPITER is assisted by its co-presence with Venus, the other benefic. However, Jupiter is distressed by the inferior square from Mars. In addition, Jupiter is maltreated by Saturn, which opposes it from an unfortunate house (the second). I am giving Jupiter a C–.

SATURN is overcome by a tenth-sign square (*epidekatesis*) from Mars. While this is problematic, and potentially severe, it is not considered maltreatment because Mars is located in a fortunate house (the eleventh). The oppositions from the benefics, Venus and Jupiter, are not at all helpful, mainly because they are located in the eighth house, which limits their good. I give Saturn a C.

THE MOON in Aries receives inferior sextiles from Venus and Jupiter in Gemini. The benefics are limited by their eighth-house location, and the inferior sextile is quite weak. But the malefics do not harm the Moon in any way. Therefore I give the Moon a B.

VENUS has the greatest difficulties of any of the planets in this chart. Although she is assisted by her co-presence with Jupiter, she is not bonified; rather, she is thrice maltreated. First, she applies to Saturn within 3° (connection/*sunaphē*); second, Saturn is casting its opposition ray from an unfortunate house; third, she is enclosed by the rays of both malefics, Saturn and Mars. I give Venus a D–.

MARS receives some help by being overcome by a superior square from both benefics, Venus and Jupiter. However, they are limited in their good because of their eighth-house location. Nevertheless, the two benefics enclose Mars with their rays and provide assistance and protection as they can. Mars also receives an inferior square from Saturn, which is not as strong as the superior square. Saturn's rays are not close enough to Mars to strike it. Therefore I give Mars a B–.

THE SUN and MERCURY are in the best shape via their aspect relationships. VENUS is in the worst condition, while JUPITER is struggling.

CHART TWO: PICASSO

SUMMARY OF MALTREATMENT CONDITIONS

ASPECT/ CONDITION	SUN 2° SCORP	JUPITER 23° TAUR	SATURN 9° TAUR	MERCURY 24° SCORP	MOON 8° SAG	VENUS 4° LIB	MARS 12° CAN
Struck by a ray from a malefic	—	—	—	—	—	—	—
Enclosed or contained by malefics	—	—	—	—	—	—	—
Connection (sunaphē) with a malefic	—	—	—	—	—	—	—
Adherence to a malefic	—	—	—	—	—	—	—
Overcome by a malefic in a bad house	—	—	—	—	—	Square from Mars in the 12th	—
Opposed by a malefic in a bad house	—	—	—	—	—	—	—
Domicile lord is a malefic in a bad house	Lord (Mars) in the 12th	—	—	Lord (Mars) in the 12th	—	—	—
Located in sixth or twelfth house	—	—	—	—	—	—	12th house

SUMMARY OF BONIFICATION CONDITIONS

ASPECT/ CONDITION	SUN 2° SCORP	JUPITER 23° TAUR	SATURN 9° TAUR	MERCURY 24° SCORP	MOON 8° SAG	VENUS 4° LIB	MARS 12° CAN
Struck by a ray from a benefic	—	—	—	—	—	—	—
Enclosed or contained by benefics	—	—	—	—	—	—	—
Connection (sunaphē) with a benefic	—	—	—	—	—	—	—
Adherence to a benefic	—	—	—	—	—	—	—
Overcome by a benefic in a good house	—	—	—	—	—	—	—
Opposed by a benefic in a good house	—	—	—	—	—	—	—
Domicile Lord a benefic in a good house	—	—	—	—	Lord (Jupiter) in 10th	—	—

The Moon is potentially bonified in this chart.

SUMMARY OF ASPECT RELATIONSHIPS

Planet and sign	Positive testimony	Negative testimony	Maltreatment	Bonification	Grade
SUN 2° SCORP	—	Saturn opposition	Domicile lord in 12th house	—	C
JUPITER 23° TAUR RX	—	Saturn co-present	—	—	C+
SATURN 9° TAUR RX	Jupiter co-present	—	—	—	B+
MERCURY 24° SCORP		Saturn opposition	Domicile lord in 12th house	—	D+
MOON 8° SAG	Sup. sextile from Venus			Domicile lord (Jupiter) in 10th (note: in aversion)	B+
VENUS 4° LIBRA		Sup. square from Mars	Overcome by sup. square from Mars in 12th		C−
MARS 12° CANCER	Sup. sextile from Jupiter		In 12th	Overcome by sup. sextile from Jupiter in 10th	B

ASSESSMENT

THE SUN receives negative testimony from the opposition by Saturn. It has a more severe problem of maltreatment due to having the malefic Mars as its domicile lord, which is immersed in all of the problematic significations of the unfortunate twelfth house. Therefore I give the Sun a D+.

JUPITER receives negative testimony due to Saturn's co-presence in the same sign. It is neither maltreated nor bonified. I give Jupiter a c+.

SATURN is somewhat improved due to its affirming, positive testimony from Jupiter's co-presence. It does not receive any negative testimony or maltreatment from Mars. B+.

MERCURY, like the SUN, receives negative adversarial testimony from Saturn's opposition, and it is maltreated by its domicile lord Mars, which resides in an unfortunate house. D+.

THE MOON receives mildly positive testimony by sextile from her sect mate, Venus. The Moon in Sagittarius also occupies the domicile of benefic Jupiter, which is well-placed in the powerful tenth house. In this case, the support can be considered beneficial even though Jupiter is in aversion to the Moon. The Moon does not receive any negative testimony and is not maltreated. B+.

VENUS does not receive any positive testimony, and she is maltreated by the superior square from Mars in the badly-placed twelfth house. c-.

MARS does not receive any negative testimony; he has some maltreatment due to his placement in the unfortunate twelfth house, but receives mild bonification by being overcome by a superior sextile from Jupiter, which is well-placed in the tenth house. Because these influences seem to balance each other out, I give Mars a B.

→ EXERCISE 37

Using your own chart, and referring to the previous exercises you have done up until now, complete exercise 37: Final Judgment of Planetary Condition based upon Testimony and Aspect Relationships

EXERCISE 37

FINAL JUDGMENT OF PLANETARY CONDITION
BASED UPON TESTIMONY AND ASPECT RELATIONSHIPS

Using your own chart, enter your results from the previous exercises into the following tables (summary of maltreatment conditions; summary of bonification conditions). Once you have done this, integrate and evaluate the results in order to make a final judgment about the condition of each planet (summary of aspect relationships).

1. *Drawing from the previous exercises, summarize the different kinds of positive and negative testimony that each planet receives from the benefics and malefics respectively.* For reasons of space, you may wish to use the glyphs for the planets, signs, and aspects.
2. *If the planet is maltreated, specify how it is maltreated and/or by which planet.*
3. *If the planet is bonified, specify how it is bonified and/or by which planet.*
4. *Give each planet an evaluation.* Ask yourself if it is improved, worsened, mixed, or not influenced.
5. *Finally, write an analysis for each planet based upon the testimony it receives.* Consider the influence of the benefics and malefics, whether or not it is maltreated or bonified, and whether it holds the superior position in any of its aspect relations.

MAKING YOUR JUDGMENT

A planet's condition is *improved* in its capacity to bring forth beneficial outcomes due to affirmative whole sign testimony from the benefics, and even more so due to special conditions of bonification. A planet's condition is *impaired* in bringing forth beneficial outcomes due to negating whole sign testimony from the malefics, and even more so due to the special conditions of maltreatment.

BENEFICS, when *enhanced*, do greater good; their benefic nature is improved. When *impaired*, they are either limited in the amount of good they can do, or the good is undone.

MALEFICS, when *enhanced*, are supported in bringing forth better outcomes. When *impaired*, they are damaged in their capacity to do good, and their malefic nature is worsened; if this is the case, they can be predisposed to do bad for the individual (and hence to others).

A planet that receives *both affirming and negating testimony*, or which is *both maltreated and bonified*, has *mixed* conditions and brings forth improved outcomes in some cases and more difficult ones in other cases. A planet that receives *neither good nor bad testimony*, or is *neither maltreated nor bonified*, is not influenced in its overall condition by aspect configurations with other planets.

SUMMARY OF MALTREATMENT CONDITIONS

ASPECT/ CONDITION	SUN	JUPITER	SATURN	MERCURY	MOON	VENUS	MARS
Struck by a ray from a malefic							
Enclosed or contained by malefics							
Connection (sunaphē) with a malefic							
Adherence to a malefic							
Overcome by a malefic in a bad house							
Opposed by a malefic in a bad house							
Domicile lord is a malefic in a bad house							
Located in sixth or twelfth house							

SUMMARY OF BONIFICATION CONDITIONS

ASPECT/ CONDITION	SUN	JUPITER	SATURN	MERCURY	MOON	VENUS	MARS
Struck by a ray from a benefic							
Enclosed or contained by benefics							
Connection (sunaphē) with a benefic							
Adherence to a benefic							
Overcome by a benefic in a good house							
Opposed by a benefic in a good house							
Domicile lord a benefic in a good house							

SUMMARY OF ASPECT RELATIONSHIPS

Planet and Sign	Positive Testimony	Negative Testimony	Maltreatment	Bonification	Grade
SUN					
JUPITER					
SATURN					
MERCURY					
MOON					
VENUS					
MARS					

REFLECTION AND ANALYSIS

1. Are any of your planets in a condition of maltreatment? If so, which ones and in what particular ways?

2. Have you had any extremely difficult experiences that are signified by this planet's symbolism in regards to the topics of the house(s) it occupies and rules, as well as its aspect configurations with other planets? (We will more fully develop this analysis in the forthcoming volume, which deals with houses).

3. Have you felt injured, mistreated, victimized, negated, deprived? Or have you experienced sorrow, loss, suffering, violence, injustice, uncontrollable anger, hatred, or jealousy around these topics?

4. Do you see repetitive actions symbolized by the maltreated planet that are often unconsciously motivated, and which continue to result in unhappy situations?

5. What kinds of spiritual or psychological practices can you employ to help purify the toxicity of long-held pain? How can you modify your unconscious reactions and responses so that the source trauma does not continue to reduplicate itself in varied expressions?

6. Are any of your planets in a condition of bonification? If so, have you encountered a steady flow of positive assistance, blessings, events, and results in the area of your life that are under the auspices of this planet?

7. Which planet (or planets) are in the best condition?

8. Which planet (or planets) have the greatest challenges?

9. Which sect is in better shape overall—the diurnal sect planets or the nocturnal sect planets?

CHAPTER 52

Doruphoria

SPEAR-BEARING BODYGUARDS

———

THE ANCIENT ASTROLOGERS PLACED CONSIDERABLE IMPORTANCE ON whether a chart had the signature of an eminent person—someone of importance who would bear power. One way that they investigated this matter was to see if the chart had *doruphoria*, or "spear-bearing bodyguards". Harkening back to the royal courts of Persia where the king was accompanied and preceded by spear-bearing guards, certain planetary configurations were seen to signify someone of sufficient importance as to warrant bodyguards.

Doruphoria thus offered protection, but they also functioned as a visual symbol of power and authority. They could signify the heralds that precede a person, announcing their arrival, or the entourage that accompanies and follows important figures, like the attendants who follow a queen (holding up her train of flowing robes).

In the ancient texts, the discussions dealing with bodyguards either followed the sections on maltreatment (Porphyry), or preceded them (Antiochus), so it is relevant to place our own discussion of the technique here. Indeed, we can speculate that bodyguards were seen as a means of protection from maltreatment, or at least provided mitigation. However, in the context of the chart examples given in the Hellenistic texts, the conditions for spear-bearing bodyguards mainly seem linked to the signatures of eminence.

The general principles behind the doctrine of spear-bearing bodyguards may be summarized as follows:

1. Planets that are strong enough to merit bodyguards must be *angular*, and in most cases, in the *first or tenth houses.*

2. THE SUN AND MOON (the planets that signify royalty; the archetypal king and queen) are the best candidates to merit having bodyguards, *when they are in the first or tenth houses.*

3. Planets in their own *domicile* or *exaltation*, when in any of the *angular houses*, may also be eligible to be guarded.

4. The bodyguards themselves ideally belong to the *sect of the chart* (JUPI-
    TER AND SATURN in a day chart; MARS AND VENUS in a night chart;
    in some cases, the Sun and Moon may also function as bodyguards).
    The diurnal bodyguards rise or cast rays *before* the Sun; the nocturnal
    bodyguards follow or cast rays *behind* the Moon.

UNRAVELING THE SOURCE TEXTS

Three kinds of spear-bearing bodyguards were identified. The conditions for
determining them are a complex synthesis of many of the concepts we have
been developing concerning sect, sign rulerships, the solar phase cycle, and aspect theory, as well as house locations. Similar to some of the maltreatment
conditions, there is disagreement and inconsistency in the definitions from one
author to the next. As the tradition went on, later astrologers provided their own
attempt to clarify the material, which seems to have been ambiguous to them. In
the presentation that follows, I will attempt to do the same.

The earliest discussion on spear-bearing bodyguards appears to come from
the first-century astrologer, Serapio. He is mostly drawing upon earlier Babylonian traditions, and on the work of Nechepso and Petosiris:

> The stars are called morning spearbearers when they appear rising
> before the Sun, but evening spearbearers when they rise before the
> Sun, but rise after the Moon.[1]

Based on the definitions in the Antiochus and Porphyry texts, THE FIRST
KIND of spear-bearing bodyguard occurs when the protecting planet is in its
own domicile or exaltation and "closely observes" the protected planet by casting a ray upon the degrees preceding that planet. Furthermore, the protected
planet should be angular and in its own domicile or exaltation. The example that
we are given has the Sun in Leo in an angular house, while Saturn is in Aquarius,
protecting the Sun with its opposition ray. It would also be possible for Jupiter
in Sagittarius or Mars in Aries to protect the Sun by casting trine rays, or Venus
in Libra by casting sextile rays (Mercury in Gemini, however, would be astro-
nomically impossible).

Here we see the respect given to a planet in its own domicile and in the au-
thoritative position of an angular house. Note, too, that the bodyguard must also

---

1   SERAPIO, in *CCAG* 8.4, p. 227.

be powerful—in its own domicile or exaltation sign. It must cast its protective rays like spears *into* the sign of the protected planet, but in the space *ahead* of it.

It is unclear whether the expression "closely observes" refers to the 3° orb or not. In any event, the exact range ahead of the protected planet is not specified. The degrees preceding the Sun refer to the primary, clockwise motion of the planets: i.e., the degrees that have risen *before* the Sun. So if the Sun is at 10° Leo, the 3° interval that *precedes* the Sun would be from 9–7° Leo.

According to the given example, a bodyguard can be a member of the opposite sect. However, according to Porphyry, a great nativity is portended if the bodyguards are the rulers of the sect. With the Sun in the tenth (i.e., a diurnal chart), Saturn and Jupiter as bodyguards would bring even greater eminence.

THE SECOND KIND of spear-bearing bodyguard involves the Sun or the Moon. The luminary must be in the first house (*hōroskopos*) or tenth house (Midheaven), but can be in any zodiacal sign. A planet belonging to the sect of the chart can potentially act as a bodyguard if it hurls a backward ray that falls within a certain amount of degrees *before* the Sun or *after* the Moon. In a diurnal chart, Jupiter and Saturn can act as bodyguards for the Sun; in a nocturnal chart, Venus and Mars for the Moon. It would therefore seem that the bodyguard should ideally be of the same sect as the protected planet, but the texts are not clear whether this is absolutely the case.

For example, if the Moon is at 15° Libra in the first house, and Venus at 25° Aquarius hurls a backward trine ray that lands at 25° Libra, that ray falls into the zodiacal section that *follows* the Moon. We might wonder what might happen if the bodyguard is a malefic. If it hurls a ray towards the luminary within a 3° interval, the luminary would technically be maltreated by connection (*sunaphē*), but if the interval were larger, this would not be the case. It is also possible that a malefic of the same sect as the luminary might be in a better position to act as a protector.

It is unclear whether intervention applies to bodyguards. That is, if another planet interposes itself bodily or by ray between the protected planet and the ray of the bodyguard, would this intervention prevent the efficacy of the bodyguard?

THE THIRD KIND of spear-bearing bodyguard allows any planet to be guarded, provided it is located in the first or tenth houses. Bodyguards must be of the sect, although they can guard a planet of the contrary sect. The diurnal sect bodyguards must rise *before* the planet being guarded, and in physical proximity. The nocturnal sect bodyguards must follow *behind* the planet being guarded. If the Moon is being guarded, her spear-bearing attendant must follow her within 7° of proximity.

Paulus suggests that the diurnal bodyguards should be in the degrees and signs that precede the Sun up to the aspect of the trine (presumably so that they are not weakening due to the imminent retrograde). He also states that body-guards are stronger when they are in the same sign as the Sun.[2]

The texts could be interpreted to suggest that the bodyguards should be more than 15° ahead of the Sun to avoid being weakened under the beams. However, one of the skills of a secret service attendant (to use a more modern example) is to remain close by, but appear inconspicuous. So the 15° interval can be argued either way. The matter is further complicated by the statement in Porphyry and Antiochus that bodyguards standing within 15° of the preceding portions do not harm the Sun when they are morning risers in the east and have power.

Paulus also tells us that the bodyguards following the Moon should simply be in the same sign as the Moon. However, for planets other than the Moon, the texts do not specify the interval that the bodyguard must occupy in order to offer protection. The description of this third kind of bodyguard concludes with the statements that the Sun and Moon can act as bodyguards to an angular sect mate. Thus, if Jupiter or Saturn are in the first or tenth house, the Sun can guard them from the front. So too for Venus or Mars: the Moon can guard them from the rear.

Finally, the third kind of bodyguard can be contrary to sect. Diurnal planets can attend nocturnal ones, and nocturnal planets diurnal ones. Hence, if Mars is angular and in the first house in a day chart, Jupiter and Saturn can guard him from the front; if Jupiter is angular in a night chart, Mars can guard him from the rear. "Whenever bodyguarding occurs by benefics", remarks Porphyry in his final comment on the topic, "the nativity will not be without significance".[3]

THREE TYPES OF BODYGUARDS

Despite these ambiguities, we will nevertheless attempt to provide some general guidelines for the three types of bodyguards. These will be based upon what we have learned about sect, sign rulerships, the solar phase cycle, and aspect theo-ry, as well as the significance of house locations. (Houses will be explored more fully in volume two).

TYPE 1: For a planet to warrant having a bodyguard, it must be located in an angular house and in its own domicile or exaltation. The bodyguard must be another planet, of either sect, which is in its own domicile or exaltation, casting

2   PAULUS, *Introduction* 14.
3   PORPHYRY, *Introduction* 29.

a ray from either the right or the left side (trine, opposition, square, sextile) upon the degrees that are in the same sign and earlier in sequence than the planet being guarded (FIGURE 81).

TYPE II: The Sun or Moon must be in the first or tenth house. This makes a luminary worthy of being guarded. It can be in any zodiacal sign. The planets that belong to the sect of the chart are the bodyguards, and they must hurl a backward ray according to one of the aspect figures into the degrees ahead of the Sun or the degrees behind the Moon. The triangular (trine) bodyguards are the best (FIGURES 82–83).

TYPE III: A planet worthy of being guarded must be in the first or tenth house, in any zodiacal sign. If the chart is diurnal, the Sun, Jupiter, or Saturn (or morning star Mercury) can be bodyguards if they are located in the portion of the chart that rises before the planet being guarded. If the chart is nocturnal, the Moon, Venus, Mars (or evening star Mercury) must be in the portion of the chart that follows behind the planet. If the Moon is being guarded, her bodyguards must be very close: within 7°. If the Sun is being guarded, the planets must be no more than 120° ahead of the Sun (FIGURES 84–85).

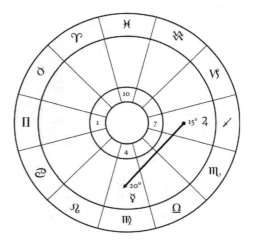

FIGURE 81.

SPEAR-BEARER, TYPE I

The protected planet (Mercury) is in its domicile (Virgo) & angular (fourth house); the bodyguard (Jupiter) is in its domicile (Sagittarius), angular (seventh house), & casts an aspect ray into the earlier degrees of the protected planet's sign (15° Virgo, earlier according to diurnal motion).

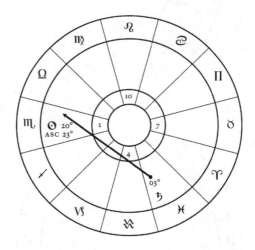

FIGURE 82.

SPEAR-BEARER, TYPE II (DIURNAL)

The Sun is angular (first house), & the chart is diurnal, qualifying Jupiter & Saturn as guards; Saturn hurls a ray to the degrees preceding the Sun.

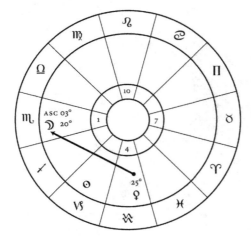

FIGURE 83.

SPEAR-BEARER, TYPE II (NOCTURNAL)

The Moon is angular, in the first house, and the chart is nocturnal, qualifying Venus and Mars as guards. Venus hurls a ray to the degrees behind the Moon (by diurnal motion), thus protecting her from the rear.

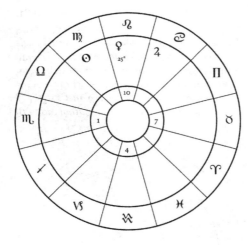

FIGURE 84.

SPEAR-BEARER, TYPE III (DIURNAL)

The protected planet (Venus) is in the tenth house in a day chart; therefore only Jupiter, Saturn, or a morning-rising Mercury, qualify to protect her—if they are located in the degrees ahead of Venus by diurnal motion. Jupiter, located in the degrees preceding Venus, thereby acts as a bodyguard, protecting Venus from the front.

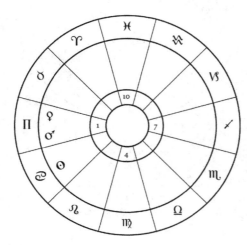

FIGURE 85.

SPEAR-BEARER, TYPE III (NOCTURNAL)

The protected planet (Venus) is in the first house in a night chart; only Mars, or an evening-rising Mercury, qualify to protect it—if they are located in the degrees behind Venus by diurnal motion. Thus, Mars acts as a bodyguard, protecting Venus from the rear.

→ EXAMPLE CHARTS

Let us examine our example charts for the presence of bodyguards, taking our analysis as far as we can based upon what we are certain of.

CHART I

THE SUN is at 5° Leo, in its own domicile, and in the tenth house. It potentially qualifies for all three bodyguard types. TYPE I is eliminated because no other planet is in its domicile or exaltation. TYPE II is eliminated because in this diurnal chart, only SATURN qualifies as a sect mate who can hurl a backward ray towards the Sun. However, in spite of the ray being the favored trine, the ray falls at 24° Leo, which is in the degrees *behind* the Sun, not ahead of the Sun. TYPE III might qualify if we were more certain of the requirements. The Sun is in the tenth house. Its diurnal sect mate, morning MERCURY, is at 2° Leo, and stands in the degrees ahead of the Sun; but because Mercury is so close to the Sun, and therefore combust under his beams, he is possibly disqualified. The Sun's diurnal sect mate, JUPITER, is at 9° Gemini, but the intervention by VENUS at 21° Gemini possibly disqualifies Jupiter. This chart *possibly* has a benefic as a bodyguard, and therefore could portend a notable nativity.

CHART II

TYPE I: THE SUN at 2° Scorpio, while in the fourth house, might qualify to have a type I bodyguard if it were in its own domicile or exaltation, but it is not. TYPE II: Neither the Sun nor the Moon is in the first or tenth houses. TYPE III: JUPITER and SATURN are located in the tenth house. They may qualify for type III bodyguards. But because this is a nocturnal chart, the bodyguards must be either MARS or VENUS, and they must stand *behind* the planets being guarded—which they do. But there is uncertainty about the interval ranges of the guards: are they restricted to 7° behind Jupiter and Saturn, to the same sign, or to the much larger interval? If we consider the possibility of Mars or Venus as bodyguards, there are several interventions by the rays of other planets into the degrees between them and Jupiter. In any event, the slim possibility of protection may be evident.

→ EXERCISE 38

Using your own chart, complete exercise 38:
Spear-bearing Bodyguards

EXERCISE 38

SPEAR-BEARING BODYGUARDS

Check to see if your chart bears any signature of eminence or special protection due to the presence of bodyguards. As the criteria are not absolute in every detail, the best you can do is to ascertain how far you can go with what is given in the texts.

1.   *First, look to see if you have any planets in angular houses. If you do not, stop. You do not have any planets that merit having spear-bearing bodyguards.*

2.   TYPE I *spear-bearing requires that the angular planet be in its domicile or exaltation. If this is so, proceed to examine if there is another planet in its own domicile or exaltation. If so, does that planet cast a ray into the degrees preceding the angular planet that is being so guarded? If so, the dignified angular planet has a bodyguard and signifies that you have a signature of eminence in your chart.*

3.   TYPE II *requires the Sun or Moon to be in the first or tenth houses (any sign). If this is so, proceed to examine if there is a planet that belongs to the sect of the chart that is hurling rays back to the luminary, which fall ahead of the Sun or behind the Moon. If so, the luminary has a bodyguard, and signifies that you have a signature of eminence in your chart.*

4.   TYPE III *requires that any planet, of any sect or zodiacal sign, is in the first or tenth house. Only a planet that is of the sect of the chart can act as a bodyguard. In a diurnal chart, the diurnal-sect bodyguards must rise before the planet being guarded. How far ahead is unclear, and the possibility of intervention from another planet must be considered. If the Sun is being guarded, the diurnal bodyguard may need to be 15–120° ahead of the Sun. In a nocturnal chart, only the nocturnal sect planets can act as body guards. They must rise after the planet being guarded, in the degrees behind the planet. Again, how far behind, or the effect of intervention, is unspecified. However, if the Moon is being guarded, the protecting planet must be behind the Moon, within 7°.*

Use the following tables to ascertain whether any of your planets might have a spear-bearing bodyguard, and thus a signature of eminence.

TYPE I

	Angular house	Domicile or exaltation	Rays cast in front of planet by another planet in its own domicile or exaltation
SUN			
JUPITER			
SATURN			
MERCURY			
MOON			
VENUS			
MARS			

TYPE II

	First or tenth house	Planet of sect casts rays to luminary	Rays fall ahead (Sun) or behind (Moon)
SUN			
MOON			

TYPE III

	First or tenth house	Diurnal chart: planet of sect bodily ahead of protected planet. If the Sun is being guarded, diurnal planet is 15–120° degrees ahead of the Sun	Nocturnal Chart: planet of sect behind protected planet. If the Moon is being guarded, nocturnal planet is behind the Moon within 7°
SUN			
JUPITER			
SATURN			
MERCURY			
MOON			
VENUS			
MARS			

REFLECTION AND ANALYSIS

1. Which planet, if any, has a bodyguard? (If so, which type? Explain
    your determination).
2. Do the significations of the protected planet stand out in your life in
    any meaningful way?
3. Do the significations of the bodyguard stand out in your life in any
    meaningful way?
4. Are there legitimate signs of eminence or protection in your life that
    match the significations of the protected planet and/or the bodyguard?

CHAPTER 53

Sign-based Sympathies

AND PLANETARY CONNECTIONS

———

THE THIRD GENERAL CATEGORY OF PLANETARY COMBINATIONS IS BASED upon zodiacal signs alone. Here, planets interact with one another in ways that are not based upon testimony from planetary aspects. Zodiacal signs that share the same *ascensional time*, the same *domicile lord*, that *see and perceive one another*, and that *command and obey one another* share sympathetic relations. This is especially significant for planets that occupy the sets of zodiacal signs that are in aversion, giving them a connection they would not otherwise have.

The aversion, a non-aspect in Hellenistic astrology, is called the quincunx, inconjunct, or disconjunt aspect (30° and 150°) in modern astrology. From a Hellenistic perspective, planets in aversion cannot "see" each other and thus have a blind spot or disconnect regarding each other's significations. Paulus writes that planets in aversion are "disharmonious":

> Sometimes they bring upon enmities and factionalisms, other times
> separations and exiles when such a stance is adopted by all, whether
> by parents towards children, by brothers, by man and wife, by an as-
> sociation, by slaves and masters, and by all such like.[1]

In some cases, the sympathies between certain zodiacal signs which we will describe below can offset, or mitigate, the difficulty that planets have when they are in aversion to one another. The planets can still share sympathetic relations, sometimes referred to as a "mitigating sympathy", and interpreted as a "reluctant conjunction". In other cases, presence in certain sets of zodiacal signs can intensify the existing aspects between planets located in those signs.

---

1   PAULUS, *Introduction* 11.

SIGNS SHARING THE SAME ASCENSIONAL TIMES

Certain sets of zodiacal signs have the same ascensional times and thus share a sympathy, which extends to planets occupying those signs. The ascensional time of a sign refers to the amount of time that the sign takes to completely rise over the horizon (based upon the number of degrees that pass over the Midheaven as that zodiacal sign rises).

The signs of long and short ascension are demarcated by the *solstitial axis* of Cancer and Capricorn (see chapter 9). However, when this zodiacal arrangement is viewed from the *equinoctial axis* of Aries and Libra, we have parallel sets of signs with the same ascensional times. Thus, the signs Aries and Pisces, Taurus and Aquarius, Gemini and Capricorn, Cancer and Sagittarius, Leo and Scorpio, and Virgo and Libra, each take the same amount of time to rise over the horizon at given latitudes in the Northern Hemisphere. Aries and Pisces have the shortest ascensional times, while Virgo and Libra have the longest. The reverse is true for the Southern Hemisphere.

Ascensional time also forms the basis of an important timing method in Hellenistic astrology. The number of degrees, which varies by latitude, is converted into a corresponding number of years in order to determine when the events associated with that sign mature and become fully manifest. Planets that share the same ascensional times are also activated at similar times. Thus their events occur simultaneously and are intertwined with one another.

Table 24. Pairs of Signs with the Same Ascensional Rising

ARIES AND PISCES	Aversion
TAURUS AND AQUARIUS	Square
GEMINI AND CAPRICORN	Aversion
CANCER AND SAGITTARIUS	Aversion
LEO AND SCORPIO	Square
VIRGO AND LIBRA	Aversion

Four of these six sets of zodiacal signs are in aversion according to the aspect configuration model, but they nevertheless have a connection because of similar ascensions. For example, while a planet in Aries and a planet in Pisces are considered to be in aversion, they still have a sympathetic relationship because their natural aversion is mitigated by sharing the same ascensional time, and they are said to have a reluctant conjunction (FIGURE 86).

If planets already form valid aspects, and they are also in signs of the same ascension, it creates a more intense bond between them. For example, planets occupying the signs of Taurus/Aquarius and Leo/Scorpio have the same ascensional times; consequently, the square aspect between them is intensified.

→ EXAMPLE CHARTS

If we were doing timing procedures, we could explore the simultaneous occurrence of planetary events in zodiacal signs that have the same ascensional times. However, our purpose in this chapter is to isolate any planets in aversion in order to see if the ill effects arising from lack of connection are mitigated by their presence in signs that share the same ascensional times.

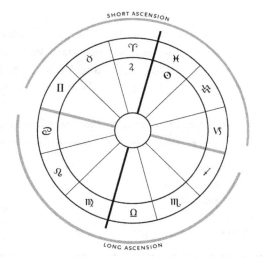

FIGURE 86.
SHARED ASCENSIONAL RISING

Jupiter and the Sun are in aversion (do not see each other by aspect ray), but because they share the signs of same ascensional rising, their aversion is mitigated and they form a "reluctant conjunction".

CHART I: The Moon in Aries is in aversion to Mars in Virgo. However, Aries and Virgo do not have the same ascensional times, so there is no reluctant conjunction between the Moon and Mars. CHART II: Mars in Cancer is in aversion to the Moon in Sagittarius. Cancer and Sagittarius share the same ascensional times. Thus there is a reluctant conjunction between Mars and the Moon.

SIGNS SHARING THE SAME
DOMICILE LORD

There is sympathy between zodiacal signs that share the same domicile lord. This sympathy extends to planets occupying those signs. Planets that occupy these paired signs are *guests of the same host*, who provides their resources and support, even though they might reside in different domiciles. They are connected insofar as they are *recipients of a similar bounty* (or lack thereof) *dispensed by the same host* in order to accomplish their goals. Note that the lord may witness one of its houses but not the other, which accounts for differences in outcomes.

The signs Aries and Scorpio share Mars as their lord; Taurus and Libra share Venus as their lord; Gemini and Virgo share Mercury as their lord; Sagittarius and Pisces share Jupiter; and Capricorn and Aquarius share Saturn.

Table 25. Pairs of Signs with the Same Domicile Lord

ARIES AND SCORPIO	Mars	Aversion
TAURUS AND LIBRA	Venus	Aversion
GEMINI AND VIRGO	Mercury	Square
SAGITTARIUS AND PISCES	Jupiter	Square
CAPRICORN AND AQUARIUS	Saturn	Aversion

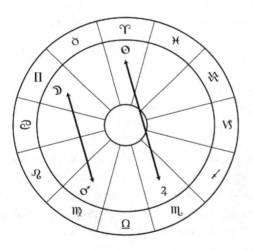

FIGURE 87.

SHARED DOMICILE LORD

Planets in aversion can establish a sympathy if they are in signs that share the same domicile lord. Here, the Sun and Jupiter are both in signs ruled by Mars, which thus mitigates their aversion. Planets forming a square aspect in signs sharing the same domicile lord have their relationship intensified. Here, the Moon and Mars are in Mercury's domiciles, and their aspect is thus intensified.

The sets of signs that are in aversion to one another by configuration, but share the same domicile lord are Aries/Scorpio, Taurus/Libra, and Capricorn/Aquarius. Leo and Cancer, the signs of the two luminaries, the Sun and the Moon, also enjoy this sympathy. Thus, in a particular chart, planets in Aries and Scorpio, considered to be in aversion, still have a sympathetic relationship because the natural aversion is offset by having the same domicile lord, i.e., Mars.

If planets are already in valid configurations, and they also have the same domicile lord, this shared sympathy creates an even more intense bond between the two planets. Planets occupying the zodiacal signs Gemini/Virgo and Sagittarius/Pisces have the same domicile and thus the square aspect between them is intensified (FIGURE 87).

→ EXAMPLE CHARTS

Let us investigate the example charts to see if any aversions are mitigated, or if any pre-existing configurations are intensified due to shared domicile lords.

CHART I: The Moon in Aries and Mars in Virgo are in aversion, and they do not share the same domicile lord. Mars is also in aversion to the Sun and Mercury in Leo, and again they do not share a domicile lord. Thus there is no reluctant conjunction. The squares between Venus and Jupiter with Mars are intensified because Gemini and Virgo share the same domicile lord, Mercury. CHART II: Venus in Libra is in aversion to Jupiter and Saturn in Taurus, but because both signs share Venus as a domicile lord, they have a reluctant conjunction. They receive much more support from a powerful Venus in Libra than they otherwise would with an aversion from one's lord. The only square aspect is between Mars in Cancer and Venus in Libra. However, they do not share a common domicile lord, so there is no aspect intensification.

We have seen that particular squares, due to their sympathy based upon similar ascensional times (Taurus/Aquarius, Leo/Scorpio) or shared domicile lords (Gemini/Virgo, Sagittarius/Pisces), stand out as being more potent. And this applies in both whole sign testimony and degree-based aspect relations. There are similar situations that intensify the sextile and trine relationships. The Hellenistic authors discuss these in terms of signs that "see and perceive" one another, and signs that "hear" or "command and obey" one another.

PLANETS IN SIGNS THAT
SEE AND PERCEIVE ONE OTHER

The zodiacal signs that see and perceive one another are equidistant from the Cancer/Capricorn or *solstitial* axis. Each pair provides equal amounts of day and night, and rises and sets from the same part of the horizon. Gemini looks at Leo, and Leo perceives Gemini; Taurus looks at Virgo, and Virgo perceives Taurus; Aries looks at Libra, and Libra perceives Aries; Scorpio looks at Pisces, and Pisces perceives Scorpio; Sagittarius looks at Aquarius, and Aquarius perceives Sagittarius.

It is important to note that when we speak of "seeing", it is not the same kind of seeing used in testimony and aspect relations. The Greek texts use different terminology to differentiate these kinds of visual relationships.

Paulus tells us that these signs contribute toward sympathy, friendship, and good will among similar members of people in every association.[2] These categories later became the model used for antiscia. Except for Aries/Libra and Cancer/Capricorn, these sets of signs have natural sextile or trine configurations, and these particular combinations intensify the sextile or trine relationship in both testimonial and aspect relations between planets occupying these signs.

Table 26. Pairs of Signs that See and Perceive One Another

GEMINI *looks at* LEO	LEO *perceives* GEMINI	Sextile
TAURUS *looks at* VIRGO	VIRGO *perceives* TAURUS	Trine
ARIES *looks at* LIBRA	LIBRA *perceives* ARIES	Opposition
SCORPIO *looks at* PISCES	PISCES *perceives* SCORPIO	Trine
SAGITTARIUS *looks at* AQUARIUS	AQUARIUS *perceives* SAGITTARIUS	Sextile

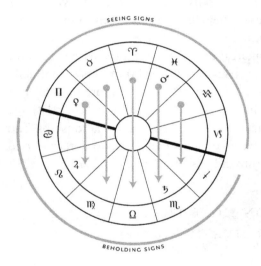

SEEING SIGNS

BEHOLDING SIGNS

FIGURE 88.

SEEING & PERCEIVING

Planets that see and perceive one another intensify their existing aspect relationship. Here, the sextile between Venus in Gemini and Jupiter in Leo is intensified due to the planets being equidistant from the solstitial axis (defined by Cancer and Capricorn). Venus "sees" Jupiter, and Jupiter "perceives" Venus. Similarly, the trine between Mars in Pisces and Saturn in Scorpio is made more potent. Mars "sees" Saturn, and Saturn "perceives" Mars.

→   EXAMPLE CHARTS

Looking at our example charts, let us ascertain if any planets are in signs that see and perceive one another, heightening their aspect relationships.

CHART I: The sextile between Venus/Jupiter in Gemini and Mercury/Sun in Leo is intensified because Gemini sees Leo. CHART II: No planets see each other according to this classification.

2   PAULUS, *Introductory Matters* 8.

SIGNS THAT COMMAND
AND OBEY ONE ANOTHER

The signs that "hear" one another are also called signs that "command and obey". They are the signs that are both equally removed from the equinoctial signs of Aries and Libra, and in opposite hemispheres. The *commanding* signs were considered more powerful than the obeying signs because they were closer to the Earth. Ptolemy tells us that these signs ascend in equal periods of time, and are on equal parallel. The signs in the summer hemisphere, where the Sun makes the day longer than the night, are *commanding*, while those in the winter hemisphere are *obedient*.[3] The reverse is the case in the Southern Hemisphere.

Table 27. Pairs of Signs that Command and Obey One Another

TAURUS *commands* PISCES	PISCES *obeys* TAURUS	Sextile
GEMINI *commands* AQUARIUS	AQUARIUS *obeys* GEMINI	Trine
CANCER *commands* CAPRICORN	CAPRICORN *obeys* CANCER	Opposition
LEO *commands* SAGITTARIUS	SAGITTARIUS *obeys* LEO	Trine
VIRGO *commands* SCORPIO	SCORPIO *obeys* VIRGO	Sextile
ARIES *commands* LIBRA	LIBRA *obeys* ARIES	Opposition

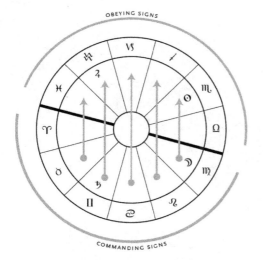

OBEYING SIGNS

COMMANDING SIGNS

FIGURE 89.

COMMANDING & OBEYING

Planets that command and obey one another intensify their existing aspect relationship. Here, the trine between Saturn in Gemini and Jupiter in Aquarius is intensified due to the planets being equidistant from the equatorial axis (defined by Aries and Libra). Saturn "commands" Jupiter, and Jupiter "obeys". Similarly, the sextile between the Moon in Virgo and the Sun in Scorpio is made more potent. The Moon "commands" the Sun, and the Sun "obeys".

3 PTOLEMY, *Tetrabiblos* 1.14.

Technically, Aries and Libra neither command nor obey one another, but some astrologers place Aries with the commanding signs because when the Sun is in Aries, the day hours increase; Libra was placed with the obeying signs because when the Sun is in Libra, the day hours decrease.

Once again, there is an intensification of the relationship in both testimony and aspect relations between planets occupying these signs, whether it is the trines between Gemini/Libra and Leo/Sagittarius; the sextiles between Taurus/Pisces and Virgo/Scorpio; or the Cancer/Capricorn opposition.

→   EXAMPLE CHARTS

Looking at our example charts, let us see if any planets are in signs that command and obey one another, thus heightening their aspect relationships.

CHART I: The Sun in Leo commands Saturn in Sagittarius, which obeys.
CHART II: No planets are in signs that command and obey one another.

SUMMARY OF SIGNS SHARING
SYMPATHETIC RELATIONS

The following table shows the signs that share sympathetic relations. *Italicized* signs are in aversion by aspect configuration, but have mitigating sympathies in accordance with these sign-based combinations.

Table 28. Signs that Share Sympathetic Relations

SAME ASCENSIONAL TIMES	SAME DOMICILE LORDS	SEEING AND PERCEIVING	COMMANDING AND OBEYING
Aries/Pisces	*Aries/Scorpio*	Aries/Libra	Taurus commands Pisces
Taurus/Aquarius	*Taurus/Libra*	Taurus/Virgo	Gemini commands Aquarius
Gemini/Capricorn	Gemini/Virgo	Gemini/Leo	Cancer commands Capricorn
Cancer/Sagittarius	Sagittarius/Pisces	Scorpio/Pisces	Leo commands Sagittarius
Leo/Scorpio	*Capricorn/Aquarius*	Sagittarius/Aquarius	Virgo commands Scorpio
Virgo/Libra	*Cancer/Leo*		Aries commands Libra

NOTE: Although Cancer and Leo do not share the same domicile lord, their signs are home to the two royal luminaries—the Sun and Moon—and host the greatest hours of daylight in the Northern Hemisphere. Therefore, when they occupy each other's signs, they enjoy sympathetic relations with one another.

→   EXAMPLE CHARTS

Let us summarize our findings, and identify the planets that have special or additional connections based upon their zodiacal signs alone.

CHART I: SIGN-BASED SYMPATHIES

	Planets/Signs	Aversions Mitigated	Aspects Intensified
SAME ASCENSIONAL TIMES	—	—	—
SAME DOMICILE LORD	*Venus/Jupiter (Gemini), Mars (Virgo)*	—	Square intensified
SEEING AND PERCEIVING	Venus/Jupiter (Gemini), Sun/ Mercury (Leo)	—	Sextile intensified
COMMANDING AND OBEYING	Sun (Leo) Saturn (Sagit- tarius)	—	Trine intensified

The SQUARE between Venus and Jupiter (both in Gemini) to Mars in Virgo is intensified because Gemini and Virgo share the same *domicile lord*, MERCURY. The SEXTILE between Venus and Jupiter (both in Gemini) and the Sun and Mercury (both in Leo) is intensified because Gemini *sees and beholds* Leo. THE SUN in Leo *commands* Saturn in Sagittarius, which *obeys*.

CHART II: SIGN-BASED SYMPATHIES

	Planets/Signs	Aversions Mitigated	Aspects Intensified
SAME ASCENSIONAL TIMES	Mars (Cancer), Moon (Sagittarius)	Reluctant conjunction	—
SAME DOMICILE LORD	Venus (Libra), Jupiter/Saturn (Taurus)	Reluctant conjunction	—
SEEING AND PERCEIVING	—	—	—
COMMANDING AND OBEYING	—	—	—

MARS in Cancer and THE MOON in Sagittarius share the same *ascensional time*, and thus have a reluctant conjunction. VENUS in Libra, and JUPITER and SATURN (both in Taurus), have a reluctant conjunction because they share the same *domicile lord*, VENUS.

EXERCISE 39

SIGN-BASED PLANETARY SYMPATHIES

Referring to the tables provided throughout this chapter, determine which planets have connections that mitigate their aversions, intensify their aspects, or share other special connections. Enter your results in the provided table.

1. *Planets sharing same ascensional times*
    Which aversions, if any, are mitigated by reluctant conjunctions?
    Which configurations, if any, are intensified?

2. *Planets sharing same domicile lord*
    Which aversions, if any, are mitigated by reluctant conjunctions?
    Which configurations, if any, are intensified?

3. *Planets that see and perceive one another*
    Which configurations, if any, are intensified?

4. *Planets that command and obey*
    Which configurations, if any, are intensified?

Planets/Signs	Aversions Mitigated	Aspects Intensified
SAME ASCENSIONAL TIMES		
SAME DOMICILE LORD		
SEEING AND PERCEIVING		
COMMANDING AND OBEYING		

REFLECTION AND ANALYSIS

1. When interpreting these particular planets in the delineation of your chart, how could you take these additional factors into consideration?
2. In what ways do they provide nuance to your understanding?

CHAPTER 54

Summary

AND SOURCE READINGS

———

MAIN POINTS
OF THE ASPECT DOCTRINE

1. Aspects between planets are operative by both whole sign and specific degree.
2. Planets that occupy zodiacal signs that are configured according to the sextile, square, and trine can see each other and can testify about what they have witnessed.
3. The sextile, square, trine, and opposition are the only valid aspects. Planets occupying the same sign, while not configured, are said to be co-present, and treated like aspects. The semi-sextile and quincunx are not configurations; they are called aversions.
4. The whole sign sextile and trine aspects indicate sympathetic testimony and helpful relations between planets. The whole sign square aspect indicates harsh, negating testimony and obstructive relations between planets. The whole sign opposition aspect indicates adversarial relations between planets. Co-presence by whole sign indicates a co-mingling of the individual planetary natures. There is no relation between planets in aversion, only estrangement (unless mitigated by certain sign-based sympathies).
5. A planet's condition is enhanced to bring forth its best outcomes when it receives positive testimony from the benefics by co-presence, sextile, or trine aspects.
6. A planet's condition is made more problematic when it receives negative testimony from the malefics by co-presence, square, or opposition aspects.

7. Planets engage in closer, friendly, or hostile relations when one planet makes a 3° (or for the Moon, 13°) applying aspect to another planet. This impacts each planet's significations, as well as the topics of the houses they rule.

8. Bonification and maltreatment refer to the specific degree-based, spatial, or directional situations whereby one planet is significantly improved and protected (bonified) or injured and harmed (maltreated) by another planet. When a benefic planet is maltreated, its benefic significations are suppressed or impeded. When a malefic planet is maltreated, it can turn violent. When a malefic planet is bonified, it is pacified. When a benefic planet is bonified, it becomes even more beneficent.

9. The conditions of maltreatment and bonification can be counteracted or neutralized.

10. Planets in aversion, and which have the same domicile lord or same ascensional time, can still enter into relations with one another. This can be interpreted as a reluctant conjunction.

11. A chart that has the presence of spear-bearing bodyguards indicates protection from harm, which is provided to eminent individuals, or to those with power and authority. These complex indications integrate the concepts of sect, zodiacal rulership, solar phase, aspects, and house locations.

CONCLUSION

As you have discovered, planets engage in many different, complex interactions. These planetary patterns mirror the complexity of human relationships with all of the attachments, loyalties, support, obligations, commitments, entanglements, betrayals, jealousies, conflicts, hurtful actions, and destructiveness that we participate in and partake of in the dance of self with other. No person is an island. The testimonial and aspectual relations between the planets demonstrate how difficult it is for a planet—or a person—to function independently of the myriad relationships that exist in the larger matrix of our lives. A close examination and reflection upon the planetary patterns in the birth chart can provide us with illumination and understanding of the challenges and blessings that we encounter when relating to others over the course of life.

The identification of maltreatment conditions, which some find to be overly complicated, tedious, and fatalistic, are nevertheless of extreme importance for anyone who approaches astrology as a healing art. Maltreated planets are the direct line into the parts of the psyche that are extremely wounded. If the issues that they represent remain ignored or unaddressed, the individual continues the self-destructive attitudes and behaviors that often serve as coping mechanisms. But their actions will still perpetuate outcomes characterized by pain, rejection, conflict, and failure. Counseling astrologers who give guidance for psychological insight and healing modalities, medical astrologers who diagnose illness, and evolutionary astrologers who address past life karmic afflictions can all benefit their clients by developing a proficiency in recognizing the serious wounds that these red flags alert us to. This is the beneficial application of the maltreatment conditions.

The fundamental teachings concerning planetary condition are now complete. In the next section, you will integrate all the previous indications—both broad and subtle—concerning sect and sect-rejoicing, zodiacal rulerships, solar phase cycles, special lunar considerations, testimony, and aspect relations. The purpose of this synthesis is to arrive at a *final judgment* of each planet's capacity to be effective and beneficial on behalf of the native.

PRIMARY SOURCE READINGS
FOR PART FIVE: ASPECTS

PETOSIRIS	A Surprising Point from Petosiris Concerning Harmonious Squares (CCAG 6, p. 62; translation in SCHMIDT, *The Astrological Record of the Early Sages*, p. 18).
MANILIUS	*Astronomica* 2.270–432.
VALENS	*Anthology* 1.19: The Co-presences of the Stars.
	Anthology 1.20: The Co-presence of Three Stars; Triangular, Hexagonal, and Diametrical Figures.
PTOLEMY	*Tetrabiblos* 1.13: The Aspects of the Zodiacal Signs.
	Tetrabiblos 1.14: Commanding and Obeying Signs.
	Tetrabiblos 1.15: Signs which Behold Each Other and Signs of Equal Power.
	Tetrabiblos 1.16: Disjunct Signs.
	Tetrabiblos 1.24: Applications and Separations.
ANTIOCHUS	*Summary* 6: Witnessing.
	Summary 7: Right and Left Figures.
	Summary 8: Passing Beyond and Connecting.
	Summary 9: Adherence, Meeting, and Separation.
	Summary 10: Domination.
	Summary 11: Traveling Together and Traveling Alone.
	Summary 12: Enclosure.
	Summary 13: Hurling a Ray.
	Summary 17: Spear-bearing Bodyguards.
	Summary 18: Maltreatment.

PORPHYRY   *Introduction* 8: Witnessing.
                  Introduction 9: Right and Left Figures.
                  Introduction 11: Connecting and Adhering.
                  Introduction 12: Separating.
                  Introduction 13: Separating.
                  Introduction 14: Containment.
                  Introduction 15: Enclosure.
                  Introduction 16: Intervention.
                  Introduction 20: Domination.
                  Introduction 21: Overcoming.
                  Introduction 22: Traveling Together.
                  Introduction 23: Traveling Alone (Void in Course).
                  Introduction 24: Hurling a Ray.
                  Introduction 28: Maltreatment.
                  Introduction 29: Spear-bearing Bodyguards.
FIRMICUS   *Mathesis* 6. 3–28.
PAULUS   *Introduction* 10: The Trine, Sextile, Square, and Opposition Aspects.
                  Introduction 11: Zodiacal Signs in Aversion with Each Other.
                  Introduction 12: Zodiacal Signs in Aversion and Sympathy
                  to Each Other.
                  Introduction 13: Zodiacal Signs in Homozone and Equal-Rising.
HEPHAISTIO   *Apotelesmatics* 1.9: Sections that Command and Obey.
                  Apotelesmatics 1.10: Sections of Equal Power and those Seeing.
                  Apotelesmatics 1.11: Unconnected Sections.
                  Apotelesmatics 1.14: Applications and Separations.
                  Apotelesmatics 1.15: Enclosure.
                  Apotelesmatics 1.16: Hurling of Rays.
                  Apotelesmatics 1.17: Spear-bearing.
RHETORIUS   *Compendium* 15: Trines, Squares, Oppositions, and Disjunctions.
                  Compendium 16: Disjunct Signs and those having Sympathy.
                  Compendium 17: Squares that are Sympathetic and those that are Not.
                  Compendium 19: Hearing and Seeing Signs.
                  Compendium 20: Beholding.
                  Compendium 21: Casting a Ray.
                  Compendium 22: Right and Left Aspects.
                  Compendium 23: Doruphory.
                  Compendium 26: Domination.
                  Compendium 27: Affliction and Ineffective Houses.
                  Compendium 34: Adherence.
                  Compendium 35: Application.
                  Compendium 36: Intervention.
                  Compendium 37: Separation.
                  Compendium 39: Void in Course.
                  Compendium 41: Besieging (Enclosure).

PART SIX
THE ART OF JUDGMENT

CHAPTER 55

The Celestial Condition

OF THE PLANETARY GODS

———

Each star is the lord of its own essence with regard to its sympathies and antipathies and mutual influences in the cosmos. They are blended with one another according to their connections and separations and overcoming, and enclosures and spear-bearing bodyguards and the hurling of rays and the approach of their masters. The Moon is the lord of foresight, the Sun is the lord of light, Saturn is the lord of ignorance and fated necessity, Jupiter is the lord of reputation, wreaths of honor, and goodwill, the star of Mars is the lord of actions and hardships, the star of Venus is the lord of love and desire and beauty, and the star of Mercury is the lord of law and custom and faith.—VALENS.[1]

EACH PLANET HAS AN AGENDA THAT IT BRINGS TO THE LIFE OF AN INDI-vidual. In addition to the worldly significations that each planet has jurisdiction over—such as occupations, personality traits, body parts, illnesses, metals, stones, plants—it also represents a certain *quality of the soul*, which is an emanation of its essential nature. A planet's essence is then filtered through the image of the zodiacal sign it occupies, and from which it draws certain characteristics, resources, and powers. Strengthened, weakened, or intensified by its relationship with the Sun, this planet is then influenced and impacted as a result of the testimonies and aspectual relationships it has with other planets.

The *science* of astrology involves the accurate calculation of the birth chart and the determination and tabulation of all the various criteria that influence the condition of a planet. In the previous chapters, we have detailed the many criteria that affect the outcomes of a planet's significations in the individual life. The fine details of a planet's sect status, zodiacal sign, solar and lunar phase, and aspect configurations all impact the planet's ability to bring about its most beneficial matters and events.

1   VALENS, *Anthology* 1.1.

The *art* of astrology entails the process of synthesizing all the indications of each planet, weighing and balancing the pros and cons, and then making a judgment about its condition relative to its capacity to bring forth its positive significations and events in the life of the individual. This requires understanding the full spectrum of the planet's strengths and weaknesses, as well as the particular ways it is able to bring about beneficial outcomes for the individual, and where it is most vulnerable to disappointment or failure for the individual.

According to basic Buddhist teachings, every sentient being desires happiness and the causes of happiness. Within an astrological context, each archetypal planetary divinity desires to bring about its own beneficial significations into the lives of the individual. However, there are a myriad of conditions that have the potential to obstruct the successful outcome of this process. The originating cause of these difficulties may have various sources—fate, karma, ignorance, bad luck, one's own actions, or trauma outside one's control. The chart does not indicate the specific environmental reasons why good and bad things happen to people (unless one views the chart through the lens of inherited karma); instead, it simply depicts the planetary signatures indicating the existence of these patterns in the life, regardless of their origin. It is important to emphasize that although we might describe a planet, house, or aspect as "good" or "bad", this does not mean that planets are inherently good or bad. It is more the case that their conditions shape the helpful or harmful outcomes of the matters and events that they represent.

When the analysis of the birth chart is approached from a healing perspective, the purpose of identifying difficulties is so that they can be remedied (if possible). The chart itself can point to factors that counteract, mitigate, or transmute the severely injured, disabled, or malignant parts of the psyche.

CHAPTER 56

Summary

FOR FINAL SYNTHESIS

———

The benefic stars, suitably and well situated, bring forth their own matters according to their nature and the nature of their zodiacal sign, with the additional mixture of the aspect testimonies and the co-presences of each star. When they are unfavorably situated, they are indicative of obstacles. Likewise, even the malefic stars, when they operate suitably and are of the sect, are givers of good and indicative of greater rank and success. But when they are in unprofitable places, they bring about banishment and accusations.—VALENS.[1]

FOR BOTH BENEFICS AND MALEFICS: THE BETTER A PLANET'S CONDITION, the better the outcome of its events for the interests of the individual. The following table summarizes the factors that predispose a planet towards a good or bad condition.

Table 29. Good and Bad Planetary Conditions

GOOD PLANETARY CONDITION	BAD PLANETARY CONDITION
Same sect as chart & sect rejoicing	Sect contrary to chart
Zodiacal signs of own domicile, exaltation, triplicity, or bound	Zodiacal signs of detriment or fall
Connected to a benefic and strong domicile lord	Not connected to its domicile lord, or badly-situated domicile lord
Fast, direct, visible	Slow, retrograde, invisible, under beams
Phase intensification: rising and direct station	Phase intensification: setting and retrograde station
Witnessed by benefics from good aspects	Witnessed by malefics from bad aspects
Bonification and spear-bearers	Maltreatment

1 VALENS, *Anthology* 1.1.

Various conditions can predispose a planet to bring forth better outcomes, act in more powerful and hence more effective ways, or weaken a planet's strength so it cannot act, leading to ineffective, problematic, or harmful outcomes. The task of the astrologer is to understand, specifically, what makes a planet's actions turn out better or worse. The final evaluation entails the careful weighing of each factor. What planetary strength might be likely to outweigh, mitigate, or counteract the weakness indicated by another factor? Which patterns can indicate the possibility of transmutation of the bad into something good, or the destruction of the good, once realized, into something bad?

→   *Turn to the* MASTER EVALUATION TABLES *at the end of this section, and familiarize yourself with the layout. After we review the guidelines for each category, we will explore the tables using our examples charts, and explicate the process of synthesis and evaluation. You will then have the opportunity to integrate your understanding using your own chart. Remember, we are not yet making final interpretations of what the planets mean in the chart. That will happen in the next volume. All we are doing now is thoroughly assessing the planet's condition. But this judgment is the foundational step that must precede all further interpretation.*

SECT

Sect is the *first consideration* in any evaluation of a planet's condition. The determination of sect is based upon the Sun's terrestrial condition—its location above or below the horizon at the time of birth. A daytime birth gives a *diurnal* chart, while a nighttime birth gives a *nocturnal* chart. Sect determination is preliminary to most other considerations because the conditions of the planets are modified according to the sect status of the chart.

The planets that belong to the sect of the chart (the diurnal planets in a day chart and the nocturnal planets in a night chart) have more potential to bring about their beneficial agendas. Their ability to actually fulfill this promise, however, is modified by all the other conditions to which they are subject. A planet's sect status thus establishes its baseline capacity to bring forth more or less beneficial outcomes.

Sect-rejoicing conditions bring the evaluation up or down from that baseline. Thus, a planet that belongs to the sect of the chart, and which meets all three rejoicing conditions, is improved. However, sect-rejoicing conditions, while improving the condition of a contrary-sect planet, cannot change the fundamental rank of that planet on its own. Other factors might, but sect rejoicing alone cannot. Sect rejoicing simply gives *nuance* to our understanding of sect.

There are some techniques for ascertaining the most qualified planet for a certain role in the native's life. When two or more planets vie for this status, sect rejoicing factors can be useful for tipping the scales in the final decision.

> In a *diurnal chart*, the SUN, JUPITER, SATURN, and a MORNING-RISING MERCURY are predisposed to bring about their agendas in more beneficial ways for the individual. Jupiter is the greater benefic, and Saturn by day can also lead to benefic outcomes. Mars, as the malefic contrary to sect, is the potential nexus of greatest difficulty in a day chart.

> In a *nocturnal chart*, the MOON, VENUS, MARS, and an EVENING-RISING MERCURY are predisposed to bring about their agendas in more beneficial ways for the individual. Venus is the greater benefic, and Mars by night can also lead to benefic outcomes. SATURN is the potential nexus of greatest difficulty in a night chart.

> THE SUN, JUPITER, SATURN, and a MORNING-RISING MERCURY *rejoice* (1) when in the same hemisphere as the Sun, (2) when rising before the Sun in the morning, and (3) when occupying the masculine/diurnal signs.

> THE MOON, VENUS, MARS, and an EVENING-RISING MERCURY *rejoice* (1) when in the opposite hemisphere to the Sun, (2) when rising after the Sun sets in the evening, and (3) when occupying the feminine/nocturnal signs.

> MARS has a mixed judgment. He is happier as a morning riser and in a masculine sign, but acts *better for the interests of the individual* when he is an evening riser in a feminine sign. This is because these conditions temper his rash nature.

ZODIACAL SIGN RULERSHIPS

After sect, a planet's zodiacal sign is perhaps the next most important factor in the evaluation of its condition. The meanings of the zodiacal signs are derived from the images formed by the fixed stars, which stand closer to the divine source in the celestial hierarchy of the cosmos. Each of the four rulership systems (domicile, exaltation, triplicity, bounds) accords a planet various kinds of powers when it occupies them. Domicile and exaltation rulership are considered to be the most potent, but following the lead of Dorotheus, many Arabic and Medieval astrologers gave precedence to the triplicity lords over the domicile lords for house rulers. Some Hellenistic astrologers, such as Firmicus Maternus, looked to the bound lord as equal in strength to the domicile lord.

> The more a planet is the lord of its own zodiacal divisions (DOMICILE, EXALTATION, TRIPLICITY, BOUNDS), *the more power and resources it has available in order to accomplish its agenda.* Occupying one or more of its own signs significantly raises the planet's overall rating.

If a planet is not the lord of its own zodiacal signs, the next best lords to have are its SECT MATES, and the *benefic sect mate* is better than the malefic sect mate (unless the malefic sect mate is quite powerful on its own). The most challenging zodiacal signs are those where the lords of those signs are planets of the contrary sect, with the malefic of the contrary sect being the most problematic placement.

If a planet occupies the signs of its DETRIMENT, it *experiences challenges obtaining the power and resources it needs* to accomplish its agenda. The resources may be lacking, scarce, or inconsistent. Therefore, the person may have to work harder for poorer results. This significantly lowers its rating. If the planet is in the sign of its fall, it suffers from a lack of influence. This arises from being held in low esteem, or simply not being recognized for its merits.

A planet that is weak on its own may be improved by being in MUTUAL RECEPTION with another planet regarding their joint endeavors. Here, *each planet contributes to and supports the other.* The Hellenistic astrologers used only domicile rulership for assessing mutual reception, but the Medieval tradition looked to mutual reception by exaltation, triplicity, and bounds as well.

A planet in its OWN DOMICILE—i.e., a planet that is its own domicile lord—*has the optimal resources that it needs* for the accomplishment of its agenda. It also has full, free, and independent access to them. The five planets are the lords of two signs each, but they *rejoice* in the zodiacal sign of their own sect, where they have even more power. Venus, for example, has more power in Taurus because it is a *feminine* sign, rather than Libra, which is a masculine sign. Venus rejoices in Taurus, Jupiter rejoices in Sagittarius, Mercury rejoices in Virgo, Mars rejoices in Scorpio, and Saturn rejoices in Aquarius.

A planet in a domicile other than its own must *look to the lord of that domicile* as its HOST, who provides it with the resources to accomplish its agenda. These resources may or may not be optimal or easily given. The condition of a planet's domicile lord also informs the long-term prognosis for the successful outcomes of the planet.

It is important for the planet to be CONFIGURED by *co-presence or whole sign aspect* (sextile, square, trine, or opposition) *to its domicile lord* in order to access those resources. If it is not, the host cannot see its guest planet, for which it is responsible. The trine is the best aspect, followed by the conjunction (in which case the lord will be in its own domicile sign), then the sextile. A square indicates that the resources are given with conditions; these conditions are harsher and more stringent from malefics than from benefics. A planet that is opposed by its domicile lord indicates that the lord is in the sign of its detriment and is therefore potentially unable to provide much help, which can make their relationship demanding, unfulfilling, and adversarial.

In your delineation, it is important not only to know if a planet has POWER, but to know *exactly what kind of power* it has to accomplish its affairs. If a planet is its own domicile lord, it has resources. If a planet is its own exaltation lord, it has influence from being held in esteem. If a planet is its own triplicity lord, it has the support of followers. If a planet is its own bound lord, it has autonomy and the freedom to play by its own rules.

Planets in MUTUAL RECEPTION should ideally be *configured* by some kind of aspect in order for them to pool their resources for mutual endeavors and benefit.

SOLAR PHASE

A planet's relationship to the Sun and Moon has a crucial impact on its performance in the life of an individual. Its relationship to the Sun during its synodic cycle shapes the observable dynamics of the planet. A planet's speed, direction, and visibility all impact its capacity to make its affairs manifest.

A planet can better bring about its matters when it is *swift* in speed, *direct* in motion, and *visible* when rising or setting on the horizon.

Its condition is weakened and its significations are less fortunate when it is *slow, retrograde* in direction, or *invisible* when rising or setting over the horizon. In techniques that entail looking for a planet's suitability for a certain role, a planet is rejected if it is under the Sun's beams or retrograde. Mercury and Venus are especially problematic when retrograde and in the combust zone.

The exception to this guideline is the protection that is accorded to planets when they are in the *heart of the Sun*, or in their *chariot*. The heart of the Sun is defined as being within 1° on either side of Sun (Hellenistic) or 17' on either side (Medieval). A planet in its chariot (its own domicile, exaltation, triplicity, or bound) is protected from being weakened when under the beams of the Sun.

The significations of a planet are intensified at its FOUR PHASE TRANSITIONS. A planet shifts to its strengthening phase at the *heliacal morning rising* (or evening rising for Mercury and Venus), and at the *direct station*. It shifts to its weakening phase at the *heliacal evening setting* (morning setting for Mercury and Venus), and at the *retrograde station*.

MARS, JUPITER and SATURN are most effective as *morning stars* from the interval of 15° from the Sun until the retrograde station near the right trine to the Sun. They are particularly effective with a sextile or with a still-direct trine aspect to the Sun. They are also effective as *evening stars* from the interval of the direct station near the left trine to the Sun, through to the 15° interval from the Sun.

MERCURY and VENUS are effective as *morning stars* from their morning rising (15° from the Sun), through to their greatest elongation, until their morning setting (15° from the Sun). As *evening stars*, they are most effective from their evening rising (15° from the Sun), through to their greatest elongation, until their evening setting (15° from the Sun).

ALL PLANETS are ineffective during their *lying-hidden phase* under the Sun's beams, unless they lie in the heart of the Sun or in their chariot. MARS, JUPITER, and SATURN are also ineffective during their *acronychal phase*, while they are *retrograde*, and particularly when in *curtailed passage*.

LUNAR CONSIDERATIONS

Several factors unique to the MOON impact its condition.

The Moon's condition is *improved* when its waxing or waning phase accords with a diurnal or nocturnal birth, causing her to rejoice; when it is *active* (making an applying aspects to other planets) rather than *slack* (void in course); and when free (not captive under the bond of the Sun).

The Moon is *precarious* when conjunct either her North or South Node, as she is making a transitional shift on the ecliptic (from below to above, or above to below). The Moon is also *intensified* when part of a lunar or solar ECLIPSE, resulting in life events that seem fated in some way.

The Moon brings forth *difficult* outcomes when it is *eclipsed, under the bond* (within 15° on either side of the conjunction or opposition to the Sun), *with the Nodes,* or *extremely slow in motion.*

Medieval astrologers added the *via combusta*, the "burnt path" of Libra and Scorpio, where the Sun and Moon have their falls.

A planet's condition is *improved* by certain contacts with the Moon. When a planet receives an *applying aspect* from the Moon, the Moon helps that planet anchor its own agenda into the everyday life of the individual.

A planet is also *enhanced* when conjunct the LOT OF FORTUNE, the special LOT OF THE MOON. Any planetary contact with the NODES partakes of the ominous quality of the eclipsing places. *The good of benefic planets is increased* when conjunct the NORTH LUNAR NODE, and *weakened* when conjunct the SOUTH LUNAR NODE. The *difficulties of the malefics are reduced* when conjunct the SOUTH NODE, but *accentuated* when conjunct the NORTH NODE.

ASPECT TESTIMONY, MALTREATMENT,
AND BONIFICATION

No man is an island, and no planet in the solar system can act independently from the influences of the other planets. They all participate in the cosmic dance. The positive and negative testimony that a planet receives from the benefics and malefics has an impact on the assessment of a planet's condition. And the special conditions of bonification and maltreatment can radically change the evaluation of a planet.

The more positive testimony a planet has from the benefic planets, the more support it has to ensure the successful completion of its objectives, general good fortune, and happiness in life. A planet's condition is *improved* by whole sign co-presences, sextiles, and trines from VENUS and JUPITER. The superior trine from Jupiter is the best aspect testimony, and even the superior square from Jupiter can be very helpful.

The more negative testimony a planet receives from the malefics, the more obstacles and conflicts there are to thwart its successful outcomes, leading to misfortune and unhappiness. A planet's condition is *impaired* by co-presences, squares, and oppositions from MARS and SATURN. The superior square from Mars is perhaps the most difficult of all aspect testimony.

If a planet receives both positive and negative testimony, its condition is *mixed*. The good fortune is lessened, but the misfortune is mitigated. The planet's circumstances are more moderate, and the protective qualities of the benefics guard one from the painful effects of the malefics.

Firmicus Maternus detailed the effects of the Moon *separating* from a benefic and then *applying* to a malefic or vice versa.[2] Medieval astrologers then generalized this principle to all planets so that a planet separating from a benefic and then applying to another benefic *amplifies* its good fortune. A planet separating from a malefic and applying to another malefic *deepens* its misfortune.

Conditions of MALTREATMENT and BONIFICATION are less frequent, but more important in dramatically raising or lowering a planet's overall rating. CONTAINMENT and ENCLOSURE are extremely potent in protection or injury, depending on whether it is done by benefics or malefics. The 3° applying conjunction, square, or opposition to a malefic is a red flag for painful outcomes. The superior square from a malefic is also cause for concern. Abu Ma'shar specifies that if a planet is in the bounds or domicile of a malefic, and that malefic overcomes the planet by a superior square, it is most harmful if the malefic does not receive the planet.

2   *Mathesis* 4.

SPEAR-BEARING BODYGUARDS can be difficult or even impossible to determine based upon the available textual evidence. However, in the cases where the pattern is obvious, spear-bearers indicate eminence in the nativity, especially in regards to the planet that is guarded or attended.

MITIGATION, COUNTERACTION, AND TRANSMUTATION

> When the benefics are not involved, the person who is ill will die immediately up to the opposition [of the Moon to the malefic planet]. When the benefics are present beholding the Moon from the right, even though the patient is endangered, he will recover.[3]

When astrologers reach a judgment about a planet that is less than optimal, and the indications point to severe difficulties in a particular area of life, the question arises as to whether anything can be done to reverse the prognosticated outcomes. Many astrologers recount situations from their client files where something seemingly bad turned out to be a blessing in disguise. This observation is often used as a warning against saying anything negative about a planet because we may not know the final outcome of the situation.

However, there are indications in the chart to guide the astrologer's judgment about the possibility of reversals, improvement, and healing. After determining the fairness or poorness of a planet's condition, other patterns in the chart may require us to alter our judgment.

Traditional astrologers saw Jupiter as the greater benefic and Venus as the lesser benefic. In medical diagnosis, if the significator of an illness was afflicted, it portended the onset of a disease that could be life-threatening. However, many texts added that if the significator was witnessed by the benefics, the patient would recover.[4] From this we can extrapolate that recovery from pain, distress, trauma, or failure is possible if a planet is in a difficult condition, but has a trine with Jupiter (especially an applying trine to Jupiter, and even better, a 3° *sunaphē* bonification). To a lesser extent, this is also true for Venus, particularly in a night chart. Other forms of bonification, such as enclosure by the benefics, or being overcome by Jupiter in a superior trine or even square aspect, lead us to

3   *Iatromathematika: From Hermes to Ammun to Egyptian*; J. L. IDELER, *Physici et Medici gracci minores*, vol. 1, Berlin 1841, pp. 387–96; 430–40.

4   Ibid.

encourage the client to find an appropriate form of healing that has the signature to be effective. Positive relationships with the benefic planets can mitigate and lessen the severity or pain produced by planets in poor condition.

Antiochus and Porphyry discuss the concept of counteraction in their series of aspect definitions, whereby certain conditions of a planet can be undone or reversed.[5] A planet may be in good condition, favorably situated by zodiacal sign and house location, but its beneficial effects can be counteracted and undone if its ruler is injured or maltreated, rendering it ineffective.

This doctrine came to have a much broader interpretation as the tradition went on; it was linked to the zodiacal sign of one's domicile lord (host planet) as well as its house location. Firmicus Maternus instructs the astrologer to examine the condition of a planet's domicile lord by both zodiacal sign and house location. If a planet's lord is in good condition, the planet will benefit from its lord's good fortune and happiness. However, if a planet's lord is in poor zodiacal condition and in an unfortunate house location, the planet shares its lord's misfortunes and sorrows.[6]

This can be taken one step further. The misfortunes of a planet in poor condition can be mitigated to some extent by the excellent condition of its lord. Over time, its own situation improves. For example, someone might be poor, but a wealthy and generous relative might help them over the course of their life and leave them an inheritance. In contrast, the affluence of a planet in good condition can dissipate over time if its domicile lord is in poor condition. For example, someone may be born into family wealth, but it is squandered by the parents or lost in a financial crash.

In evaluating a planet that is distressed, check to see if its domicile lord is strong, well-placed, and connected by aspect: this indicates that healing and recovery are possible or that the life circumstances will improve over time. If its domicile lord is in poor condition, and badly placed in an unfavorable house, the prognosis for improvement is considerably lessened. As a counseling astrologer, it is important to know when to encourage the client to pursue healing, and when to acknowledge (at least to yourself) that some things simply must be accepted, and to do whatever is possible within limited parameters.

In some instances, a planet has the capacity to go beyond mitigation and counteraction to actively transmute the ill effects portended by its condition, transforming the negative situation into positive outcomes. We will detail these indications more thoroughly in the next volume in our discussion of houses.

---

5   ANTIOCHUS, *Summary* 16; PORPHYRY, *Introduction* 27.
6   FIRMICUS MATERNUS, *Mathesis* 2.22. 8–9, trans. HOLDEN.

After making your evaluations for each category separately, the final step is to synthesize them into a final judgment. The order of importance and weighting is generally the order in which we have presented the concepts above. First of all, look at sect status. A planet that belongs to the same sect as the chart is ahead of the game from the start in its capacity to effect beneficial outcomes. Next, factor in zodiacal rulerships. A planet that is in one or more of its own rulership positions is powerful, but in its detriment or fall, weakened. Then check solar phase. A planet that is swift, direct, and visible is effective. Finally, look at witnessing by benefics and malefics for assistance or obstruction. Bonification for protection, and maltreatment for damage, are the final considerations, but they can overturn the previous evaluations.

Although this can seem like a very subjective process, and your conclusions may differ from those of other astrologers, the strength of your judgment arises from the precision of your reasoning. With practice, you will develop increasing speed, precision, and confidence in the process.

Keep in mind that the final judgments for each planet have different implications depending upon whether the planet is a benefic or a malefic. Benefics in good condition bring about beneficial outcomes. Benefics in poor condition are limited in the amount of good they can do, or the good they do can be reversed. Malefics in good condition also bring about beneficial outcomes for the individual, but often with strife, hard work, and at the expense of others. Malefics in poor condition are challenged in bringing about good, and are predisposed to bring about difficult outcomes for the individual. Be clear: this does not mean that the individual is a bad person, or that their actions are bad; it just means that, in the best case scenario, things don't turn out that well for them, and in the worst case, it can lead to active harm.

You will find that most planets have a mixed condition. They provide a blend of good and bad results, either at the same time, or at different times throughout the native's life. Look for the extreme cases to give very positive or very challenging delineations. Planets of mixed condition often give an average or muddled performance.

→ EXAMPLE CHARTS

IN THE NEXT TWO CHAPTERS we will look at our example charts in detail, performing a final synthesis and judgment, taking into account everything that we have examined so far. For your convenience, we have reproduced the charts again, followed by detailed master tables to assist a complete evaluation of each planet's condition.

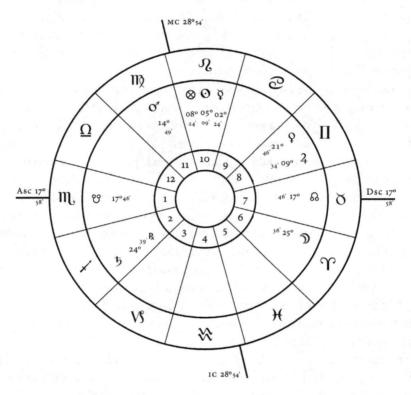

FIGURE 90.
CHART OF JACQUELINE KENNEDY ONASSIS

CHAPTER 57

Chart One

JACQUELINE KENNEDY ONASSIS

———

THE SUN IN LEO

THIS IS A DAY BIRTH, SO THE SUN IS THE SECT LEADER OF THE CHART and has the authority to set the beneficial agenda for the life of this person. The Sun rejoices and gains power in its masculine diurnal sign of Leo, which is its only sect-rejoicing option. This further amplifies its ability to actualize its beneficial nature in this chart. The Sun in its own domicile of Leo has royal power and full and easy access to its optimal resources. It is also its own triplicity lord, which gives it additional power from the support of followers, and it operates within the parameters of a generous and lenient bound lord, its benefic sect mate, Jupiter. The Sun's good evaluation is raised higher because it occupies two of its own signs of rulership, plus the bounds of a benefic sect mate that is of the same sect as this diurnal chart.

None of the solar phase criteria apply to the Sun because the Sun is the reference point for those conditions. The Sun does not receive an applying aspect from the Moon to help ground its significations. Both benefics, Venus and Jupiter, overcome the Sun with superior, harmonious, sextile testimony, impressing it with more positive influences. Neither of the malefic planets give negative testimony. The Sun is not maltreated.

I give the Sun a grade of A+ because it is the leader of the sect in favor, occupies two of its own places of rulership, receives positive testimony from both benefics, and no negative testimony or maltreatment. Its only weakness is that it does not receive an application from the Moon, but that is not enough to warrant lowering the evaluation. When, in the next chapters, we place the Sun in its house, we can give an excellent delineation of its capacity to bring about the most fortunate and stable significations of that house. When the Sun becomes a time lord, we can predict great things about that period in the life.

JUPITER IN GEMINI

Diurnal Jupiter is the greater benefic and belongs to the same sect as the chart in this diurnal nativity. Like the Sun, he has the authority to set its most fortunate agenda for the life. Jupiter rejoices in all three sect-rejoicing conditions: the diurnal sign Gemini, the same hemisphere as the Sun, and as a morning star in the interval of 15–120° ahead of the Sun.

We begin to see some of Jupiter's problems emerge from his location in Gemini, the sign of his detriment. This can lead to scarcity or instability in the supply of resources, or to reversals of fortune. But Jupiter is configured to Mercury, his domicile lord, by the harmonious sextile aspect; and Mercury is a diurnal sect mate, strong in the angular tenth house. Jupiter has Saturn for its triplicity lord; Saturn is Jupiter's sect mate and is a guest in Jupiter's own domicile of Sagittarius, obligating Saturn to give whatever support it can to Jupiter. And Jupiter is his own bound lord: autonomous and playing by his own rules. Even though Jupiter is weak by domicile, having the power of the Sun and Mercury as his other lords, and being his own bound lord, mitigate many of the ill effects of the detriment. Jupiter is also strong by solar phase criteria—fast, direct, visible—and effective as a morning star.

Jupiter's greatest difficulties arise from the negative testimony given by Mars, the contrary-sect malefic (although this is somewhat lessened by Mars being in the inferior square position). Jupiter is also maltreated by Saturn, who opposes him from the unfortunate second house. This is somewhat mitigated by the co-presence of Venus in Jupiter's sign.

I am giving Jupiter a C+. His sect condition is excellent; the zodiacal rulerships, though initially problematic, turn out fine in the end. The solar phase conditions are excellent, but the negative testimony, and especially the maltreatment, pull his evaluation down. When we delineate Jupiter in the house he occupies and the houses he rules, we can expect a mixture of some very good outcomes, and also some very bad ones.

SATURN IN SAGITTARIUS

Saturn is the malefic that belongs to the same sect as the chart. He has the potential ability to bring about his benefic significations for the individual. He rejoices in the diurnal sign of Sagittarius, but does not rejoice in the two other sect-rejoicing conditions. He is of the evening, rising after the Sun, and located in the opposite hemisphere to the Sun. Thus, according to sect-rejoicing, his happiness index is marginal; this causes the evaluation to drop a little from its baseline.

Saturn occupies the domicile of his benefic sect mate, Jupiter, to whom he is configured by opposition. This points to an adversarial relationship with his host and sect mate, but at least Saturn is seen by and connected to Jupiter. He is more beneficially connected by the trine to his sect leader, the powerful Sun, who as his triplicity lord, provides the support of the community. Saturn occupies his own bounds, which greatly strengthens his power of autonomy. He therefore sits in the zodiacal sector of one of his own rulership positions (bounds), and his two sect mates are his lords for the other rulership powers (domicile and triplicity). He is doing quite well in this category.

Saturn is retrograde and thus moving very slowly, but is visible. However, being in the acronychal phase, he falls outside the effective evening star range (120–15° behind the Sun). The retrograde can indicate reversal or the taking back of what has been given. Saturn does not receive any benefic testimony from Venus and Jupiter. His predicament becomes even more severe due to the superior square he receives from the contrary-to-sect malefic Mars, who overcomes him from the tenth sign (*epidekatesis*). However, this is not a case of maltreatment, because Mars is not in an unfortunate house.

I am going to give Saturn a B. Even though he is retrograde, he is doing somewhat better than Jupiter because, like Jupiter, he has one zodiacal position of power (being in his own bounds), but he is not in detriment (as is Jupiter). Moreover, while he is overcome by Mars, he is not maltreated (as is Jupiter). Jupiter holds his own as an essential benefic, but Saturn, functionally speaking, is slightly more benefic. When we delineate Saturn according the houses that he occupies and rules, we can expect some relatively good outcomes—albeit with a certain measure of fear, struggle and hardship—as well as some reversals in fortune.

MERCURY IN LEO

Rising ahead of the Sun in the morning, Mercury belongs to the diurnal sect. As such, he rejoices in the diurnal, masculine sign of Leo, and enjoys its proximity to the Sun in the same hemisphere. Mercury has the powerful Sun, his sect leader, as his domicile and triplicity lord, with whom he is co-present. His benefic sect mate, Jupiter, who is a guest in his own domicile of Gemini, is his bound lord. As such, while Mercury is not the lord of any of his zodiacal places, the planets who govern them are his friends and hold power in their own right. Mercury is traveling very fast, since he is direct and conjunct the Sun. However, because he is within a 3° applying interval to the Sun, he is in the combust zone. Mercury is weakened by the overwhelming heat of a very hot Sun in Leo (though some Medieval traditions dispute that Mercury is debilitated when under the Sun's beams if located in Leo or Aries, the signs of the Sun's domicile and exaltation). Being under the beams also serves to conceal Mercury's significations for good or for ill. The Sun absorbs the significations of Mercury into itself and becomes more mercurial in its expression. Both Venus and Jupiter overcome Mercury with their positive testimony, giving good fortune by means of superior sextiles. Neither of the malefic planets interferes by presenting negative testimony.

I give Mercury a B+. The uncertainty of being under the beams of the Sun is his main problem. Otherwise, he is in good condition, even though he is not in any of its own positions of power. When we delineate Mercury in the house he occupies and rules, we can surmise that while moderately beneficial overall, there is some weakness in the topics of the houses he rules. We also suspect that some of what is going on is behind closed doors, and is not visible or apparent to the outside observer.

MOON IN ARIES

In this day birth, the Moon does not belong to the same sect as the chart. Thus, she has less authority to bring about her beneficial agenda, and she does not rejoice in her masculine diurnal sign of Aries. However, removed from the glaring light of the Sun, she is the undisputed queen of her own hemisphere.

Her domicile lord is Mars, to whom she is in aversion. Although Mars is a sect mate, he cannot see her and thus cannot provide for nor protect her. The Sun is her exaltation and triplicity lord, and Saturn is her bound lord. The Sun and Saturn are not her sect mates, but both are configured to her by sympathetic trines. She is in a tenuous situation where she is tacitly supported by powerful members of the opposite sect. The Moon is waning and thus not rejoicing in this day chart, which provides further reason for feeling unhappy or out of sync. Mildly supportive testimony comes from the inferior sextiles of Venus and Jupiter.

I give the Moon a c+. While there is no active detriment, maltreatment, or affliction, she nevertheless suffers from a lack of substantial support from her sect mates, particularly from her host, Mars. When we delineate the Moon in the house she occupies, we will see that the delineation turns toward outcomes of unhappiness.

VENUS IN GEMINI

Nocturnal-sect Venus is contrary to the sect in this diurnal birth chart, and is thus not positioned to bring forth her best outcomes. Venus does not rejoice in any of the three sect-rejoicing conditions. She occupies a diurnal masculine zodiacal sign, she is of the morning solar phase, and is located in the same hemisphere as the Sun. Thus, Venus is uncomfortable. Her environment is too bright and active for her more nocturnal sense of pleasure. Her domicile lord is Mercury, "the friend to all", and she enjoys a mildly harmonious sextile with him. Her triplicity and bound lords—Saturn and Mars—are the two malefics, whose support is begrudging and contentious. She does not occupy any of her own signs of rulership, and two of her three lords are not her sect mates. In regards to sign, she is relatively powerless.

Venus is of average speed, direct, and visible, so she is able to make manifest her significations, but she would be more effective as an evening star than as a morning star. As a consequence, her events do not contribute to lasting happiness. The greatest and most formidable difficulties regarding her condition are the negative testimony from both malefics, compounded by triple maltreatment. Mars and Saturn enclose her with their rays, and she is injured by running into an opposition ray cast by Saturn, the malefic of the contrary sect, within a 3° applying connection (*sunaphē*). Furthermore, Saturn casts his opposition ray from the unfortunate second house. These lead to outcomes that are fraught with danger and pain. Benefic Jupiter, co–present in Gemini, mitigates some of the hardship and adds to a mixed delineation of good with bad. Venus also benefits mildly from a harmonious relationship with her domicile lord, Mercury, so there is some improvement of her condition over time.

I give Venus a D in the evaluation of her condition. She is unhappy by sect and sect rejoicing, powerless in her zodiacal sign, and severely injured by both malefics. When we delineate Venus according to the house she occupies and the houses she rules, we will see that Venus represents some of the greatest challenges that the native faces, and that the topics and outcomes are painful and disappointing.

MARS IN VIRGO

Nocturnal-sect Mars in this day chart is not automatically in a position to bring about his most positive outcomes. His naturally hot nature is overheated and made more reckless by his presence in the same hemisphere as the Sun. However, he occupies the nocturnal sign of Virgo, and is of the evening phase in relation to the Sun. The later Hellenistic astrologers understood that, while Mars would prefer occupying a masculine sign and thrive in the activity of day, his outcomes are more beneficial to the individual when his nature is tempered by the cooling, nocturnal conditions. So he has a mixed reading for sect-rejoicing conditions: "you may not like it, but it's good for you".

His domicile and exaltation lord is Mercury; but Mercury is in aversion to Mars, does not see him, and thus does not readily provide resources or honors. Mars' triplicity and bound lord is his benefic sect mate, Venus; but while she is willing due to her intrinsic nature, she is limited in what she can and will do for him due to his maltreatment of her and her own challenges.

Mars is moving fast, is visible, and in the effective evening star interval; thus, solar phase conditions allow him to actively manifest his significations. Mars' essential malefic nature is subdued and overcome by the superior square testimony from both Venus and Jupiter, which also enclose and bonify him, thus dramatically improving his condition and ability to do good. He receives negative testimony via the square from Saturn, but Saturn's inferior, backward-hurled ray does not maltreat him.

I give Mars a B–. According to sect, he is in the position to bring about the most malefic outcomes. He does not have much power from his zodiacal sign, is not seen by his domicile lord, and receives negative testimony from Saturn. However, his solar phase conditions make him active and effective in doing his job, and his bonification from both benefics predisposes him to doing good in spite of himself, at least some of the time. When we delineate Mars in the house he occupies and the houses he rules, we will see that the tendency toward bad outcomes is often mitigated, and in the final account, the topics eventuate better than expected.

Table 30. Ranking of Planets from Best to Worst: Onassis

SUN	A+
MERCURY	B+
SATURN	B
MARS	B–
JUPITER	C+
MOON	C+
VENUS	D

MASTER TABLES: ONASSIS

BIRTH DATA: *Sunday July 28, 1929; 2:30 pm; Southampton, New York*
SECT OF CHART: *Diurnal*

SUN: 5° LEO 09'

NATURE *Benefic/malefic/* *common/luminary*	Luminary
SECT *Day/night,* *Same/contrary*	Day, same (sect leader)
SECT REJOICING *Hemisphere, Sign,* *Solar Phase*	Rejoices by sign
LORDS *Domicile, Exaltation,* *Triplicity, Bound*	Sun*, —, Sun*, Jupiter
ESSENTIAL DIGNITY *Domicile, Detriment,* *Exaltation, Fall, Bound* *Mutual Reception*	Domicile, triplicity
SOLAR PHASE *Speed, Direction, Station,* *Visibility/Beams/Chariot,* *Morning/Evening, Phasis*	n/a (Sun defines category)
LUNAR ASPECTS *Lunar application* *Nodal Connection*	Sun squares nodes (by sign)
TESTIMONY *Favorable/Unfavorable* *Maltreated/Bonified*	Favorable from Venus and Jupiter
CONDITION OF DOMICILE LORD *Helps/Hinders*	Own domicile lord
JUDGMENT GRADE *A/B/C/D/F*	A+

* = PLANET IS ITS OWN LORD

JUPITER: 9° GEMINI 34'

NATURE *Benefic/malefic/ common/luminary*	Benefic
SECT *Day/night, Same/contrary*	Day, same (benefic of sect)
SECT REJOICING *Hemisphere, Sign, Solar Phase*	Rejoices by hemisphere, sign, phase
LORDS *Domicile, Exaltation, Triplicity, Bound*	Mercury, —, Saturn, Jupiter*
ESSENTIAL DIGNITY *Domicile, Detriment, Exaltation, Fall, Bound Mutual Reception*	Detriment, Bound
SOLAR PHASE *Speed, Direction, Station, Visibility/Beams/Chariot, Morning/Evening, Phasis*	Fast, direct, visible, morning star
LUNAR ASPECTS *Lunar application Nodal Connection*	None
TESTIMONY *Favorable/Unfavorable Maltreated/Bonified*	Favorable from Venus, unfavorable from Mars, maltreated by Saturn
CONDITION OF DOMICILE LORD *Helps/Hinders*	Helped by Mercury
JUDGMENT GRADE *A/B/C/D/F*	C+

SATURN: 24° SAGITTARIUS 39' RX

NATURE *Benefic/malefic/* *common/luminary*	Malefic
SECT *Day/night,* *Same/contrary*	Day, same (malefic of sect)
SECT REJOICING *Hemisphere, Sign,* *Solar Phase*	Rejoices by sign Does not rejoice by hemisphere or phase
LORDS *Domicile, Exaltation,* *Triplicity, Bound*	Jupiter, —, Sun, Saturn*
ESSENTIAL DIGNITY *Domicile, Detriment,* *Exaltation, Fall, Bound* *Mutual Reception*	Bound
SOLAR PHASE *Speed, Direction, Station,* *Visibility/Beams/Chariot,* *Morning/Evening, Phasis*	Slow, retrograde, visible, acronychal
LUNAR ASPECTS *Lunar application* *Nodal Connection*	None
TESTIMONY *Favorable/Unfavorable* *Maltreated/Bonified*	Unfavorable from Mars
CONDITION OF DOMICILE LORD *Helps/Hinders*	Some reluctant help from Jupiter
JUDGMENT GRADE *A/B/C/D/F*	B

MERCURY: 02° LEO 24'

___

NATURE *Benefic/malefic/* *common/luminary*	Common; in this chart, benefic
SECT *Day/night,* *Same/contrary*	Day, same
SECT REJOICING *Hemisphere, Sign,* *Solar Phase*	Rejoices by hemisphere, sign, and phase
LORDS *Domicile, Exaltation,* *Triplicity, Bound*	Sun, —, Sun, Jupiter
ESSENTIAL DIGNITY *Domicile, Detriment,* *Exaltation, Fall, Bound* *Mutual Reception*	None
SOLAR PHASE *Speed, Direction, Station,* *Visibility/Beams/Chariot,* *Morning/Evening, Phasis*	Fast, direct, combust, lying hidden
LUNAR ASPECTS *Lunar application* *Nodal Connection*	Squares the Nodes
TESTIMONY *Favorable/Unfavorable* *Maltreated/Bonified*	Favorable from Venus and Jupiter
CONDITION OF DOMICILE LORD *Helps/Hinders*	Much help from the Sun
JUDGMENT GRADE *A/B/C/D/F*	B+

MOON: 25° ARIES 36'

NATURE
Benefic/malefic/
common/luminary   Luminary

SECT
Day/night,
Same/contrary   Night, contrary

SECT REJOICING
Hemisphere, Sign,   Rejoices by hemisphere
Solar Phase   Does not rejoice by sign or phase

LORDS
Domicile, Exaltation,
Triplicity, Bound   Mars, Sun, Sun, Saturn

ESSENTIAL DIGNITY
Domicile, Detriment,
Exaltation, Fall, Bound
Mutual Reception   None

SOLAR PHASE
Speed, Direction, Station,
Visibility/Beams/Chariot,
Morning/Evening, Phasis   Average speed

LUNAR ASPECTS
Lunar application
Nodal Connection   n/a, none.

TESTIMONY
Favorable/Unfavorable
Maltreated/Bonified   Favorable from Venus and Jupiter

CONDITION OF DOMICILE LORD
Helps/Hinders   Not helped by Mars (in aversion).

JUDGMENT GRADE
A/B/C/D/F   C+

VENUS: 21° GEMINI 46'

NATURE *Benefic/malefic/* *common/luminary*	Benefic
SECT *Day/night,* *Same/contrary*	Night, contrary
SECT REJOICING *Hemisphere, Sign,* *Solar Phase*	Does not rejoice by hemisphere, sign, or phase
LORDS *Domicile, Exaltation,* *Triplicity, Bound*	Mercury, —, Saturn, Mars
ESSENTIAL DIGNITY *Domicile, Detriment,* *Exaltation, Fall, Bound* *Mutual Reception*	None
SOLAR PHASE *Speed, Direction, Station,* *Visibility/Beams/Chariot,* *Morning/Evening, Phasis*	Average, direct, visible, morning star
LUNAR ASPECTS *Lunar application* *Nodal Connection*	N/A, none.
TESTIMONY *Favorable/Unfavorable* *Maltreated/Bonified*	Favorable from Jupiter Triple maltreatment
CONDITION OF DOMICILE LORD *Helps/Hinders*	Some help from Mercury
JUDGMENT GRADE *A/B/C/D/F*	D

MARS: 14° VIRGO 49'

NATURE
Benefic/malefic/
common/luminary   Malefic

SECT
Day/night,
Same/contrary   Night, contrary

SECT REJOICING
Hemisphere, Sign,   Does not rejoice by hemisphere
Solar Phase   Rejoices by sign and phase

LORDS
Domicile, Exaltation,
Triplicity, Bound   Mercury, Mercury, Venus, Venus

ESSENTIAL DIGNITY
Domicile, Detriment,
Exaltation, Fall, Bound
Mutual Reception   None

SOLAR PHASE
Speed, Direction, Station,
Visibility/Beams/Chariot,
Morning/Evening, Phasis   Faster, direct, visible, evening star

LUNAR ASPECTS
Lunar application
Nodal Connection   None

TESTIMONY
Favorable/Unfavorable   Unfavorable from Saturn
Maltreated/Bonified   Bonified by enclosure from benefics

CONDITION OF DOMICILE LORD
Helps/Hinders   Not helped (aversion to Mercury)

JUDGMENT GRADE
A/B/C/D/F   B−

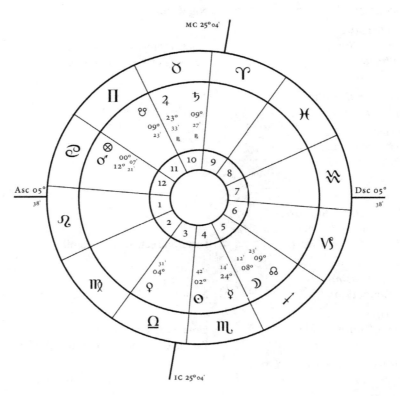

FIGURE 91.
CHART OF PABLO PICASSO

CHAPTER 58

Chart Two

PABLO PICASSO

———

SUN IN SCORPIO

IN THIS NOCTURNAL CHART, THE DIURNAL SUN IS CONTRARY TO SECT and thus not positioned to bring about his best outcomes. He does not rejoice in the nocturnal feminine sign of Scorpio, his only sect-rejoicing option. The Sun is in the domicile, triplicity, and bounds of Mars, the malefic that is of the sect, and this points to a contentious relationship with his only lord. Even though Mars is configured to the Sun by the trine aspect, Mars is in the zodiacal sign of his fall, and placed in the unfortunate twelfth house. This, in fact, is an instance of maltreatment: the planet occupies the domicile of a malefic that is itself in a bad house. The sympathetic assistance given is questionable: it is like help from a shadowy stranger involved in nefarious dealings.

The Sun does not receive positive testimony from the benefics (unless one considers Petosiris' statement that an opposition from the benefics is never bad in relation to the lights). Saturn is giving negative testimony by his opposition. Given all of this, and placing due weight on the maltreatment, which accentuates the planet's difficulty, I give the Sun a c.

JUPITER IN TAURUS

In this nocturnal chart, diurnal Jupiter is contrary to the sect of the chart, and thus not positioned to bring about his best outcomes. He does not rejoice in the opposite hemisphere from his sect leader, the Sun; he does not rejoice in the nocturnal feminine sign of Taurus; but he does rise ahead of the Sun. Overall, Jupiter is rather weak in terms of sect-related conditions.

Jupiter is in the domicile of Venus, in the exaltation and triplicity of the Moon, and within the bounds of Saturn. Three of his four lords are not his own sect mates, and Saturn, while Jupiter's sect mate, is still a harsh malefic in the marginalized sect. However, Venus, as his domicile lord, is relatively friendly and generous as the in-sect benefic, and she is also powerful in Libra, her sign of rulership. The problem is that Venus is in aversion to Jupiter and cannot see him. But because she is also the lord of Jupiter's sign, Taurus, she does have some familial relationship to his domicile, even if that connection is not linked by an aspect. Thus Jupiter has access to Venus' rich æsthetic resources and assistance.

Jupiter is slow, retrograde, and while visible, is in the ineffective acronychal phase. There is no applying aspect from the Moon. His only testimony is negative, from his co-presence with his sect mate, Saturn. He is neither bonified nor maltreated. I give Jupiter a c+, with the proviso that the Jupiterian significations of the native's life will improve over time because of a powerful Venus as his lord.

SATURN IN TAURUS

In this nocturnal chart, diurnal Saturn is contrary to the sect of the chart, and thus not positioned to bring about its best outcomes. Similar to Jupiter, it does not rejoice in the hemisphere opposite the Sun, nor in the feminine nocturnal sign of Taurus. However, it is technically of the morning in terms of its solar phase. Saturn is also in the domicile of Venus, in the exaltation and triplicity of the Moon, and within the bounds of Mercury, none of whom are his sect mates. He does not derive any power from his zodiacal sign placement. Saturn is in aversion to his domicile lord, a potent Venus who turns away from him. But because Venus has a shared sympathy with both signs (as domicile lord of both Taurus and Libra), she nevertheless continues to provide artistic and romantic resources.

Saturn is slow in speed, retrograde in motion, and invisible rising over the eastern horizon, as it is in curtailed passage within a 7½° opposition to the Sun. It is especially ineffective in its acronychal phase. There is no help from the Moon, which, also in aversion, does not make an applying aspect. Saturn is helped by positive testimony received from Jupiter, which is co-present in the same sign, but is not bonified or maltreated. I give Saturn the same grade as Jupiter. Its sect and sect-rejoicing conditions are weak, it has no power in its zodiacal sign, no steady and consistent flow of resources from a reluctant domicile lord, and its solar phase conditions make it quite ineffective. While it is better than Jupiter because of the positive testimony, it is worse than Jupiter because of the invisibility on the horizon due to curtailed passage. I therefore give Saturn a c+.

MERCURY IN SCORPIO

Traveling behind the Sun, Mercury belongs to the nocturnal sect in this night chart. He is thus positioned to bring forth his more positive significations. Mercury rejoices in the nocturnal feminine sign of Scorpio, but as a nocturnal planet he does not rejoice in the same hemisphere as the diurnal Sun. Mercury is in the domicile and triplicity of Mars, and in the bounds of Saturn. There is no exaltation lord of Scorpio. While Mars is a sect mate of Mercury and looks upon him with a trine aspect, Mars is in his fall in the 12th house, and cannot offer much positive help. In fact, this is a condition of maltreatment. And restrictive Saturn is not a friend to nocturnal Mercury.

Mercury is moving very slowly as he will make a retrograde station a few days later. He is still visible and effective in the evening star phase, but about to make his heliacal set within the seven-day *phasis* range. Both the retrograde station and heliacal set intensify Mercury's significations, but the tendency is moving towards weakening. Mercury is in aversion to his sect leader, the Moon, and thus does not receive any applying aspect that would help ground his significations. Mercury does not receive testimony from Venus, and receives negative testimony from the Saturn opposition, the malefic of the contrary sect. Mercury's biggest problem is the maltreatment that comes from being in the domicile of the malefic Mars, which is located in the unfortunate 12th house.

Mercury is middling by sect conditions, does not receive any power from his zodiacal sign, and is actively maltreated by his domicile lord. While visible and mildly effective, he is about to take a dramatic plunge into the lying-hidden retrograde phase, and will experience a weakening of what power he has. I give Mercury a c–.

MOON IN SAGITTARIUS

The Moon is the sect leader of this nocturnal chart, so theoretically she is in a good position to bring forth a benefic agenda. The Moon does not rejoice in the same hemisphere as the Sun, nor in the masculine diurnal sign Sagittarius. The Moon is in the domicile, triplicity, and bounds of benefic Jupiter, but Jupiter in Taurus is in aversion to the Moon, does not see her, and thus cannot provide for her needs.

The Moon is traveling with average speed, but her close conjunction with the North Node places her in a precarious transition: she leaves the south latitude situations, which seem tenuous, and heads north, where her significations tend towards increase. The Moon receives mild positive testimony due to the inferior sextile from her well-endowed sect mate, Venus, and some possible bonification from being in the domicile of a well-placed benefic, Jupiter. Because Jupiter cannot see the Moon, his potential help is questionable. There is no negative testimony or maltreatment. The Moon's condition is problematic, not because she is being injured by the malefics, but rather because she navigates a challenging and turbulent course with uncertain help from her lord. I give the Moon a B–.

VENUS IN LIBRA

Venus belongs to the sect of this nocturnal chart. However she is not happy in any of her sect-rejoicing conditions, as she is in the same hemisphere as the diurnal Sun, the masculine diurnal sign of Libra, and rising ahead of the Sun in the morning. Venus' greatest power comes from being in her own domicile of Libra, replete with æsthetic sensitivities. Venus' exaltation and bound lord is the harsh and disciplined taskmaster, Saturn—the malefic of the contrary sect—who relentlessly demands enormous productivity; her triplicity lord is an intense, unpredictable Mercury.

Venus is moving faster than average, direct in motion, is visible, and effective (but not rejoicing) as a morning star. However she is suffering severe maltreatment due to being overcome and dominated (*epidekatesis*) by a superior square from Mars in the unfortunate 12th house. In spite of the maltreatment and lack of sect rejoicing, I give Venus a B+ because of the power that comes from being in her own domicile, and the effectiveness from her solar phase conditions. She is the strongest of the native's planets.

MARS IN CANCER

Mars belongs to the sect of this night chart and, as such, is positioned to do good for this individual. As a nocturnal planet, he rejoices in the opposite hemisphere from the Sun and in the feminine nocturnal sign of Cancer, but not as a morning star. Mars has a mixed rulership situation. While he is in the domicile of his sect leader the Moon, Cancer is the sign of his fall, where Mars does not receive the honors of respect. And he is in aversion to the Moon: the gaze of his lady is averted from him; she is indifferent to providing resources for his needs. However, because Cancer and Sagittarius share a sympathy due to having the same ascensional times, a reluctant connection exists, as both of their events occur simultaneously. Mars is his own triplicity lord, and this place of rulership accords the power of support from his followers. Mars' location in the 12th house brings to mind the image of the thief and his merry band of robbers. Mars is further helped by having the two benefics, Jupiter and Venus, as his exaltation and bound lords, who give him the benefit of the doubt and act to mitigate the unfortunate repercussions of his actions. Mars is maltreated due to his placement in the twelfth house.

Mars is traveling with slower-than-average speed, direct in motion, visible, and effective in the morning star range. He does not receive any negative testimony, and is mildly bonified by a superior sextile from Jupiter, who is well-placed in the tenth house. I give Mars a B–, despite being in his fall and maltreated by house placement. He is the malefic of the sect of the chart, has two of three sect rejoicing conditions, is in one of his own places of rulership along with benefics as his lords, does not receive any negative testimony, and has some mild bonification.

Table 32. Ranking of Planets from Best to Worst: Picasso

VENUS	B+
MOON	B–
MARS	B–
JUPITER	C+
SATURN	C+
SUN	C
MERCURY	C–

* * *

MASTER TABLES: PICASSO

BIRTH DATA: *October 25, 1881; 11:15 pm; Málaga, Spain*
SECT OF CHART: *Nocturnal*

THE SUN: 02° SCORPIO 42'

NATURE *Benefic/malefic/* *common/luminary*	Luminary
SECT *Day/night,* *Same/contrary*	Day, contrary
SECT REJOICING *Hemisphere, Sign,* *Solar Phase*	Does not rejoice by sign
LORDS *Domicile, Exaltation,* *Triplicity, Bound*	Mars, —, Mars, Mars
ESSENTIAL DIGNITY *Domicile, Detriment,* *Exaltation, Fall,* *Mutual Reception*	None
SOLAR PHASE *Speed, Direction, Station,* *Visibility/Beams/Chariot,* *Morning/Evening, Phasis*	n/a (Sun defines category)
LUNAR ASPECTS *Lunar application* *Nodal Connection*	None
TESTIMONY *Favorable/Unfavorable* *Maltreated/Bonified*	Unfavorable from Saturn Maltreated by Mars
CONDITION OF DOMICILE LORD *Helps/Hinders*	Sympathetic trine of dubious assistance
JUDGMENT GRADE *A/B/C/D/F*	C

* = PLANET IS ITS OWN LORD

JUPITER: 23° TAURUS 33' RX

NATURE
Benefic/malefic/
common/luminary   Benefic

SECT
Day/night,
Same/contrary   Day, contrary

SECT REJOICING
Hemisphere, Sign,   Does not rejoice by hemisphere or sign
Solar Phase   Rejoices by phase

LORDS
Domicile, Exaltation,
Triplicity, Bound   Venus, Moon, Moon, Saturn

ESSENTIAL DIGNITY
Domicile, Detriment,
Exaltation, Fall,
Mutual Reception   None

SOLAR PHASE
Speed, Direction, Station,
Visibility/Beams/Chariot,
Morning/Evening, Phasis   Slow, retrograde, visible, acronychal

LUNAR ASPECTS
Lunar application
Nodal Connection   None

TESTIMONY
Favorable/Unfavorable
Maltreated/Bonified   Unfavorable from Saturn

CONDITION OF DOMICILE LORD
Helps/Hinders   Aversion mitigated by shared sympathy of
                                         domicile lord Venus

JUDGMENT GRADE
A/B/C/D/F   C+

SATURN: 09° TAURUS 27' RX

NATURE *Benefic/malefic/* *common/luminary*	Malefic
SECT *Day/night,* *Same/contrary*	Day, contrary
SECT REJOICING *Hemisphere, Sign,* *Solar Phase*	Does not rejoice by hemisphere or sign Rejoices by phase
LORDS *Domicile, Exaltation,* *Triplicity, Bound*	Venus, Moon, Moon, Mercury
ESSENTIAL DIGNITY *Domicile, Detriment,* *Exaltation, Fall,* *Mutual Reception*	None
SOLAR PHASE *Speed, Direction, Station,* *Visibility/Beams/Chariot,* *Morning/Evening, Phasis*	Slow, retrograde, invisible, curtailed passage, acronychal
LUNAR ASPECTS *Lunar application* *Nodal Connection*	None
TESTIMONY *Favorable/Unfavorable* *Maltreated/Bonified*	Favorable from Jupiter
CONDITION OF DOMICILE LORD *Helps/Hinders*	Aversion mitigated by shared sympathy of domicile lord Venus
JUDGMENT GRADE *A/B/C/D/F*	C+

MERCURY: 24° SCORPIO 14'

NATURE *Benefic/malefic/* *common/luminary*	Common
SECT *Day/night,* *Same/contrary*	Night, same
SECT REJOICING *Hemisphere, Sign,* *Solar Phase*	Does not rejoice by hemisphere Rejoices by solar phase and sign
LORDS *Domicile, Exaltation,* *Triplicity, Bound*	Mars, —, Mars, Saturn
ESSENTIAL DIGNITY *Domicile, Detriment,* *Exaltation, Fall,* *Mutual Reception*	None
SOLAR PHASE *Speed, Direction, Station,* *Visibility/Beams/Chariot,* *Morning/Evening, Phasis*	Slow, direct, visible
LUNAR ASPECTS *Lunar application* *Nodal Connection*	None
TESTIMONY *Favorable/Unfavorable* *Maltreated/Bonified*	Unfavorable from Saturn, Maltreated by Mars
CONDITION OF DOMICILE LORD *Helps/Hinders*	Sympathetic trine of dubious assistance from sect mate, Mars
JUDGMENT GRADE *A/B/C/D/F*	C−

MOON: 08° SAGITTARIUS 12'

NATURE
Benefic/malefic/
common/luminary   Luminary

SECT
Day/night,
Same/contrary   Night, same

SECT REJOICING
Hemisphere, Sign,   Does not rejoice by hemisphere, sign, or
Solar Phase   solar phase

LORDS
Domicile, Exaltation,
Triplicity, Bound   Jupiter, —, Jupiter, Jupiter

ESSENTIAL DIGNITY
Domicile, Detriment,
Exaltation, Fall,
Mutual Reception   None

SOLAR PHASE
Speed, Direction, Station,
Visibility/Beams/Chariot,
Morning/Evening, Phasis   Average speed

LUNAR ASPECTS
Lunar application   Does not rejoice as waxing in night chart
Nodal Connection   Conjunct North Node

TESTIMONY
Favorable/Unfavorable
Maltreated/Bonified   Favorable from Venus

CONDITION OF DOMICILE LORD
Helps/Hinders   Aversion to Jupiter

JUDGMENT GRADE
A/B/C/D/F   B−

VENUS: 04° LIBRA 31'

NATURE *Benefic/malefic/* *common/luminary*	Benefic
SECT *Day/night,* *Same/contrary*	Night, same
SECT REJOICING *Hemisphere, Sign,* *Solar Phase*	Does not rejoice by hemisphere, sign, or phase
LORDS *Domicile, Exaltation,* *Triplicity, Bound*	Venus*, Saturn, Mercury, Saturn
ESSENTIAL DIGNITY *Domicile, Detriment,* *Exaltation, Fall,* *Mutual Reception*	Domicile
SOLAR PHASE *Speed, Direction, Station,* *Visibility/Beams/Chariot,* *Morning/Evening, Phasis*	Faster, direct, visible, morning star
LUNAR ASPECTS *Lunar application* *Nodal Connection*	None
TESTIMONY *Favorable/Unfavorable* *Maltreated/Bonified*	Unfavorable from Mars Maltreated by Mars
CONDITION OF DOMICILE LORD *Helps/Hinders*	Best condition (own domicile lord)
JUDGMENT GRADE *A/B/C/D/F*	B+

MARS: 12° CANCER 21'

NATURE
*Benefic/malefic/
common/luminary*   Malefic

SECT
*Day/night,
Same/contrary*   Night, same

SECT REJOICING
Hemisphere, Sign,   Rejoices by hemisphere and sign
Solar Phase   Does not rejoice by phase

LORDS
Domicile, Exaltation,
Triplicity, Bound   Moon, Jupiter, Mars*, Venus

ESSENTIAL DIGNITY
Domicile, Detriment,
Exaltation, Fall,
Mutual Reception   Triplicity, fall

SOLAR PHASE
Speed, Direction, Station,
Visibility/Beams/Chariot,
Morning/Evening, Phasis   Slower, direct, visible, morning star

LUNAR ASPECTS
Lunar application
Nodal Connection   None

TESTIMONY
Favorable/Unfavorable   Favorable from Jupiter
Maltreated/Bonified   Mild bonification from Jupiter

CONDITION OF DOMICILE LORD   Aversion to Moon mitigated by shared
Helps/Hinders   sympathy of same ascensional times

JUDGMENT GRADE
A/B/C/D/F   B−

CHAPTER 59

Final Evaluation

OF PLANETARY CONDITION

———

In this final exercise, you will integrate all the criteria that we have studied thus far. You will make a complete evaluation of each planet's condition, and assess its capacity to bring forth its significations in ways that are beneficial for the individual. Using the *Master Tables of Planetary Condition*, enter all the criteria that apply to each planet. Be sure to review the earlier chapters or exercises in order to refresh anything you are unclear on.

> BIRTH DATA: Enter the name, date, time, and place of birth.
> SECT: Is the chart diurnal or nocturnal: *day/night*.
> PLANET: Enter the zodiacal sign and degree of the planet.

1. NATURE: Enter the nature of the planet: *benefic/malefic/common/luminary*.

2. SECT OF PLANET: (1) Enter the sect of the planet: *day/night*, (2) note if the planet is of the same sect or contrary to the sect of the chart: *same/contrary*.

3. SECT REJOICING: Note if the planet rejoices by (1) *hemisphere*, (2) *sign*, and (3) *solar phase*. Remember that Venus, Jupiter, Mars, and Saturn have all three possible sect-rejoicing conditions; the Moon and Mercury have two possible options (hemisphere and sign); and the Sun has only one option (sign).

4. LORDS: Referring to the rulership tables, enter the (1) *domicile lord*, (2) *exaltation lord*, (3) *triplicity lord*, and (4) *bound lord* of each planet, based upon the sign, degree, and sect of the planet in question. (Remember to round up to the next degree for the bound lord: e.g., 6° Aries 01' = 7° Aries). If a planet is its own domicile, exaltation, trigon, or bound lord, mark it with an asterisk.

5. DIGNITY: Note if the planet is in its sign of *domicile, exaltation, detriment*, or *fall*, or if it has *mutual reception*.

6. SOLAR PHASE: Note any relevant solar phase information. (1) Is the planet fast or slow in *speed*, (2) direct or retrograde in *direction*, (3) *visible* (greater than 15° degrees before or after the Sun), or *under the beams* (less than 15° before or after the Sun)? If the planet is under the beams, check to see if it is in its *chariot* (domicile, exaltation, triplicity, or bound) or *cazimi* (Hellenistic: 1° on either side; Medieval: 17'). (4) *Phase*: is the planet effective as a *morning star* (15–120° degrees ahead of the Sun for Mars, Jupiter, and Saturn; or heliacal rise to morning set for Mercury and Venus), or as an *evening star* (120–15° degrees behind the Sun for Mars, Jupiter, and Saturn; or evening rise to evening set for Mercury and Venus). (5) Is the planet is making a phase transition (*phasis*): heliacal morning rising/setting (Mercury and Venus only), heliacal evening setting/rising (Mercury or Venus only); does it make a direct or retrograde station within seven days before/after the birth.

7. LUNAR ASPECTS: (1) Note if the Moon is making an applying aspect to the planet, (2) note if a planet is conjunct one of the Nodes.

8. ASPECT TESTIMONY: Note if a planet has *favorable testimony* (whole sign conjunction, sextile, or trine from Venus or Jupiter), or *unfavorable testimony* (whole sign conjunction, square, or opposition from Saturn or Mars). For each of these aspects, note if it is superior (stronger) or inferior (weaker). Note if the planet is *maltreated* or *bonified*.

9. CONDITION OF DOMICILE LORD: Note of the planet is *helped* or *hindered*. A planet is *helped* and made more fortunate if its domicile lord is in good condition and well-placed by house location. A planet is *hindered* and shares in the afflictions of its lord if that lord is in a bad condition and in an unfortunate house. If a planet's lord is in aversion to it, check to see if their zodiacal signs have any shared sympathies that could mitigate the aversion.

10. JUDGMENT: The *best condition* is when a planet: belongs to the same sect as the chart; is in all of its sect-rejoicing conditions; occupies one or more zodiacal signs of its own rulership; is fast, direct, and visible; receives favorable testimony from the benefics and no unfavorable testimony from the malefics; is bonified. The *worst condition* is when a planet: belongs to the opposite sect of the chart; has no sect-rejoicing conditions; occupies none of its signs of rulership; is in detriment or fall; is under the Sun's beams and not in its chariot; is retrograde; is witnessed unfavorably by the malefics and not witnessed favorably by the benefics; is maltreated. Judge each planet's overall condition and give it a grade from A to F with plus or minus gradations.

MASTER TABLES OF PLANETARY CONDITION

BIRTH DATA:
SECT OF CHART:

SUN:

NATURE
Benefic/malefic/
common/luminary

SECT
Day/night,
Same/contrary

SECT REJOICING
Hemisphere, Sign,
Solar Phase

LORDS
Domicile, Exaltation,
Triplicity, Bound

ESSENTIAL DIGNITY
Domicile, Detriment,
Exaltation, Fall, Triplicity,
Bound, Mutual Reception

SOLAR PHASE
Speed, Direction, Station,
Visibility/Beams/Chariot,
Morning/Evening, Phasis

LUNAR ASPECTS
Lunar application
Nodal Connection

TESTIMONY
Favorable/Unfavorable
Maltreated/Bonified

CONDITION OF DOMICILE LORD
Helps/Hinders

JUDGMENT GRADE
A/B/C/D/F

---

* = PLANET IS ITS OWN LORD

JUPITER:

NATURE
Benefic/malefic/
common/luminary

SECT
Day/night,
Same/contrary

SECT REJOICING
Hemisphere, Sign,
Solar Phase

LORDS
Domicile, Exaltation,
Triplicity, Bound

ESSENTIAL DIGNITY
Domicile, Detriment,
Exaltation, Fall, Triplicity,
Bound, Mutual Reception

SOLAR PHASE
Speed, Direction, Station,
Visibility/Beams/Chariot,
Morning/Evening, Phasis

LUNAR ASPECTS
Lunar application
Nodal Connection

TESTIMONY
Favorable/Unfavorable
Maltreated/Bonified

CONDITION OF DOMICILE LORD
Helps/Hinders

JUDGMENT GRADE
A/B/C/D/F

SATURN:

NATURE
Benefic/malefic/
common/luminary

SECT
Day/night,
Same/contrary

SECT REJOICING
Hemisphere, Sign,
Solar Phase

LORDS
Domicile, Exaltation,
Triplicity, Bound

ESSENTIAL DIGNITY
Domicile, Detriment,
Exaltation, Fall, Triplicity,
Bound, Mutual Reception

SOLAR PHASE
Speed, Direction, Station,
Visibility/Beams/Chariot,
Morning/Evening, Phasis

LUNAR ASPECTS
Lunar application
Nodal Connection

TESTIMONY
Favorable/Unfavorable
Maltreated/Bonified

CONDITION OF DOMICILE LORD
Helps/Hinders

JUDGMENT GRADE
A/B/C/D/F

MERCURY:

NATURE
Benefic/malefic/
common/luminary

SECT
Day/night,
Same/contrary

SECT REJOICING
Hemisphere, Sign,
Solar Phase

LORDS
Domicile, Exaltation,
Triplicity, Bound

ESSENTIAL DIGNITY
Domicile, Detriment,
Exaltation, Fall, Triplicity,
Bound, Mutual Reception

SOLAR PHASE
Speed, Direction, Station,
Visibility/Beams/Chariot,
Morning/Evening, Phasis

LUNAR ASPECTS
Lunar application
Nodal Connection

TESTIMONY
Favorable/Unfavorable
Maltreated/Bonified

CONDITION OF DOMICILE LORD
Helps/Hinders

JUDGMENT GRADE
A/B/C/D/F

MOON:

NATURE
Benefic/malefic/
common/luminary

SECT
Day/night,
Same/contrary

SECT REJOICING
Hemisphere, Sign,
Solar Phase

LORDS
Domicile, Exaltation,
Triplicity, Bound

ESSENTIAL DIGNITY
Domicile, Detriment,
Exaltation, Fall, Triplicity,
Bound, Mutual Reception

SOLAR PHASE
Speed, Direction, Station,
Visibility/Beams/Chariot,
Morning/Evening, Phasis

LUNAR ASPECTS
Lunar application
Nodal Connection

TESTIMONY
Favorable/Unfavorable
Maltreated/Bonified

CONDITION OF DOMICILE LORD
Helps/Hinders

JUDGMENT GRADE
A/B/C/D/F

VENUS:

NATURE
Benefic/malefic/
common/luminary

SECT
Day/night,
Same/contrary

SECT REJOICING
Hemisphere, Sign,
Solar Phase

LORDS
Domicile, Exaltation,
Triplicity, Bound

ESSENTIAL DIGNITY
Domicile, Detriment,
Exaltation, Fall, Triplicity,
Bound, Mutual Reception

SOLAR PHASE
Speed, Direction, Station,
Visibility/Beams/Chariot,
Morning/Evening, Phasis

LUNAR ASPECTS
Lunar application
Nodal Connection

TESTIMONY
Favorable/Unfavorable
Maltreated/Bonified

CONDITION OF DOMICILE LORD
Helps/Hinders

JUDGMENT GRADE
A/B/C/D/F

MARS:

NATURE
*Benefic/malefic/
common/luminary*

SECT
*Day/night,
Same/contrary*

SECT REJOICING
*Hemisphere, Sign,
Solar Phase*

LORDS
*Domicile, Exaltation,
Triplicity, Bound*

ESSENTIAL DIGNITY
*Domicile, Detriment,
Exaltation, Fall, Triplicity,
Bound, Mutual Reception*

SOLAR PHASE
*Speed, Direction, Station,
Visibility/Beams/Chariot,
Morning/Evening, Phasis*

LUNAR ASPECTS
*Lunar application
Nodal Connection*

TESTIMONY
*Favorable/Unfavorable
Maltreated/Bonified*

CONDITION OF DOMICILE LORD
Helps/Hinders

JUDGMENT GRADE
A/B/C/D/F

RANKING AND JUDGMENT

After you have completed the tables for each individual planet, make a final evaluation of each planet's condition by weighing up all the results.

REMEMBER

> *Sect* is primary
> *Domicile and exaltation* rulerships give power and resources
> *Solar phase* indicates effectiveness and intensity
> *Testimony* helps or harms
> *Bonification and maltreatment* are rarer but radically tip the scales

At the end of your analysis of each planet, rank them in order from best to worst, and then step back and reflect upon the questions presented at the end of this section. Write out a complete evaluation for each planet, being sure to give the reasons for your judgments.

Ranking of Planets from Best to Worst

PLANET	GRADE
1.	
2.	
3.	
4.	
5.	
6.	
7.	

REFLECTION AND ANALYSIS

1. *Which planet is in overall best condition?* What are the planet's significations and essential nature? Does it belong to the sect of the chart? What are its strengths? Does it have any weaknesses that could lead to less than ideal outcomes? Keep in mind that when you place this planet in the house it occupies and determine the house it rules, it can marshal its powers to bring forth the best outcomes for your self-interest. And when it becomes a time

lord by any of the various time-lord procedures, you can prognosticate that this will be a good period for you.

2. *What planet is in the worst overall condition?* What are this planet's significations and essential nature? Does it belong to the sect of the chart? What are its specific weaknesses that could lead to problematic experiences, reversals of fortune, or outcomes that are not in your best interests? Does it have any mitigating strengths that can point to transformation of the difficulties into something ultimately more positive? Keep in mind that when you place this planet in the house it occupies and determine the house it rules, it can indicate obstacles, limitations, ineffectiveness, conflicts, and failure in successfully bringing about the best outcomes regarding the house topics. Know that you may have to work harder than others in this area, or some things just may not happen, or they may not happen easily or consistently. And when this planet becomes a time lord by any of the various time-lord procedures, you can prognosticate that this may be a difficult period for you, or one in which things just don't happen as expected or hoped.

3. *What planets are in middling condition, or are between the best and worst?* In general, their significations and those of the houses they occupy and rule will be more moderate in their outcome. Often there will be a mixture of some good and some difficult outcomes and events.

4. *As a whole, which sect is in better condition?* Is it the sect of the chart, or the sect contrary to the chart? Think about the interpretive implications of this judgment. When planets of the same sect as the chart are in good condition, and are well connected to each other and to their sect leader, they function as a strong team that is able to bring about its collective agenda in a clear and decisive manner on behalf of the individual. When they are in bad condition, and unconnected to each other and to their sect leader, they are unable to take leadership, or cannot effectively bring about their best for the person. When the planets of the contrary sect are in good condition, and well connected to each other and their sect leader, they may demonstrate great potential and results. But in the final accounting, the matters they bring forth may not work out for the best interests of the individual, or may not be consistent over the course of the life. When they are in poor condition, they can lead to less than optimal outcomes because they are ineffective and powerless in accomplishing their significations. If they have negative testimony or maltreatment, their events are harmful and damaging to the person.

5. Heeding the maxim, "physician, heal thyself", reflect upon the planet that is in the best condition. *How can you support and fortify that which is most*

positive in yourself by bringing forth the best that you have to offer to others and to the world? Turning to the planet that is most impaired, *try to understand the ways in which it is the cause of your suffering, so that the propensity to bring harm to yourself and others is decreased.* The natal chart can provide the key to diagnosing the good and bad conditions of your life, but in the end you must follow the prescription in order to benefit from the knowledge it provides.

CHAPTER 60

Afterword

———

I FIRST IMAGINED WRITING THIS BOOK IN THE SUMMER OF 2006 WHILE presenting at the Project Hindsight Conclave. All that week there was a palpable excitement in the room as we uncovered long-hidden treasures of ancient astrological wisdom for more than one hundred attendees. Robert Schmidt and Ellen Black were the presiding luminaries, attended by Bill Johnston and Alan White, who had spent years working through the Hellenistic doctrines with Bob during many long nights on the back porch. Ben Dykes, Kenneth Johnson, Ken Bowser, Robert Corre, and myself were the support team, so to speak.

I looked at the sea of eager faces, desirous of learning and at the same time overwhelmed with the seeming complexity of the concepts, the strange foreign terminology, and the daily dismantling of their previous astrological structures. Wouldn't it be a good idea, I thought to myself, to make a simple workbook, in the style of *Astrology For Yourself*, that would help people learn this material in a clear, straightforward, and concise manner?

It took the next ten years to actually complete the work, and another two to publish it. As I began to write, more and more words kept coming, with more and more details. I tried to delete paragraphs, pages, and entire sections only to have them show up again. At a certain point I realized that the richness of the Hellenistic tradition—and the core of its value—was the conceptual thinking that underpinned its techniques. To strip away the elegant rationales and evocative language from the techniques was like disrobing the revered Queen of the Sciences of her glorious raiment before presenting her to her audience. As a double Leo, I found that I was simply unable to do that.

This first volume, *Assessing Planetary Condition*, as long and labyrinthine as it may seem, is but the foundational teachings for understanding the entirety of the ancient astrological tradition. In the nautical metaphor that suffuses ancient astrology and philosophy, this is the gangplank that gets you onto the ship, which will have many ports of call before reaching its destination. But then, each of you can embark upon your own journey of uncovering additional buried treasures, using arcane tools to benefit your clients, and sharing your knowledge with other colleagues.

I have faith, based upon having guided students through the program in this book, that if you do the exercises step by step, in the order presented, that you can master the material. You may become frustrated with the repetition of certain points. This is the voice of my oral teachings to students; motivated by the understanding that some things just don't sink in until you have said them over and over in the same words. I apologize if you have found this irritating and ask for your patience with the process. Brick by brick, you are laying the foundation for the temple where you can have many kinds of conversations with the planetary gods, to which Valens alluded two thousand years ago.

Much of the material will come together in the second volume, *Delineating Planetary Meaning*, which focuses upon the twelve astrological houses. There you will see how the celestial planetary influences come down to earth into the realm of the experiences of the human condition.

My final words go to acknowledging the editorial expertise and æsthetic vision of Aaron Cheak. When the initial publication of this book was stalled—too long, complex and difficult to edit—Chris Brennan and Tony Howard forged the links to bring it to Rubedo Press. To the extent that the overall clarity, tone, look, and feel of this book sparkles like diamond stars in the night sky, my gratitude is to Aaron Cheak.

DEMETRA GEORGE
September 14, 2018

ABOUT THE AUTHOR

DEMETRA GEORGE (MA, Classics) is a pioneering mythic-archetypal astrologer, who studies Greek astrological texts, as well as the transmission of classical doctrines into the Arabic and Medieval worlds. An international lecturer since 1992, she has taught the history of astrology at both Kepler College and the University of Oregon. She presently lives in Eugene, Oregon, maintains a private practice, offers mentoring and educational programs, and leads tours to archæological sites in the Mediterranean. Recipient of the Regulus Award, her work provides the keys to understanding all forms of traditional astrology.

Her previous books include *Asteroid Goddesses: The Mythology, Psychology, and Astrology of the Re-emerging Feminine* (ACS, 1986; revised ed., Ibis, 2003), *Astrology for Yourself: How to Understand and Interpret your own Birth Chart: A Workbook for Personal Transformation* (Wingbow, 1987; revised ed., Ibis, 2006), *Mysteries of the Dark Moon: The Healing Power of the Dark Goddess* (HarperCollins, 1992), *Finding Our Way through the Dark* (ACS, 1994; AFA, 2008), and *Astrology and the Authentic Self: Integrating Traditional and Modern Astrology to Uncover the Essence of the Birth Chart* (Ibis, 2008).

CPSIA information can be obtained
at www.ICGtesting.com
Printed in the USA
LVHW060331180621
690354LV00024B/185